THE FUNCTION OF THE ORGASM

Books by Wilhelm Reich

CHARACTER ANALYSIS
(third, enlarged edition, newly translated)
THE FUNCTION OF THE ORGASM
THE INVASION OF COMPULSORY SEX-MORALITY
(third edition)

LISTEN, LITTLE MAN!
(illustrated by William Steig)

THE MASS PSYCHOLOGY OF FASCISM
(a new translation)

THE MURDER OF CHRIST
REICH SPEAKS OF FREUD
(edited by Mary Higgins and Chester M. Raphael, M.D.)
WILHELM REICH: SELECTED WRITINGS
THE SEXUAL REVOLUTION
(fourth edition, revised)

WILHELM REICH

THE FUNCTION OF THE ORGASM

SEX-ECONOMIC PROBLEMS OF
BIOLOGICAL ENERGY

Volume I of *The Discovery of the Orgone*

*Newly translated from the German
by Vincent R. Carfagno*

**WRM
PRESS**

WRM Press
19 Orgonon Circle
Rangeley, ME 04970

This translation is copyright © 1973 by mary Boyd Higgins as Trustee of the Wilhelm Reich Infant Trust Fund
Die Entdeckung des Orgons, Erster Teil: Die Function des Orgasmus, Copyright © 1968 by Mary Boyd Higgins as Trustee of the Wilhelm Reich Infant Trust Fund
Earlier translation published under the title *The Discovery of the Orgone, Volume 1, The Function of the Orgasm*, copyright 1942, 1948 by the Orgone Institute Press, Inc.
All rights reserved
Printed in the United States of America
Library of Congress catalog card number: 72-81011
First Noonday paperback edition, 1973
Seventh printing, 1999

ISBN-13: 978-1-952000-01-0
ISBN-10: 1-952000-01-7

Love, work and knowledge are the well-springs of our life. They should also govern it.

WILHELM REICH

CONTENTS

	FOREWORD	vii
	PREFACE TO SECOND EDITION	ix
	GENERAL SURVEY	3
I	BIOLOGY AND SEXOLOGY BEFORE FREUD	20
II	PEER GYNT	38
III	GAPS IN PSYCHOLOGY AND IN THE THEORY OF SEX	51
IV	THE DEVELOPMENT OF THE ORGASM THEORY	84
V	THE DEVELOPMENT OF THE CHARACTER-ANALYTIC TECHNIQUE	117
VI	AN ABORTIVE BIOLOGICAL REVOLUTION	190
VII	THE BREAKTHROUGH INTO THE BIOLOGICAL REALM	250
VIII	THE ORGASM REFLEX AND THE TECHNIQUE OF CHARACTER-ANALYTIC VEGETOTHERAPY	299
IX	FROM PSYCHOANALYSIS TO BIOGENESIS	368
	INDEX	395

FOREWORD

In the death of Wilhelm Reich, the emotional plague claimed its most formidable opponent. Throughout all of recorded history those who had been killed by the effects of this specifically human disease were invariably its "innocent" victims. Reich, however, did not become a victim innocently. He was the first man to deliberately study and to satisfactorily understand the biopathological basis of this scourge which is created by the suppression of genital love life on a mass scale. Throughout his entire life, he sought a practical method of combatting it. He never failed to draw attention to the fact that the emotional plague was the one enemy of man which, unless accurately understood and effectively fought, would make impossible the elimination of the agony of the child, the adolescent, and of the masses of biophysically and emotionally sick human beings. Consequently, when he too fell victim to this disease, it was not unexpected. He realized the risk involved, and with the courage of a true scientist he exposed himself to its destructive effects; seeking in the process, without compromising the scientific truth, to find a way out of the legalistic rigmarole in which the plague had enmeshed him.

Since Reich's death, there has been an insistent demand for his writings, which strongly indicates that the plague has fallen short of its intention—the concealment of the truth.

The slanderous assaults upon his person, designed to discredit him and, thereby, to divert attention from his significant discoveries, have lost some—unfortunately, not all—of their impact, and it now may be possible to turn to a sober scrutiny of his work.

The Function of the Orgasm was the first of Reich's writings to be translated into English. It is not a textbook. It is rather a scientific biography. "A systematic presentation could not have given the reader a picture of how . . . one problem and its solution led to another; nor would it show that this work is not pure invention; and that every part of it owes its existence to the peculiar course of scientific logic."

That Wilhelm Reich, who was the instrument of this logic, should die in a federal penitentiary is shocking. That those who cared were helpless, and that there were many who knew and who did not care, is tragic. It is no longer possible to stand aside and to say, "Forgive them for they know not what they do." It is time that we all know what we do—and why we do it. It is time that we find a way to end this chronic murder of life and of the knowledge of life. This knowledge exists, and with the republication of Reich's works, it is again made available. We must learn to tolerate the truth. We must learn to understand and to respect the bioenergetic function of the orgastic convulsion, and we must learn to know what we become and what we do when this function is thwarted and denied.

In this book, there is knowledge; and in this knowledge, there is hope.

                    Mary Higgins, Trustee
                    The Wilhelm Reich Infant Trust Fund

New York, 1961

PREFACE TO SECOND EDITION

The discovery of the orgone was the result of the consistent, clinical application of the concept of "psychic energy," initially in the field of psychiatry. The present volume can be considered an extensive introduction to the newly opened field of orgone biophysics. The results of biophysical and physical research since 1934 were set forth in special treatises in the *International Journal for Sex-economy and Orgone Research* (1942–5). In the near future, they will be collected and published as Volume II, under the title *The Cancer Biopathy*. It has been clearly shown that knowledge of the emotional functions of biological energy is indispensable for the understanding of its *physical* and *physiological* functions. The biological emotions which govern the psychic processes are themselves the direct expression of a strictly physical energy, the cosmic orgone.

The second edition of this book appears unchanged.

W. R.

New York
February 1947

THE FUNCTION OF THE ORGASM

GENERAL SURVEY

This book comprises my medical and scientific work on the living organism over the course of the past twenty years. It was not initially intended for publication. Thus, I had no hesitation in expressing what I might otherwise have left out owing to material considerations, good reputation in the general sense of the word, and some still unresolved trains of thought.

To most people, it is a riddle that I can be active simultaneously in disciplines as different as depth psychology, sociology, physiology, and now even biology. Some psychoanalysts wish that I would return to psychoanalysis; the politicians relegate me to natural science and the biologists to psychology.

The subject of "sexuality" virtually cuts through all scientific fields of research. In its central phenomenon, the sexual orgasm, we meet with questions deriving from the field of psychology as well as from that of physiology, from the field of biology no less than from that of sociology. Natural science offers hardly another field of research that is so well equipped to exhibit the fundamental unity of everything that lives and to guard against narrow, fragmentizing specialization. *Sex-economy* became an independent discipline, having its own methods of research and its own body of knowledge. It is a *natural-scientific, empirically founded theory of sex-*

uality. Now it has become essential to describe its development. In doing so, I am very happy to be able to take the opportunity to clear up what I can claim as my own contribution, how my work is related to other fields of research, and what is concealed behind the hollow rumors about my activity.

Sex-economy grew in the womb of Freud's psychoanalysis between 1919 and 1923. The material separation from this matrix took place around 1928, but it was not until 1934 that I was separated formally from the International Psychoanalytic Association.

The present volume is more a narrative of facts and events than it is a textbook. A systematic presentation of the material could not have shown the reader how, in the course of these twenty years, problems and solutions followed one upon the other. Nothing could have been contrived; everything owes its existence to the remarkable course of scientific logic. It is not false modesty when I say that I feel myself to be merely the instrument of this logic.

The functional method of research acts like a compass in an unfamiliar region. I do not know of any finer proof of the validity of the sex-economic theory than the circumstance that the "orgastic potency" discovered in 1922, the most important element of sex-economy, led to and found its natural-scientific substantiation in the discovery of the *orgasm reflex* (1935) and *orgone radiation* (1939). This inherent logic in the development of sex-economy is its fulcrum in a welter of opinions. It is its citadel in the struggle against misunderstandings and in the overcoming of grave doubts at a time when confusion threatens to stifle clear thinking.

There are certain advantages in writing scientific biographies in one's younger years. Some of the illusions one still has during that period, namely that people will be prepared to accept revolutionary insights, enable one to stick to the basic facts, to resist the manifold temptations to make compromises and not to shy away from incisive conclusions for the sake of intellectual complacency, peace of mind, or worldly acceptance. The temptation to deny the sexual etiology of so many illnesses is far greater in the case of sex-economy than it was in psychoanalysis. It was only with great effort that I succeeded in establishing the term "sex-economy." This concept is intended to cover a new scientific field: the investigation of biopsychic energy. According to the prevailing view of life, "sexuality" is an offensive term. It is very tempting to wipe out its importance for human life altogether. It will no doubt require the work of many generations before sexuality is taken seriously by official science and the laity, probably not until the social questions of life and death bear in upon us the absolute necessity of comprehending and mastering the sexual process, free of social constraints.

One such question is cancer; another is the psychic plague which gave rise to dictatorships.

Sex-economy is a natural-scientific discipline. It is not ashamed of the subject of sexuality, and it rejects as its representative everyone who has not overcome the inculcated social fear of sexual defamation. The term "vegetotherapy," used to describe the sex-economic therapeutic technique, is actually a concession to the squeamishness of the world in sexual matters. "Orgasmotherapy" would have been a much better, indeed more correct term, for this medical technique: that is precisely what vegetotherapy basically is. It had to be taken into consideration, however, that this term would have entailed too great a strain on the young sex-economists in their practice. Well, it can't be helped. Speak of the core of their natural longings and religious feelings and people will either laugh derisively or snicker sordidly.

There is reason to fear that in a decade or two, the school of sex-economists will split up into two mutually hostile groups. One group will claim that the sexual function is subordinate to the general functions of life, and hence of no real account. The other group of sex-economists will raise a strong, radical protest and attempt to save the honor of research on sexuality. In this controversy, the fundamental identity between sexual process and life process could become totally obscured. I, too, could give in and deny what was an honest scientific conviction in my younger years of struggle. For there is no reason to suppose that the fascist world will cease to threaten our difficult work with annihilation through moralistic, hereditary-oriented psychiatrists and party bureaucrats, as it has done and continues to do. Those friends who are familiar with the Norwegian scandal created by the fascist press campaign against sex-economy know what I mean. Without delay, therefore, it is imperative to establish what is meant by sex-economy, before I myself begin to think differently under the pressure of obsolete social conditions and obstruct with my authority the search for truth by future young scientists.

The theory of sex-economy and its investigation of living phenomena can be stated in a few sentences.

Psychic health depends upon orgastic potency, i.e., upon the degree to which one can surrender to and experience the climax of excitation in the natural sexual act. It is founded upon the healthy character attitude of the individual's capacity for love. Psychic illnesses are the result of a disturbance of the natural ability to love. In the case of orgastic impotence, from which the overwhelming majority of people suffer, damming-up of biological energy occurs and becomes the source of irrational actions. The essential requirement to cure psychic disturbances is the re-establishment of the natural capacity for love. It is dependent upon social as well as psychic conditions.

Psychic illnesses are the consequences of the sexual chaos of society. For thousands of years, this chaos has had the function of psychically subjecting man to the prevailing conditions of existence, of internalizing the external mechanization of life. It has served to bring about the psychic anchoring of a mechanized and authoritarian civilization by making man incapable of functioning independently.

The vital energies regulate themselves naturally, without compulsive duty or compulsive morality—both of which are sure signs of existing antisocial impulses. Antisocial actions are the expression of secondary drives. These drives are produced by the suppression of natural life, and they are at variance with natural sexuality.

People who are brought up with a negative attitude toward life and sex acquire a pleasure anxiety, which is physiologically anchored in chronic muscular spasms. This neurotic pleasure anxiety is the basis on which life-negating, dictator-producing views of life are reproduced by the people themselves. It is the core of the fear of an independent, freedom-oriented way of life. This fear becomes the most significant source of strength for every form of political reaction, and for the domination of the majority of working men and women by individual persons or groups. It is a biophysiological fear, and it constitutes the central problem of the psychosomatic field of investigation. It has been until now the greatest obstruction to the investigation of the involuntary functions of life, which the neurotic person can experience only in a mysterious and fear-ridden way.

The character structure of modern man, who reproduces a six-thousand-year-old patriarchal authoritarian culture, is typified by characterological armoring against his inner nature and against the social misery which surrounds him. This characterological armoring is the basis of isolation, indigence, craving for authority, fear of responsibility, mystic longing, sexual misery, and neurotically impotent rebelliousness, as well as pathological tolerance. Man has alienated himself from, and has grown hostile toward, life. This alienation is not of a biological but of a socio-economic origin. It is not found in the stages of human history prior to the development of patriarchy.

Since the emergence of patriarchy, the natural pleasure of work and activity has been replaced by compulsive duty. The average structure of masses of people has been transformed into a distorted structure marked by impotence and fear of life. This distorted structure not only forms the psychological basis of authoritarian dictatorship, it enables these dictatorships to justify themselves by pointing to human attitudes such as irresponsibility and childishness. The international catastrophe through which we are living is the ultimate consequence of this alienation from life.

The structuring of masses of people to be blindly obedient to authority is brought about not by natural parental love, but by the authoritarian family. The suppression of the sexuality of small children and adolescents is the chief means of producing this obedience.

Nature and culture, instinct and morality, sexuality and achievement become incompatible as a result of the split in the human structure. The unity and congruity of culture and nature, work and love, morality and sexuality, longed for from time immemorial, will remain a dream as long as man continues to condemn the biological demand for natural (orgastic) sexual gratification. Genuine democracy and freedom founded on consciousness and responsibility are also doomed to remain an illusion until this demand is fulfilled. Helpless subjugation to chaotic social conditions will continue to typify human existence. The destruction of life by means of coercive education and war will prevail.

In the field of psychotherapy, I worked out the technique of character-analytic vegetotherapy. Its basic principle is the re-establishment of biopsychic motility through the dissolution of the character and muscular rigidifications ("armorings"). This technique of treating neuroses was experimentally substantiated by the discovery of the bioelectric nature of sexuality and anxiety. Sexuality and anxiety are functions of the living organism operating in opposite directions: pleasurable expansion and anxious contraction.

The orgasm formula which directs sex-economic research is as follows: MECHANICAL TENSION → BIOELECTRIC CHARGE → BIOELECTRIC DISCHARGE → MECHANICAL RELAXATION. It proved to be the formula of living functioning as such. It led to the experimental investigation of the organization of living from non-living matter, to experimental bion research, and, more recently, to the discovery of orgone radiation. Research in the field of sexuality and bions opened a new approach to the problem of cancer and a number of other disturbances of vegetative life.

The immediate cause of many devastating diseases can be traced to the fact that man is the sole species which does not fulfill the natural law of sexuality. The death of millions of people in war is the result of the overt, social negation of life. This negation, in turn, is the expression and consequence of psychic and somatic disturbances of the life function.

The sexual process, i.e., the expansive process of biological pleasure, is the productive life process per se.

This is saying a lot all at once, and it sounds almost too simple. This "simplicity" constitutes the secret which some people sense in my work. I want to try to describe how the difficulties were solved which have blocked human insight into these problems until now. I very much hope to persuade the reader that there was no magic involved. On the contrary, my theory is general but unadmitted human knowledge about the functioning of life. It is to be ascribed to the universal alienation from life that the facts and relationships which I discovered have been overlooked or consistently concealed.

The history of sex-economy would be incomplete without mentioning the part played in it by its friends and co-workers. They will understand why, in the scope of the present volume, I have to refrain from paying due respect to their accomplishments. I can assure everyone who fought and often suffered for sex-economy that, without their efforts, the entire development would not have been possible.

This presentation of sex-economy proceeds exclusively from the perspective of the European conditions which led to catastrophe. The victory of the dictatorships is ascribable to the psychic illness of the European masses who were not capable of mastering any of the various forms of democracy, economically, socially, or psychologically. I have not been in the United States long enough to judge to what extent my presentation does or does not apply to American conditions. The conditions which I have in mind are not solely external human relationships and social circumstances; what I have in mind is the deep psychic structure of American men and women and their society. It requires time to gain an understanding of this structure.

I can foresee that the English-language edition of this book will be objected to on various grounds. The many years of experience I had in Europe enabled me to use certain indications to assess the importance of an attack, a critique, or an expression of praise. Since there is no reason to assume that the reactions of certain circles in this country will be fundamentally different from those of certain circles in Europe, I should like to answer possible objections in advance.

Sex-economy has nothing to do with any one of the existing political organizations or ideologies. The political concepts which separate the various strata and classes of society are not applicable to sex-economy. The social distortion of *natural* sexuality and its suppression in children and adolescents are universal human conditions, transcending all state and group boundaries.

Sex-economy has been persecuted by the representatives of political parties of all persuasions. My publications have been prohibited by the communists as well as the fascists; they have been attacked and denounced by police authorities as well as by the socialist and bourgeois liberals. On the other hand, they have met with recognition and respect in all strata and circles of the population. The elucidation of the function of the orgasm, particularly, was well received by professional-scientific and cultural-political groups of all kinds.

Sexual suppression, biological rigidity, moralism, and asceticism are not confined to certain classes or strata of the population. They are found everywhere. I know of clergymen who willingly accept the distinction between natural and unnatural sexuality, and who acknowledge the scientific view that the concept of God and the law of nature are equivalent; I know of other clergymen who look upon the elucidation and concrete realization of child and adolescent sexuality as a threat to the existence of the Church and hence take strong measures to combat it. Praise and hatred quoted the same ideology in their defense. Liberalism and democracy felt as threatened as the dictatorship of the proletariat, the honor of socialism as much as the honor of the German woman. In reality, only one attitude and only one kind of social and moral arrangement is threatened by the elucidation of the function of life, namely the authoritarian dictatorial regime of every kind which seeks through compulsive morality and compulsive work to destroy the spontaneous decency and natural self-regulation of the vital energies.

However—and let us put the matter straight this time—it is not solely in totalitarian states that we find authoritarian dictatorship. It is found in the Church as well as in academic organizations, among the communists as well as in parliamentary governments. It is a universal human tendency produced by the suppression of life; authoritarian upbringing constitutes the psychological basis in the masses of people of all nations for the acceptance and establishment of dictatorship. Its basic elements are mystification of the life process, actual helplessness of a material and social nature, fear of assuming the responsibility for determining one's own life, and, therefore, craving for illusionary security and authority, whether actively or passively. The genuine, age-old striving for the democratization of social life is based on self-determination, on natural sociality and morality, on pleasurable work and on earthly happiness in love. It regards every illusion as a danger. Hence, it will not only not fear the natural-scientific comprehension of life, it will make use of it to master decisive problems of the development of human structure in a scientific and practical and not in an illusionary way. Efforts are being made everywhere to transform formal democracy into a genuine democracy of all working men and women, into a work democracy, in keeping with the natural organization of the work process.

In the field of mental hygiene, the first and foremost task is to replace sexual chaos, prostitution, pornographic literature, and sexual trafficking, with natural happiness in love secured by society. This implies neither the intent "to destroy the family" nor "to undermine morality." Family and morality are already undermined by the compulsive family and compulsive morality. Professionally, we are faced with the task of mastering the infirmities, in the form of psychic illnesses, caused by sexual and familial chaos. To master the psychic plague, it is necessary to draw a clear-cut distinction between the natural love which exists between parents and children and every form of familial compulsion. The endemic illness, "familitis," destroys everything which honest human strivings are attempting to achieve.

Though I do not belong to any political or religious organization, I nonetheless have a very definite view of social life. It is, in contrast to every form of political, purely ideological, or mystical view of life, scientifically rational. On the basis of this view, it is my belief that our earth will never find lasting peace and that it will seek in vain to fulfill the function of social organization as long as untutored and naïve politicians and dictators of whatever persuasion continue to contaminate and to lead sexually sick masses of people. The social organization of man has the natural function of protecting work and the natural fulfillment of love. From ancient times, these two biological activities of man have been dependent upon scientific research and thought. Knowledge, work, and natural love are the sources of our life. They should also govern it, and the full responsibility should be borne by working men and women everywhere.

Mental hygiene on a mass scale requires the power of knowledge against the power of ignorance; the power of vitally necessary work against every form of parasitism, whether of an economic, intellectual, or philosophic nature. Taking itself seriously, natural science can become a citadel against those forces which destroy life, no matter who perpetuates this destruction or where. Quite obviously, there is no one person who possesses the knowledge necessary to safeguard the natural function of life. The scientifically rational view of life excludes dictatorship and demands work democracy.

Social power, exercised by the people, through the people, and for the people, borne by the natural feeling for life and respect for the performance of work, would be invincible. However, this power presupposes that the working masses of people will become psychically independent and capable of bearing full responsibility for social existence and the rational determination of their own lives. What prevents this from happening is the psychic mass neurosis which is materialized in all forms of dictatorship and in all forms of political hullabaloo. To master the mass neurosis and the irrationalism in social life, i.e., to implement genuine mental hygiene, a social framework is required which must first of all eliminate material distress and safeguard the free development of the vital energies in each and every individual. This social framework can only be genuine democracy.

However, genuine democracy is not a condition of "freedom" which can be given, granted, or guaranteed to a group of people by an elected or totalitarian government. Genuine democracy is a difficult, lengthy process in which the people, socially and legally protected, have (i.e., do not "receive") every possibility of schooling themselves in the administration of vital individual and social life and of advancing to ever better forms of living. In short, genuine democracy is not a finished development which, like some old man, now enjoys its glorious, militant past. It is, rather, a process of unceasing wrestling with the problems of the unbroken development of *new* ideas, *new* discoveries, and *new* forms of living. The development will be continuous and incapable of being disrupted only when the antiquated and senescent, which fulfilled its role at an earlier stage of democratic development, becomes sagacious enough to make room for the young and the new and does not stifle them by appealing to dignity or formal authority.

Tradition is important. It is democratic when it fulfills its natural function of providing the new generation with a knowledge of the good and bad experiences of the past, i.e., of enabling it to learn from old errors and not repeat them. Tradition becomes the bane of democracy when it denies the rising generation the possibility of choice, when it attempts to dictate what is to be regarded as "good" and what as "bad" under new conditions of life. Traditionalists easily and readily forget that they have lost the ability to decide what is *not* tradition. For instance, the improvement of the microscope was not brought about by destroying the first model: the improvement was achieved by preserving and developing the first model in keeping with a more advanced stage of human knowledge. A microscope of Pasteur's time does not enable the modern researcher to study viruses. Now suppose the Pasteur microscope had the power and the impudence to prohibit the electron microscope.

The young would not feel any hostility toward tradition, would indeed have nothing but respect for it if, without jeopardizing themselves, they could say, "*This* we will take over from you because it is strong, honest, still relative to our times and capable of development. *That,* however, we cannot take over. It was useful and true for your time—it would be useless to us." These young people will have to be prepared to hear the same thing from their children.

The development of prewar democracy into complete and genuine work democracy means that the general public must acquire concrete determination of its existence in place of the formal, fragmentary, and defective sort of determination it has at present. It means that the irrational political molding of the will of the people has to be replaced by rational mastery of the social process. This requires the progressive self-education of the people toward responsible freedom, instead of the childish expectation that freedom can be received as a gift or can be guaranteed by someone else. If democracy wants to eradicate the tendency to dictatorship in the masses of the people, it will have to prove that it is capable of eliminating poverty and of bringing about the rational independence of people. This and only this can be called organic social development.

It is my opinion that the European democracies were defeated in the fight against dictatorship because the democratic systems were far too laden with formal elements and much too deficient in objective and practical democracy. Fear of vital living determined every educational measure. Democracy was looked upon as a condition of guaranteed "freedom" and not as the development of responsibility in the masses. Even in the democracies, the people were taught, and still are taught, to be blind followers. The catastrophic events of the times have taught us that people brought up to be blindly loyal in any form whatever will deprive themselves of their own freedom; they will slay the giver of freedom and run off with the dictator.

I am not a politician and I am not versed in politics, but I am a socially conscious scientist. As such, I claim the right to say what I have recognized to be true. If my scientific observations have the capacity to be conducive to a better organization of human conditions, the purpose of my work shall have been fulfilled. When the dictatorships have come to naught, human society will have need of truths, and precisely unpopular truths. Those truths which have to do with the unadmitted reasons of the present social chaos will eventually prevail, whether people want this to happen or not. One such truth is that dictatorship is rooted in the irrational fear of life in the masses. He who expounds such truths is very much endangered—but he can wait. He does not feel compelled to fight for power for the purpose of enforcing truth. His power is his knowledge of facts which pertain to mankind as a whole. No matter how distasteful such facts may be, in times of extreme social exigency, the society's will to life will force it to acknowledge them, in spite of everything else.

The scientist is duty-bound to insist on the right of free speech under all conditions; this right must not be left to those whose intent is to suppress life. We hear so much about the duty of a soldier to be willing to sacrifice his life for his country; we hear too little about the duty of a scientist to expound a truth once it has been recognized, cost what it may.

The physician or the teacher has but one responsibility, namely to practice his profession unflinchingly, irrespective of the powers which suppress life, and to have in mind solely the welfare of those entrusted to him. He must not represent any ideologies which contradict medical science or pedagogy.

Those who call themselves democrats and want to contest this right on the part of the researcher, physician, educator, technician, or writer are hypocrites or at least victims of the plague of irrationalism. Without firmness and seriousness in vital questions, the fight against the plague of dictatorship is hopeless, for dictatorship thrives—and can only thrive—in the obscurity of unrecognized issues of life and death. Man is helpless when he lacks knowledge; helplessness due to ignorance is the fertilizer of dictatorship. A social system cannot be called democratic if it is afraid of posing decisive questions, finding unaccustomed answers, and engaging in a discussion about such questions and answers. In such a case, it is defeated by the slightest attack on its institutions by would-be dictators. This is what happened in Europe.

"Freedom of religion" is dictatorship when it does not go hand in hand with freedom of science; for, when this is not the case, there is no free competition in the interpretation of the life process. It must be decided once and for all whether "God" is a bearded, all-powerful, divine figure, or whether he represents the cosmic law of nature which governs us. Only if God and the law of nature are identical is an understanding possible between science and religion. It is but one step from the dictatorship of an earthly representative of God to the dictatorship of a divinely ordained savior of peoples.

"Morality" is dictatorial when it lumps natural feelings of life together with pornography. In doing so, it perpetuates sexual smut and blights natural happiness in love, whether this is what it intends or not. It is necessary to raise a strong protest when those who determine their social behavior on the basis of inner laws instead of external compulsive codes are labeled immoral. A man and a woman are husband and wife not because they have received the sacrament, but because they feel themselves to be husband and wife. The inner and not the external law is the yardstick of genuine freedom. Moralistic bigotry cannot be fought with another form of compulsive morality, but only with knowledge of the natural law of the sexual process. Natural moral behavior presupposes that the natural life process can develop freely. On the other hand, compulsive morality and pathological sexuality go hand in hand.

The line of compulsion is the line of least resistance. It is easier to demand discipline and to enforce it authoritatively than it is to bring up children to take pleasure in doing independent work and to have a natural attitude toward sexuality. It is easier to declare oneself to be an omniscient Führer ordained by God, and to decree what millions of people are to think and do, than it is to expose oneself to the struggle between rationality and irrationality in the clash of opinions. It is easier to insist on legal fulfillment of respect and love than it is to win friendship through humane behavior. It is easier to sell one's independence for material security than it is to lead a responsible, independent existence and to be master of oneself. It is more convenient to dictate the behavior of subordinates than it is to guide this behavior, while preserving what is singular in it. This is also why dictatorship is always easier than genuine democracy. This is why the complacent democratic leader envies the dictator and incompetently seeks to imitate him. It is easy to stand up for what is commonplace. It is difficult to stand up for truth.

Hence, those who do not have or have lost faith in the life process are at the mercy of the subterranean influence of the fear of life which produces dictatorship. The life process is inherently "rational." It becomes distorted and grotesque when it is not allowed to develop freely. When the life process is distorted, it can only engender fear. Hence, only knowledge of the life process can dispel fear.

Our world has indeed become out of joint. But no matter how the bloody struggles of the present shape the centuries to come, the fact remains that the science of life is more powerful than tyranny and all forms of life-negation. It was Galileo and not Nero who laid the foundation of technology; Pasteur and not Napoleon who combatted diseases; Freud and not Schicklgruber who plumbed the psychic depths. It was these scientists, in short, who ensured our existence. The others have merely misused the achievements of great men to destroy life. However, the roots of natural science go infinitely deeper than any transitory fascist tumult.

Wilhelm Reich

New York
November 1940

Chapter I

BIOLOGY AND SEXOLOGY BEFORE FREUD

The scientific position which I have just sketched has its roots in the Vienna seminar on sexology, 1919 to 1922. No system, no preconceived opinion has directed the development of my views. There are some who would like to contend that we are dealing here with a man who, having a peculiar personal history of complexes and excluded from "respectable" society, wants to impose his fantasies about life on other people. Nothing could be further from the truth. The fact is that a youth filled with activity and experience enabled me to perceive and represent data, peculiarities of research, and results which remained closed to others.

Before I became a member of the Vienna Psychoanalytic Society in October 1920, I had acquired as extensive a knowledge in the field of sexology and psychology as I had acquired in the field of natural science and natural philosophy. This sounds immodest. Be that as it may; misplaced modesty is no virtue. There was no witchcraft involved. Intellectually starved after four years of doing nothing in World War I and endowed with the ability to learn quickly, thoroughly, and systematically, I plunged into everything of interest which came my way. I did not idle away very much of my time in cafés and soirées, nor did I spend any time going on sprees or in clowning around with fellow students.

It was quite by chance that I came into contact with psychoanalysis. During a lecture on anatomy in January 1919, a handbill was passed around from desk to desk. It called upon interested students to set up a seminar on sexology. I went to the initial meeting. There were some eight young medical students present. It was said that a seminar on sexology was necessary for medical students because the University of Vienna was neglecting this important question. I regularly attended the seminar, but I did not take part in the discussion. The manner in which this subject was treated in the first sessions sounded strange to me; it lacked the tone of naturalness. There was something in me that rejected it. One of my notes of March 1919 runs as follows: "Perhaps it is the moralism with which the subject is approached that disturbs me. From my own experience, from observations made on myself and others, I have reached the conclusion that sexuality is the center around which the life of society as a whole as well as the inner intellectual world of the individual . . . revolves."

Why did I object? It was not until some ten years later that I found out the reason. I had experienced sexuality differently from the way it was dealt with in that course. There was something bizarre and strange about the sexuality of those first lectures. A natural sexuality did not appear to exist at all; the unconscious was full of perverse instincts only. For instance, the psychoanalytic theory denied the existence of a primary vaginal eroticism in young girls and ascribed female sexuality to a complicated combination of other drives.

The suggestion was made to invite an older psychoanalyst to deliver a series of lectures on sexuality. He spoke well and what he said was interesting, but I had an instinctive dislike for the manner in which he treated the subject. I heard a great deal that was new, and I was very much interested, but somehow the lecturer was not worthy of the subject. I would not have been able to say why this was so.

I procured a number of works on sexology: Bloch's *Sexualleben unserer Zeit*, Forel's *Die sexuelle Frage*, Back's *Sexuelle Verirrungen*, Taruffi's *Hermaphroditismus und Zeugungsunfähigkeit*. Then I read Jung's *Libido*, and finally I read Freud. I read voluminously, quickly, and thoroughly —some works I read two and three times. Freud's *Three Contributions to the Theory of Sex* and *Introductory Lectures to Psychoanalysis* decided my choice of profession. I immediately separated sexologic literature into two groups: one serious and the other "moralistic and lascivious." I was enthusiastic about Bloch, Forel, and Freud. Freud was a tremendous intellectual experience.

I did not immediately become a devoted disciple of Freud. I assimilated his discoveries gradually, at the same time studying the ideas and discoveries of other great men. Before I committed myself completely to psychoanalysis and threw myself into it totally, I acquired a general grounding in natural science and natural philosophy. It was the basic theme of sexuality which compelled me to undertake these studies. I studied Moll's *Handbuch der Sexualwissenschaft* very thoroughly. I wanted to know what others had to say about the instincts. This led me to Semon. His theory of "mnemonic sensations" gave me food for thought on the problems of memory and instinct. Semon contended that the involuntary acts of all living creatures consist in "engrams," i.e., in historical imprints of experiences. The eternally self-perpetuating protoplasm is continually absorbing impressions which, responding to corresponding stimuli, are "ecphorized." This biological theory fit in very well with Freud's concept of unconscious remembrances, the "memory traces." The question "What is life?" prompted each new acquisition of knowledge. Life was characterized by a remarkable rationality and purposefulness of instinctive, involuntary action.

Forel's investigations on the rational organization of ants

drew my attention to the problem of vitalism. Between 1919 and 1921, I became familiar with Driesch's *Philosophie des Organischen* and his *Ordnungslehre*. I understood the first book but not the second. It was clear that the mechanistic conception of life, which also dominated our medical studies, could not provide a satisfactory explanation. Driesch's contention seemed incontestable to me. He argued that, in the sphere of the life function, the whole could be developed from a part, whereas a machine could not be made from a screw. On the other hand, his use of the concept of "entelechy" to explain living functioning was unconvincing. I had the feeling that an enormous problem was evaded with a word. Thus, in a very primitive way, I learned to draw a clear distinction between facts and theories about facts. I gave considerable thought to Driesch's three proofs of the specific totally different characteristic of living matter as opposed to inorganic matter. They were well-grounded proofs. However, I couldn't quite accept the transcendentalism of the life principle. Seventeen years later I was able to resolve the contradiction on the basis of a formula pertaining to the function of energy. Driesch's theory was always present in my mind when I thought about vitalism. The vague feeling I had about the irrational nature of his assumption turned out to be justified in the end. He landed among the spiritualists.

I had more success with Bergson. I made an exceedingly careful study of his *Matter and Memory, Time and Freedom,* and *Creative Evolution.* Instinctively, I sensed the correctness of his efforts to refute mechanistic materialism as well as finalism. Bergson's elucidation of the perception of time duration in psychic experience and of the unity of the ego confirmed my own inner perceptions of the non-mechanistic nature of the organism. All of this was very obscure and vague—more feeling than knowledge. My present theory of the identity and unity of psychophysical functioning originated in Bergsonian thinking, and has become a new theory of the functional relationship between body and mind. For a time I was looked upon as a "crazy Bergsonian." While I agreed with Bergson in principle, I was not able to point out the hiatus in his theory. His "élan vital" very much reminded me of Driesch's "entelechy." The principle of a creative force which governed life could not be gainsaid. Yet, it was not satisfactory as long as it could not be made tangible, described, and dealt with concretely. Practical applicability was justifiably looked upon as the supreme goal of natural science. The vitalists always seemed to me to be closer to an understanding of the life principle than the mechanists, who cut life to pieces before endeavoring to comprehend it. On the other hand, the idea that the organism operated like a machine was intellectually more accessible. One could draw parallels to known material in the field of physics.

I was a mechanist in my medical work, and my thinking tended to be oversystematic. Of my preclinical subjects, I was most interested in systematic and topographic anatomy. I mastered the anatomy of the brain and all of the nervous system. I was fascinated by the complexity of the nerve tracts and by the ingenious arrangement of the ganglia. I learned far more than was required for the medical degree. At the same time, however, I was drawn to metaphysics. I liked Lange's *Geschichte des Materialismus* because it clearly showed the indispensability of the idealistic philosophy of life. Some of my colleagues were annoyed by my "erraticism" and "inconsistency of thinking." It was not until seventeen years later, when I succeeded in experimentally resolving the contradiction between mechanism and vitalism, that I myself understood this seemingly confused attitude. It is easy to think correctly in known fields. It is difficult, when one is beginning to feel one's way into unknown areas, not to be intimidated by the welter of concepts. Fortunately, it did not take me long to recognize that I had a gift for grappling with a profusion of seething thoughts and emerging with practical results. I owe the invention of the orgonoscope through which flashes of biological energy can be seen, to this unpopular characteristic.

The versatility of my intellectual interests made me realize that "everyone is right in some way"—it is merely a matter of knowing "how." I studied two or three books on the history of philosophy, which acquainted me with the immemorial controversy over whether the body or the mind is primary. These early stages of my scientific development were important, for they prepared me for the correct comprehension of Freud's theory. In the textbooks of biology, which I did not study until after I had taken the oral examination in biology—the value of which is very questionable— I found a rich world, no end of material suited for demonstrative science as well as for idealistic reverie. Later, my own problems forced me to make more clear-cut distinctions between fact and hypothesis. Hertwig's *Allgemeine Biologie* and *Das Werden der Organismen* provided well-grounded knowledge, but they failed to show the interrelation between the various branches of natural science. I could not have put it into these words at that time, but I was not satisfied. I was disturbed by the application of the "teleological principle" in the field of biology. According to this principle, the cell had a membrane in order to better protect itself against external stimuli. The male sperm cell was so agile in order to have greater facility in getting to the female egg. The male animals were bigger and stronger than the female animals and were often more colorful in order to be more attractive to the female, or they had horns in order to be more adept at dealing with their rivals. It was even contended that the female workers among the ants were sexless in order to be able to perform their work better. The swallows built their nests in order to warm their young, and nature arranged this or that in such and such a way in order to fulfill this or that purpose. In short, a mixture of vitalistic finalism and causal materialism reigned over the field of biology. I attended Kammerer's very interesting lectures on his theory of the heredity of acquired characteristics. Kammerer was very much influenced by Steinach, who gained prominence at that time with his great works on the hormonal interstitial tissues of the genital apparatus. The influencing of sexual and secondary sexual characteristics by means of the implantation experiment and Kammerer's modification of the mechanistic theory of heredity made a strong impression on me. Kammerer was a convinced champion of the natural organization of life from inorganic matter and of the existence of a specific biological energy. Naturally, I was not able to make any concrete judgments. It was merely that I was attracted by these scientific views. They brought life into the material which was dryly dished out to us at the university. Both Steinach and Kammerer were sharply opposed. I once made an appointment to see Steinach. When I saw him, I had the impression that he was tired and worn. Later I had a better understanding of how one is wantonly maltreated because of good scientific work. Kammerer later committed suicide. It is so easy to mount the high horse of criticism when one lacks objective arguments.

I again ran across the "in order to" of biology in various doctrines of salvation. I read Grimm's *Buddha* and was stunned by the inner logic of the theory of Nirvana, which also rejected joy because it inevitably entailed suffering. I found the theory of the transmutation of souls ridiculous, but I was at a loss to explain why millions of people adhered to such a belief. Fear of death could not be the full explanation. I never read Rudolf Steiner, but I knew many theosophists and anthroposophists. All of them had something peculiar about them; on the other hand, they were usually more fervent than the dry materialists. They too had to be right in some way.

In the summer semester of 1919, I read the final paper to the seminar on sexology, "The Concept of Libido from Forel to Jung." This paper was published two years later in the *Zeitschrift für Sexualwissenschaft*. I had examined the various conceptions of sexuality as expounded by Forel, Moll, Bloch, Freud, and Jung. It was striking just how differently these scientists regarded sexuality. With the exception of Freud, they all believed that sexuality seized man at the age of puberty from out of a clear blue sky. It was said that "sexuality awakened." No one was able to say where it had been before this time. Sexuality and procreation were regarded as one and the same thing. Behind this one erroneous conception lay concealed a mountain of psychological and sociological errors. Moll spoke of a "tumescence" and a "detumescence," but no one was quite able to say what their origin was, nor what function they had. Sexual tension and relaxation were ascribed to various special instincts. In the sexology and psychiatric psychology of that time, there were as many, or almost as many, instincts as there were human actions. There was a hunger instinct, a propagation instinct, an exhibition instinct, an instinct for power, an instinct for self-assertion, a survival instinct, a maternal instinct, an evolutionary instinct, a cultural and a herd instinct, naturally also a social instinct, an egoistic and an altruistic instinct, a separate instinct for algolagnia (instinct to suffer pain) and one for masochism, a sadistic instinct, and a transvestism instinct. In short, it was very simple and yet terribly complicated. There was no making heads or tails of it. Worst of all was the "moral instinct." Today very few people know that morality was once regarded as a phylogenetically, indeed supernaturally, determined instinct. This was said in complete seriousness and with great dignity.

It was altogether a terribly ethical period. Sexual perversions were matters of pure diabolism, moral "degeneracy." The same was true of psychic illnesses. A person suffering from mental depression or neurasthenia had a "hereditary taint," that is to say, he or she was "bad." Mental patients and criminals were looked upon as biologically tainted, severely deformed creatures, for whom there was no help and no excuse. The man of "genius" was looked upon as something akin to an abortive criminal, at best a caprice of nature —and not as a person who had shunned the cultural sterility of the world around him and had preserved a contact with nature. Listening to Beethoven's symphonies, the rich, i.e., the good and the just, would like to obliterate the ignominy of Beethoven's death in wretched isolation and poverty.

It is merely necessary to read Wulffen's book on criminality or the psychiatry of Pilcz, Kraepelin, or anyone else of that time. One does not quite know whether one is dealing with moral theology or science. Nothing was known about psychic and sexual illnesses; their existence merely aroused indignation, and the gaps in knowledge were filled in with an utterly contemptible morality. Everything was hereditary, i.e., biologically determined, and that was the end of it. The fact that such a hopeless and intellectually cowardly attitude was able to conquer the German nation fourteen years later, in spite of all the scientific efforts which were made in the interim, is to be ascribed in part to the social indifference of the pioneers of science. I intuitively rejected this metaphysics, moral philosophy, and "ethicizing." I looked in vain for facts in substantiation of these doctrines. In the biological works of a man such as Mendel, who had studied the laws of heredity, I found far greater confirmation of the variability of hereditary succession than I did of its proclaimed rigid uniformity. It did not dawn upon me that 99 percent of the theory of heredity is one stupendous subterfuge. On the other hand, I was very much taken by de Vries's mutation theory, Steinach's and Kammerer's experiments, Fliess's and Swoboda's theory of frequency. Darwin's theory of natural selection fulfilled the reasonable expectation that, while basic natural laws govern life, circumstantial influences must be allowed the greatest possible latitude. There was nothing eternally immutable here; nothing was traced back to unseen hereditary factors. Everything was capable of development.

It never entered my mind to relate the sexual instinct to these biological theories. I had no inclination for speculations. The sexual instinct eked out a meager existence in the field of science.

One has to be familiar with this atmosphere in the fields of sexology and psychiatry before Freud to understand the enthusiasm and relief which I felt when I encountered him. Freud had paved a road to a clinical understanding of sexuality. He showed that adult sexuality proceeds from stages of sexual development in childhood. It was immediately clear: sexuality and procreation are not the same. The words "sexual" and "genital" could not be used interchangeably. The sexual experience comprises a far greater realm than the genital experience, otherwise perversions such as pleasure in coprophagy, in filth, or in sadism could not be called sexual. Freud exposed contradictions in thinking and brought in logic and order.

The pre-Freudian writers used the concept of "libido" to denote simply the conscious appetite for sexual activity. It was not known what "libido" was or should be. Freud said, We cannot concretely grasp what instinct is. What we experience are merely derivatives of instinct: sexual ideas and affects. Instinct itself lies deep in the biological core of the organism; it becomes manifest as an affective urge for gratification. We sense the urge for relaxation but not the instinct itself. This was a profound thought; it was understood neither by those sympathetic to nor those inimical toward psychoanalysis. It constituted a foundation of natural-scientific thinking upon which one could build with confidence. This is how I interpreted Freud: it is altogether logical that the instinct itself cannot be conscious, for it is what rules and governs us. We are its object. Take electricity, for example. We do not know what it is or how it originates. We recognize it only through its manifestations, such as in light and in electrical shock. True, an electrical wave can be measured, but it too is only a characteristic of what we call electricity. Just as electricity is capable of being measured through its manifestations of energy, the instincts are capable of being recognized only through the manifestation of their affects. Freud's "libido," I concluded, is not the same as the "libido" of pre-Freudians. The latter denotes the conscious sexual longings. *Freud's "libido" is and can be nothing other than the energy of the sexual instinct.* It is possible that someday we shall be capable of measuring it. It was entirely without conscious premeditation that I used the simile of electricity and its energy. I had no idea that sixteen years later I would have the good fortune of demonstrating the identity between bioelectric and sexual energy. Freud's consistent, natural-scientific thinking in terms of energy captivated me. It was objective and lucid.

The seminar on sexology enthusiastically accepted my elucidation. They had heard that Freud interpreted symbols and dreams and did other curious things. I had succeeded in establishing a connection between Freud and known theories of sex. In the fall of 1919, I was elected to the chairmanship of the seminar. In this position, I learned to bring order into scientific work. Groups were formed to study the various branches of sexology: endocrinology and the general theory of hormones, the biology of sex—above all, psychoanalysis. In the beginning, we studied the sociology of sex from the books of Müller-Lyer. One medical student delivered lectures on Tandler's ideas on social hygiene, another taught us embryology. Of the original thirty participants, only some eight remained, but they did serious work. We moved into the basement of the Hayek Clinic. Rather insinuatingly, Hayek asked me whether we also wanted to practice "practi-

BIOLOGY AND SEXOLOGY BEFORE FREUD   31

cal sexology." I put his mind at ease. We were already well acquainted with the attitude of the university professors toward sexuality. It no longer bothered us. We looked upon the omission of sexology in our studies as a severe disadvantage, and we sought to inform ourselves as best we could. I learned a great deal in preparing a course on the anatomy and physiology of the sexual organs. I had gathered my material from various textbooks in which the sexual organs were represented solely as serving the purpose of reproduction. This did not even seem strange. Nothing was said about how the sexual organs were related to the autonomic nervous system; what was said about their relation to the sexual hormones was vague and unsatisfactory. We learned that "substances" were produced in the interstitial glands of the testicle and of the ovary and that these "substances" determined secondary sexual characteristics and brought about sexual maturity in puberty. They were also represented as the cause of sexual excitation. These researchers did not notice the contradiction that men castrated *before* puberty have a reduced sexuality, while men castrated *after* puberty do not lose their sexual excitability and are capable of the sexual act. The fact that eunuchs develop a singular sadism was not regarded as a problem. It was not until many years later, when I was afforded an insight into the mechanisms of sexual energy, that I understood these phenomena. After puberty, sexuality is fully developed, and castration cannot affect it. Sexual energy operates in the whole body and not solely in the interstitial tissues of the gonads. The sadism which eunuchs develop is nothing other than the sexual energy which, deprived of its normal genital function, seizes the musculature of the whole body. In the physiology of that time, the concept of sexuality did not extend beyond the comprehension of the individual points of attachment of the sexual mechanism, e.g., the interstitial tissues of the testicles and/or ovaries; it described nothing more than the secondary sexual characteristics. It was for this reason that Freud's explanation of the sexual function had a liberating effect. True, in *Three Contributions to the Theory of Sex,* he still assumed the existence of "chemical substances," which were said to be the cause of sexual excitation. He investigated the phenomena of sexual excitation, spoke of an "organ libido," and ascribed to each cell that strange "something" which influences our life to such a large extent. I was later able to experimentally confirm these intimations on Freud's part.

Psychoanalysis gradually gained supremacy over all other disciplines. My first analysis was of a young man whose chief symptom was the compulsion to walk fast. He was not able to walk slowly. The symbolism which he offered in his dreams did not appear very unusual to me. Indeed, its logic very often surprised me. Most people found Freud's interpretation of symbols rather fantastic. I was familiar with symbolism not only from Freud's *Interpretation of Dreams,* but also from my own dreams, which I had often unraveled. I have a series of my own dream analyses.

The work on my first patient went very well—too well, as is usually the case with beginners. The beginner has a way of being insensitive to the inscrutable depth of the unconscious and of overlooking the complexity of the problems. I was very proud when I succeeded in analyzing the meaning of the compulsive action. As a small boy, the patient had once stolen something from a store and had run off in fear of being pursued. He had repressed this incident. It reappeared in his "having to walk fast." In connection with this, it was easy to demonstrate his childhood fear of being caught in the act of clandestine masturbation. There was even an improvement in his condition. I also discovered a number of indications of the patient's deep sexual attachment to his mother.

On the point of technique, I proceeded exactly in accordance with the instructions set forth in Freud's works. This is how the analysis took place: the patient lay flat on the couch, the analyst sitting behind him. If possible, the patient was to avoid turning around. Looking back at the analyst was regarded as "resistance." The patient was urged to "free associate." He was not supposed to suppress anything that came to mind. He was supposed to say everything—but do nothing. The main task was to lead him "from acting to remembering." Dreams were analyzed fragment by fragment, one after the other in succession. The patient was supposed to produce associations to every fragment. There was a logical conception behind this procedure. The neurotic symptom is the manifestation of a repressed instinctual impulse which has broken through the repression in a disguised form. It followed from this that, if the analyst proceeded in a technically correct way, the unconscious sexual desire and the moralistic defense against it would have to be discovered in the symptom. For instance, a hysterical girl's anxiety about being attacked by men armed with knives is a disguised representation of the desire for sexual intercourse inhibited by morality and thrust into the unconscious through repression. The symptom results from the unconsciousness of the prohibited instinctual impulse, e.g., to masturbate or to engage in sexual intercourse. In the above case, the pursuer represents the girl's own qualms of conscience which preclude direct expression of the instinctual desire. Barred from direct manifestation, the impulse seeks disguised possibilities of expression, e.g., stealing or fear of being attacked. The cure, according to Freud, is brought about by making the repressed drive conscious and thus accessible to the condemnation of the mature ego. Since the unconsciousness of a desire is the condition of the symptom, making it conscious must produce a cure. Some years later, Freud himself questioned this formulation. Initially, however, cure was said to be dependent upon the making conscious of the repressed instinctual impulse and on its condemnation or sublimation.

I want to lay particular stress upon this point. When I began to develop my genital theory of therapy, people ascribed it to Freud or rejected it totally. To comprehend my later disagreement with Freud, it is important to note its roots in these early stages of my work. In the first years of my psychoanalytic work, I partially cured and even completely eliminated many symptoms. I did this by adhering to the principle of making unconscious impulses conscious. In 1920, there was no hint of "character" and "character neurosis." Quite the contrary: the individual neurotic symptom was explicitly regarded as an alien element in an otherwise healthy psychic organism. This is a decisive point. It was said that a part of the personality had failed to go along with the total development toward adulthood, thus remaining behind at an earlier stage of sexual development. This resulted in a "fixation." What happened then was that this isolated part came into conflict with the remainder of the ego, by which it was held in repression. My later theory of character, on the other hand, maintained that *there cannot be a neurotic symptom without a disturbance of the character as a whole*. Symptoms are merely peaks on the mountain ridge which the neurotic character represents. I developed this conception wholly in accord with the psychoanalytic theory of neurosis. It made definite demands upon technique and led finally to formulations which were at variance with psychoanalysis.

As chairman of the student seminar on sexology, it was my job to procure literature. I paid visits to Kammerer, Steinach, Stekel, Bucura (a professor of biology), Alfred Adler, and Freud. Freud's personality made the greatest, strongest, and most lasting impression. Kammerer was discerning and kind, but was not especially interested. Steinach complained about his own difficulties. Stekel sought to be impressive. Adler was disappointing. He railed against Freud. He, not Freud, was the one who had the real insight.

According to Adler, the Oedipus complex was nonsense; the castration complex was a wild fantasy; and, furthermore, his theory of masculine protest contained a much better version of it. The fruit of his ultimate "science" was a petty bourgeois community of reformers. At some other time, I shall have to describe the areas in which he was right, the injustices he suffered, and the reasons why his theory did not hold up.

Freud was different. Whereas the others all played some kind of role, whether that of the professor, the great discerner of human character, or the distinguished scientist, Freud did not put on any airs. He spoke with me like a completely ordinary person. He had bright, intelligent eyes, which did not seek to penetrate another person's eyes in some sort of mantic pose, but simply looked at the world in an honest and truthful way. He inquired about our work in the seminar and found it very sensible. We were right, he said. It was regrettable that people demonstrated no interest or only a sham interest in sexuality. He would be only too happy to provide us with literature. He knelt down in front of his bookcase and eagerly picked out a number of books and pamphlets. They were special editions of *The Vicissitudes of Instincts, The Unconscious,* a copy of *The Interpretation of Dreams,* a copy of *The Psychopathology of Everyday Life,* etc. Freud spoke rapidly, objectively, and animatedly. The movements of his hands were natural. There was a hint of irony in everything he said. I had been apprehensive in going to him—I went away cheerful and happy. From that day on, I spent fourteen years of intensive work in and for psychoanalysis. In the end, I was severely disappointed in Freud. Fortunately, this disappointment did not lead to hatred and rejection. Quite the contrary; today I can appreciate Freud's achievement in a far better and deeper way than I could in those days of youthful enthusiasm. I am happy to have been his student for such a long time, without having criticized him prematurely, and with complete devotion to his cause.

Unreserved devotion to a cause is the loftiest precondition of intellectual independence. During the years of hard struggle for Freud's theory, I saw any number of individuals appear on the stage and disappear again. Like comets, some of them rose to the top—promising much, accomplishing nothing. Others were like moles, laboriously working themselves through difficult problems of the unconscious without ever once savoring the comprehensive view which Freud offered. Then there were others who sought to compete with Freud, without having grasped the fact that Freud was set apart from conventional academic science by his adherence to the subject of "sexuality." And finally there were those who quickly seized a fragment of the theory and translated it into a profession. Objectively seen, however, it was not a matter of competing with Freud or of establishing a profession, but of advancing an enormous discovery. At issue was more than the elaboration of known material; essentially, it was a matter of discovering the biological basis of the libido theory through experimentation. It was necessary to bear responsibility for a piece of momentous knowledge, which presented a direct challenge to a world of superficiality and formalism. It was necessary to be able to stand alone—which did not exactly foster popularity. It is clear today to many people working in this new, psychobiological branch of medicine that the character-analytic theory of structure is the legitimate continuation of the theory of unconscious psychic life. The opening of a new approach to biogenesis was the most important result of the consistent application of the libido concept.

The history of science is a long unbroken chain of elaboration, deviation, and rectification, re-creation, followed by reassessment, renewed deviation and rectification, and renewed creation. It has been a long, arduous course, and we have hardly begun. It adds up to a mere two thousand years, interspersed with long arid stretches. The living world is hundreds of thousands of years old and will probably go on existing for many centuries to come. Life is constantly moving forward, never backward. Life is growing ever more complex, and its tempo is accelerating. Honest pioneer work in the field of science has always been, and will continue to be, life's pilot. On all sides, life is surrounded by hostility. This puts us under an obligation.

Chapter II

PEER GYNT

The impact of psychoanalysis was enormous and far-reaching. It was a blow in the face to conventional thinking. You think that you determine your actions with free will? Far from it! Your conscious action is only a drop on the surface of a sea of unconscious processes, of which you can know nothing—about which, indeed, you are afraid to know. You are proud of the "individuality of your personality" and of the "broadness of your mind"? What conceit! Actually, you are the mere toy of your instincts, which do with you whatever they please. This, no doubt, strongly offends your vanity! And you were just as vexed when you were told that you were a descendant of the apes and that the earth on which you crawl is not the center of the universe you were once so happy to think it was. You still believe that the earth, one of millions of planets, is the sole planet which bears living matter. In short, you are ruled by processes which you do not control, do not know, are afraid of, and erroneously interpret. There is a psychic reality which extends far beyond your conscious mind. Your unconscious is like Kant's "thing in itself." In itself, it cannot be grasped; it reveals itself to you only in its manifestation. Ibsen's Peer Gynt feels this:

Backward or forward, it's just as far. —Out or in, the way's as narrow. It's there!—and there!—and all about me! I think I've got out, and I'm back in the midst of it. What's your name! Let me see you! Say what you are!

It is the "great Boyg!" I read *Peer Gynt* again and again. I read many interpretations of it. Only that of Brandes, the great Nordic scholar, came close to my own feeling about Ibsen's drama.

The affective rejection of Freud's theory of the unconscious cannot be fully explained on the basis of the traditional fear of new and great ideas. Man has to exist, materially and psychically; has to exist in a society which follows a prescribed pattern and has to hold itself together. Everyday life demands this. Deviation from what is known, from what is familiar, from the beaten path, can mean total confusion and ruin. Man's fear of what is uncertain, bottomless, cosmic, is justified, or at least understandable. He who departs from the normal course easily becomes a Peer Gynt, a visionary, a mental patient. It seemed to me that Peer Gynt wanted to reveal a deep secret, without quite being able to do so. It is the story of a young man who, though insufficiently equipped, tears himself loose from the closed ranks of the human rabble. He is not understood. People laugh at him when he is harmless; they try to destroy him when he is strong. If he fails to comprehend the infinity into which his thoughts and actions reach, he is doomed to wreak his own ruin. Everything was seething and whirling in me when I read and understood Peer Gynt and when I met and comprehended Freud. I was ostensibly like Peer Gynt. I felt his fate to be the most likely outcome if one ventured to tear oneself loose from the closed ranks of acknowledged science and traditional thinking. If Freud's theory of the unconscious was correct—and I had no doubt that it was—then the inner psychic infinity had been grasped. One became an infinitesimal speck in the flux of one's own experiences. I felt all this in a nebulous way—not at all "scientifically."

Viewed from the standpoint of unarmored life, scientific

theory is a contrived foothold in the chaos of living phenomena. Hence, it serves the purpose of a psychic protection. There is little danger of being engulfed in this chaos when one has neatly classified, indexed, described, and hence believes to have comprehended the phenomena. In this way, it is even possible to master a certain portion of the chaos. This was of little consolation to me. In view of the infinite possibilities of life, it has been a constant effort for me during the past twenty years to limit the scope of my scientific investigations. In the background of every detailed piece of work was the feeling of being an infinitesimal speck in the universe. Flying at an altitude of one thousand meters, how wretchedly the cars appear to be creeping along down below.

In the years that followed, I studied astronomy, electronics, Planck's quantum theory, and Einstein's theory of relativity. Heisenberg and Bohr became living concepts. Although the similarity between the laws governing electrons and those governing the planetary system could be recognized with appropriate scientific detachment, it could not fail to arouse feelings of a cosmic nature as well—just as one cannot disregard the fantasy of floating in the cosmos all alone as merely a womb fantasy. With such a view, the creeping cars and the lectures on whirling electrons appear very insignificant. I knew that the experience of mental patients fundamentally moved in that direction. Psychoanalysis contended that in mental patients consciousness is inundated by the unconscious. This results in the breaking down of the barriers against the chaos in one's own unconscious, and the ability to assess outer reality is lost. The fantasy of the schizophrenic that doomsday is at hand is the harbinger of psychic breakdown.

I was deeply moved by the earnestness with which Freud sought to comprehend mental patients. His views were head and shoulders above the "priggishly conceited" opinions which the psychiatrists of the old school expressed about mental illness. As they saw it, some things were simply "crazy." After I read the questionnaire for mental patients, I wrote a short skit in which I depicted the despair of a mental patient who, unable to cope with his strong inner experiences, pleads for help and tries to find clarity. For instance, there are catatonics with stereotypies who sit for hours with their finger pressed against their forehead as if in deep thought. Think of the deep, self-estranged, searching, far-roving look and facial expression of these mental patients. And what does the psychiatrist ask them? "How old are you?" "What's your name?" "How much is three times six?" "What is the difference between a child and a dwarf?" He diagnoses the patient as being disoriented, schizophrenic, and megalomanic, period! There were some twenty thousand such persons in the Vienna "Steinhof." Each and every one of them had experienced the inner collapse of his world and, in order to keep afloat, had constructed a new delusional world in which he could exist. Hence, Freud's view was very clear to me, namely that madness is actually an attempt to reconstruct the lost ego. Yet, Freud's explanation was not wholly satisfying. For me, his theory of schizophrenia got stuck in the premature conclusion that this illness is ascribable to autoerotic regression. He represented the view that a fixation of the child's psychic development in the period of infantile primary narcissism constitutes a disposition to mental illness. I held this view to be correct but incomplete. It was not tangible. It seemed to me that the point in common between the self-absorbed infant and the adult schizophrenic lay in the manner in which they experienced their environment. For the infant, the environment with its innumerable stimuli can be nothing but a chaos in which the sensations of his own body are a part. In terms of experience, no differentiation exists between self and world. It was my opinion that initially the psychic apparatus distinguished between pleasurable and unpleasurable stimuli. Everything pleasurable became part of an expanding ego; everything unpleasurable became part of the non-ego. As time goes on, this condition changes. Parts of the ego sensations which are localized in the outer world are absorbed into the ego. In the same way, parts of the environment which are pleasurable (e.g., the mother's nipple) are recognized as belonging to the outer world. Thus, the child's ego gradually crystallizes from the chaos of internal and external sensations and begins to sense the boundary between ego and outer world. If, during this process of separation, the child experiences a severe shock, the boundaries between self and world remain blurred and nebulous, and the child becomes uncertain in his perceptions.[1] When this is the case, impressions from the outer world can be experienced as something internal or, vice versa, internal physical sensations can be felt to belong to the outside world. In the first instance, external admonitions are internalized and become melancholic self-reproaches. In the second instance, the patient might have the feeling that he is being electrified by a secret enemy, whereas he is merely perceiving his own bioelectric currents. At that time, I knew nothing about the reality of the mental patient's sensations of his body. I merely attempted to establish a relation between what is experienced as self and what is experienced as world. These observations formed the basis of my later conviction that the schizophrenic's loss of a sense of reality sets in with the misinterpretation of his own burgeoning organ sensations. All of us are merely a specially organized electric machine which is correlated with the energy of the cosmos. I shall have more to say about this later. At any rate, I had to assume a consonance between world and self. This seemed to be the only way out of the impasse. I know today that mental patients experience this consonance without differentiating be-

---

[1] Cf. Reich, *Der triebhafte Charakter*, Internationaler Psychoanalystischer Verlag, 1925.

tween self and world, and that the average citizen has no inkling of consonance and merely experiences his beloved ego as a sharply delineated center of the world. The profundity of the mental patient is humanly more valuable than the average citizen with nationalistic ideals! The former at least has an inkling of what the cosmos is. The latter derives all his grand ideas from his constipation and inferior potency.

It was all these observations and intimations that made me read *Peer Gynt* again and again. Through Peer Gynt, a great poet gave voice to his perceptions of world and life. In 1920 I studied the drama and everything that had been written about it. I saw the play at the Vienna Burgtheater and later in Berlin. In 1936 I saw a performance of the play by the Oslo National Theater, with Maurstad as Peer Gynt. It was there that I finally understood my interest in the meaning of the play. Ibsen had simply dramatized the misery of unconventional people. At first Peer Gynt has a great many fantastic ideas and feels strong. He is out of tune with everyday life, a dreamer, an idler. The others diligently go to school or to work and laugh at the dreamer. Deep down, they too are Peer Gynts. Peer Gynt feels the pulse of life, which dashes on impetuously. Everyday life is narrow and demands a strict course. On the one hand, there is Peer Gynt's imagination; on the other hand, there is *Realpolitik*. Fearing the infinite, the practical man shuts himself off on a patch of earth and establishes security for his life. It is a modest problem to which he as a scientist devotes his whole life. It is a modest trade that he plies as a shoemaker. He does not think about life: he goes to the office, into the fields, to the factory, pays visits to patients, goes to school. He does his duty and holds his peace. He has long since disposed of the Peer Gynt in himself. Thinking is too troublesome and too dangerous. The Peer Gynts are a threat to his peace of mind. It would be too tempting to be like them. True, he (the practical man) is becoming more and more impotent, but he has an uncreative "critical mind"; he has ideologies or fascistic self-confidence. He is a slave, a nobody, but his nation is a "pure nation" or Nordic; he knows that "spirit" governs the body and that generals defend "honor."

Peer Gynt is bursting with energy and sensuous joy. The others identify with the feelings of the elephant's child in Kipling's story. It ran away from its mother, reached the river, and tickled the crocodile. It was so curious and full of life. The crocodile grabbed it by the nose—still very short at that time—the elephants didn't have long trunks yet. The elephant's child defended itself as best it could. It planted both of its forelegs firmly on the ground. The crocodile pulled and pulled. The elephant's child pulled and pulled. Its nose grew longer and longer. When the nose had become quite long, the crocodile let go. But the elephant's child cried out in despair, "This is too buch for be!" Then it was ashamed of its long nose. This is the punishment for folly and disobedience. Peer Gynt will get his neck broken with his folly. People will see to it that he gets his neck broken. It will be drummed into his ears time and again! The cobbler must stick to his last! The world is wicked, otherwise there would not be any Peer Gynts. He dashes off, but he is dragged back like a chained dog chasing after a passing bitch. He deserts his mother and the girl to whom he is betrothed. Inwardly, he remains tied to both—he can't get away. He has a bad conscience and becomes entangled in allurements and dangerous deviltry. He turns into an animal and gets a tail. Once again he tears himself away and escapes the danger. He sticks to his ideals, but the world knows only business. Everything else is crazy nonsense. He wants to conquer the world, but it refuses to be conquered. It has to be overpowered. But it is too complicated, too brutal. Ideals are for the stupid people. To overpower it, one needs knowledge, a great deal of thorough, cogent knowledge. But

Peer Gynt is a dreamer who has not learned anything "sensible." He wants to change the world, and he carries it in himself. He dreams of a great love for his woman, his girl, who is mother, lover, and friend, and who bears his children. But Solveig is inaccessible as a woman; his mother scolds him, even if affectionately. He reminds her too much of his crazy father. And the other woman, Anitra, is nothing but a common whore! Where is the woman whom one can love, who matches up to one's dreams? One has to be a Brand to achieve what Peer Gynt wants. But Brand does not have enough imagination. Brand has the strength—Peer feels life. How stupid that everything is allotted in such a way. He ends up among the capitalists. He loses his fortune according to the rules; the others are "practical" capitalists and not dreamers. They know their business when it comes to money; in business matters, they are not duffers like Peer. Broken and weary, he returns as an old man to the hut in the woods, to Solveig, who takes the place of his mother. He is cured of his delusion; he has learned what life has to offer when one dares to feel it. That is how it is for most people who refuse to toe the line. And the others aren't going to make fools of themselves—you can be sure of that! They have been clever and superior from the beginning.

That was Ibsen and that is his Peer Gynt. It is a drama which will lose its relevance only when the Peer Gynts finally *do* win out in the end. Until then, the good and the just will have their laugh.

I wrote a long scholarly paper on "The Libido Conflict and Delusion of Peer Gynt." In the summer of 1920, I became a guest member of the Vienna Psychoanalytic Society. That was shortly before the Hague congress. Freud moderated the sessions. Most of the speeches dealt with clinical material. The speakers gave objective and good reports on the questions under discussion. Freud was very good at summarizing the essential points of a paper and briefly stating his own opinion at the end. It was a real treat to listen to him. He spoke precisely and unaffectedly, yet with wit and often with biting irony. He was finally enjoying the success which followed upon many lean years. There were still no orthodox psychiatrists in the society at that time. The sole active psychiatrist, a gifted man by the name of Tausk, had committed suicide shortly before. His work, *Über den Beeinflussungsapparat bei der Schizophrenie,* was important. He demonstrated that the apparatus which influences the schizophrenic is a projection of his own body, in particular of the sexual organs. It was not until I discovered bioelectric excitations in the vegetative currents that I correctly understood this matter. Tausk had been right: It is his own body that the schizophrenic patient experiences as the persecutor. I can add to this that he cannot cope with the vegetative currents which break through. He has to experience them as something alien, as belonging to the outer world and having an evil intent. The schizophrenic merely represents in grotesquely magnified condition what characterizes modern man in general. Modern man is estranged from his own nature, the biological core of his being, and he experiences it as something alien and hostile. He has to hate everyone who tries to restore his contact with it.

The Psychoanalytic Society was like a community of people who had to put up a united fight against a world of enemies. It was wonderful. Such scientists commanded respect. I was the sole young physician among "grown-ups," most of whom were ten to twenty years older than I.

On October 13, 1920, I delivered my lecture as a candidate for membership in the society. Freud did not like it when lectures were read from the manuscript. In such cases, he said, the listener feels like a person who, his tongue hanging out, is chasing after a speeding car in which the lecturer rides at leisure. He was right. Hence, I made thorough preparations to deliver my talk extemporaneously. Prudently, I kept the manuscript at hand, and I was right in having done so. Hardly had I spoken three sentences when I lost my thread in a maze of thoughts. Fortunately, I readily found where I had left off. The lecture came off well, except that I had not complied with Freud's wishes. Such details are important. If people were not inhibited by a fear of authority, they would speak far less nonsense and far more sense. It is possible for everyone to speak extemporaneously on material which has been mastered, and still maintain one's poise. But I had wanted to be particularly impressive, wanted to be sure not to make a fool of myself. I felt all eyes focused on me—and hence thought best to refer to my manuscript. Since then I have delivered hundreds of speeches extemporaneously and become well known as a speaker. I owe this to my early determination never again to take a manuscript to a lecture, preferring rather "to swim."

My paper was very well received. At the next session, I was admitted as a member in the Psychoanalytic Society.

Freud knew very well how to remain detached and to command respect. He was not arrogant—on the contrary, he was very friendly. But behind this façade, one sensed coldness. Only seldom did he become affable. He was great when, with biting severity, he took a callow know-it-all to task or when he spoke out against the psychiatrists who treated him deplorably. He was inflexible when discussing a crucial point of theory. There were but few lectures on technique, an omission which I felt very keenly in my work with patients. There was neither a training institute nor a set training program. Everyone was left to his own resources. I often went to the older analysts for advice. They were not of much help. "Just keep on analyzing," they said, "you'll get there." Where one was supposed to "get," no one seemed to know. To know how to deal with inhibited or even silent patients was most difficult. Analysts who came later did not experience this "floundering" in matters of technique in such a bleak way. When a patient did not produce any associations, did not "want to have" any dreams, or had nothing to say about them, the analyst sat there session after session, not knowing what to do. True, the technique of resistance analysis had been theoretically established, but it was not used in practice. I knew that the inhibitions represented resistances against the uncovering of unconscious contents; also that I had to eliminate them. But how? That was the crucial question. If the patient was told, "You have a resistance!" he would look at the analyst vacantly. Indeed, this was not a very intelligent communication. Nor was it any better to tell him that he "was defending himself against his unconscious." If the analyst tried to persuade the patient that his silence or resistance served no purpose, that it was merely an expression of his anxiety or distrust, this was somewhat better and more intelligent, but to no avail nonetheless. And the advice of the older analysts was always the same: "Just keep on analyzing." My entire character-analytic method of proceeding derives from this "just keep on analyzing." I had no idea of this in 1920. I went to Freud. Freud was a master in theoretically unraveling the intricacies of a complicated situation. But, regarding technique, his explanations were unsatisfying. Above all, he said, analysis means patience. The unconscious is timeless. One has to keep one's therapeutic ambitions in check. Other times he encouraged me to intervene energetically. Finally, I understood that therapeutic work can be efficacious only when the analyst has the patience to comprehend the therapeutic process itself. Too little was known about the nature of psychic illness. These details may appear unimportant in view of our intent to describe the function of the life process, but they are very important. *The question of how and why the encrustations and rigidifications of human emotional life are brought about led directly into the realm of vegetative life.*

At one of the later congresses, Freud modified the original therapeutic formula. Originally, it was stated that the symptom *had* to disappear when its unconscious meaning had been made conscious. Now Freud said, "We have to make a correction. The symptom can but it does not have to disappear when the unconscious meaning has been uncovered." This modification made a strong impression on me. It led me to ask what condition changes "can disappear" to "must disappear." If making the unconscious conscious does not of necessity eliminate the symptom, what other factor must be added to guarantee its disappearance? No one knew the answer. Freud's modification of his formula regarding the cure of symptoms did not even attract much attention. The analyst continued to interpret dreams, slips, and chains of associations. He felt little responsibility for the mechanism of cure. It did not occur to him to ask, "Why do we fail to effect a cure?" This is understandable in terms of the situation in psychotherapy at that time. The usual neurological therapeutic approach, namely the use of bromide or telling the patient, "You are only nervous—there's nothing wrong with you," were such a tedium to the patient that just to be able to lie on the couch and give free rein to his thoughts made him feel good. Indeed, it was not merely that he could give free rein to his thoughts, he was actually told "to say everything that came into his head." It was not until many years later that Ferenczi asserted that no one really followed or could follow this rule. This is so clear to us today that we do not even expect it.

In 1920 it was believed that the average neurosis could be "cured" in three to, at most, six months. Freud referred patients to me with the notation, "For psychoanalysis, impotence, three months." It seemed impossible. Meanwhile the suggestionists and psychiatrists raged against the "depravity" of psychoanalysis. There was a deep commitment to the work; one was firmly convinced of its correctness. Each case was an additional proof of just how right Freud had been. And the older colleagues never tired of repeating, "Just keep on analyzing"! My first writings dealt not with technique but with clinical and theoretical material. It was clear that a great deal more would have to be comprehended before better results could be obtained. This awareness made one want to fight harder and dig deeper. One belonged to an elite of scientific fighters, completely set apart from the quackery which existed in the therapy of neuroses. Perhaps these historic details will put today's orgone therapists in a more patient frame of mind when they do not readily reach the goal of "orgastic potency" in their patients.

CHAPTER III

GAPS IN PSYCHOLOGY AND IN THE THEORY OF SEX

1. "PLEASURE" AND "INSTINCT"

On the basis of my biological studies, and in accordance with Freud's definition of instinct, I ventured to investigate a puzzling aspect of the pleasure-unpleasure problem. Freud had pointed out the peculiar phenomenon that, contrary to the otherwise unpleasurable nature of tension, sexual tension has a pleasurable character. Tension, thus ran the usual conception, could only be unpleasurable. It was solely the relaxation that afforded pleasure. This was different in the case of sexuality. I interpreted the matter in this way: the tension generated in the forepleasure would have to be felt as unpleasurable if gratification failed to take place. However, the fantasized pleasure of gratification does not only generate tension—it also discharges a small quantity of sexual excitation. This small gratification, and the promise of the great pleasure in the climax, overshadow the unpleasure of the tension prior to the complete discharge. This piece of information was the first clue to my later functional explanation of the activity of the sexual instinct. It was in this way that *I came to consider the instinct as nothing more than the "motor aspect of pleasure."* Modern psychoanalytic research disproved the idea that our perceptions are merely passive experiences without any activity on the part of the ego. It was more correct to say that every perception was determined by an active "attitude" toward the particular stimulus ("Wahrnehmungsintention," "Wahrnehmungsakt"). This was an important step forward, for now it was possible to understand that the same stimuli which, in one case, usually produce a sensation of pleasure are, in the case of a different inner attitude, not perceived. In terms of sexology, this meant that, whereas gentle stroking of a sexual zone produces a pleasurable sensation in one person, this is not the case in another person. The latter merely perceives a touching or a rubbing. This is the basis of the differentiation between the experience of full orgastic pleasure and the experience of purely tactile sensations, i.e., fundamentally the differentiation between orgastic potency and orgastic impotence. Those who are familiar with my bio-electrical research are aware that the "active attitude of the ego in the act of perception" is identical with the flowing of the electrical charge of the organism toward the periphery.

I differentiated pleasure into a motor-active and a sensory-passive component, both of which merge into one. At one and the same time, the motor component of pleasure is experienced passively and the sensation is actively perceived. My scientific thinking at that time, for all its cumbersomeness, was definitely on the right track. Later I learned to formulate my findings more succinctly. A drive is no longer something here which seeks a pleasure there. It is the motor pleasure itself. This created a problem. How was one to explain the longing to repeat a once-experienced pleasure? Semon's engrams were of use here. *The sexual drive is nothing other than the motor remembrance of previously experienced pleasure.* In this way, the concept of drives was reduced to the concept of pleasure. There was still the question as to the nature of pleasure. In accordance with the false modesty of that time, I expressed a *semper ignorabimus*.

Notwithstanding, I continued to grapple with the problem of the relation between the quantitative concept of "drive" and the qualitative concept of "pleasure." According to Freud, the drive was determined by the quantity of the excitation, i.e., by the amount of libido. Yet, I had just discovered pleasure to be the nature of drives—it is a psychic quality. In keeping with the systems of thought known to me at that time, the quantitative factor and the qualitative factor were incompatible, absolutely separate spheres. I had reached a dead end. Yet, wholly unaware of it, I had made the first step toward my later functional unification of the quantitative concept of excitation and the qualitative concept of pleasure. With my clinical-theoretical solution of the problem of drives, I had come very close to the border line of mechanistic thinking. Opposites are opposites and nothing but that. They are incompatible. I had the same experience later with concepts such as "science" and "politics," or the supposed incompatibility between research and evaluation.

This retrospective review is proof that correct clinical observation can never lead one astray. Philosophy is simply wrong! Correct observation must always lead to functional, bioenergetic formulations, if one does not turn aside too soon. The fear of functional thinking on the part of so many good researchers is in itself a riddle.

I recorded these modest findings in a short essay entitled "Zur Triebenergetik," and presented it to the Vienna Psychoanalytic Society on June 8, 1921. It was published in the *Zeitschrift für Sexualforschung* in 1923. I remember that it was not understood. From that time on, I presented clinical material only, and stayed away from theoretical essays.

I soon acquired a good name as a psychoanalytic clinician. People extolled the clarity and exactness of my observations as well as my ability to present them.

2. GENITAL AND NON-GENITAL SEXUALITY

The following diagrams illustrate the identity between drive and pleasure:

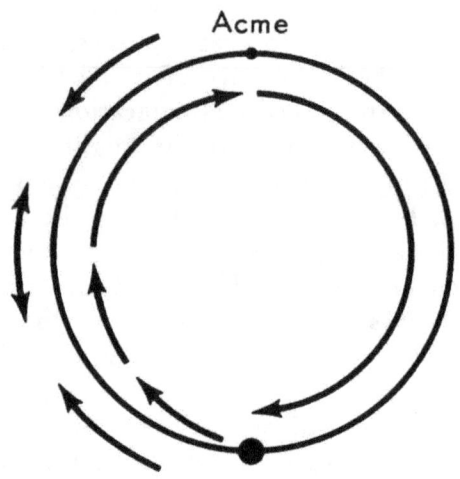

Diagram depicting identity between instinct and pleasure.

This diagram enables us to *differentiate the non-genital mechanism from the genital mechanism*. On the outside of the circle, we see that the excitation retrogresses before reaching the peak. On the inside, we see that the discharge fully resolves the accumulated tension and reduces the excitation to zero. Let us visualize the diagram differently:

In figure 1, we see that in the forepleasure the gratification is always less than the tension which, in fact, increases. Only in the end-pleasure (figure 2) is the energy discharge equal to the accumulated tension.

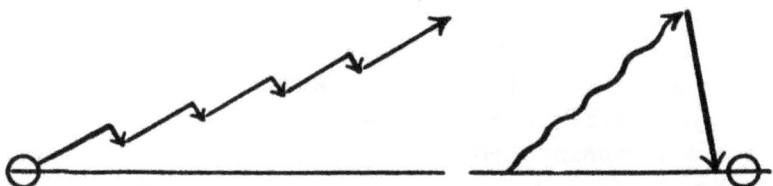

Fig. 1. Forepleasure mechanism.   Fig. 2. End-pleasure mechanism.

This idea has continually been the fulcrum of all my conceptions and representations in the field of sex-economy. Figure 1 also depicts the sexual stasis that develops when gratification fails to take place and is the cause of various disturbances of psychic and vegetative balance. Figure 2 depicts the orgastic potency which guarantees energy equilibrium.

The above theoretical conceptions are based on definite clinical experiences. For example, I had once treated a waiter who had never experienced an erection. A medical examination did not offer any evidence of an organic deficiency. A clear-cut distinction was made at that time between psychic and somatic illness. Psychoanalytic treatment was automatically excluded in cases in which somatic symptoms were found. From the point of view of our present knowledge, this was of course fundamentally incorrect. However, it was correct in terms of the assumption that psychic illnesses are brought about by psychic causes. Mistaken conceptions prevailed about the relation between psychic and somatic functioning.

I began to treat this patient in January 1921 and had continued without success six hours per week until October 1923. The absence of any genital fantasies in this patient drew my attention to various masturbatory practices in other patients. It soon became evident that the way in which a patient masturbated was dependent upon definite pathological fantasies. *In the act of masturbation, not a single patient conceived of experiencing pleasure through the natural genital act.* When I inquired more closely into what fantasies the patients had while masturbating, I learned that they had no definite conceptions. The term "sexual intercourse" was used mechanically. It usually denoted the desire "to prove oneself a man." It included infantile desires to rest in the arms of a woman, usually an older woman, or "to thrust into a woman." In short, the term could denote a great variety of things, except genital sexual pleasure. This was new and strange to me. I could not have surmised the existence of such a disturbance. True, psychoanalytic literature had a lot to say about disturbances of potency—but it had nothing to say about this. From that time on, I began to make a careful study of the contents of masturbation fantasies and the way in which masturbation was practiced. There was no end of curious phenomena to be observed here. The strangest practices were concealed behind such meaningless expressions as "I masturbated yesterday," or "I slept with this or that person."

I was soon able to distinguish two large groups. One was characterized by the fact that the penis as such functioned in the fantasy. An ejaculation took place, but it did not provide genital pleasure. The penis was a murderous weapon or it was used to "prove" that one is potent. The patients achieved an ejaculation by pressing the genital against the mattress. In this, the body was "as if dead." The penis was squeezed with a towel, pressed between the legs, or rubbed against the thigh. Only a rape fantasy was capable to compel an ejaculation. In a large number of cases, the patient would not allow an ejaculation to take place or would allow it only after one or more interruptions. Yet, in spite of everything, the genital became erect and participated. In the second group, on the other hand, there was neither activity nor fantasies which could be called genital. These patients squeezed a penis which was not erect. They excited themselves with their finger in their anus. They tried to get their penis into their own mouth. They squeezed it between their thighs and tickled it from behind. There were fantasies of being beaten, bound, or tortured, eating excrement or having the penis sucked, in which case it represented a nipple. In short, though making use of the genital organ, the fantasies had a non-genital goal.

It followed from these observations that the form in which the sexual act was fantasized, and the manner in which the manipulation took place, offered an easy approach to the unconscious conflicts. I wrote a brief report on this subject entitled "Über Spezifität des Onanieformen," which I presented to the Vienna Psychoanalytic Society on October 10, 1922. It was published in the *Internationale Zeitschrift für Psychoanalyse* in 1922. This report contained only a few remarks on the possible prognostic and therapeutic importance of these specific practices. But this was how I got on the track of the role of genitality in the therapy of neuroses.

At the same time, I was concerned with the question as to the limits of the patients' memory in the analysis. The recalling of repressed infantile experiences was the main task of the treatment. True, Freud himself did not regard the possibility as being very great that early childhood ideas would emerge accompanied by the sensation of recognition ("remembering"). In his opinion, the analyst had to content himself with the fact that the early remembrances emerged in the form of fantasies from which the "primal situation" could be reconstructed. For good reasons, great importance was attached to the reconstruction of early infantile situations. Those who had never taken the trouble to probe the innermost depths of a case could have no real idea of the profusion of the child's unconscious attitudes and of the nature of infantile experience. They had of necessity to be ignorant of analytic thinking. In the long run, this knowledge was far more important than the achieving of quick superficial successes. The analyst who had it would later be able to achieve more in therapy. None of my present views on the biological functions in the psychic sphere would have been possible or sufficiently substantiated if I had not carried out extensive investigations of unconscious fantasy life. The goal of my work is the same today as it was twenty years ago: the reawakening of the earliest childhood experiences. However, the method of achieving this has changed considerably, so much so in fact that it can no longer be called psychoanalysis. The study of the genital practices of patients molded my clinical views. It enabled me to see new connections in psychic life. However, my work, including that on the activity of memory, was carried out wholly within the framework of general psychoanalytic empiricism.

After three years of clinical work, I saw that the patient's memory activity was very poor and unsatisfactory. It was as if an essential specific barricade blocked access to the unconscious. I delivered a report on this subject to the Psychoanalytic Society in November 1922. My colleagues were more interested in my theoretical explanation of déjà vu, which I took as my point of departure, than they were in the questions involving therapy and technique. I had little of a practical nature to say about this, and there really is not much point in merely raising a question.

3. FOUNDING OF THE VIENNA SEMINAR FOR PSYCHOANALYTIC TECHNIQUE

In September 1922, the International Psychoanalytic Congress convened in Berlin. The German analysts led by Karl Abraham took great pains to make it a success. Analysts from the United States were present. The wounds of the war were beginning to heal. The International Psychoanalytic Association was the sole organization which had, as well as it could, maintained international connections during the war. Freud spoke on "The Ego and the Id." After *Beyond the Pleasure Principle,* which had appeared the year before, it was a clinical treat. The basic idea was as follows: until then, we had been solely concerned with the repressed instincts. They were more accessible to us than the ego. This was very odd really, for one would think the ego lay closer to consciousness. Strangely enough, however, it is far more difficult to reach than repressed sexuality. The only explanation for this is that essential parts of the ego itself are unconscious, i.e., are repressed. It is not solely the prohibited sexual desire that is unconscious, but also the defensive forces of the ego. From this, Freud inferred an "unconscious guilt feeling." He did not at that time equate it to an unconscious *need for punishment.* Alexander and Reik in particular later equated the two. Freud also discussed the curious phenomenon of the so-called "negative therapeutic reaction." This meant that, instead of showing signs of improvement when the meaning of their unconscious contents were interpreted to them, many patients became worse. This was contrary to expectations. There must be a force in the unconscious ego, Freud argued, which prevents the patient from getting well. Eight years later, this force revealed itself to me as the physiological fear of pleasure and the organic incapacity to experience pleasure.

At that same congress, Freud proposed a competition. An exact investigation was to be made of the correlation between theory and therapy. To what extent does theory improve therapy? And, conversely, to what extent does an improved technique enable better theoretical formulations? It is evident that Freud was very much concerned at that time with the wretched state of therapy. He felt called upon to find a solution. His speech already contained hints of the later theory of the death instinct as a central clinical factor, the decisively important theory of the repressed defense functions of the ego, and the unity of theory and practice.

Freud's proposal to investigate the correlation between theory and technique determined my clinical work during the subsequent five years. It was a proposal which was simple, clear, and in keeping with clinical demands. At the very next congress, in Salzburg in 1924, three well-known psychoanalysts presented papers toward a solution of the proposed task, for which there was to be a cash prize. They did not take a single practical everyday question into account and got lost in a maze of metapsychological speculations. The problem was *not* solved, nor did the contestants receive a prize. Though I was extremely interested in this problem, I had not submitted a paper. However, I was already engaged in several projects designed to lead to a well-grounded solution. The character-analytic vegetotherapy of 1940 is the answer to the question posed by psychoanalysis in 1922. A decade of systematic work was necessary to arrive at an answer. The gains were far greater than I could have dreamed at that time. It was very annoying that these findings should cost me my membership in the Psychoanalytic Association, but the scientific reward was great.

On the return trip from Berlin to Vienna, I spoke with younger colleagues who were not yet members of the Psychoanalytic Association but who had already begun to practice psychoanalysis. I suggested that we set up a "seminar on technique." We wanted to study cases systematically to achieve the highest mastery in technique. I further suggested that we organize a *Kinderseminar,* i.e., that we "young ones" should get together regularly, without the "old ones." The purpose of this would be to allow the young analysts to discuss their theoretical troubles and doubts and, above all, to learn to speak freely. Both of these suggestions were acted upon. At one of the Vienna meetings following the Berlin congress, I officially proposed the creation of the seminar on technique. Freud heartily approved. In the beginning, only the active members met. Hitschmann assumed the position of official chairman. He was the director of the Vienna Psychoanalytic Clinic, which had been founded on May 22, 1922. It was not my desire to be the chairman of the seminar, for I did not feel that I had the necessary experience for such a task. Nunberg took over the chairmanship a year later. It was not until the fall of 1924 that I assumed this position. The seminar was under my leadership until I moved to Berlin in November 1930. It became the cradle of systematic analytic therapy. The Berlin analysts later set up a seminar on technique similar to the Vienna seminar. The Vienna seminar produced the generation of young Viennese analysts who took part in the early development of character analysis. While they incorporated elements of it in their practice, they did not participate in its later development, to which they were opposed and even hostile. I want to describe the many clinical sources from which the subsequently famous seminar on technique derived its force. Those psychological convictions were formed in it which made possible the breakthrough into the realm of biological functioning.

4. PSYCHIATRIC AND PSYCHOANALYTIC DIFFICULTIES
IN COMPREHENDING PSYCHIC ILLNESS

In the summer of 1922, I received my medical degree from the University of Vienna. I had already been analyzing patients for more than three years, was a member of the Psychoanalytic Association, and was involved in a number of clinical investigations.

My interests were chiefly directed toward schizophrenia. Psychiatry merely described and classified—there was no treatment. The patients either recovered spontaneously, or they were sent to Steinhof, the asylum for chronic patients. In Vienna, they did not even use the more and more widely adopted methods of the Bleuler clinic at Burghölzli. Strict discipline was maintained. The attendants had their hands full, especially in the "disturbed ward," where I was an intern for a year. Wagner-Jauregg was working on his now famous malaria therapy for general paresis, for which he later received the Nobel prize. He was good to the patients and had a marvelous ability to diagnose neurological diseases. But he knew nothing about psychology and he made no bones about it. He had a rough peasant candor that was very engaging. I had been to the psychotherapeutic out-patient clinic only a few times. The neurotic patients were treated with bromide and suggestion. The director boasted of "curing" better than 90 percent of the patients. Since I knew beyond a shadow of doubt that he did not really cure a single patient, and that his "successes" were to be ascribed to suggestion, I was interested in finding out what the suggestionists meant by "cure."

It was in this way that the question of the theory of psychotherapy came to be discussed in the psychoanalytic seminar on technique. It also tied in with my own difficulties in technique. At that time, a patient was usually considered "cured" when he said that he felt better, or when the individual symptom for which he had sought therapy in the first place disappeared. The psychoanalytic concept of cure had not been defined. I want to mention only those impressions of the psychiatric clinic which contributed to the development of sex-economy. It was not possible to categorize them at that time. Later, however, they fitted in very well with the basic conception of my theory on the relation between mind and body. I was working in psychiatry when Bleuler's modern theory of schizophrenia, based on Freud, was beginning to gain prominence. Economo was publishing his great work on postencephalitic lethargica, and Paul Schilder was making his brilliant contributions on depersonalization, the posture reflexes, psychic disturbances in general paresis, etc.

At that time Schilder was collecting material for his treatise on the "body image." He demonstrated that the body is psychically represented in definite unitary sensations of form and that this "psychic image" roughly corresponds to the actual functions of the organs. He also attempted to establish a correlation between the numerous ego-ideals which a person forms and the organic disturbances in aphasia and paresis. (Pötzl had worked on brain tumors in a similar way.) Schilder contended that the Freudian unconscious could indeed be perceived in some nebulous form, "in the background of consciousness," so to speak. The psychoanalysts rejected this view. Philosophically oriented physicians, such as Fröschels, also rejected the view that psychic ideas are completely unconscious. Behind all such attempts lay the intent to discredit the theory of the unconscious and, in view of the difficult situation created by the sex-negating attitude of scientific workers, it was necessary to take a sharp stand against them. These clashes of opinion were important. For instance, experimental work in the field of sex-economy soon succeeded in demonstrating that *the Freudian "unconscious" is present and concretely comprehensible in the form of vegetative organ sensations and impulses.*

My present view of the antithetical functional identity between psychic and somatic impulses originated in the following way: An older girl with totally paralyzed arms and muscular atrophy was admitted to the clinic. The neurological examination revealed no organic cause. A psychological examination was not customary at that time. I learned from the patient that a shock had precipitated the paralysis of her arms. Her fiancé had wanted to embrace her and, half terrified, she had stretched her arms forward "as if paralyzed." Afterward, she could no longer move them. Atrophy gradually began to set in. I did not, if I recall correctly, write this episode into the patient's case history. In a psychiatric clinic at that time, such an entry would have caused embarrassment. The ward chiefs either laughed derisively or they became angry. Wagner-Jauregg took every opportunity to poke fun at sexual symbolism. What impressed me most about this case was the fact that *a psychic experience can cause a somatic response which produces a permanent change in an organ.* Later, I called this phenomenon the physiological anchoring of a psychic experience. It differs from hysterical conversion by virtue of the fact that it cannot be psychologically influenced. In my later clinical work, I had ample opportunity to apply this view of organic illnesses, e.g., in the case of gastric ulcers, bronchial asthma, pylorospasm, rheumatism, and various skin diseases. Sex-economic cancer research is also based on the idea of the physiological anchoring of libidinal conflicts.

A great impression was made on me once by a catatonic patient who veered from stupor to rage. It was a tremendous discharge of destructive rage. Following this seizure, he was clear and accessible. He assured me that the frenzy had been a pleasurable experience. He had been happy. He remembered nothing of the apathetic phase. It is known that patients suffering from a sudden catatonic stupor readily become normal again if they are capable of fits of rage. In contrast to them, such forms of schizophrenia as hebephrenia, which set in gradually, destroy the patient slowly but surely. I knew of no explanation for these phenomena, but later I understood them. When I eventually learned to produce fits of rage in affect-blocked, muscular-hypertonic neurotics, I regularly brought about a considerable improvement in the patient's general condition. In patients suffering from catatonic stupor, the muscular armoring grips the entire body. The discharge of energy becomes more and more restricted. In a fit of rage, a strong impulse breaks out of the vegetative center, which is still mobile, and through the armor, thus releasing bound muscular energy. By its very nature, such an experience has to be pleasurable. It was impressive, and the psychoanalytic theory of catatonia could not explain it. It was said that the catatonic patient "completely regressed to the womb and autoeroticism." This explanation was not satisfactory, for the bodily reaction entailed in this experience was too strong. The psychic content of the catatonic patient's fantasy could not be the cause of the somatic process. This content could only be activated by a peculiar general process which, in turn, retained the condition.

There was a serious contradiction in psychoanalytic theory. Freud had postulated a physiological basis for his psychology of the unconscious, but there were still no signs of it. His theory of the instincts was the first step in this direction. A connection to orthodox medical pathology was also sought. Gradually a tendency became evident which some ten years later I criticized as the "psychologization of the somatic." It culminated in the unscientific, psychologistic interpretations of somatic processes, using the theory of the unconscious. If a woman missed her period and yet was not pregnant, it was said that this was an expression of her rejection of her husband or child. According to this conception, just about all physical illnesses resulted from unconscious desires or anxieties. A person became sick with cancer "in order to . . ." Another person destroyed himself through tuberculosis because he unconsciously wished to. In the psychoanalytic clinic, strangely enough, there was a profusion of data which seemed to confirm this view. The data were incontestable. Nonetheless, careful deliberation rebelled against such a conclusion. How could an unconscious desire produce a carcinoma? Little was known about cancer, and still less was known about the real nature of this strange unconscious, the existence of which could not be doubted! Groddeck's *The Book of the It* abounds in such examples. It was metaphysics, but even mysticism is "right in some way." And it was mystical only to the extent to which one could not say precisely when it was right, or when it was expressing correct data incorrectly. A "desire" in the meaning of the word at that time could not conceivably bring about deep organic changes. The act of desiring had to be grasped in a much deeper way than analytic psychology was capable of doing. Everything pointed to deep biological processes, of which the "unconscious desire" could only be an expression.

The controversy between the psychoanalytic explanation of psychic illnesses on one hand, and the neurological, physiological explanation on the other, was just as vehement. "Psychogenic" and "somatogenic" were absolute antitheses. The young psychoanalyst working in the field of psychiatry had somehow to find his way around in this confusion. Conceiving of psychic illnesses as having "multiple causes" offered some comfort against the difficulties.

Postencephalitic paralysis and epilepsy came under the same complex of problems. In the winter of 1918, Vienna was stricken with a virulent influenza epidemic which claimed many lives. No one knew why it was so malignant. Even worse were the illnesses of many stricken people who survived the epidemic. Several years later, they were afflicted with a general paralysis of their vital activity. Their movements were retarded, their faces acquired a masklike rigid expression, their speech became lethargic, every impulse of their will appeared to be held back as by a brake. Their inner psychic activity was unimpaired. The disease was called postencephalitic lethargica. It was incurable. Our wards were full of patients suffering from this disease. They were an extremely depressing sight. Some of them were under my care. In my perplexity, I hit upon the idea of having them do muscular exercises in an effort to overcome the extrapyramidal rigidity. True, it was assumed that the lateral spinal tracts were damaged—the same was assumed about the nerve centers in the brain. Economo even went so far as to assume that the "sleep center" was impaired. Wagner-Jauregg felt that my plan was a sensible one. I got several pieces of equipment and had the patients do exercises on them, each according to his particular condition. I was struck by the peculiar facial expressions of the patients while performing these exercises. One patient displayed the exaggerated facial features of a "criminal." His movements with the equipment corresponded to these features. A high school teacher had a strict "schoolmaster face." In the performance of the exercises, he was somehow "professorial." It was clearly noticeable that postencephalitic adolescents tended to be hyperactive. In adolescents, the disease produced more overexcitement; in older people, it produced more lethargic forms. I did not publish anything about this, but it made a lasting impression. At that time, disturbances of the vegetative nerve functions were diagnosed wholly according to the scheme of disturbances of the voluntary sensorimotor nervous system. Certain nerve areas and nerve centers were said to be affected by the illness. Impulses were said to be disturbed or reshaped. Mechanical lesions of the nerves were considered the causes of the disturbance. No one thought of the possibility of a general disturbance of vegetative functioning. Even today, in my opinion, the problem has not been solved. I don't know what to say about it. Most likely, the postencephalitic disease is a disturbance of the total body impulse, a disturbance in which the nerve tracts play an intermediary role only. There can be no doubt that there is a connection between the specific character structure and the particular form of the vegetative inhibition. That it originates from an infection is beyond doubt. In short, the disturbance of the total body impulse and the inhibition of the general vegetative function were the essential factors which made a lasting impression and became decisive for my later work. Nothing was known about the nature of vegetative impulses.

The obviousness of the sexual disturbance in schizophrenia and related disturbances of the ego firmly convinced me of the correctness of Freud's assertions of the sexual etiology of neuroses and psychoses. What the analyst had to spend months in unraveling and interpreting in compulsive patients was expressed in plain language by the psychotic patient. Strangest of all was the attitude of the psychiatrists who simply refused to take cognizance of this and outdid one another in jeering at Freud. There is no case of schizophrenia which, once a slight contact has been established, does not reveal unmistakable sexual conflicts. The nature of these conflicts can be very different, but blatant sexual elements are always uppermost. Official psychiatry is solely interested in classifying, and the content of the conflicts is merely a nuisance. For official psychiatry, it is important whether the patient is only disoriented in space or whether he is also disoriented in time. The psychiatrist is not interested in what caused the patient to become disoriented in one way or another. The psychotic patient is besieged by the sexual ideas which, in others, are very carefully concealed, repressed, or only half admitted. The sexual act, perverse activities, intercourse with the mother or father, the smearing of excrement over the genitals, the seduction of or by the wife or husband of a friend, grossly sensuous sucking fantasies, and more of the same, inundate the psychotic's conscious thinking. It is not surprising, therefore, that the patient reacts by losing his inner orientation. The strange inner situation breeds anxiety.

A person who has allowed prohibited sexuality, while retaining his defenses against it, must begin to sense the outer world as strange. That world, for its part, labels such a person a freak and excludes him from its regimented ranks. Indeed, sexual sensations are experienced by the psychotic with such immediacy that he *has* to become estranged from usual thinking and living. In turn, he is often clearly aware of the sexual hypocrisy of his environment. Hence, he ascribes to the physician or to his own relatives what he himself directly feels. And what he experiences is reality—*not fantasies* about reality. People are "polymorphously perverse," and so are their morality and their institutions. Strong barriers have been erected against this flood of refuse and asociality: moralistic views and inhibitions on the inside and the vice squad and public opinion on the outside. To be able to exist, therefore, people have to disown their own most vital interests; they have to adopt artificial forms of living and attitudes, which they themselves have made necessary. The result of this is that they experience as innate what is a constant burden and alien to their nature; they conceive of it as the "eternally moral nature of man," as "the truly human," as opposed to the "animal." The many fantasies which psychotic patients have about the reversal of a real state of affairs can be explained on the basis of this split. They often conceive of locking up their attendants and physicians as the ones who are really sick. It is they who are in the right—not the others. This idea is not as fanciful as one would like to believe. Great and sensible men have concerned themselves with this phenomenon, e.g., Ibsen in *Peer Gynt*. Everyone is right in some way. Even psychotic patients have to be right in principle in some definite places. But where? Certainly not where they claim to be. Yet, when one succeeds in establishing contact with them, one finds that they are capable of conversing very sensibly and seriously about the numerous peculiarities of life.

The reader who has carefully followed the presentation thus far will be somewhat puzzled. He will want to know whether the bizarre, perverse sexual sensations felt by the psychotic patient truly represent a breakthrough of what is "natural" in him. Are coprophagia, homosexual fantasies, sadism, etc., natural experiences of life? The reader is right to be puzzled about these things. The instincts which initially break through in the schizophrenic patient are indeed perverse. But in the background of schizophrenic experience there is something else which is hidden by the perversion.

The schizophrenic patient experiences his organ sensations, the vegetative currents, in the form of concepts and ideas which have been borrowed partly from the world around him and acquired partly in the warding off of his natural sexuality. The average normal person also thinks of sexuality in unnatural or perverse concepts, e.g., "fucking." Hand in hand with the deterioration of the natural sexual organ sensations went the words and terms to express it. If only perversions broke through in the schizophrenic, there would be no fantasies of doomsday and cosmic processes— but only perversions. What belongs specifically to the schizophrenic patient is that, though he experiences the vital biology of the body, he cannot cope with it. He is bewildered and begins to conceive of his vegetative currents in terms of perverse sexuality. With respect to their experiencing of life, the neurotic patient and the perverted individual are to the schizophrenic as the petty thief is to the daring safecracker.

And so, to the impressions of postencephalitic lethargica were added those of schizophrenia. The ideas of a gradual or rapid "vegetative deterioration," of the "splitting of the unitary, ordered, vegetative functioning," became essential sources of my later investigations. To me, schizophrenic lack of concentration and helplessness, confusion and disorientation, catatonic block, and hebephrenic deterioration were merely various forms of one and the same process, i.e., the progressive splitting of the normally unitary function of the vital apparatus. It was not until twelve years later that the unity of the life function became clinically comprehensible in the form of the *orgasm reflex*.

If one has one's doubts about the absolute rationality and correct way of thinking of this "respectable" world, one will have an easier time in gaining access to the nature of psychotic patients. I observed a young girl who had lain in bed in the clinic for years and did nothing but move her pelvis and rub her finger over her genital. She was totally withdrawn. Once in a while, a vague smile appeared on her face. Only seldom did one get through to her. She did not answer any questions. On occasion, however, an intelligible expression took shape on her face. If a person really knows the shocking anguish of small children who are forbidden to masturbate, he will understand such behavior on the part of psychotic patients. They give up the world and, in a demented state, practice what an irrationally governed world once denied them. They do not revenge themselves; they do not punish; they cause no harm. They merely lie in bed and try to salvage the last, pathologically distorted, remnants of pleasure.

Psychiatry understood nothing of all this. It was afraid to understand it. It would have had to undertake a radical change. Freud had provided an approach to the problem, but his "interpretations" were laughed at. Thanks to my knowledge of the theory of childhood sexuality and the repression of instincts, I had a better understanding of psychotic patients. I took up Freud's cause in earnest. It was clear to me that the sole function of psychiatric science was to divert attention from a true elucidation of the sexual conditions of existence. It made every effort to "prove" that psychotic patients are tainted from birth, are degenerate in their very protoplasm. It had to prove at all cost that disturbances of the brain function or inner secretion caused mental illnesses. Psychiatrists gloated over the fact that patients suffering from general paresis exhibit some symptoms of genuine schizophrenia or melancholia. "See, that's what comes of immorality" was and still is an often-assumed attitude. It did not occur to anyone that the ravages of the body functions, in whatever form, could just as well be the results of a general disturbance of vegetative functioning.

There were three basic conceptions on the relation between the somatic sphere and the psychic sphere:

1. Every psychic illness or manifestation has a physical cause. This was the formula of *mechanistic materialism*.

2. Every psychic illness or manifestation can have only a psychic cause. For religious thinking, all somatic illnesses are also of psychic origin. This was the formula of *metaphysical idealism*. It corresponded to the view that "spirit creates matter" and not vice versa.

3. The psychic and the somatic are two parallel processes which have a reciprocal effect on one another—*psychophysical parallelism*.

There was no unitary-functional conception of the body-mind relation. Philosophic questions played no role in my clinical work, nor did my clinical work proceed from philosophy. On the contrary, on the basis of my clinical work, I developed a method which, at first, I applied quite unconsciously. This method required clarity about the connection between the somatic and the psychic realms.

So many researchers had correctly observed the same data. And yet, in scientific work, one scientist was the rival of another, e.g., Adler's theory of the "nervous character" opposed Freud's theory of the sexual etiology of neuroses. As much as one hesitates to admit it, it is nonetheless true: "character" and "sexuality" constituted two irreconcilable poles of psychoanalytic thinking. Too much talk about character was not exactly appreciated in the Psychoanalytic Association. I understood the reasons for this. There was hardly another subject that was caviled about as much as "character." There were few who made a clear-cut distinction between the valuation of ("good" or "bad") character and its natural-scientific investigation. Characterology and ethics were, and still are, almost identical. Even in psychoanalysis, the concept of character was not free of moral valuations. There was a stigma attached to the "anal" character; less so to the "oral" character, but the latter was looked upon as an infant. Freud had demonstrated the origin of a number of typical character traits from early childhood impulses. Abraham had furnished brilliant data on the character traits in melancholia and manic-depressive states. Hence, the confusion between moral valuations and empirical investigations was all the more perplexing. It was said, to be sure, that scientific work had to be "objective" and "non-evaluative." Yet every sentence on character attitudes was a judgment, not—which would have been correct —a judgment on the "health" or "sickness" of a particular form of behavior, but a judgment in the sense of "good" and "bad." The view was held that there were certain "bad characters" who were unsuitable for psychoanalytic treatment. It was said that psychoanalytic treatment required a certain level of psychic organization in the patient, and that many were not worth the effort. Besides, many patients were so "narcissistic" that the treatment was not capable of breaking through the barrier. Even a low IQ was considered an obstruction to psychoanalytic treatment. Hence, psychoanalytic work was limited to circumscribed neurotic symptoms in intelligent persons capable of free association and having "correctly developed" characters.

This feudalistic conception of psychotherapy, which, by its very nature, is extremely individualistic, naturally came into immediate conflict with the requirements of medical work when the Vienna Psychoanalytic Clinic for destitute persons was opened on May 22, 1922. At the Budapest congress in 1918, Freud had spoken of the necessity of founding public psychoanalytic clinics for those who could not afford private treatment. However, the pure gold of psychoanalysis would have, he said, to be mixed "with the copper of suggestive therapy." Mass treatment would make this necessary.

As early as 1920, a psychoanalytic clinic had been set up in Berlin under Karl Abraham. In Vienna, both the local medical authorities, who had to give their authorization to the psychoanalytic clinic, as well as the state board of health, raised considerable difficulties. The psychiatrists were flatly against it and advanced all sorts of quibbling excuses, while the doctors' union feared that the medical profession would suffer pecuniary damages. In short, the founding of a clinic was considered altogether useless. Eventually, however, the necessary authorization was received. We moved into a few rooms in the cardiac ward of Kaufmann and Meyer. Six months later, an injunction was issued against our continuation. And so it went, back and forth, because the medical authorities did not know what to make of it. Nor did it fit into the framework of their thinking. Hitschmann, the director of the psychoanalytic clinic, described the difficulties in a booklet written in honor of its tenth anniversary. However, I want to return to my main theme.

The psychoanalytic clinic became a fountainhead of insights into the mechanisms of neuroses in inpecunious people. I worked in this clinic from the day of its opening as the chief assistant physician; altogether, I worked there for eight years, ultimately as its deputy director. The consultation hours were jammed. There were industrial workers, office clerks, students, and farmers from the country. The influx was so great that we were at a loss to deal with it, especially when the clinic became known among the populous. Every psychoanalyst agreed to give one session every day without charge. But this was not enough. We had to sort out those cases which were more suited for analysis. This forced us to try to find ways of assessing the prospects of treatment. Later, I persuaded analysts to make a monthly contribution. I wanted to use this money to employ one or two paid physicians. In this way, it could be hoped that the name "clinic" would one day be justified. According to the standards of that time, it was believed that treatment required one session per day for at least six months. One thing became immediately clear: *psychoanalysis is not a mass therapy*. The idea of preventing neuroses did not exist—nor would one have known what to say about it. Work in the clinic soon made the following very clear:

Neurosis is a mass sickness, an infection similar to an epidemic, and not the whim of spoiled women, as was later contended in the fight against psychoanalysis.

Disturbance of the genital sexual function was by far the most frequent reason given for coming to the clinic.

Accountability as to the results of the psychotherapeutic treatment was indispensable if we wanted to make any headway at all. What were the criteria for determining the prognosis of therapy? This question had not been previously considered.

Why an analyst succeeded in curing one patient and not another was also a question of the first magnitude. If this were known, then it would be possible to make a better selection of patients. There was no theory of therapy at that time.

Neither the psychiatrist nor the psychoanalyst thought to inquire into the social living conditions of the patients. It was known, of course, that there was poverty and material distress, but somehow this was not regarded as being relevant to the treatment. Yet, the patient's material conditions were a constant problem in the clinic. It was often necessary to provide social aid first. All of a sudden there was a tremendous gap between private practice and practice in the clinic.

After we had been working for two years or so, it became clear that individual psychotherapy has a very limited significance. Only a fraction of the emotionally ill patients could receive treatment. And hundreds of hours of work with those who were treated were lost in fruitless efforts because of the unsolved therapeutic problems pertaining to technique. One's efforts were rewarded in a small percentage of cases only. Psychoanalysis never made any secret about the wretchedness of actual practice.

Then there were patients whom private practice afforded no opportunity to observe, patients who were so mentally deranged that they were wholly outside of society. The usual psychiatric diagnosis for such cases was "psychopathy," "moral insanity," or "schizoid degeneracy." Severe "hereditary taint" was looked upon as the sole essential cause. Their symptoms could not be classified under any of the known categories. Compulsive actions, hysterical comas, murder fantasies and impulses completely uprooted them from the everyday world. While these private manias were, in the case of the well-to-do, socially harmless, they had, in the case of the poor, a grotesque and dangerous character. As a result of material distress, the moralistic inhibitions had been broken down to such an extent that the criminal and perverse impulses clamored for action. My book, *Der triebhafte Charakter,* is an investigation of this type. For three years, I had to deal predominantly with such difficult cases in the clinic. They were put in the disturbed ward and left there until they settled down. Then they were discharged, or they were put in a mental institution as soon as a psychosis broke out. They stemmed almost exclusively from the milieu of the laborer and the clerk.

One day, a pretty young working woman came to the clinic. She had two boys and a small child with her. She had lost her voice, a symptom known as "hysterical mutism." She wrote on a slip of paper that she had suddenly lost her voice a few days before. Since an analysis was not possible, I made an attempt to eliminate the speech disturbance through hypnosis and was successful after a few sessions. Now she spoke in a low, hoarse, and apprehensive voice. For years she had been suffering from a compulsive impulse to kill her children. The father of the children had deserted her. She was alone, and she and the children had hardly anything to eat. She did sewing at home, but earned hopelessly little from it. Then she was struck by the idea of murder. She was on the verge of pushing her children into the water when she was seized by terrible anxiety. From then on she was tormented by the impulse to confess to the police to protect the children from herself. This intention put her in a state of deadly fear. She was afraid of being hanged for her crime. The thought of it produced a constriction in her throat. The mutism, in turn, protected her from carrying out her impulse. In reality, her mutism was an extreme spasm of the vocal cords. It was not difficult to put one's finger on the childhood situation which lay behind it. She had been an orphan and had been boarded with strangers. She had lived with as many as six and more people in one room. As a small girl she had been sexually violated by grown men. She was tormented by a longing for a protective mother. In her fantasies, she was a suckling infant. Throat and neck had always been the site of the choking anxiety and the longing. Now she was a mother and saw her children in a situation similar to the one in which she had been as a child. She did not want them to live. In addition, she had transferred to the children the bitter hatred she felt toward her husband. It was a terribly complicated situation. No one understood her. Though totally frigid, she slept with many different men. I succeeded in helping her overcome a number of difficulties. I had the boys put in a respectable boarding school. She plucked up enough courage to start working again. We took up a collection for her. In reality, the misery continued —merely somewhat alleviated. The helplessness of such people drives them to commit unaccountable acts. She would come to my house at night and threaten to commit suicide or infanticide unless I did this or that, unless I agreed to protect her in this or that situation, etc. I visited her in her apartment. There I had to grapple not with the exalted question of the etiology of neuroses but with the question of how a human organism could put up with such conditions year in and year out. There was nothing, absolutely nothing, to bring light into this life. There was nothing but misery, loneliness, gossip of the neighbors, worries about the next meal—and, on top of it all, there were the criminal chicaneries of her landlord and employer. In spite of the fact that she was severely hampered in her work by acute psychic disturbances, she was ruthlessly exploited. She received some two schillings per day for ten hours' work. That is to say, she was expected to support herself and her three children on some sixty to eighty schillings per month! The phenomenal thing about it was: she did it! I was never able to find out how she managed. In spite of everything, she was not at all neglected in her appearance. She even read books, including some which she borrowed from me.

Later, when the Marxists never tired of telling me that the sexual etiology of psychic illnesses was a bourgeois whim, that it was "only material distress" which produced neuroses, I always had to think of cases such as these. As if sexual distress were not a "material distress"! It is not "material distress" in the sense of Marxian economy that produces neuroses. Rather it is the neuroses of these people that ruins their ability to do something sensible about their distress, to assert themselves more effectively, to stand up to the competition of the labor market, to come to an understanding with others who are in a similar social situation, to keep their heads clear for rational thinking. Objections to the effect that such cases are exceptions, particularly if such objections are raised by people who dismiss neurosis as a "luxury of bourgeois damsels," can be refuted by facts.

The neuroses of the working population are merely lacking in cultural finesse. They are crude, blunt rebellions against the psychic massacre to which everybody is subjected. The well-to-do citizen bears his neurosis with dignity, or he manifests it materially in one form or another. Among the broad masses of the working population, the neurosis comes out in all its tragic grotesqueness.

Another patient was suffering from so-called nymphomania. She was never able to experience gratification. Hence, she slept with any man who was available, without gratification. She masturbated with a knife handle, or even with the knife blade in her vagina until she bled. Only those who know the torment which an insatiable, high-strung sexual excitation can cause cease to speak about the "transcendence of phenomenological spirituality." In this patient, too, the destructive influence of a large, poor, materially harassed laborer family was ruthlessly revealed. Mothers of such families have neither the time to nor the possibility of bringing up their children carefully. When the mother notices that her child is masturbating, she simply throws a knife at the child. And the child associates the knife with the fear of being punished for sexual activity and the accompanying guilt feelings; the child does not allow gratification to take place and attempts later, tormented by unconscious feelings of guilt, to experience orgasm with the same knife. This case was described in detail in *Der triebhafte Charakter*.

Such cases were not in the same category as simple neuroses or psychotic illnesses. Impulsive characters seemed to represent a transitional stage between neurosis and psychosis. The ego still functioned properly, but it was torn between affirmation of instinct and affirmation of morality, between negation of morality and negation of instinct, at one and the same time. It seemed to be in a rage against its own conscience, seemed to want to rid itself of it by exaggerating the impulsive actions. And the conscience was clearly ascertainable as the product of a contradictory, brutal upbringing. Compulsive neurotics and hysterical patients are brought up from an early age in a consistently antisexual way. In early childhood, these people had been without sexual guidance or had been prematurely active. Then, suddenly, they were brutally punished, and this punishment lived in the unconscious as sexual guilt feeling. The ego defended itself against the overwrought conscience by repressing it, in the same way in which it usually would repress only sexual desires.

The stasis of sexual energy in these patients was far greater and more drastic than it was in instinct-inhibited patients. In treating them, I had first of all to wrestle with their entire being, their character. The difficulties which they presented were directly dependent upon the degree of the sexual tension or the extent to which sexual gratification had been experienced. Every discharge of sexual tension through genital gratification immediately mitigated the effect of the breakthrough of pathological impulses. Those familiar with the basic ideas of sex-economy will have noticed that everything was present in these patients which was later incorporated into my basic theory: the character resistance, the curative role of genital gratification, the accumulative effect of sexual stasis on the asocial and perverse sexual impulses. I was able to put all this data together only after I had had similar experiences with instinct-inhibited neuroses. I wrote an eight-page monograph in which I explained for the first time the necessity of "character-analytic work" on the patient. Freud read the manuscript within three days and wrote me a letter of appreciation. It was possible, he said, that from now on mechanisms similar to those which had been found to be operative between ego and id would be found to be operative between ego and superego.

The idea was new that perverse and asocial impulses increase owing to the impairment of the normal sexual function. Psychoanalysts had been in the habit of explaining such cases on the basis of the "constitutional intensity of a drive." The anal sexuality of compulsive neurotic patients was said to be caused by a "strong erogenic predisposition of the anal zone." Abraham contended that, in melancholia, a "strong oral disposition" existed which predetermined the tendency to depressive moods. It was assumed that an especially "strong skin eroticism" lay at the basis of the masochistic beating fantasy. Exhibitionism was accounted for by an especially strong erogenicity of the eyes. An "exaggerated muscle eroticism" was said to be responsible for sadism. These conceptions are important in order to comprehend the research which I had to carry out before I was able to incorporate my clinical experiences on the role of genitality. What was difficult to understand in the beginning was the misunderstandings with which I had continually to contend.

The fact that the intensity of asocial actions is dependent upon the disturbance of the genital function had been correctly perceived. It contradicted the psychoanalytic conception of isolated "partial instincts." Although Freud had assumed a development of the sexual instinct from a pregenital to a genital stage, this view had become obscured in mechanistic conceptions. These are some of the contentions that were made: every erogenic zone (mouth, anus, eyes, skin, etc.) has a corresponding partial instinct, e.g., the pleasure of sucking, the pleasure of defecating, etc. Ferenczi, indeed, was of the opinion that genital sexuality was made up of pregenital qualities. Freud clung to the view that girls have only a clitoral sexuality and that they do not experience vaginal eroticism in early childhood. I went over my handwritten notes time and again. There was nothing to be done. My observations showed quite clearly that pregenital sexual impulses increased with impotence and decreased with potency. In the process of collating my observations, it occurred to me that a completely developed sexual tie between parent and child could exist at any stage of childhood sexual development. It was possible that, even at the age of five, a boy could desire his mother in an oral way only, while a girl of the same age could desire her father in an anal or oral way only. The relationships of children to adults of both sexes could have any number of variations. Freud's formula "I love my father or my mother and hate my mother or my father" was only a beginning. For my own convenience, I differentiated pregenital from genital child-parent relationships. Clinically, the former demonstrated far deeper regressions and psychic damages than the latter. In terms of sexual development, I had to conceive of the genital relationship as normal and the pregenital relationship as pathologic. A boy having a fully developed genital relationship to his mother would have a much easier time in establishing a genital relationship to a woman than a boy who loved his mother in an anal, i.e., perverse, way only. In the former, it was merely necessary to loosen the fixation; in the latter, the boy's entire personality had taken on passive and feminine characteristics. For the same reason, it was easier to cure a girl who had a vaginal or anal attachment to her father than it was to cure a girl who had assumed the sadistic male role. Hence, hysteria with its genital incest fixation offered fewer therapeutic difficulties than compulsive patients with their pregenital structure.

Why it was easier to dissolve the genital fixation than it was to dissolve the pregenital fixation was still not clear. At that time, I knew nothing about the fundamental difference between genital and pregenital sexuality. In psychoanalysis, no distinction was or is made between the two. Genitality was assumed to be as capable of sublimation as anality and orality. Gratification in the case of the latter was regarded as the same as "gratification" in the case of the former. There was "cultural suppression" and "condemnation" in both the former and the latter.

It is necessary at this point to go into these ideas in more detail. There is no basis to the contention of psychoanalysts that they have incorporated the theory of genitality into their theory of neuroses. It is imperative, therefore, to define precisely what is meant by genitality. It is true that my publications on this subject since 1922 have been partially incorporated into psychoanalytic thinking. It is also true, however, that there is still no understanding for the most essential elements of my ideas. The independent development of sex-economy began with the question of the difference between pregenital and genital pleasure. Not a single point of my theory is valid without it. Its correct solution leads automatically to the path which I had to pursue. To have evaded it would have been to compromise my work.

Chapter IV

THE DEVELOPMENT OF THE ORGASM THEORY

1. INITIAL EXPERIENCES

In December 1920, Freud sent me a young student for treatment. He was suffering from a compulsion to ruminate and to count, compulsive anal fantasies, habitual masturbation, acute neurasthenic symptoms, e.g., headaches and back pains, absent-mindedness and nausea. I treated him for several months. The compulsion to ruminate immediately became a compulsion to associate. His case seemed quite hopeless. Suddenly, an incest fantasy broke through, and for the first time the patient masturbated with gratification. All his symptoms vanished at once. In the course of eight days, they gradually returned. He masturbated again. The symptoms again disappeared, only to return a few days later. This went on for several weeks. Finally we succeeded in getting at the root of his guilt feelings about masturbation and in correcting some damaging modes of behavior. His condition visibly improved. After a total of nine months, I terminated the treatment. The patient was now capable of working and his condition was significantly better. My records show that I was informed about the patient's condition over a period of six years. He later married and remained healthy.

Parallel with this case, I was also analyzing a waiter who was totally incapable of having an erection. The treatment ran a smooth course. In the third year, we arrived at a perfect reconstruction of the "primal scene." He was about two years old when it occurred. His mother gave birth to a child. From the adjacent room, he had been able to observe every detail of the delivery. The impression of a large bloody hole between her legs became firmly ingrained in his mind. On a conscious level, there remained only the sensation of an "emptiness" in his own genitals. According to the psychoanalytic knowledge of that time, I merely connected his inability to have an erection with the severely traumatic impression of the "castrated" female genital. This was no doubt correct. However, it wasn't until a few years ago that I began to pay special attention to and to understand the "feeling of emptiness in the genitals" in my patients. It corresponds to a withdrawal of biological energy.

At that time, I incorrectly assessed the total personality of my patient. He was very quiet, well-mannered, and well-behaved, and did everything that was asked of him. He never got excited. In the course of three years of treatment, he never once became angry or exercised criticism. Thus, according to the prevailing concepts, he was a fully "integrated," "adjusted" character, with only one acute symptom (monosymptomatic neurosis). I delivered a report on this case to the seminar on technique and was praised for the correct elucidation of the primal traumatic scene. Theoretically, I had given a complete explanation of the symptom, the patient's inability to have an erection. Since the patient was industrious and orderly—"adjusted to reality" as we used to say—it did not occur to any one of us that it was precisely this emotional tranquility, this unshakable equanimity, which formed the pathological characterological basis on which erective impotence could be maintained. The older analysts considered the analytic work that I had performed complete and correct. For my part, I left the meeting unsatisfied. If everything was indeed just as it should be, why was there no change in the patient's impotence? There must be something missing some place, but none of us knew where. I terminated the analysis several months later—the patient had not been cured. The imperturbability with which he bore it was as stoical as the imperturbability with which he had accepted everything throughout the entire treatment. This patient impressed upon me the important character-analytic concept of "affect-block." I had hit upon the far-reaching connection between the present-day formation of the human character and emotional coldness and genital deadness.

This was when psychoanalysis was requiring longer and longer periods of treatment. When I first began to treat patients, six months was considered a long time. In 1923, one year was already a matter of course. The idea gained ground that two or more years for a treatment would be even better. There was no getting around it: neuroses are complicated and severe illnesses. Freud wrote his now famous *History of an Infantile Neurosis* on the basis of a case which he treated for five years. Freud of course had acquired a deep knowledge of a child's world of experience from this case. The psychoanalysts, on the other hand, made a virtue of necessity. Abraham contended that years were needed to understand a chronic depression, and that the "passive technique" was the only true technique. Psychoanalysts made sly jokes about their drowsiness during the analytic session. If a patient did not produce any associations for hours on end, then the analyst had to smoke a great deal in order not to fall asleep. There were analysts, indeed, who deduced grandiose theories from this. If the patient was silent, then the analyst too had to be silent, whether for hours or weeks on end. This was regarded as "consummate technique." From the very beginning, I sensed that something was fundamentally wrong here. Yet I too attempted to follow this "technique." Nothing came of it. The patients merely developed a deep sense of helplessness, a bad conscience, and the stubbornness which went hand in hand with both. Matters were not made any better by the jokes about the analyst who woke up from a deep sleep during a session and found his couch empty, nor with convoluted explanations to the effect that it was quite all right for the analyst to drowse for a while, for his unconscious would keep a careful watch over the patient. It was even contended that the analyst's unconscious was able, upon waking up from sleep during a treatment, to pick up precisely where the patient's unconscious was continuing. It was both depressing and hopeless. On the other hand, Freud warned us not to be overly ambitious in our therapeutic efforts. It was not until many years later that I understood what he meant. The allegations which were made by the psychotherapists were simply not true. Following the discovery of the unconscious mechanisms, Freud himself had initially cherished the definite hope of being able to tread upon secure ground toward the development of a causal psychotherapy. He had deceived himself. He must have been greatly disappointed. His conclusion was correct that further research was most imperative. A rash desire to cure is not conducive to the recognition of new facts. I had as little notion as anyone about the nature of the area into which this indispensable research had to lead. Nor did I have any notion that it was the psychoanalyst's fear of the social consequences of psychoanalysis which caused him to assume such bizarre attitudes in questions of therapy. At issue were the following questions:

1. Is the Freudian theory on the etiology of the neurosis complete?

2. Is it possible to arrive at a scientific theory of technique and therapy?

3. Is the Freudian theory of instinct correct? Is it complete? If not, where is it lacking?

4. What made sexual repression (which led to the epidemic of neurosis) necessary in the first place?

These questions contained the germ of everything that later came to be called sex-economy. It is only in retrospect that I can pose these orientating questions. At that time, the conscious formulation of any one of them might well have prematurely held me back from any kind of research. I am grateful that I had no concrete conception of these questions in those initial years, that I innocently went about my work in the psychoanalytic clinic and worked on the development of the psychoanalytic system—all in the belief that my activity was in Freud's name and for his life work. Deeply committed to my own life work, I have not the slightest regret today that this not very self-confident attitude later caused me considerable suffering. This attitude was the prerequisite for my later discoveries.

2. SUPPLEMENTATION OF FREUD'S CONCEPTION OF THE ANXIETY NEUROSIS

I would remind the reader that I came to Freud from sexology. It is not at all surprising, therefore, that I found his theory of the actual neuroses, which I called sexual stasis neuroses, far more appealing and scientific than the "interpretation" of the "meaning" of symptoms in the psychoneuroses. Freud designated as actual neuroses those illnesses which were caused by contemporary disturbances of sexual life. According to his conception, the anxiety neurosis and neurasthenia were illnesses which did not have a "psychic etiology." He held the view that they were direct manifestations of dammed-up sexuality. They were just like toxic disturbances. Freud assumed that the body contained "chemical substances" of a "sexual nature" which, if they were not adequately "metabolized," produced nervous palpitations, cardiac irregularity, acute attacks of anxiety, perspiration, and other symptoms of the vegetative life apparatus. It was far from Freud's intent to establish a relation between the anxiety neurosis and the vegetative system. On the basis of his clinical experience, he contended that the anxiety neurosis was the result of sexual abstinence or coitus interruptus. It was different from neurasthenia which, in contrast to the anxiety neurosis, was brought about by "sexual abuses," that is, by unregulated sexuality, e.g., excessive masturbation. The symptoms of neurasthenia were back pains and lumbago, headaches, general irritability, disturbances of memory and attentiveness, etc. In other words, Freud classified syndromes which were not understood by official neurology and psychiatry according to their etiology. It was for this reason that he was attacked by the psychiatrist Löwenfeld, who, like hundreds of other psychiatrists, completely denied the sexual etiology of neuroses. Freud stuck to the official clinical terminology. He contended that the abovementioned symptoms did not reveal any psychic content, whereas such contents were revealed by psychoneuroses, particularly hysteria and compulsion neurosis. The symptoms of these illnesses showed a concretely comprehensible content which was always sexual. It was merely necessary to have a sufficiently broad and sensible conception of sexuality. The incest fantasy and the fear of being injured in one's genitals were at the core of every psychoneurosis. The unconscious fantasies which were expressed in the psychoneurotic symptom were clearly of an infantile sexual nature. Freud made a clear-cut distinction between the actual neuroses and the psychoneuroses. Understandably, the psychoneuroses were of central importance in psychoanalytic clinical work. It was Freud's view that the actual neuroses could be cured by ridding the patient of the detrimental sexual activities, i.e., abstinence or coitus interruptus in the case of anxiety neurosis, and excessive masturbation in the case of neurasthenia.

Psychoneuroses, on the other hand, have to be treated psychoanalytically. In spite of this sharp dichotomization, he admitted a connection between the two groups. He was of the opinion that every psychoneurosis centered around "an actual-neurotic core." It was this very illuminating comment that formed the point of departure of my investigations of stasis anxiety. Freud no longer published anything on this subject.

According to Freud's conception of the actual neurosis, sexual energy is inadequately disposed of. Its access to consciousness and motility is blocked. The actual anxiety and the concomitant physiologically determined nervous symptoms are, so to speak, proliferations of a malignant nature which are nourished by non-resolved sexual excitation. But even the strange psychic formations of the compulsion neurotic and hysterical patients had the appearance of biologically meaningless, malignant proliferations. *Where did they derive their energy?* Could there be any doubt that it was from the "actual-neurotic core" of dammed-up sexual excitation. In other words, this must also be the energy source of the psychoneuroses. Freud's hint admitted of no other interpretation. This could be the only possible way of seeing it. The objection which most psychoanalysts raised to the theory of the actual neuroses had a disturbing effect. They contended that there was no such thing as an actual neurosis. This illness also, they said, was "psychically determined." Unconscious psychic contents could also be shown to exist in so-called "free-floating anxiety." Stekel was the chief exponent of this view. He argued that all forms of anxiety and nervous disturbances were psychically determined and not somatically determined, as was contended in the case of the actual neuroses. Like many others, Stekel failed to see the fundamental difference between the psychosomatic excitation and the psychic content of a symptom. Freud did not clear up the contradiction, but he stuck to his initial differentiation. I, on the other hand, saw any number of somatic symptoms in the psychoanalytic clinic. However, it could not be denied that the symptoms of the actual neurosis also had a psychic superstructure. Cases of pure actual neuroses were rare. The differentiation was not as clear-cut as Freud had assumed. Such specific questions of scientific research may well appear unimportant to the layman. It will be shown that very decisive problems of human health were concealed in them. In short, *there was no doubt that the psychoneuroses had an actual (stasis) neurotic core and that the stasis neuroses had a psychoneurotic superstructure.* Was there still any point in differentiating the two? Was it not merely a quantitative question?

While most analysts attached the greatest importance to the psychic contents of the neurotic symptoms, leading psychopathologists like Jaspers (cf. his *Psychopathologie*) completely denied the scientific character of psychological interpretation of meaning and, hence, denied the scientific character of psychoanalysis itself. He argued that the "meaning" of a psychic attitude or action could be grasped only "philosophically" and not scientifically. The natural sciences, he said, were concerned solely with *quantities* and energies, whereas philosophy was concerned with psychic *qualities*. There was no bridge between the quantitative and qualitative factors. At issue was a decisive question: did psychoanalysis and its methods have a natural scientific character? In other words: can there be a natural scientific psychology in the strict sense of the word? Can psychoanalysis claim to be a natural science, or is it merely one of the many philosophic disciplines? Freud paid no attention to these methodological questions and unconcernedly published his clinical observations. He disliked philosophic discussions. But I had to fight against narrow-minded opponents in these arguments. They wanted to relegate psychoanalysts to the ranks of the spiritualists and thus dispose of us. However, we knew that, for the first time in the history of psychology, we were practicing natural science. We wanted to be taken seriously. It was in the difficult struggle to gain clarity about these questions in the dialogue with our opponents that the weapons were forged with which I later defended Freud's cause. If it were true that only Wundt's experimental psychology is "scientific" because it measures reactions quantitatively; if, moreover, psychoanalysis is not scientific because it does not measure quantities but merely describes and constructs the relation of meanings between psychic phenomena which have been torn apart; then natural science is false. For Wundt and his students knew nothing of man in his living reality. They made evaluations about man on the basis of how many seconds it took him to react to the stimulus-word "dog." They still do this today. We, however, made evaluations on the basis of the manner in which a person dealt with his conflicts and the motives which prompted his actions. In the background of this dispute was the question of whether it was possible to arrive at a more concrete understanding of the Freudian concept of "psychic energy" or, best of all, to classify it under the general concept of energy.

Facts are not of much use in countering philosophic arguments. Allers, the Viennese philosopher and physiologist, declined to enter into the question of unconscious psychic life because, from the point of view of philosophy, the assumption of an "unconscious" was a priori false. I still run across such arguments today. When I maintain that highly sterilized substances can be alive, people say no—that is not possible. The slide must have been dirty, or else what I saw was "Brownian movement." The fact that it is easy to distinguish dirt on the slide from the bions, and Brownian movement from vegetative movement, does not make any difference to them. In short, "objective science" is a problem in itself.

Unexpectedly, a number of observations in the everyday

DEVELOPMENT OF THE ORGASM THEORY

life of the clinic, such as those made on the two patients mentioned earlier, helped me to find my way in this confusion. It gradually became clear that *the intensity of a psychic idea depends upon the quantity of somatic excitation with which it is combined.* Emotion originates in the instincts, thus in the somatic realm. An idea, on the other hand, is a purely "psychic," non-physical formation. What, then, is the relation between the "non-physical" idea and the "physical" excitation? When a person is fully aroused sexually, the idea of sexual intercourse is vivid and urgent. After gratification, on the other hand, it cannot be immediately reproduced; it is feeble, colorless, and somehow nebulous. There can be no doubt that this fact contained the secret of the relation between the physiogenic anxiety neurosis and the psychogenic psychoneurosis. My one patient had momentarily lost all his psychic compulsive symptoms after experiencing sexual gratification. With the reappearance of excitation, the symptoms also reappeared and remained until the next gratification. My other patient, however, had thoroughly worked through all the material in the psychic sphere, but there had not been any sexual excitation. The unconscious ideas which made him incapable of having an erection had not been influenced by the treatment. Suddenly, things began to fit together. I understood now that a psychic idea endowed with a very small amount of energy can provoke an increase in the excitation. In turn, this provoked excitation makes the idea urgent and vivid. If the excitation ceases, the idea also vanishes. If, as in the case of the stasis neurosis, a conscious idea of the sexual act fails to materialize because of a moralistic inhibition, what happens is that the excitation becomes attached to other ideas which can be thought of more freely. I concluded from this that the stasis neurosis is a *physical* disturbance caused by inadequately disposed of, i.e., unsatisfied, sexual excitation. However, without a psychic inhibition, the sexual excitation would always be adequately discharged. I was surprised that Freud had overlooked this fact. Once an inhibition has produced a sexual stasis, it can easily happen that the latter intensifies the inhibition and reactivates infantile ideas that take the place of normal ideas. As a result of a contemporary inhibition, childhood experiences which are not in themselves pathologic could, so to speak, receive an excess of sexual energy. Once this happens, they become urgent, come into conflict with the adult psychic organization, and have, from now on, to be held in check with the help of repression. It is in this way that a chronic psychoneurosis with its infantile sexual contents develops from a contemporaneously caused, at first "harmless," sexual inhibition. This is the essence of what Freud described as the neurotic "regression to infantile mechanisms." All the cases which I treated demonstrated this mechanism. If the neurosis had not existed from childhood, if it had developed later, it always turned out that a "normal" sexual inhibition or difficulty in one's sexual life had produced a stasis, and this stasis in turn had activated the infantile incest desires and sexual anxieties.

The next question was this: is the sexual inhibition and the concomitant rejection of sexuality that develops at the beginning of a chronic illness "neurotic" or "normal"? No one spoke about this. It appeared that the sexual inhibition of a well-brought-up middle-class girl was quite the way it should be. I, too, was of the same opinion; that is to say, I simply did not give it any thought at that time. If, owing to an ungratifying marriage, a young lively woman developed a stasis neurosis, e.g., nervous cardiac anxiety, it did not occur to anyone to ask about the inhibition that prevented her from experiencing sexual gratification in spite of her marriage. In time, it is even possible that she might develop a real hysteria or compulsion neurosis. In this case, the primary cause would have been the moralistic inhibition, while the ungratified sexuality would have been its driving force.

This was the point of departure for the solution of many problems. But it was very difficult to tackle them immediately and energetically. For seven years I thought I was working in complete accordance with the Freudian school of thought. No one divined that this line of questioning would lead to a fatal clash between fundamentally incompatible scientific views.

3. ORGASTIC POTENCY

The case of the uncured waiter called into question the correctness of the Freudian formula of therapy. The other case clearly revealed the actual mechanism of cure. For a time, I tried to bring these opposing views into harmony. In his *History of the Psychoanalytic Movement,* Freud tells about the time he heard Charcot relating to a colleague the case history of a young woman who was suffering from acute symptoms. Her husband was impotent or very clumsy in the sexual act. Seeing that the colleague did not grasp the connection, Charcot suddenly exclaimed with great vivacity, "Mais, dans des cas pareils, c'est toujours la chose génitale, toujours! toujours! toujours!" "I know," Freud writes, "that for a moment I was paralyzed with astonishment, and I said to myself, 'Yes, but if he knows this, why does he never say so?'"

A year later, the Viennese physician Chrobak referred a patient to Freud. She was suffering from acute anxiety attacks and was still a virgin, after eighteen years of marriage to an impotent man. Chrobak had written the following comment: "We know only too well what the only prescription is for such cases, but we can't prescribe it. It is: 'Penis normalis, dosim. Repetatur!'" In other words, the hysterical patient falls ill owing to a lack of genital gratification. This put Freud on the track of the sexual etiology of hysteria, but he shrank from the full consequences of Charcot's statement.

It is banal and sounds rather hackneyed, but I maintain that every person who has succeeded in preserving a certain amount of naturalness knows this: those who are psychically ill need but one thing—complete and repeated genital gratification. Instead of simply investigating this matter, substantiating it, expressing it, and immediately taking up its fight, I entangled myself for years on end in the psychoanalytic formulation of theories, which detracted from it. Most of the theories which psychoanalysts have advanced since the publication of Freud's *The Ego and the Id* have had but one function: to wipe out Charcot's statement, "In these cases, it is always a question of genitality, and I mean always." The fact that man's sexual organs do not function in a normal way, thus precluding sexual gratification for both sexes, that this is the cause of most psychic misery and even has a bearing on the cancer scourge, was too simple to be perceived. Let us see if this is an exaggeration.

The facts of medical experience were confirmed again and again wherever I was working—in my private practice, the psychoanalytic clinic, and the psychiatric-neurologic clinic.

The severity of every form of psychic illness is directly related to the severity of the genital disturbance.

The prospects of cure and the success of the cure are directly dependent upon the possibility of establishing the capacity for full genital gratification.

Of the hundreds of cases which I observed and treated in the course of several years of extensive and intensive work, there was not a single woman who did not have a vaginal orgastic disturbance. Roughly 60 to 70 percent of the male patients had gross genital disturbances. Either they were incapable of having an erection during the act or they suffered from premature ejaculations. The disturbance of the ability to experience genital gratification, to experience, that is, the most natural of what is natural, proved to be a symptom which was always present in women and seldom absent in men. At that time, I did not give any further thought to the 30 to 40 percent of the men who appeared to be genitally healthy but were otherwise neurotic. This negligence in clinical thinking was consistent with the psychoanalytic view that impotence or frigidity was "merely one symptom among many."

In November 1922, I read a paper before the Vienna Psychoanalytic Society on the "Limits of Memory Activity in the Psychoanalytic Cure." The presentation met with enthusiastic approval, for all therapists were tormented in applying the basic rule, to which the patients did not adhere, and in obtaining the memories which the patients were supposed to produce but could not. In the hands of mediocre analysts, the primal scene remained a not very convincing, rather arbitrary reconstruction. I emphasized that there could be no doubt about the Freudian formulation concerning the existence of primal traumatic experiences in children between the ages of one and four. It was all the more important, therefore, to investigate the limitations of the method.

In January 1923, I presented the case history of a psychogenic tic. The patient was an older woman suffering from a diaphragmatic tic, which subsided when it became possible for her to masturbate. My presentation was praised and affirmed.

In October 1923, I read a paper before the society on introspection in a schizophrenic patient. I had been treating a female schizophrenic patient who had particularly clear insights into the mechanisms of her persecution ideas. She confirmed the finding of Tausk regarding the influence of the genital apparatus.

On November 28, 1923, following three years of investigation, I read my first major paper, "On Genitality, from the Point of View of the Prognosis and Therapy of Psychoanalysis." It was published in the *Internationale Zeitschrift für Psychoanalyse* the following year.

During my presentation, I became aware of a growing chilliness in the mood of the meeting. I was a good speaker and had always been listened to attentively. When I had finished, an icy stillness hung over the room. Following a break, the discussion began. My contention that the genital disturbance was an important, perhaps the most important, symptom of the neurosis was said to be erroneous. The same was said about my contention that valuable prognostic and therapeutic data could be derived from the assessment of genitality. Two analysts literally asserted that they knew any number of female patients who had a "completely healthy genital life." They appeared to me to be more excited than was in keeping with their usual scientific reserve.

I was at a disadvantage in this controversy, for I had to admit that there were many male patients who did not appear to have any genital disturbance. Among female patients, on the other hand, this was clearly not the case. I was looking for the *energy source of the neurosis*, its somatic core. This core could be nothing other than dammed-up sexual energy, but I could not explain the origin of this stasis if potency was unimpaired. Two cardinal views of psychoanalysis led me astray. A man was said to be "potent" when he was able to carry out the sexual act. He was said to be very potent when he could do so several times in the course of one night. The most cherished topic of conversation among men of all circles centers around the question of which one could sleep with a woman the most number of times in one night. The psychoanalyst Roheim even went so far as to define potency as the ability of a man to embrace a woman in such a way as to cause an inflammation of the vagina.

The other misleading view was that a partial instinct, e.g., the desire to suck on the mother's breast, could be blocked separately. In this way, it was argued, the existence of neurotic symptoms in patients having "full potency" could be explained. This view was wholly in keeping with the idea of non-related erogenous zones. In addition, the psychoanalysts denied my contention that there is not a single female patient capable of full genital gratification. A woman was considered genitally healthy when she was capable of having a clitoral orgasm. At that time, the sex-economic differentiation between clitoral and vaginal excitation was unknown.* In short, no one had any idea of the natural function of the orgasm. Still to be accounted for was a questionable remainder of genitally healthy men who, if they were indeed capable of experiencing genital gratification, threw overboard all assumptions about the prognostic and therapeutic role of genitality. For it was clear: *if my assumption was correct, i.e., if the genital disturbance constituted the energy source of neurotic symptoms, then there could not be a single case of neurosis with undisturbed genitality.*

My procedure in this was much the same as in all my other scientific achievements. A general hypothesis was derived from a series of clinical observations. There were gaps in it here and there; it was open to objections which appeared justified. One's opponents seldom fail to ferret out such gaps and, on the basis of them, to reject the hypothesis as a whole. As Du Teil † once said, "Scientific objectivity is not of this world. Indeed, its existence is altogether doubtful." There is little hope of objective cooperation on any one problem. It was precisely through their "fundamental" objections that the critics helped me to overcome difficulties,

---

* Controversy still rages on this subject. Masters and Johnson are the most recent authorities to deny that there is a distinction. Yet it would seem that the only true authority is the woman who has experienced both clitoral and vaginal orgasms. Invariably, she will insist that there is a distinct difference. [Editor]

† Roger Du Teil did control work on the bion experiments at the University in Nice. [Editor]

though this was hardly their intent. Such was the case then, too. The objection that there are any number of genitally healthy neurotics prompted me to take a closer look at "genital health." As incredible as it may seem, it is nonetheless true that the precise analysis of genital behavior, which goes deeper than "I slept with a woman" or "I slept with a man," was strictly forbidden in psychoanalysis. It took me more than two years of experience to rid myself completely of this cultivated reserve and to realize that people confuse "fucking" with the loving embrace.

The more precisely my patients described their behavior and experiences in the sexual act, the more firm I became in my clinically substantiated conviction that *all patients, without exception, are severely disturbed in their genital function*. Most disturbed of all were those men who liked to boast and make a big show of their masculinity, men who possessed or conquered as many women as possible, who could "do it" again and again in one night. It became quite clear that, though they were erectively very potent, such men experienced no or very little pleasure at the moment of ejaculation, or they experienced the exact opposite, disgust and unpleasure. The precise analysis of fantasies during the sexual act revealed that the men usually had sadistic or conceited attitudes and that the women were afraid, inhibited, or imagined themselves to be men. For the ostensibly potent man, sexual intercourse means the piercing, overpowering, or conquering of the woman. He merely wants to prove his potency or to be admired for his erective endurance. This "potency" can be easily undermined by uncovering its motives. Severe disturbances of erection and ejaculation are concealed in it. In none of these cases is there the slightest trace of *involuntary behavior or loss of conscious activity in the act*. Gradually, groping my way ahead step by step, I acquired a knowledge of the characteristics of *orgastic impotence*. It took me a decade to gain a full understanding of

DEVELOPMENT OF THE ORGASM THEORY

this disturbance, to describe it and to learn the correct technique for eliminating it.

Orgastic impotence has always been in the forefront of sex-economic research, and all of its details are still not known. Its role in sex-economy is similar to the role of the Oedipus complex in psychoanalysis. Whoever does not have a precise understanding of it cannot be considered a sex-economist. He will never really grasp its ramifications. He will not understand the difference between health and sickness, nor will he comprehend human pleasure anxiety or the pathological nature of the parent-child conflict and the misery of marriage. It is even possible that he will endeavor to bring about sexual reforms, but he will never touch upon the core of sexual misery. He might admire the bion experiments, even imitate them perhaps, but he will never really conduct research in the field of sex-economy. He will never comprehend religious ecstasy, nor have the least insight into fascist irrationalism. Because he lacks the most important fundamentals, he will of necessity adhere to the antithesis between nature and culture, instinct and morality, sexuality and achievement. He will not be able to really solve a single pedagogic problem. He will never understand the identity between sexual process and life process. Nor, consequently, will he be able to grasp the sex-economic theory of cancer. He will mistake sickness for health and health for sickness. He will end up misinterpreting man's fear of happiness. In short, he might be anything, but he will never be a sex-economist, who knows that man is the sole biological species that has destroyed its own natural sexual function and is sick as a consequence of this.

Instead of a systematic presentation, I want to describe the theory of the orgasm in the way in which it developed. This will enable the reader to grasp more easily its inner logic. It will be seen that no human brain could have invented these relationships.

Until 1923, the year the orgasm theory was born, only ejaculative and erective potency were known to sexology and psychoanalysis. Without the inclusion of the functional, economic, and experiential components, the concept of sexual potency has no meaning. Erective and ejaculative potency are merely indispensable preconditions for orgastic potency. *Orgastic potency is the capacity to surrender to the flow of biological energy, free of any inhibitions; the capacity to discharge completely the damned-up sexual excitation through involuntary, pleasurable convulsions of the body.* Not a single neurotic is orgastically potent, and the character structures of the overwhelming majority of men and women are neurotic.

In the sexual act free of anxiety, unpleasure, and fantasies, the intensity of pleasure in the orgasm is dependent upon the amount of sexual tension concentrated in the genitals. The greater the excitation and the steeper its "drop," the more intense the pleasure.

The following description of the orgastically gratifying sexual act pertains only to the course of a few typical, naturally determined phases and modes of behavior. I did not take into account the biological foreplay which is determined by the individual needs and does not exhibit a universal character. In addition, we must note that the bioelectric processes of the orgasm function have not been explored and therefore this description is incomplete.

Phase of voluntary control of the excitation

1.[2] Erection is not painful as it is in priapism, spasm of the pelvic floor, or of the spermatic duct. It is pleasurable. The penis is not overexcited as it is after a prolonged period of abstinence or in cases of premature ejaculation. The female genital becomes hyperemic and moist in a specific way

---

[2] The arabic figures in the text correspond to the arabic figures in the legend to the diagram.

through the profuse secretion of the genital glands; that is, in the case of undisturbed genital functioning, the secretion has specific chemical and physical properties which are lacking when the genital function is disturbed. An important characteristic of male orgastic potency is the urge to penetrate. Erections can occur without this urge, as is the case in some erectively potent narcissistic characters and in satyriasis.

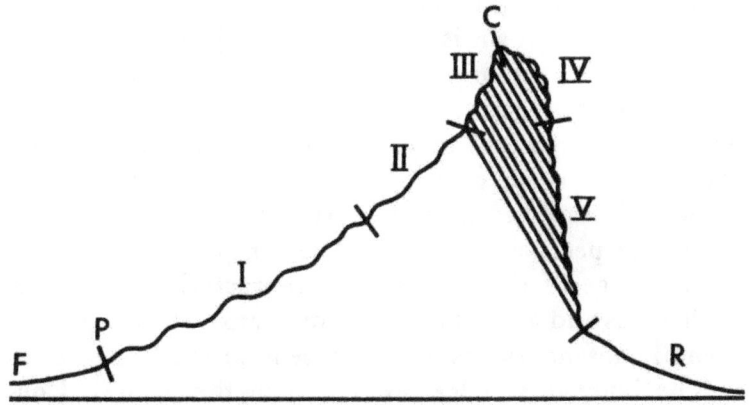

Diagram depicting the typical phases of the sexual act in which both male and female are orgastically potent

F = forepleasure (1, 2). P = penetration of penis (3). I (4, 5) = phase of voluntary control of the excitation and prolongation which is still unharmful. II (6 a-d) = phase of involuntary muscle contractions and automatic increase of excitation. III (7) = sudden and steep ascent to the climax (C). IV (8) = orgasm. The shaded part represents the phase of involuntary convulsions of the body. V (9, 10) = steep drop of the excitation. R = pleasant relaxation. Duration from five to twenty minutes.

2. The man and the woman are tender toward each other, and there are no contradictory impulses. The following are pathological deviations from this behavior: aggressiveness stemming from sadistic impulses, as in some erectively potent compulsion neurotics, and the inactivity of the passive-feminine character. Tenderness is also absent in

"onanistic coitus" with an unloved object. Normally, the activity of the woman does not differ in any way from that of the man. The widespread passivity on the part of the woman is pathological, usually the result of masochistic rape fantasies.

3. The pleasurable excitation, which has remained at approximately the same level during forepleasure activity, suddenly increases in both man and woman with the penetration of the penis into the vagina. The feeling on the part of the man that he is "being sucked in" is the counterpart of the woman's feeling that she is "sucking in" the penis.

4. The man's urge to penetrate deeply increases, but does not take on the sadistic form of "wanting to pierce through," as in the case of compulsion neurotic characters. Through the mutual, gradual, spontaneous, effortless friction, the excitation becomes concentrated on the surface and glans of the penis and on the posterior parts of the mucous membrane of the vagina. The characteristic sensation which heralds and accompanies the discharge of the semen is still wholly absent; this is not the case in premature ejaculation. The body is still less excited than the genital. Consciousness is fully attuned to the assimilation of the streaming sensations of pleasure. The ego actively participates insofar as it attempts to explore all possible avenues of pleasure and to achieve the highest degree of tension before the onset of the orgasm. Conscious intentions obviously play no part in this. It all takes place spontaneously on the basis of the individually different forepleasure experiences, through change of position, the nature of the friction, its rhythm, etc. According to most potent men and women, the slower and more gentle the frictions are and the more closely synchronized, the more intense are the sensations of pleasure. This presupposes a high degree of affinity between the partners. A pathological counterpart to this is the urge to produce vio-

lent frictions. This is especially pronounced in sadistic compulsive characters who suffer from penis anesthesia and the inability to discharge semen. Another example is the nervous haste of those who suffer from premature ejaculations. Orgastically potent men and women never laugh and talk during the sexual act, except possibly to exchange words of endearment. Both talking and laughing are indicative of severe disturbances of the ability to surrender; surrender presupposes complete immersion in the streaming sensation of pleasure. Men who feel that surrender is "feminine" are always orgastically disturbed.

5. In this phase, interruption of the friction is in itself pleasurable because of the special sensations of pleasure which attend this pause and do not require psychic exertion. In this way, the act is prolonged. The excitation subsides a little during the pause. However, it does not, as in pathological cases, subside altogether. Interruption of the sexual act by withdrawing the penis is not unpleasurable as long as it occurs after a restful pause. When friction continues, the excitation steadily increases beyond the level which had been previously attained. It gradually takes more and more possession of *the entire body,* while the genital itself maintains a more or less constant level of excitation. Finally, as a result of a fresh, usually sudden increase of genital excitation, the phase of involuntary muscular contraction sets in.

Phase of involuntary muscle contractions

6. In this phase, voluntary control of the course of the excitation is no longer possible. It exhibits the following characteristic features:

a. The increase of the excitation can no longer be controlled; rather it grips the entire personality and causes an acceleration of pulse and deep exhalation.

b. The physical excitation becomes more and more concentrated in the genital; there is a sweet sensation which can be best described as the flowing of excitation from the genital to other parts of the body.

c. To begin with, this excitation causes involuntary contractions of the entire musculature of the genitalia and pelvic floor. These contractions are experienced in the form of waves: the rise of the wave coincides with the complete penetration of the penis, while the fall of the wave coincides with the retraction of the penis. But as soon as the retraction goes beyond a certain limit, immediate spasmodic contractions take place which accelerate ejaculation. In the female, it is the smooth musculature of the vagina which contracts.

d. At this stage, the interruption of the act is altogether unpleasurable for both the man and the woman. When an interruption takes place, the muscular contractions which lead to the orgasm in the woman and the ejaculation in the man are spasmodic instead of rhythmic. The sensations which this produces are highly unpleasurable and occasionally pains in the pelvic floor and the sacrum are experienced. As a result of the spasms, moreover, the ejaculation takes place earlier than it does in the case of undisturbed rhythm.

The voluntary prolongation of the first phase of the sexual act (1 to 5) is not harmful up to a certain degree and has a pleasure-intensifying effect. On the other hand, the interruption or voluntary change of the course of the excitation in the second phase is harmful because of the involuntary nature of this phase.

7. Through the further intensification and increase in the frequency of the involuntary muscle contractions, the excitation mounts rapidly and sharply to the climax (III to C in the diagram); normally this coincides with the first ejaculatory muscle contractions in the man.

8. At this point, consciousness becomes more or less clouded; following a brief pause at the "height" of the climax, the frictions increase spontaneously and the urge to

penetrate "completely" becomes more intense with every ejaculatory muscle contraction. The muscle contractions in the woman follow the same course as they follow in the man; there is merely a psychic difference, namely that the healthy woman wants "to receive completely" during and just after the climax.

9. The orgastic excitation takes hold of the entire body and produces strong convulsions of the musculature of the whole body. Self-observations on the part of healthy persons of both sexes, as well as the analysis of certain disturbances of the orgasm, show that what we call the resolution of tension and experience as motor discharge (descending curve of the orgasm) is essentially the result of the reversion of the excitation from the genital to the body. This reversion is experienced as a sudden reduction of the tension.

Hence, the climax represents the turning point in the course of the excitation, i.e., prior to the climax, the direction of the excitation is toward the genital; subsequent to the climax, the excitation flows away from the genital. It is this complete return of the excitation from the genital to the body that constitutes the gratification. This means two things: flowing back of the excitation to the entire body and relaxation of the genital apparatus.

10. Before the neutral point is reached, the excitation fades away in a gentle curve and is immediately replaced by a pleasant physical and psychic relaxation. Usually, there is also a strong desire to sleep. The sensual relations are extinguished, but a "satiated" tender attitude to the partner continues, to which is added the feeling of gratitude.

In contrast to this, the orgastically impotent person experiences a leaden exhaustion, disgust, repulsion, weariness, or indifference and, occasionally, hatred toward the partner. In the case of satyriasis and nymphomania, the sexual excitation does not subside. Insomnia is one of the essential characteristics of lack of gratification. It cannot be automatically concluded, however, that a person has experienced gratification when he falls asleep immediately following the sexual act.

If we re-examine the two phases of the sexual act, we see that the first phase is characterized essentially by the sensory experience of pleasure, while the second phase is characterized by the motor experience of pleasure.

Involuntary bioenergetic convulsion of the organism and the complete resolution of the excitation are the most important characteristics of orgastic potency. The shaded part of the diagram represents the involuntary vegetative relaxation. There are partial resolutions of the excitation which are similar to the orgastic resolution. They have until now been looked upon as the actual release. Clinical experience shows that, as a result of universal sexual suppression, men and women have lost the ability to experience the ultimate surrender to the involuntary. It is precisely this previously unrecognized phase of final excitation and resolution of tension that I have in mind when I speak of "orgastic potency." It constitutes the primal and basic biological function which man has in common with all living organisms. All experiencing of nature is derived from this function or from the longing for it.

The course of excitation in the woman is exactly the same as that of the man. The orgasm in both sexes is more intense when the peaks of genital excitation coincide. This is very frequently the case among men and women who are capable of concentrating affection and sensuality on *one* partner who reciprocates this affection and sensuality. It is the rule when the love relationship is disturbed neither by internal nor external factors. In such cases, at least conscious fantasy activity is completely suspended; the ego absorbs and is fully focused on the sensations of pleasure. The ability to focus the entire affective personality upon the orgastic experience, in spite of any contradictions, is another characteristic of orgastic potency.

It cannot be easily determined whether unconscious fantasy activity is also at rest. Certain factors would indicate that it is. Fantasies which are not allowed to become conscious can only detract from the experience. It is necessary to distinguish two groups of fantasies which could accompany the sexual act, those in harmony with the sexual experience and those at variance with it. If the partner is capable of attracting all sexual interests to herself or himself at least momentarily, then the unconscious fantasies are also superfluous. In terms of their very nature, these fantasies are opposed to the real experience, for one fantasizes only what one cannot have in reality. There is a genuine transference from the primal object to the partner. It is possible for the partner to replace the object of the fantasy because of the identity between their basic characteristics. If, however, the transference of sexual interests takes place solely on the basis of a neurotic desire for the primal object, without the inner ability for genuine transference and in spite of the fact that there is no identity between the partner and the fantasized object, then no illusion can drown out the vague feeling of artificiality in the relationship. In the former instance, coitus is not followed by disappointment. In the latter, disappointment is inevitable, and we can assume that the fantasy activity during the act did not cease: it served, rather, to maintain the illusion. In the former, one loses interest in the original object and, consequently, its fantasy-generating force is also lost. The original object is regenerated by the partner. In a genuine transference, there is no glorification of the sexual partner; characteristics at variance with the primal object are correctly assessed and tolerated. In an artificial transference, the sexual partner is inordinately idealized and the relationship is full of illusions. The negative characteristics are not recognized, and fantasy activity must be continued, otherwise the illusion is lost.

The more intensively the fantasy has to work to make the partner approximate the ideal, the more the sexual pleasure loses in the way of intensity and sex-economic value. It depends entirely upon the nature of the disagreements, that occur in every extended relationship, whether and to what extent they reduce the intensity of the sexual experience. The reduction tends to become a pathological disturbance much sooner when there is a strong fixation on the primal object and an inability to achieve a genuine transference; when, moreover, a great deal of energy is required to overcome those characteristics in the partner which are at variance with the primal object.

4. SEXUAL STASIS—THE ENERGY SOURCE OF THE NEUROSIS

Since my first clinical observations in 1920, I had carefully singled out and noted genital disturbances in the patients whom I treated at the clinic. Over the course of two years, I had collected sufficient material to permit me to make this formulation: the disturbance of genitality is not, as was previously believed, one symptom among others. It is *the* symptom of the neurosis. Little by little all the evidence pointed to one conclusion: psychic illness is not only a result of a sexual disturbance in the broad Freudian sense of the word; even more concretely, it is the result of the disturbance of the genital function, in the strict sense of orgastic impotence.

If I had redefined sexuality to mean solely genital sexuality, I would have relapsed to the pre-Freudian, erroneous conception of sexuality. Sexual would be only what is genital. By amplifying the concept of genital function with the concept of orgastic potency and defining it in terms of energy, I added a new dimension to the psychoanalytic theory of sexuality and libido within its original framework. The arguments in support of this were as follows:

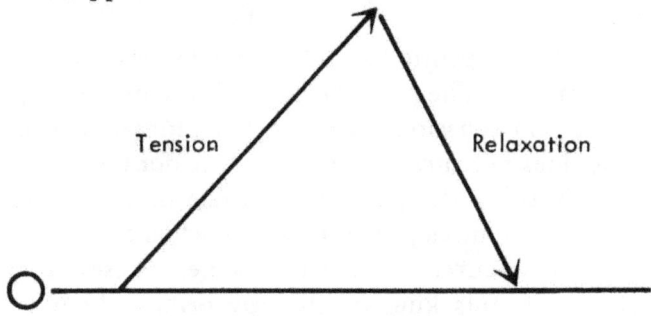

1. Sex-economic energy process.

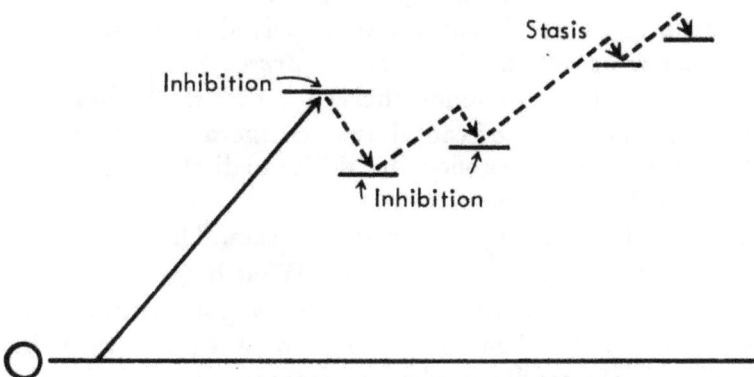

2. Inhibition. Disturbed sex-economy (stasis).

1. If every psychic illness has a core of dammed-up sexual excitation, it can be caused only by the disturbance of the capacity for orgastic gratification. Hence, impotence and frigidity are the key to the understanding of the economy of neuroses.

2. *The energy source of the neurosis is created by the difference between the accumulation and discharge of sexual energy.* The ungratified sexual excitation which is always

present in the neurotic psychic apparatus distinguishes it from the healthy psychic apparatus. This holds true not only for the stasis neuroses (in Freudian terminology, actual neuroses) but for all psychic illnesses, with or without symptom formation.

3. Freud's therapeutic formula for neuroses, though correct, is incomplete. The primary prerequisite of therapy is to make the patient conscious of his or her repressed sexuality. This alone does not cure, i.e., it *can* but it does not *of necessity* do so. Making the patient conscious of his or her repressed sexual impulses guarantees cure when this also eliminates the energy source of the neurosis, i.e., the sexual stasis. In other words, this kind of therapy brings about a cure when the consciousness of the instinctual demands also restores the capacity for full orgastic gratification. In this way, the pathological proliferations are deprived of the source of their energy (*principle of energy withdrawal*).

4. There can be no doubt, therefore, that the highest and most important goal of causal analytic therapy is the establishment of orgastic potency, the ability to discharge accumulated sexual energy completely.

5. Sexual excitation is a somatic process. The conflicts of the neurosis are of a psychic nature. What happens is that a minor conflict, in itself normal, causes a slight disturbance in the balance of sexual energy. This minor stasis intensifies the conflict, and the conflict in turn increases the stasis. Thus, the psychic conflict and the stasis of somatic excitation mutually augment one another. The central psychic conflict is the sexual relationship between child and parent. It is present in every neurosis. It is the historical storehouse of experience from which the content of the neurosis is nourished. All neurotic fantasies can be traced back to the child's early sexual relationship to the parents. However, if it were not continually nourished by the contemporary stasis of excitation which it initially produced, the child-parent conflict could not by it-

self cause a permanent disturbance of the psychic equilibrium. Hence, the stasis of excitation is the ever-present contemporary factor of the illness; it does not add to the content of the neurosis but supplies it with energy. The pathological incestuous ties to parents and brothers and sisters lose their force when the contemporary energy stasis is eliminated, i.e., when full orgastic gratification is experienced in the actual present. Hence, *whether the Oedipus conflict becomes pathological or not depends upon the degree to which the sexual energy is discharged.* In short, actual neurosis and psychoneurosis overlap: they cannot be conceived as separate types of neuroses.

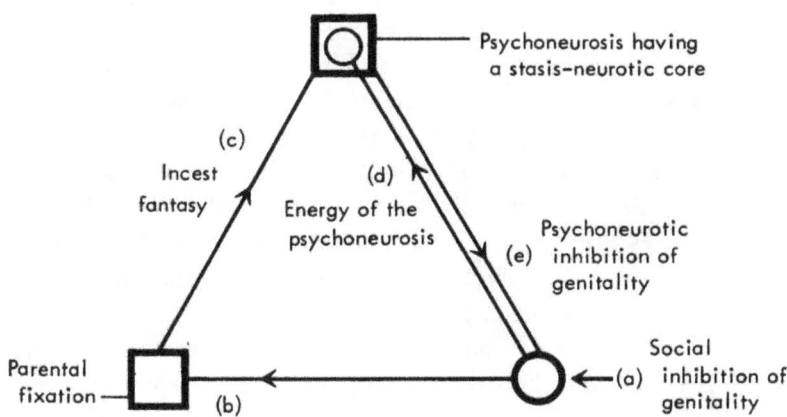

Diagram depicting the relation between the content of childhood experience and sexual stasis

- a. Socially induced sexual inhibition (O)
- b. Stasis results in fixation on parents (historical content □)
- c. Incest fantasy
- d. Energy source of the neurosis
- e. Neurosis maintains the stasis (contemporary stasis of energy)

6. The dynamics of pregenital sexuality (oral, anal, muscular, etc.) are fundamentally different from the dynamics

of genital sexuality. If non-genital sexual activities are retained, the genital function becomes disturbed. This disturbance incites pregenital fantasies and actions. The pregenital sexual fantasies and activities which we find in neuroses and perversions are not only the cause of the genital disturbance but, at least as much the result of this disturbance. These insights and observations constitute the groundwork of the distinction I made in 1936 between natural and secondary drives. With reference to the theory of instinct and the theory of culture, the most decisive formula was: the general sexual disturbance is a result of genital disturbance, i.e., orgastic impotence. What I understood by genital sexuality was a function that was unknown and did not conform to the usual ideas about man's sexual activities. "Genital" in the sex-economic sense of the word and "genital" in the usual sense of the word do not mean the same thing, any more than "sexual" and "genital" mean the same thing.

7. Moreover, a question of the theory of neurosis which harassed Freud in the following years was solved in a simple way. Psychic illnesses represent qualities only. Nonetheless, they always appear to be dependent upon so-called quantitative factors, upon the strength and force, the energy cathexis, of the psychic experiences and actions. At a meeting of the inner circle of analysts, Freud once exhorted us to be cautious. We had, he said, to be prepared to expect dangerous challenges to the psychic therapy of the neurosis by a future *organotherapy*. There was no way of knowing what it would be like, but one could already hear its exponents knocking at the door. Psychoanalysis must one day be established on an organic basis. This was a genuine Freudian intuition! When Freud said this, I understood that the solution of the quantity problem in the neurosis presupposed the solution of the problem of organotherapy. Access to the latter could be provided only by the understanding and handling of the physiological sexual stasis. I had already begun

to work along these lines. Indeed, the first significant breakthrough had been achieved five years before: the advancement from character analysis to the formulation of the fundamental principles of the technique of the vegetotherapy of the neurosis. The interim was taken up with fifteen years of hard work and difficult struggles.

In the years 1922 to 1926, the theory of the orgasm was formulated and substantiated piece by piece, followed by the development of the technique of character analysis. Every subsequent experience, success as well as failure, confirmed this theory, which had developed by itself on the basis of those first decisive observations. For my work, the problems loomed up rapidly and clearly.

Clinical work led in one direction to the present level of experimental work in the field of sex-economy. A second direction proceeded from the question: what is the source and what is the function of the social suppression of sexuality?

Much later, from 1933 on, a biological offshoot of sex-economy developed from the first complex of problems: bion research, sex-economic cancer research, and the investigation of the phenomena of orgone radiation. Some seven years later, the second complex of problems split up into actual sexual sociology on the one hand and political psychology on the other.[3] The orgasm theory has determined the psychological, psychotherapeutic, physiobiological, and sociological sectors of sex-economy. I do not claim that the framework of sex-economy could replace these specialized fields. But it does claim today to be a unitary natural-scientific theory of sex, on the basis of which it will be possible to resuscitate and fecundate all aspects of human life. This imposes upon us the obligation of giving a thorough presentation of its

---

[3] Cf. Reich, *The Sexual Revolution*, 1974, *The Invasion of Compulsory Sex-Morality*, 1971, and *The Mass Psychology of Fascism*, 1970, all Farrar, Straus and Giroux.

framework in all related fields. Since the life process and the sexual process are one and the same, it goes without saying that *sexual, vegetative energy is active in everything that lives*. This statement is very dangerous precisely because it is simple and absolutely correct. To apply it correctly, care must be taken to prevent it from becoming a platitude or deteriorating into a fixed system. Followers tend to make matters easy for themselves. They take over arduously worked-out material and operate with it in the most comfortable way possible. They make no effort to find new applications for all the subtleties of the method. They become torpid and the complex of problems ceases to be a challenge. I hope that I shall succeed in saving sex-economy from this fate.

Chapter V

THE DEVELOPMENT OF THE CHARACTER-ANALYTIC TECHNIQUE

1. DIFFICULTIES AND CONTRADICTIONS

The psychoanalytic technique made use of free association to ferret out and interpret unconscious fantasies. However, the therapeutic effect of interpretation proved to be limited. There were but few patients who were capable of free, involuntary association. The improvements which were achieved were ascribable to breakthroughs of genital energy. They were usually brought about accidentally through the loosening of the psychic apparatus, as a consequence of free association. I could see that the release of genital energies had enormous therapeutic effect, but I did not know how to direct and control this factor. It was never really possible to say which processes in the patient were responsible for the accidental breakthrough. It became necessary, therefore, to make a careful study of the psychoanalytic technique itself.

I have already described the hopelessness of the technical situation at that time. When I became chairman of the Vienna seminar on technique in the fall of 1924, I had a good idea of the work that had to be done. In the preceding two years, the lack of systematic presentation in the case reports was disturbingly conspicuous. I sketched a plan for systematic reports. The cases offered a bewildering profusion of experiences. Hence, I suggested that only that material should be presented which pertained to the problems of technique. Other matters would come up by themselves in the discussion. Prior to this, it was the custom to give a thorough presentation of the childhood history of the case without reference to the therapeutic problem and, at the conclusion, to offer random suggestions. I saw no point in this. If psychoanalysis was a causal scientific therapy, then the specifically necessary technique had to result by itself from the structure of the case. The structure of the neurosis could be determined only by the fixations in childhood situations. It was further shown that the resistances were circumvented, partly because they were not recognized and partly because it was believed that they were an obstruction to the analytic work and, hence, to be avoided as much as possible. For this reason, only situations having to do with resistance were discussed during the first years of my activity as head of the seminar. In the beginning, we were completely helpless. However, we soon learned a great deal and rapidly added to our knowledge. The most important fruit of the first years of our work in the seminar was the decisive insight that, in speaking of "transference," the analysts meant only positive transference and not negative transference, though the theoretical differentiation between the two had been made by Freud long before. The analysts were afraid to listen to, examine, confirm, or refute deprecatory opinions and embarrassing criticism by the patient. In short, the analyst felt insecure both personally and professionally, because of the sexual material and the vast complexity of human nature.

It was further shown that unconscious hostile attitudes on the part of the patient formed the basis of the neurosis as a whole. Every interpretation of the unconscious material glanced off this secret repressed hostility. It followed, therefore, that no unconscious material should be interpreted until the hidden deprecatory attitudes had been uncovered and eliminated. True, this was in line with known principles of practical work—but its application still had to be learned.

The discussion of practical questions removed many incorrect and complacent attitudes on the part of therapists, e.g., so-called "waiting," which was supposed to have a meaning. Usually, it was sheer helplessness. We condemned the habit of many analysts who simply reproached the patient when he or she demonstrated resistance to the treatment. For it was wholly inherent in psychoanalytic principles that we had to try to comprehend the resistance and to eliminate it with analytic means. At that time analysts were in the habit of setting termination dates when the treatment stagnated. The idea behind this practice was that the patient was supposed to decide before a certain date "to give up the resistance to getting well." If he or she was not able to do so, then he or she simply had "insurmountable resistances." It must be borne in mind, however, that the clinic was constantly making high demands on our skills. No one had any idea of the physiological anchoring of such resistances.

There were a number of incorrect technical procedures that had to be eliminated. Since I myself had made these mistakes for five years and had treated many patients unsuccessfully as a result of them, I knew precisely what they were and recognized them in other analysts. One of these incorrect procedures was the unsystematic way in which the analyst dealt with the material which the patient produced. It was interpreted "just as it came," without taking into account its depth and the resistances which precluded genuine understanding. This procedure often resulted in grotesque situations. The patients readily divined what the psychoanalyst expected in terms of theory, and they produced the appropriate "associations." In short, they produced material to oblige the analysts. If they were cunning individuals, they half-consciously led the analyst astray, e.g., produced extremely confusing dreams so that no one knew what was going on. It was precisely this continual confusion of the dreams, not their content, that was the crucial problem. Or they produced one symbol after another—the sexual meaning of which they readily divined—and in no time they were able to operate with concepts. They would speak about the "Oedipus complex" without any trace of affect. Inwardly, they did not believe in the interpretations of their associations, which the analysts usually took at face value. Almost all treatments were chaotic. There was no order in the material, no organization in the treatment, and, therefore, no evolving of a process. Most analyses broke down after two or three years of treatment. There were improvements now and then, but no one could explain precisely what had brought them about. Thus, we came to realize the importance of orderly and systematic work on the resistances. In the treatment, the neurosis breaks up, so to speak, into individual resistances. These the analyst must keep clearly separated from one another and eliminate individually, always proceeding from the one closest to the surface, i.e., nearest to the patient's conscious perception. This was not new—merely a consistent application of the Freudian conception.

I dissuaded analysts from trying to "convince" patients that an interpretation was correct. If the resistance to an unconscious impulse has been comprehended and eliminated, the patient will proceed further of his own accord. That element of the instinct against which the resistance is directed is contained in the resistance. If the patient recognizes the meaning of the defense, then he is also well on his way to comprehending what is being warded off. This means, however, that the analyst must consistently and precisely uncover every minute trace of distrust and rejection on the part of the patient. Every patient is deeply skeptical about the treatment. Each merely conceals it differently. I once presented a report on a patient who concealed his secret distrust in an extremely clever way, i.e., he was very polite and agreed with everything. Behind this politeness and acquiescence lay the real source of anxiety. Hence, he revealed a great deal, but always very cleverly concealed his aggression. The situation demanded that I should not interpret his very clear dreams of incest with his mother until he had manifested his aggression toward me. This was flatly at variance with the practice at that time of interpreting each individual dream fragment or association. Yet, it was in keeping with the principles of resistance analysis.

I very soon sensed that I had become entangled in a conflict. Since psychoanalytic practice was not commensurate with psychoanalytic theory, it was clear that some analysts would take issue with my approach. For, in effect, they were required to bring their practice into conformity with theory, i.e., to make readjustments in technique. This, in their eyes, was an unreasonable demand. Without having any inkling of it, we had come up against the peculiarity of modern man's character, i.e., the tendency to ward off genuine sexual and aggressive impulses with spurious, contrived, deluded attitudes. The adaptation of technique to the patient's characterological hypocrisy had consequences which no one divined and everyone unconsciously feared. At issue was the concrete releasing of aggression and sexuality in the patient. At issue was the personal structure of the therapist who had to deal with and handle this aggression and sexuality. But we analysts were the children of our times. We were operating with subject matter which, though acknowledged in theory, we shied away from in practice. We did not want to experience it. It was as if we were fettered in formal academic conventions. The analytic situation required freedom from conventional standards and an attitude toward sexuality untrammeled by moral prejudices. During the first years of the seminar, there was no mention of establishing the capacity to experience orgasm. I instinctively avoided the subject. It was touchy, and one generally became very excited in discussing it. I myself did not feel completely secure about it. Nor was it at all easy to comprehend correctly the toilet habits and sexual peculiarities of the patient and still maintain one's social and academic dignity. One preferred to speak of "anal fixation" or "oral desires." The animal was and remained untouched.

The situation was difficult in other respects also. On the basis of a number of clinical observations, I had formulated a hypothesis on the therapy of the neurosis. To compass the desired goal in practice required considerable skill in technique. It was like an arduous march toward a definite goal which, clearly visible, seemed to move further and further away with each step. While, on one hand, clinical experience repeatedly confirmed that neuroses were cured quickly when genital gratification was made possible, it revealed, on the other hand, that cases in which this gratification was not (or inadequately) achieved were all the more difficult. This spurred one on to make a conscientious study of the obstructions to the goal and of the many stages to it. It is not easy to give a lucid exposition of this. Nonetheless, I want to try to give as vivid a picture as possible of how the orgasm theory of the therapy of neuroses gradually became more and more closely related to the development of the character-analytic technique. In the course of a few years, they became an inseparable unity. As the foundation of this work gained in clarity and firmness, conflicts with the psychoanalysts of the old school became more frequent.

There were no conflicts during the first two years, but then a growing opposition began to make itself felt from the older colleagues. They simply refused to grasp what we were doing; they were afraid of losing their reputations as "experienced authorities." Hence, they had to take one of two attitudes toward the new material which we were investigating: (1) "There is nothing new here—Freud knew all about it"; or (2) they declared that our approach was all "wrong." In the long run, the role of genital gratification in the therapy of neuroses could not be kept hidden. It came up inevitably in the discussion of every case. This fortified my position but it also made enemies for me. The goal of enabling the patient to experience "orgastic genital gratification" shaped technique in the following way: all patients are disturbed in their genital function; this function must be made whole again. Hence, all pathological attitudes that obstruct the establishment of orgastic potency have to be sought out and destroyed. This became the task of technique for a generation of analytic therapists, for the obstructions to the genital function were legion and had an endless variety of forms. They were anchored in the social no less than in the psychic framework. Most importantly, as was later discovered, they were anchored in the body.

I began by laying the main stress of the work on the study of pregenital fixations, the devious modes of sexual gratification, and the social difficulties which obstruct a gratifying sexual life. Without intending it, questions pertaining to marriage, adolescence, and the social inhibition of sexuality gradually cropped up in the discussions. All this still appeared to be very much within the framework of psychoanalytic research. My young colleagues were very enthusiastic and demonstrated a great determination to work. They made no secret of their enthusiasm for my seminar. Their distinctly unprofessional and unscientific conduct later, when the rupture in my relations with the Psychoanalytic Assocation occurred, cannot diminish my appreciation of their achievements in the seminar.

The publication of Freud's *The Ego and the Id* in 1923 had a disconcerting impact on everyday analytic practice, the central concern of which was the patient's sexual difficulties. In practice, it was very difficult to know what to make of the "superego" and the "unconscious guilt feelings" which were theoretical formulations about facts that were still very obscure. A technique for dealing with these "phenomena" had not been specified. Thus, one preferred to operate with masturbation anxiety and sexual guilt feelings. In 1920, Freud had published *Beyond the Pleasure Principle,* in which, initially as a hypothesis, the death instinct was placed on an equal footing with the sexual instinct, indeed was accorded deeper instinctual force. Young analysts who had not yet begun to practice and those analysts who did not grasp the structure of the sexual theory began to apply the new ego theory. It was a very disturbing situation. Instead of sexuality, analysts began to speak of "Eros." Mediocre therapists claimed that they were able "to put their hands on" the superego, a concept that had been theoretically postulated to help grasp the psychic structure. They operated with it as if it were a concretely established fact. The id was "wicked," the superego sat on a throne with a long beard and was "strict," and the poor ego endeavored to "mediate" between the two. The vivid and fluid description of facts was replaced by a mechanical schema which seemed to make further thinking unnecessary. Clinical discussions drifted more and more into the background and speculation began. Soon strangers who had never analyzed came along and delivered "brilliant" lectures on the ego and superego or on schizophrenics they had never seen. In 1934, when my break with the International Psychoanalytic Association occurred, they functioned officially as the "transcendental" exponents of psychoanalysis against the sex-economic principle of depth psychology. Clinical investigation stagnated. Sexuality became something shadowy; the "libido" concept was deprived of every trace of sexual content and became a figure of speech. Seriousness in psychoanalytic communications disappeared. It was more and more replaced by a pathos reminiscent of moral philosophers. Little by little, the theory of the neuroses was translated into the language of "ego psychology." The atmosphere was becoming "purified"!

Slowly but surely, it was cleansed of all Freud's achievements. Bringing psychoanalysis into line with the world, which shortly before had threatened to annihilate it, took place inconspicuously at first. Analysts still spoke of sexuality, but they had something else in mind. At the same time, they had retained a trace of the old pioneer pride. Hence, they developed a bad conscience and usurped my new findings, declaring them traditional components of psychoanalysis, with the intent of destroying them. Form eclipsed content; the organization became more important than its task. The process of deterioration, which has destroyed every great social movement in history, set in. Just as the primitive Christianity of Jesus was transformed into the Church, and Marxist science became fascistic dictatorship, many psychoanalysts soon became the worst enemies of their own cause. The rift within the movement was no longer reparable. Today, fifteen years afterward, this is evident to everyone. It was not until 1934 that I grasped it clearly. It was too late. Until then, suppressing my inner conviction of my own cause, I had fought within the framework of the International Psychoanalytic Association, officially and for myself in the name of psychoanalysis.

Around 1925, a cleavage occurred in the formulation of psychoanalytic theory that initially was not perceived by the representatives, but is clearly evident today. To the same extent to which a cause loses ground, it becomes susceptible to personal intrigue. What is outwardly passed off as objective interest is backstage politics, tactics, diplomacy. It is perhaps to the painful experiences of this development within the International Psychoanalytic Association that I owe the most important fruits of my efforts: the knowledge of the mechanism of every kind of politics.

The description of these facts is by no means irrelevant. The critical stand I took against these signs of disintegration within the psychoanalytic movement (e.g., the theory of the death instinct) provided the groundwork for my successful breakthrough, several years later, into the realm of vegetative life.

Reik published a book, *Geständniszwang und Strafbedürfnis* [*Compulsion to Confess and Need of Punishment*], in which the whole original conception of psychic illness was turned upside down. The worst of it was that the book met with approval. Reduced to the simplest terms, his innovation can be described as the elimination of the fear of punishment for sexual transgressions committed in childhood. In *Beyond the Pleasure Principle* and in *The Ego and the Id,* Freud assumed the existence of an unconscious need for punishment. This need ostensibly explained the patient's resistance to getting well. At the same time, the "death instinct" was made a part of psychoanalytic theory. Freud assumed that living substance was governed by two antithetical instinctual forces. On one hand, he postulated the life instincts, which he equated to the sexual instinct (Eros). According to Freud, these instincts had the task of rousing the living substance out of its inorganic state of repose, creating tension, and concentrating life into larger and larger entities. These instincts were loud, clamorous; they were responsible for the hubbub of life. However, operating behind these life instincts was the "mute" but "far more important" death instinct (Thanatos), the tendency to reduce living substance to an inanimate condition, to nothingness, to Nirvana. According to this conception, life was really only a disturbance of the eternal silence, of nothingness. In the neurosis, according to this view, the death instinct counteracted the creative life, i.e., sexual, instincts. To be sure, the death instinct could not be perceived. But its manifestations were said to be too evident to be overlooked. In everything he did, man demonstrated the tendency toward self-annihilation. The death instinct manifested itself in masochistic strivings. It was because of these strivings that neurotic patients "refused" to get well. They nourished the unconscious feeling of guilt, which could also be called the need for punishment. The patients simply did not want to get well, because this need for punishment, which found gratification in the neurosis, prevented them.

Reik made me realize where Freud had begun to go wrong. Disregarding all Freud's precautions, Reik simply used the patient's death instinct to excuse his own psychotherapeutic inadequacies. Reik exaggerated correct insights, e.g., that criminals easily betray themselves or that many people feel relieved when they can confess a crime.

Until this point, a neurosis was looked upon as the result of a conflict between sexual demand and fear of punishment. Now it was said that a neurosis was a conflict between sexual demand and demand for punishment, i.e., the exact opposite of fear of punishment for sexual activities. This was a complete liquidation of the psychoanalytic theory of neurosis. It was at variance with every clinical insight. The latter left no doubt that Freud's first formulation was correct, i.e., neuroses were caused by fear of punishment for sexual activity and not by desire to be punished for it. On the basis of the complications in which some patients became involved due to the inhibition of their sexuality, they subsequently developed the masochistic attitude of wanting to be punished, to injure themselves, or to stick to their illness. It was undoubtedly the task of the analyst to treat these desires for self-punishment as a secondary neurotic formation, to eliminate the patient's fear of punishment, and to liberate his sexuality. It was not the task of the treatment to confirm these self-injuries as the manifestations of deep biological strivings. The exponents of the death instinct, who appeared in greater and greater numbers and with increasing dignity, because now they could speak of "Thanatos" instead of sexuality, traced the neurotic self-injurious intent of the sick psychic organism to a primary biological instinct of the living substance. Psychoanalysis never recovered from this.

Reik was followed by Alexander, who investigated a number of criminals and ascertained that, in the main, crime was the consequence of an unconscious need for punishment which compelled the person to commit a criminal act. He did not inquire into the origin of this unnatural behavior. He did not devote a single word to the powerful social basis of criminality. This saved the trouble of any further questioning. If the analyst failed to cure a patient, it was the death instinct that was responsible. If people committed murder, they did so to get themselves put in jail. Children stole to free themselves from the pressure of a tormenting conscience. Today, I look back in amazement at the energy expended at that time in the discussion of such views. Nevertheless, Freud had meant something worthy of great effort. I shall go into this later. Indolent analysts, however, fastened upon his idea and frittered away decades of effort.

The "negative therapeutic reaction" of the patient later proved to be the result of the analyst's technical and theoretical inability to establish orgastic potency in the patient, in other words, his inability to deal with the patient's pleasure anxiety.

With these concerns in mind, I paid a call on Freud. I asked him whether he had intended to introduce the death instinct as a clinical theory. He himself, I pointed out, had denied that the death instinct was a tangible clinical phenomenon. Freud reassured me. It was "merely a hypothesis," he said. It could just as well be omitted. Its elimination would change nothing in the basic structure of the psychoanalytic system. He had merely allowed himself to venture a speculation for once. He was well aware that his speculation was being misused. I should not let it bother me, he said, but just go on working clinically. I went away relieved. But I was determined, in my sphere of work, to put up a strong fight against any chatter about the death instinct, and I wrote a polemic against Alexander in which I proved the untenability of his views.

My negative critique of Reik's book and the polemic against Alexander were published in 1927. In my seminar on technique, hardly any mention was made of the death instinct and the unconscious need for punishment as the causes of therapeutic failure. The meticulously precise clinical presentation of the individual cases precluded this. Only occasionally, one of the death-instinct theorists attempted to set forth his views. I carefully avoided any direct attack on this erroneous theory. It was clear that its complete untenability would have to be proven by clinical work itself. The more minutely we studied the mechanisms of the neuroses, the more certain we were to triumph. In the Psychoanalytic Association, on the other hand, the incorrect interpretation of the ego theory gained ever greater influence. The situation grew more and more tense. All of a sudden, it was discovered that I was very aggressive, "riding my own hobbyhorse," and wholly exaggerating the importance of genitality.

At the Psychoanalytic Congress in Salzburg in April 1924, I added "orgastic potency" to my initial formulations on the therapeutic importance of genitality. My presentation dealt with two basic facts: (1) *neurosis is the manifestation of a genital disturbance and not solely of sexuality in general;* (2) *relapse into neurosis subsequent to analytic treatment is avoided to the extent to which orgastic gratification in the sexual act has been secured.* My presentation was well received. Abraham congratulated me on my successful formulation of the economic factor of the neurosis.

To establish orgastic potency in patients, it was not enough to liberate existing genital excitations from their inhibitions and repressions. Sexual energy is bound in the symptoms. Hence, the dissolution of every symptom releases a quantity of psychic energy. At that time, the two concepts "psychic energy" and "sexual energy" were by no means identical. The liberated sexual energy was spontaneously conveyed to the genital system: *potency improved*. The patient ventured to approach a partner, gave up abstinence, or experienced more gratifying sexual embraces. However, only in a few cases was the expectation fulfilled that this liberating of sexual energy would also entail the establishment of the orgastic function. The conclusion to be drawn from this seemed to be that insufficient energy had been liberated from the neurotic bindings. Symptoms did, to be sure, disappear, and the patient's ability to work more or less improved. On the whole, however, the patient remained blocked. Thus, the question suggested itself: where, apart from the neurotic symptoms, is sexual energy bound? This was a new question in psychoanalysis, but it was not outside its framework. On the contrary, it was merely a consistent application of the analytic method of thinking, using the individual neurotic symptom as its point of departure. At first, I had no answer to this question. Clinical and therapeutic problems can never be solved by musing about them. They solve themselves in the process of mastering practical tasks. This is true generally of every form of scientific work. The correct formulation of a practical problem automatically leads to further formulations, which gradually become concentrated in a uniform picture of a general problem.

On the basis of the psychoanalytic theory of neurosis, it seemed obvious to look for the energy necessary to establish full orgastic potency in the non-genital, i.e., early childhood, pregenital activities and fantasies. If a large amount of sexual interest is focused on sucking, biting, the desire to be loved, anal habits, etc., the capacity for genital experience is reduced. This gave further credence to the view that the individual sexual instincts do not function independently of one another but form a unity, as a liquid in connecting pipes. There can be only *one uniform sexual energy which seeks gratification in various erogenous zones and psychic ideas.* This was at variance with views which were beginning to gain ground at that time. Ferenczi published his theory of genitality, according to which the genital excitation function is made up of pregenital excitations, anal, oral, and aggressive. This was at variance with my clinical experience. I had observed the exact opposite of this: every admixture of nongenital excitations in the sexual act or in masturbation weakened orgastic potency. A woman who unconsciously equates vagina and anus might be afraid of breaking wind during excitation and thus making a fool of herself. Such an attitude can have a paralyzing effect on her entire life activity. A man who unconsciously regards his penis as a knife or uses it to prove his potency is incapable of total surrender in the sexual act. Helene Deutsch published a book on female sexuality in which she contended that, for the woman, the culmination of sexual gratification lay in the act of giving birth. According to her conception, there is no primary vaginal excitation. The latter, she argued, was made up of excitations which were shifted to the womb from the mouth and the anus. Right at that time, Otto Rank published his *Trauma der Geburt,* in which he contended that the sexual act corresponded to a "return to the womb." I was on good terms with these psychoanalysts and valued their views, but there was a wide divergency between my experiences and ideas and theirs. Gradually, it became clear that it was fundamentally incorrect to try to give the experience in the sexual act a psychological interpretation, to seek a psychic meaning in it as one would seek a psychic meaning in a neurotic symptom. The exact opposite is true: every psychic idea during the sexual act can only hinder one's immersion in the excitation. Moreover, such interpretations of genitality constitute a denial of its biological function. By seeing it as the concentration of non-genital excitations, one denies its existence. It was precisely in the function of the orgasm that I, on the other hand, recognized the basic qualitative difference between genitality and pregenitality. Only the genital apparatus is capable of bringing about orgasm and fully discharging biological energy. Pregenitality can only increase vegetative tensions. One notices the deep cleavage that was taking place here in the psychoanalytic view of the function of instincts.

The therapeutic implications deriving from these two views were incompatible with one another. If genital excitation is merely a mixture of non-genital excitations, then cure must consist in a shifting of anal and oral eroticism to the genital. If, however, my view was correct, then genital excitation had to be liberated from and purified of (so to speak, "distilled from") admixtures with pregenital excitations. There was nothing in Freud's writings that suggested an answer one way or another.

Freud stated that libido development in the child proceeded from the oral to the anal and from the anal to the phallic stage. He ascribed the phallic genital position to both sexes. The phallic eroticism of the girl became concentrated in the clitoris, just as the phallic eroticism of the boy became concentrated in the penis. It was not until puberty, Freud said, that all infantile sexual excitations became subordinated to "genital primacy," at which time the latter "began to fulfill the function of procreation." This formulation retained the old identification between genitality and procreation—genital pleasure continued to be regarded as a function of procreation. I had failed to see this in the beginning. A Berlin psychoanalyst pointed it out to me some years later when the rift had become flagrantly obvious. I was able to remain in the International Psychoanalytic Association with my theory of genitality for such a long time only because I continually referred to Freud in substantiating my views. This was an injustice to my theory, and it made separation from the psychoanalytic organization difficult for my associates.

Today, such views appear impossible. I am amazed at how seriously analysts discussed at that time whether or not there is an original genital function. No one had any inkling of the social reasons for this scientific naïveté. The further development of the theory of genitality revealed them all too flagrantly.

2. THE SEX-ECONOMY OF NEUROTIC ANXIETY

The wide divergencies in the formulation of psychoanalytic theory after 1922 are also evident in the central problem of anxiety. The original hypothesis ran as follows: if the path to the perception and discharge of physical sexual excitation is blocked, then the excitation is converted into anxiety. Nothing was said about how this "conversion" took place. Since I was continually confronted with the task of liberating sexual energy from its neurotic fixations, this problem demanded clarification. Stasis anxiety was undischarged sexual excitation. To reconvert it into sexual excitation, it was necessary to know how the initial conversion into anxiety had taken place. In 1924, I treated two female patients with cardiac neurosis. With the emergence of genital excitation, the cardiac anxiety diminished. In one of these patients, I could observe, over a period of weeks, the alternation between cardiac anxiety and genital excitation. Every inhibition of vaginal excitation immediately evoked a feeling of constriction and anxiety "in the cardiac region." This was an eloquent confirmation of the original Freudian conception of the relation between libido and anxiety. But there was more to it than that. I was now able to localize the site of the anxiety sensation. It was the region of the heart and the diaphragm. The other patient exhibited the same alternating function, but also urticaria. If the patient was afraid to accede to her vaginal excitation, the result was cardiac anxiety or large itching wheals on various parts of the skin. Clearly, therefore, the sexual excitation and the anxiety had something to do with the functions of the vegetative nervous system. This was further borne out by the fact that anxiety is localized in the cardiac region. I reformulated the Freudian formula to read: *there is no conversion of sexual excitation. The same excitation which appears in the genitals as the sensation of pleasure is perceived as anxiety when it takes hold of the cardiac system, i.e., it is perceived as the exact opposite of pleasure.* The vasovegetative system can, in one instance, express itself in the form of sexual excitation and, in another instance, when the excitation is blocked, in the form of anxiety. This idea proved to be very fortunate. Its development led step by step directly to my present view that *sexuality and anxiety are manifestations of two antithetical directions of vegetative sensations of excitation.* It took some ten years to clarify the bioelectric nature of these sensations and excitations.

Freud had not mentioned the vegetative nervous system in connection with his theory of anxiety. I had not the least doubt that my supplementation would be evident to him. However, when I presented my concept at a meeting in his apartment toward the end of 1926, he rejected the relation between anxiety and the vasovegetative system. I have never understood why.

It became more and more clear that the overloading of the vasovegetative system with undischarged sexual excitation is the central mechanism of anxiety and, hence, of neurosis. Every new case confirmed the initial observations. Apparently, anxiety always developed when the vasovegetative system became overexcited in a certain way. Cardiac anxiety is found in angina pectoris, bronchial asthma, nicotine poisoning, and exophthalmic goiter. Thus, anxiety always develops when the cardiac system is affected by some abnormal excitation. In short, the sexual stasis anxiety ties in very well with the problem of anxiety as a whole. It is merely that, here, the undischarged sexual excitation burdens the cardiac system, as nicotine or toxic substances do in other cases. The question remained as to the nature of this overexcitation. In this connection, I still had no knowledge of the antithesis between sympathetic and parasympathetic reactions.

For my own clinical needs, I differentiated the concept of anxiety from that of fear or apprehension. "I am 'afraid' of being beaten, punished, or castrated" is something different from the "anxiety" which one experiences when faced with a real danger. "Fear" or "apprehension" becomes an affective "anxiety experience" only when the stasis of physical excitation overloads the autonomic system. There were patients who experienced castration "anxiety" without any affect of anxiety. And there were others who experienced affects of anxiety without any idea of danger, e.g. patients who were sexually abstinent. Thus, it was necessary to differentiate the anxiety which was the result of a stasis of excitation and the anxiety which became the cause of a sexual repression. The former determined the stasis neuroses, the latter the psychoneuroses. But both kinds of anxiety operated simultaneously in either case. Initially, the fear of being punished or of being socially ostracized produces a damming-up of sexual excitation. This excitation is shifted from the genital-sensory system to the cardiac system and accumulates there as stasis anxiety. Even the anxiety experienced in fright, I thought, can be nothing other than severely dammed-up sexual excitation suddenly flowing back to the cardiac system. It takes only a *small* quantity of stasis anxiety to produce the experience of apprehension. Even a vivid idea of a possible danger can create it. In such a case, the danger situation is, so to speak, physically anticipated by imagining it. This tied in very well with the earlier consideration that the intensity of a psychic idea, whether in the nature of pleasure or anxiety, is determined by the intensity of the amount of excitation currently operative in the body. In the fantasy or expectation of a danger, the organism acts as if the danger were already present. Possibly, fantasizing in general is based upon such reactions on the part of the life apparatus. At that time, I was working on my book *Die Funktion des Orgasmus*. In special chapters on the "vasomotor neurosis" and "anxiety and the vasovegetative system," I set forth the above-mentioned relationships.

In the fall of 1926, Freud published *Hemmung, Symptom und Angst*. In this work, many of the original formulations on actual anxiety were retracted. Neurotic anxiety was defined as a "signal" of the ego. Anxiety was said to be an alarm signal of the ego when prohibited drives were stirred, as well as when an actual danger threatened from the outside. It was not possible, Freud contended, to establish a connection between actual anxiety and neurotic anxiety. This was, he said, most regrettable, but he concluded his observations with a *non liquet*. Anxiety was no longer to be understood as the result of sexual repression but as its actual cause. The question as to the substances out of which anxiety is manufactured was of no interest. The contention that it was the libido which was converted into anxiety diminished in importance. Freud failed to see that anxiety, a biological phenomenon, cannot appear in the ego unless it is first prepared in the biological depth.

This was a hard blow for my work on the anxiety problem. I had just succeeded in making a big step forward toward the differentiation between anxiety as a cause and anxiety as a result of repression. From now on it would be more difficult to represent the view that stasis anxiety resulted from sexual stasis because Freud's formulations, of course, carried considerable authority. It was not very easy to hold a different opinion, certainly not in matters of central importance. In my book on the orgasm, I had passed over this difficulty with a harmless footnote. It was generally agreed, I pointed out, that anxiety in neurosis is the cause of sexual repression. At the same time, I stuck to my own view that anxiety is the result of sexual stasis. This Freud abrogated.

The rift deepened rapidly and to an alarming degree. Unfortunately, I was right. Since *Hemmung, Symptom und Angst,* there is no longer any psychoanalytic theory of anxiety that satisfies the clinical needs. I was firmly convinced of the correctness of my amplification of Freud's original concept of anxiety. It was very gratifying that I was getting closer and closer to its physiological source. At the same time, this entailed a sharpening of the conflict.

In my clinical work, it became increasingly important to convert the stasis anxiety back into genital excitation. When I succeeded in doing this, I achieved good and lasting results. However, I did not always succeed in liberating the cardiac anxiety and in bringing about its oscillation with genital excitation. Thus, the next question was: what is it that prevents the biological excitation from becoming manifest as cardiac anxiety as soon as the genital excitation is blocked? Why did stasis anxiety not appear in all cases of psychoneurosis? Here, too, original formulations of psychoanalysis came to my help. Freud had demonstrated that anxiety in neurosis becomes bound. The patient evades anxiety if, for example, he develops a compulsive symptom. If the function of the compulsion is disturbed, anxiety appears. But not always. Many cases of protracted compulsion neurosis and chronic depression could not be disturbed. They were somehow inaccessible. I had an especially hard time with the affect-blocked compulsive characters. They could produce associations, but no trace of affect was ever revealed. All one's efforts bounced back as from a "thick, hard wall." They were "armored" against any attack. In psychoanalytic literature, there were no technical procedures for getting beneath the surface of this rigidified condition. It was the character as a whole that resisted. With this insight, I was on the threshold of *character analysis*. Apparently, the character armor was the mechanism which bound all energy. It was also the mechanism that enabled so many psychoanalysts to maintain that there is no stasis anxiety.

3. CHARACTER ARMOR AND THE DYNAMIC STRATIFICATION OF THE DEFENSE MECHANISMS

The theory of "character armor" was the result of my efforts, which were at first very tentative, to extract the patient's resistances one by one. Between 1922, when the therapeutic role of genitality was comprehended, and 1927, when *Die Funktion des Orgasmus* was published, I collected the countless minor and major experiences which, taken together, pointed in one direction: it is the patient's total "personality" or "character" that constitutes the difficulty of cure. "Character armor" is expressed in treatment as "character resistance."

I want to describe the main features of the preliminary work. This will enable the reader to grasp the sex-economic theory of character and the theory of structure more easily than a reading of the systematic presentation which I gave in my book *Character Analysis*. In that work, the analytic theory of character might still appear to be an amplification of the Freudian theory of neurosis. However, the two theories soon came into conflict with one another. My theory was developed in the struggle against the mechanistic conceptions of psychoanalysis.

The task of psychoanalytic therapy was to uncover and eliminate resistances. It was not supposed to interpret unconscious material directly. Hence, the analyst had to pro-

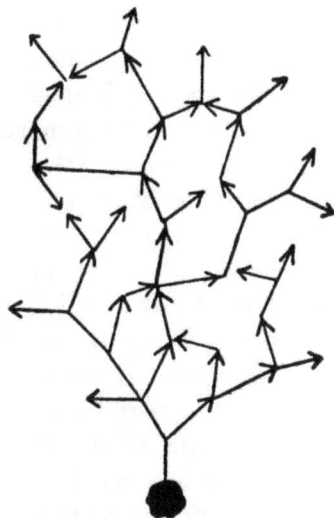

Structure of the armor resulting from the interplay of dynamic forces.

ceed from the psychic warding off of unconscious impulses by the moralistic ego. But there was not just one layer of ego defenses to break through, behind which lay the great realm of the unconscious. In reality, instinctual desires and defense functions of the ego are interlaced and permeate the entire psychic structure.

This is where the difficulty lies. Freud's schema of the interrelation of "unconscious," "preconscious," and "conscious" and his other schema of the psychic structure consisting of "id," "ego," and "superego" did not coincide. Indeed, they often contradicted. Freud's "unconscious" is not identical with the "id." The latter encompasses more. The unconscious comprises the repressed desires and important elements of the moralistic superego. Since the superego has its origin in the incestuous child-parent relationship, it bears that relationship's archaic characteristics. The superego itself is equipped with great instinctual intensity, particularly of an aggressive and destructive nature. The "ego" is not identical with the "system conscious." The ego defense against prohibited sexual desires is itself repressed. Moreover, the ego originates from, and is merely a specially differentiated part of, the id, even if later, under the influence of the superego, it comes into conflict with it. If one understands Freud correctly, then early infantile is not necessarily "id" or "unconscious," and adult is not necessarily "ego" or "superego." In the above, I have merely pointed out some of the inconsistencies of psychoanalytic theory, without discussing or drawing any conclusions about them. I am only too happy to leave that part of it to the psychoanalytic theorists. At any rate, sex-economic research on the human character structure has clarified a number of these questions. The sex-economic conception of the psychic apparatus is not of a psychological but of a biological nature.

The differentiation between what is repressed and what is capable of becoming conscious played the major role in the clinical work. Also of importance was the differentiation of the child's individual stages of sexual development. This was something the analyst could operate with in a practical way. At that time, it was not possible to operate with the id, which was not tangible, nor with the superego, which was merely a theoretical hypothesis, overtly expressed in the form of conscience-anxiety. Nor was it possible to operate with the unconscious in the strict sense for, as Freud had correctly pointed out, it can be reached only through its derivatives, i.e., manifestations that are already conscious. For Freud, the "unconscious" was never anything more than an "indispensable hypothesis." Capable of immediate and practical comprehension were the manifestations of the patient's pregenital impulses and the various forms of the moralistic or apprehensive warding off of instincts. The fact that in their theoretical works psychoanalysts did not render any account whatever on the differences between theory, hypothetical construction, and phenomena which were overtly visible and changeable; the fact that they referred to the unconscious as if it were something concrete greatly contributed to the confusion. This acted as a block to the investigation of the vegetative nature of the id and, consequently, shut off the approach to the biological foundation of psychic functioning.

I acquired my first insight into the stratification of the psychic apparatus in the previously-mentioned case of a passive-feminine young man suffering from hysterical symptoms, inability to work, and ascetic impotence. Overtly, he was very polite; covertly, his fear caused him to be very cunning. Thus, he yielded in everything. The politeness represented the topmost layer of his structure. He produced material on his sexual tie to his mother in superabundance. He "produced" without any inner conviction. I did not enter into any of this material but continually focused his attention on his politeness as a defense against really affective insight. The concealed hate appeared more and more in his dreams. As his politeness diminished, he became insulting. Thus, the politeness warded off hate. I brought it out completely by breaking down every one of his inhibitions. Until then, the hate had been an unconscious attitude. Hate and politeness were antitheses. At the same time, his excessive politeness was a disguised expression of hate. Excessively polite people are usually the most ruthless and the most dangerous.

For its part, the liberated hate warded off acute fear of his father. It was simultaneously a repressed impulse and an unconscious ego defense against anxiety. The more clearly the hate was brought to the surface, the more distinctly manifestations of anxiety appeared. Eventually, the hate gave way to new anxiety. The former was by no means the original childhood aggression but a new formation from a later period. The new anxiety which broke through was the manifestation of a defense against a deeper layer of destructive hate. The superficial layer of hate had been content with ridicule and disparagement. The deeper destructive attitude consisted of murder impulses against his father. As fear of these impulses ("destructive anxiety") was eliminated, the deeper destructive attitude became manifest in feelings and fantasies. Thus, this deeper layer of destruction was the repressed element with respect to the anxiety, by which it was held in repression. At the same time, however, it was identical with this fear of destruction. It could not stir without producing anxiety, and the fear of destruction could not rise to the surface without, at the same time, betraying the destructive aggression. In this way I gained insight into the antithetical *functional unity between what wards off and what is warded off.* I did not publish anything about this until eight years later, when I illustrated it in the following diagram.

As a result of the manner in which the character struc-

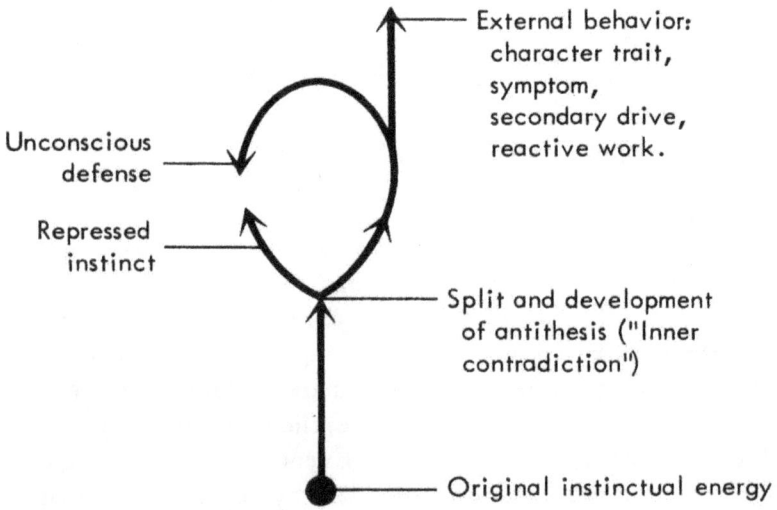

Diagram depicting the antithetical functional unity between instinct and defense.

ture of modern man is developed, an "inner resistance" is constantly interpolated between the biological impulse and its realization: man acts "reactively," and is inwardly divided against himself.

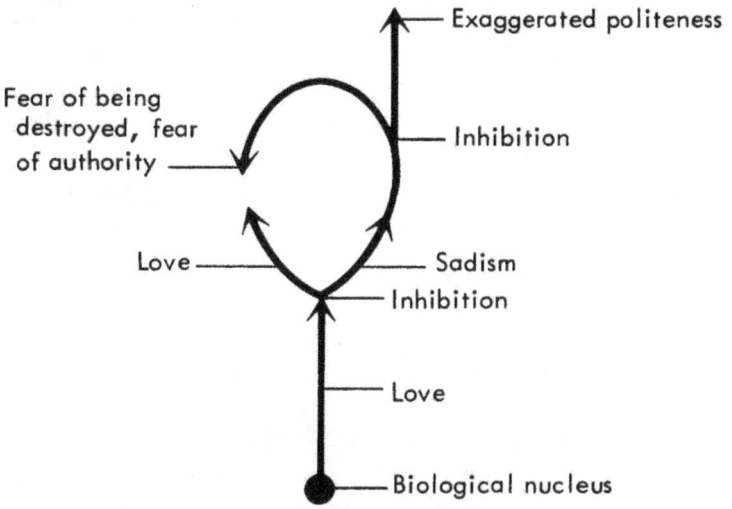

The same diagram illustrating specific impulses

The destructive impulse toward the father was, in turn, a defense of the ego against destruction *by* the father. When I began to take this apart and unmask it as defense, genital anxiety came to the surface. Thus, the destructive intentions against the father had the function of protecting the patient against castration by the father. The fear of being castrated, that was held in repression by the destructive hatred of the father, was itself a defense against a still deeper layer of destructive aggression—namely the desire to deprive the father of his penis and thus eliminate him as a rival. The second layer of destructiveness was solely destructive. The third layer was destructive with a sexual overtone. It was held in check by fear of castration; at the same time, it warded off a very deep and strong layer of passive, loving, feminine attitude toward the father. To be a woman toward the father had the same meaning as being castrated, i.e., to be without a penis. Hence, the ego of the small boy had to protect itself against this love by means of a strong destructive aggression against the father. It was the healthy "young man" who defended himself in this way. And this "young man" desired his mother passionately. When his warded-off femininity, i.e., the same femininity visible on the surface of his character, was taken apart, the genital incest desire appeared and, with it, his full capacity for genital excitability. Though still orgastically disturbed, he became erectively potent for the first time.

This was my first success with a systematic, orderly, layer by layer resistance and character analysis. A thorough description of this case appears in my book *Character Analysis*.

The concept of "armor stratification" opened many possibilities for clinical work. The psychic forces and contradictions no longer presented a chaos, but a systematic, historically and structurally comprehensible organization. The neurosis of each individual patient revealed a specific structure. There was a correlation between the structure and the development of the neurosis. That which had been repressed latest in point of time in childhood lay closest to the surface. But early childhood fixations which had a bearing on later stages of conflicts had a dynamic effect in the depth and on the surface at one and the same time. For instance, it is possible that a woman's oral tie to her husband, which stemmed from a deep fixation to her mother's breast, is a part of the most superficial layer when she has to ward off genital anxiety toward the husband. In terms of energy, the ego defense is nothing other than a repressed impulse in its reverse function. This is true of all modern man's moralistic attitudes.

Usually, the structure of the neurosis corresponds to its development in reversed sequence. The "antithetical functional unity between instinct and defense" made it possible to comprehend contemporary and early childhood experiences simultaneously. There was no longer any dichotomy between historical and contemporary material. *The entire world of past experience was embodied in the present in the form of character attitudes. A person's character is the functional sum total of all past experiences.* These explanations, academic-sounding as they may be, are of the utmost importance for the understanding of human restructurization.

This structure was not a schema which I imposed upon the patients. The logic with which layer after layer of the defense mechanisms were exposed and eliminated through the correct dissolution of resistances showed me that the stratification was actually and objectively present, independent of me. I compared the stratification of the character with the stratification of geological deposits, which are also rigidified history. A conflict which is fought out at a certain age always leaves behind a trace in the person's character. This trace is revealed as a hardening of the character. It functions automatically and is difficult to eliminate. The patient does not experience it as something alien; more often than not, he is aware of it as a rigidification or as a loss of spontaneity. Every such layer of the character structure is a piece of the person's life history, preserved and active in the present in a different form. Experience showed that the old conflicts can be fairly easily reactivated through the loosening of these layers. If the layers of rigidified conflicts were especially numerous and functioned automatically, if they formed a compact, not easily penetrable unity, the patient felt them as an "armor" surrounding the living organism. This armor could lie on the "surface" or in the "depth," could be "as soft as a sponge" or "as hard as a rock." Its function in every case was to protect the person against unpleasurable experiences. However, it also entailed a reduction in the organism's capacity for pleasure. Experiences of severe conflict

Fear of losing love and protection	Politeness; impotence; asceticism; condition of anxiety
Fear and feeling of inferiority toward authority	Contempt; ridicule; distrust; craving for power
Fear of aggression	Aggression toward authority
Self-protection; fear of being destroyed	Murder impulses toward father
Fear of being castrated	Desire to castrate father
Fear of being a woman; i.e., castrated	Passive-feminine attitude toward father; anal eroticism
Disappointment by mother; fear of the vagina	Sadistic attitude toward mother; piercing; phallic
	Genital object love toward the mother

Diagram depicting the defensive forces and the stratification of the neurotic structure made up the latent content of the armor. The energy which held the armor together was usually inhibited destructiveness. This was shown by the fact that aggression immediately began to break free when the armor was penetrated. What was the source of the destructive and hateful aggression that came to the surface in this process? What was its function? Was it primary, biological destructiveness? Many years elapsed before such questions were answered. I found that people reacted with deep hatred to every disturbance of the neurotic balance of their armor. This was one of the greatest difficulties in investigating character structure. The destructiveness itself was never free. It was held in check by opposite character attitudes. Hence, in life situations in which it was necessary to be aggressive, to act, to be decisive, to take a definite stand, the person was ruled by pity, politeness, reticence, false modesty, in short by virtues that are held in high esteem. But there could be no doubt that they paralyzed every rational reaction, every living active impulse in the person.

If natural aggression was sometimes expressed in an action, it was fragmentary, lacked direction, concealed a deep feeling of insecurity or a pathological selfishness. Thus, it was pathological aggression—not healthy, goal-directed aggression.

I gradually began to comprehend the patients' latent attitude of hate. It was never missing. If the analyst did not get stuck in emotionless associations, if he refused to be content with dream interpretations and attacked the character defenses concealed in the patient's attitude, then the patient became angry. At first, I did not understand this reaction. The patient would complain about the emptiness of his experiences. But when I pointed out the same emptiness in the nature of his communications, in his coolness, in his grandiloquent or hypocritical nature, he became angry. He was aware of the symptom, a headache or a tic, as something alien. *But his character was the person himself.* He was disturbed when it was pointed out to him. What was it that prevented a person from perceiving his own personality? After all, it is what he is! Gradually, I came to understand that it is the entire being that constitutes the compact, tenacious mass which obstructs all analytic efforts. The patient's whole personality, his *character,* his individuality resisted analysis. But why? *The only explanation is that it fulfills a secret function of defense and protection.* I was familiar with Adler's theory of character. Was I, too, destined to go astray as Adler had done? I saw the self-assertion, the feeling of inferiority, the will to power—all of which were ill suited to be examined in the open. Vanity and concealment of weaknesses were also there. Was Adler right, after all? But he had contended that character, *"not sexuality,"* was the cause of psychic illness. In what way, then, were the *character* mechanisms and the *sexual* mechanisms related? For I had not the least doubt that Freud's and not Adler's theory of neuroses was the correct one.

It took me years to become clear about this: *the destructiveness bound in the character is nothing but the rage the person feels, owing to his frustration in life and his lack of sexual gratification.* When the analyst proceeds into the depth, every destructive impulse gives way to a sexual impulse. The desire to destroy is merely the *reaction* to disappointment in or loss of love.

If a person encounters insurmountable obstacles in his efforts to experience love or the gratification of sexual urges, he begins to hate. But the hate cannot be expressed. It has to be bound to avoid the anxiety it causes. In short, thwarted love causes anxiety. Likewise, inhibited aggression causes anxiety; and anxiety inhibits demands of hate and love.

I now had a theoretical understanding of what I had experienced analytically in the dissolution of the neurosis. I also had an analytic understanding of what I knew theoretically, and I recorded the most important result: *the orgastically ungratified person develops an artificial character and a fear of spontaneous, living reactions, thus, also, a fear of perceiving his own vegetative sensations.*

About this time, the theories about destructive instincts began to move into the forefront of psychoanalysis. In his essay on primary masochism, Freud made an important change in an earlier formulation. Initially, it was said that hate was a biological instinctual force parallel to love. Destructiveness was first directed against the outside world. Under the latter's influence, however, it turned inward against itself and thus became masochism, i.e., the desire to suffer. Now it appeared that the reverse was true: "primary masochism," or the "death instinct," was in the organism from the beginning. It was an integral part of the cells. Its outward projection against the world caused destructive aggression to emerge, which, for its part, could again be turned back against the ego as "secondary masochism." It was argued that the patient's secret negative attitude was nourished by his masochism. According to Freud, masochism also accounted for the "negative therapeutic reaction" and the "unconscious feeling of guilt." After many years of work on various forms of destructiveness that caused guilt feelings and depressions, I finally began to see its significance for the character armor and its dependence on sexual stasis.

Having obtained Freud's consent, I began to think seriously about writing a book on psychoanalytic technique. In this book, I had to take a clear stand on the question of destructiveness. I did not yet have a view of my own. Ferenczi took issue with Adler in an essay entitled *Weitere Ausbau der 'aktiven Technik.'* "Character investigations," he wrote, "never play a prominent role in our technique." Only at the termination of the treatment are they "of some importance." "The character assumes importance only when certain abnormal, psychosis-like traits disrupt the normal continuation of the analysis." In these sentences, he correctly formulated the attitude of psychoanalysis toward the role of character. At that time, I was deeply immersed in characterological investigations. Adler had advocated the analysis of character in place of the analysis of the libido. I, however, was in the process of developing psychoanalysis into "character analysis." Real cure, I argued, can be achieved only through the elimination of the basis of the symptoms in the patient's character. The difficulty of the task lay in the comprehension of those analytic situations which required not symptom analysis but character analysis. My technique differed from Adler's inasmuch as I approached the analysis of character through the analysis of the patient's sexual behavior. Adler, however, had said, "Not libido analysis but character analysis." There is no parallel between my concept of character armor and Adler's conception of individual character traits. Any reference to Adler in discussing the sex-economic theory of structure is indicative of a deep misunderstanding. Character traits such as "inferiority complex" or "will to power" are merely surface manifestations in the process of armoring in the biological sense of the vegetative inhibition of vital functioning.

In *Der triebhafte Charakter* (1925), on the basis of my experiences with impulsive patients, I moved from symptom analysis to character analysis. This was a logical move, but I did not have sufficient clinical and technical knowledge to follow it through at that time. Thus, I stuck to Freud's theory of the ego and the superego. However, a character-analytic technique could not be worked out with the auxiliary concepts of psychoanalysis. What was necessary was a functional, biologically substantiated theory of psychic structure.

At this same time, my clinical experiences clearly revealed that the goal of therapy was to establish the capacity for full sexual gratification. I knew this was the goal even if I had succeeded in bringing it about in only a few patients. But I had no idea whatever of a technique that would enable me to achieve it consistently. Indeed, the more firm I became in my contention that orgastic potency is the goal of therapy, the more aware I was of the imperfections of our skill in technique. Instead of diminishing, the gap between goal and the ability to achieve it became greater.

Therapeutically, the Freudian schemata of the psychic function turned out to be efficient to a limited extent only. The making conscious of unconscious desires and conflicts had a healing effect only when genitality was also established. As for the unconscious need for punishment, it had no therapeutic usefulness whatever. For, if there is a deeply ingrained biological instinct to remain sick and to suffer, then therapy is hopeless!

Many analysts lost their bearing owing to the desolation which prevailed in the field of therapy. Stekel rejected the work on psychic resistance against the uncovering of unconscious material, choosing rather "to shoot at the unconscious with interpretations." This practice is still followed by many "wild psychoanalysts." It was a hopeless state of affairs. Stekel rejected the actual neuroses and the castration complex. He wanted to effect quick cures. This was why he detached himself from Freud's plow which, though slow, cultivated thoroughly.

Adler could not come to grips with the theory of sexuality when he perceived guilt feelings and aggression. He ended up as a finalistic philosopher and social moralist.

Jung generalized the concept of libido to such an extent that it completely lost its meaning as sexual energy. He ended up in the "collective unconscious" and, therewith, in mysticism, which he later officially represented as a National Socialist.

Ferenczi, that highly gifted and humanly outstanding man, was well aware of the desolateness in the field of therapy. He sought for the solution in the body. He developed an "active technique," focused on states of physical tension. But he was not familiar with the stasis neurosis, and he made the mistake of not taking the orgasm theory seriously.

Rank, too, was aware of the therapeutic desolateness. He recognized the longing for peace, for a return to the womb. However, he misconstrued man's fear of living in this dreadful world, interpreting it biologically as the trauma of birth, which was supposed to be *the* core of the neurosis. It did not occur to him to ask why people want to flee from real life back into the protective womb. He came into conflict with Freud, who held onto the libido theory, and withdrew from the association.

They all foundered on the one question that every psychotherapeutic situation raises: where and how is the patient to express his natural sexuality when it has been liberated from repression? Freud neither alluded to nor, as it later turned out, even tolerated this question. And, eventually, because he refused to deal with this central question, Freud himself created enormous difficulties by postulating a biological striving for suffering and death.

Such problems could not be solved theoretically. The examples of Rank, Adler, Jung, and others deterred one from making contentions that had not been clinically substantiated in minute detail. I could have run the risk of oversimplifying the entire complex of problems. Just tell the patients to have sexual intercourse if they live abstinently, tell them to masturbate, and everything will be just right! It was in this way that analysts attempted to misinterpret my theory of genitality. Indeed, this was precisely what many physicians and psychiatrists were telling their patients at that time. They had heard that Freud said sexual stasis was responsible for the neurosis, so they encouraged their patients to "gratify themselves." They were after quick results. They failed to see that it was precisely the inability to experience gratification which characterized neurosis. The concept of "orgastic impotence" contained the essence of the question which, though it sounded simple, was quite complicated. My first premise stated that genital gratification resolves symptoms. However, clinical experience showed that few patients had at their disposal the genital energy necessary to experience genital gratification. Thus, it was necessary to find the places and mechanisms where it was bound or had been misdirected. The pathological pleasure in destructiveness (more simply expressed, human maliciousness) was one such biological deviation of genital energy. Extensive, strictly controlled theoretical work had been necessary to arrive at this conclusion. The patient's aggressiveness was misdirected, burdened with guilt feelings, excluded from reality, and usually deeply repressed. Freud's theory of primary biological destructiveness complicated the solution. For, if the overt and covert everyday manifestations of human sadism and brutality were the expression of a *biological* and, therefore, natural instinctual force, there was little hope for the therapy of neuroses, or for the highly esteemed cultural perspectives. And if, indeed, the impulses to self-annihilation were biological and immutable, there remains only the prospect of mutual human slaughter. In that case, neuroses would be *biological* manifestations. Why, then, did we practice psychotherapy? I had to have clarity about these matters—I did not want to indulge in speculations. One sensed that affective blocks against truths lay concealed behind such contentions. On the other hand, my clinical experience indicated a specific direction toward the realization of a practical goal: *sexual stasis is the result of a disturbance of the orgasm function. Fundamentally, neuroses can be cured by eliminating their energy source, the sexual stasis.* This direction led through hidden and dangerous areas. Genital energy was bound, concealed, and disguised in many places and in myriad ways. The official world had banned this subject. The technique of research and therapy had to be extracted from the dismal state of affairs in which it was immersed. Only a viable dynamic method of psychotherapy could keep one out of dangerous sidetracks. In the course of the next ten years, character analysis became the technique that helped to open the buried sources of genital energy. Its task as a method of cure was fourfold:

1. The thorough investigation of human behavior, including the sexual act.
2. The comprehension and mastery of human sadism.
3. The investigation of the most important manifestations of psychic illness which have their roots in periods prior to the genital phase of childhood. It had to be made clear how non-genital sexuality obstructs the genital function.
4. The investigation of the social cause of genital disturbances.

I shall begin by describing the second part of the task.

4. DESTRUCTION, AGGRESSION, AND SADISM

In psychoanalysis, the terms "aggression," "sadism," "destruction," and "death instinct" were used randomly and interchangeably. Aggression seemed identical with destruction, which, in turn, was "the death instinct directed against the world." And sadism remained the primary partial instinct which begins to be active at a certain stage of sexual development. On the basis of their origins and intentions, I attempted to assess all the human actions that are included under the concept of "hate." In my clinical work, I never encountered a death instinct, a will to die, as a primary instinct corresponding to sexuality or hunger. All psychic manifestations that could be interpreted as "death instinct" proved to be products of the neurosis. Such, for instance, was the case in suicide, which was either an unconscious revenge on another person with whom one identified, or an action to escape the enormous unpleasure caused by an extremely embroiled life situation.

The patient's fear of death could always be traced back to a fear of catastrophes and this fear, in turn, could be traced back to genital anxiety. Moreover, analysts who accepted the theory of the death instinct frequently confused anxiety and instinct. It was not until eight years later that the matter became clear to me: *fear of death and dying is identical with unconscious orgasm anxiety, and the alleged death instinct, the longing for disintegration, for nothingness, is the unconscious longing for the orgastic resolution of tension.* In short, I had not "generalized the orgasm theory all too quickly and schematically."

A living creature develops a destructive impulse when it wants to destroy a source of danger. In this case, the destruction or killing of the object is the biologically meaningful goal. The original motive is not pleasure in destruction. Rather the destruction serves the "life instinct" (I intentionally use the term which was current at that time) and is an attempt to *avoid anxiety* and to *preserve the ego in its totality. I destroy in a dangerous situation because I want to live and do not want to have any anxiety.* In short, the impulse to destroy serves a primary biological will to live. As such, it does not have a sexual connotation. Its goal is not pleasure, even though liberation from unpleasure is an experience similar to pleasure.

All this is important for many basic concepts of sex-economy, which deny the primary biological character of destructiveness. An animal does not kill another animal because it takes pleasure in killing. This would be sadistic murder for the sake of pleasure. It kills because it is hungry or because it feels that its life is threatened. Thus, here too, the destruction serves the "life instinct." What the "life instinct" is we do not yet know.

Aggression, in the strict sense of the word, has to do neither with sadism nor with destruction. The word means "approach." *Every positive manifestation of life is aggressive;* the act of sexual pleasure as well as the act of destructive hate, the sadistic act as well as the act of procuring food. Aggression is the life expression of the musculature, of the system of movement. The reassessment of aggression is of enormous importance for the rearing of children. Much of the inhibition of aggression which our children have to endure, to their own detriment, is the result of equating "aggressive" with "wicked" or "sexual." Aggression is always an attempt to provide the means for the gratification of a vital need. Thus, aggression is not an instinct in the strict sense of the word; rather it is the indispensable means of gratifying every instinctual impulse. The latter is inherently aggressive because the tension demands gratification. Hence, there is a destructive, a sadistic, a locomotor, and a sexual aggressiveness.

If aggressive sexuality is denied gratification, the urge to gratify it in spite of the denial continues to make itself felt. Indeed, the impulse arises to experience the desired pleasure *at all cost*. The need for aggression begins to drown out the need for love. If the pleasurable goal is completely eliminated, i.e., made unconscious or imbued with anxiety, then aggression, which originally was only a means, becomes a tension-releasing action in itself. It becomes pleasurable as an expression of life, thus giving rise to sadism. Hate develops as a result of the exclusion of the original goal of love. And the hate is most intense when the act of loving or being loved is blocked. This is what brings the sexually motivated destructive intention into the aggressive action. An example of this would be sexual murder. Its precondition is the complete blocking of the ability to enjoy genital pleasure in a natural way. Thus, the perversion "sadism" is a mixture of primary sexual impulses and secondary destructive impulses. It does not exist anywhere else in the animal kingdom, and it is a characteristic of man acquired late in his development, a secondary drive.

Every seemingly arbitrary destructive action is a reaction of the organism to the frustration of a vital need, especially of a sexual need.

Between 1924 and 1927, as these connections became clear to me in their basic characteristics, I nonetheless continued to use the term "death instinct" in my publications in order not to have to "break from the ranks." In my clinical work, I rejected the death instinct. I did not discuss its biological interpretation because I had nothing to say about it. In everyday practice, it always appeared as a destructive impulse. However, I had already formulated the dependence of the destructive impulse on sexual stasis, initially, according to its intensity. I left open the question as to the biological nature of destructiveness. It was also necessary to be cautious in view of the scantiness of the facts. What was clear even then, however, was that every suppression of sexual impulses provokes hate, non-directed aggressiveness (i.e., motor restlessness without a rational goal), and destructive tendencies. Numerous examples from clinical experience, everyday life, and the animal kingdom readily come to mind.

It was impossible to overlook the reduction of hate impulses in patients who had acquired the ability to obtain natural sexual pleasure. Every conversion of a compulsion neurosis into a hysteria was accompanied by a reduction of hate. Sadistic perversions or sadistic fantasies in the sexual act decreased to the extent to which gratification increased. These insights enabled us to understand the increase in marital conflicts when sexual attraction and gratification decrease; it also enabled us to understand the disappearance of marital brutality when another gratifying partner is found. I inquired into the behavior of wild animals and learned that they are harmless when they are well-fed and sexually gratified. Bulls are wild and dangerous only when they are led to, not when they are led away from, the cow. Chained dogs are very dangerous because their motor activity and sexual satisfaction are impeded. I came to understand the brutal character traits exhibited under conditions of chronic sexual dissatisfaction. I could observe this phenomenon in spiteful spinsters and ascetic moralists. By contrast, persons capable of genital gratification were conspicuously gentle and good. A person capable of sexual gratification is never sadistic. If such a person became sadistic, it could be safely assumed that a sudden disturbance had obstructed the usual gratification. This was also borne out by the behavior of women in the menopause. There are climacterical women who show no trace of spitefulness or irrational hate, and others who develop hateful characteristics in the menopause insofar as they did not already have them. There can be no question that the difference in behavior is due to their prior genital experience. The second type are always women who had never had a gratifying love relationship and now regret this lack, consciously or unconsciously sensing the consequences of sexual stasis. Hateful and envious, they become the most vicious opponents of every form of progress. Thus, it becomes clear that the sadistic pleasure of destruction so evident in our times can be traced to the general inhibition of natural sexuality.

An important source of genital excitation had been disclosed: by eliminating destructive aggressiveness and sadism, energy can be liberated and transferred to the genital. Soon it was shown that orgastic potency is incompatible with strong destructive or sadistic impulses. One cannot want to gratify the partner genitally and simultaneously want to destroy the partner. Thus, there was no substance to the talk about "sadistic masculine and masochistic feminine sexuality." Nor was there any substance to the contention that the rape fantasy was part of normal sexuality. In these matters, psychoanalysts simply failed to think beyond man's present sexual structure.

When frustrated, genital energies become destructive. By the same token, this destructiveness disappears with genital gratification. The theory of the biological origin of sadism and destructiveness was clinically untenable, and it was hopeless from a cultural point of view. But even this realization was still far from a conclusive solution to the problem. It did not suffice to achieve the therapeutic goal of orgastic potency. Destructive energy was also bound in many places and in myriad ways. In most cases, it lapses into repression. Thus, as far as technique was concerned, it was necessary to find the mechanisms that inhibited the reactions of hate in order to liberate bound energy. In this connection, character armor, in the form of the *affect block*, became the most fruitful soil for research.

The development of systematic resistance analysis to character analysis did not take place until after 1926. Until then, I had concentrated our work in the technical seminar on the study of the latent resistances and pregenital disturbances in the neurotic process. Patients demonstrated a typical behavior when liberated sexual energy excited the genital system. Most patients reacted to an increase in excitation by taking flight into non-genital attitudes. It was as if sexual energy oscillated back and forth between genital and pregenital zones of excitation.

In 1925–6, I treated a young American woman who had been suffering from severe bronchial asthma from earliest childhood. Every situation of sexual excitation produced an attack. The attacks appeared whenever she was about to have sexual intercourse with her husband, or when she flirted with somebody and began to get excited. In such cases, she suffered acute dyspnea, from which she could obtain relief only through the use of antispasmodic drugs. Her vagina was hypesthetic. Her throat, on the other hand, was hypersensitive. Unconsciously, she suffered from strong impulses to bite and to suck, which were directed toward her mother. There was a choking sensation in her throat. The fantasy of having a penis stuck in her throat appeared clearly in dreams and actions. As these fantasies became conscious, the asthma disappeared for the first time. But it was replaced by acute vagotonic bowel excitations in the form of diarrhea. This alternated with sympatheticotonic constipation. The throat was free, whereas the bowel was overexcited. The fantasy of having a penis in her throat gave way to the fantasy of "having a child in her stomach and of having to spew it out." With the diarrhea, the genital disturbance worsened. She ceased to have any feeling whatever in her vagina and completely rejected the sexual act. She was afraid of having an attack of diarrhea during coitus. As the bowel symptoms were alleviated, preorgastic vaginal excitations appeared for the first time. However, they did not go beyond a certain degree. To every increase of excitation, the patient reacted with anxiety or with an attack of asthma. For a while, the asthma reappeared in its original form, accompanied by the oral excitations and fantasies as if they had never been treated. At every relapse, they arose again, while the excitation advanced closer and closer to the genital system. Each time she was more capable of enduring vaginal excitations. The intervals between relapses became longer. This went on for several months. The asthma disappeared with every advance toward vaginal excitation and returned with every withdrawal of the excitation to the respiratory organs. The oscillation of the sexual excitation between the throat and the pelvis was accompanied by the corresponding fantasies of oral and genital childhood sexuality. When the excitation was "above," she became petulant and depressive. When it was concentrated in the genital, she became feminine and desired the male. The genital anxiety that caused her to withdraw every time appeared initially as fear of being injured in the sexual act. After this fear had been worked through, she was seized by the anxiety that she would disintegrate or burst due to the excitation. Gradually, the patient got used to the vaginal excitation and eventually experienced orgasm. This time, there was no spasm in the throat and, consequently, no asthma. It disappeared completely. I remained in contact with the patient for several years. I last heard from her in 1932, at which time she was still well.

This case was a further confirmation of my view of the therapeutic function of the orgasm and revealed additional important processes. I now understood that the non-genital excitations and forms of gratification are retained out of fear of the intense orgastic sensations in the genitals, for the non-genital forms provide a far lesser degree of excitation. Here, then, lay an important key to the problem of instinct anxiety.

The inhibition of sexual excitation produces a contradiction that grows steadily worse. *The inhibition increases the stasis of excitation; the increased stasis weakens the ability of the organism to reduce the stasis. As a consequence, the organism acquires a fear of excitation, in other words, sexual anxiety.* Hence, sexual anxiety is caused by the external frustration of instinctual gratification and is internally anchored by the fear of the dammed-up sexual excitation. This leads to *orgasm anxiety,* which is the ego's fear of the overpowering excitation of the genital system due to its estrangement from the experience of pleasure. *Orgasm anxiety constitutes the core of the universal, biologically anchored pleasure anxiety.* It is usually expressed as a general anxiety about every form of vegetative sensation and excitation, or the perception of such excitations and sensations. The pleasure of living and the pleasure of the orgasm are identical. Extreme orgasm anxiety forms the basis of the general fear of life.

The outward forms and mechanisms of orgasm anxiety are manifold. Common to all forms is the fear of the overpowering orgastic genital excitation. There are various mechanisms of inhibition. It took roughly eight years to investigate them thoroughly. Until 1926, only a few typical mechanisms were known. Female patients offered the best possibilities of studying them. In males, the sensation of ejaculation often conceals orgasm anxiety. In females, the orgasm anxiety is unadulterated. Their most frequent anxieties are that they will soil themselves during excitation, break wind, or involuntarily have to urinate. The intensity of the inhibition and, consequently, of the orgasm anxiety depends on how severely the function of vaginal excitation is impaired and how tenaciously non-genital ideas and fantasies absorb genital energy. When it is inhibited, orgastic excitation is experienced as a threat of annihilation. Women are afraid of falling under "the power of the man," of being injured or exploded internally by him. Hence, in fantasy, the vagina is transformed into a biting organ, the intent of which is to remove the threat of the penis. Every spasm of the vagina is developed in this way. If the spasm appears before the sexual act, it means the penis is denied entrance. If it appears during the act, it means there is an unconscious desire to retain or bite off the penis. If strong destructive impulses are present, the organism is afraid of fully surrendering itself to the experience out of fear that destructive rage might break through.

Women react to orgasm anxiety in various ways. Most of them hold their bodies still, always dimly aware of the sexual activity. Others move their bodies in a very forced manner, because gentle movement produces too great an excitation. The legs are pressed together. The pelvis is pulled back. As a means of inhibiting the orgastic sensation, they always hold their breath. Strangely enough, I did not become aware of this until 1935.

A female patient having masochistic beating fantasies was plagued by the unconscious fantasy that she would soil herself with excrement during excitation. As a four-year-old child, she had developed the masturbation fantasy that her bed was equipped with an apparatus that automatically eliminated the dirt. Holding still in the sexual act out of fear of soiling oneself is a widespread symptom of inhibition.

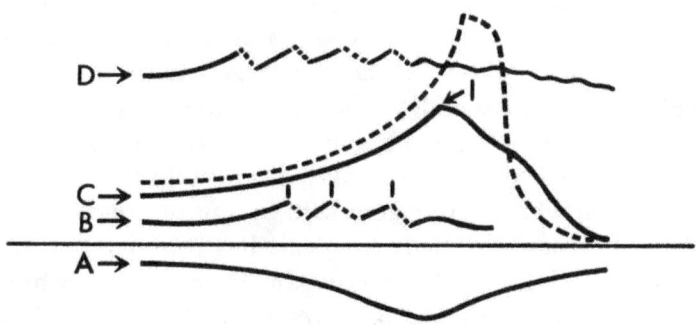

Diagram depicting typical genital disturbances in both sexes

A = Unpleasure and aversion marked by complete absence of feeling in the sexual act

B = Genital hypesthesia, minor preorgastic pleasure, intermittent inhibition (I) marked by emotional deadness

C = Normal preorgastic excitation of the genitals, decrease of excitation without orgasm: isolated orgastic impotence

D = Orgasm disturbance in nymphomania and satyriasis: intense preorgastic excitation, no decrease in excitation, no orgasm

I = Inhibition

- - - - - Normal orgasm curve

Orgasm anxiety is often experienced as a fear of death or fear of dying. If the patient suffers from a hypochondriacal fear of catastrophes, then every strong excitation is blocked. The loss of consciousness in the sexual experience, instead of being pleasurable, is fraught with anxiety. Thus, it is necessary "not to lose one's head," necessary to be constantly "on one's guard." It is necessary "to be on the alert." This attitude of watchfulness is expressed in the forehead and eyebrows.

Every form of neurosis has a genital disturbance which corresponds to it. Hysteria in women is characterized by a localized disturbance of vaginal excitation together with general hypersexuality. Abstinence due to genital anxiety is hysteria's typical genital disturbance. Hysterical men are either incapable of experiencing an erection during the sexual act, or they suffer from premature ejaculations. Compulsion neuroses are characterized by ascetic, rigid, well-rationalized abstinence. The women are frigid and generally incapable of being excited, while compulsively neurotic men are often erectively potent, but never orgastically potent. From the group of neurasthenias, I was able to separate a chronic form which is characterized by spermatorrhea and a pregenital structure. Here, the penis has completely lost its role as a penetrating pleasure organ. It represents a breast being extended to a child or a feces which is pressed out, etc.

A fourth group is composed of men who, out of fear of the woman and to ward off unconscious homosexual fantasies, are erectively superpotent. They must constantly demonstrate to themselves that they are potent, using the penis as a piercing organ, accompanied by sadistic fantasies. They are the phallic-narcissistic males, always to be found among Prussianistic officers, promiscuous charmers, and compulsively self-confident types. All of them have severe orgastic disturbances. The sexual act is nothing but an evacuation, followed by a reaction of disgust. Such men do not embrace the woman—they "fuck" her. Among women, their sexual behavior creates a deep aversion to the sexual act.

I presented a part of these findings at the Homburg Con-

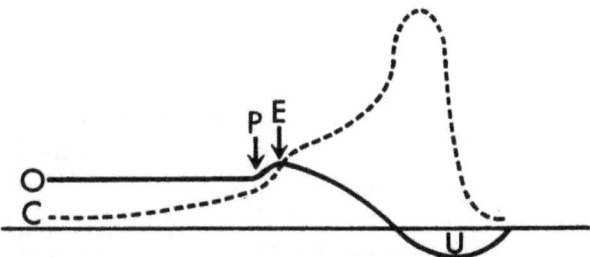

Diagram depicting the excitation curve in the case of premature ejaculation

O = Overexcitation of penis
P = Penetration of penis
E = Ejaculation
U = Unpleasure following ejaculation
C = Curve of normal orgasm

gress in 1925, under the title "On Chronic Hypochondriacal Neurasthenia." Specifically, my presentation dealt with what I referred to as "genital asthenia." This develops when genital excitation occurs with ideas of a pregenital but not a genital nature. I subsumed a second part of the subject under the title "Sources of Neurotic Anxiety." This paper was published in the volume presented to Freud to commemorate his seventieth birthday, in May 1926. In this work, I discussed the differences between the anxiety that develops from repressed aggression, the anxiety that develops from conscience, and the anxiety which is caused by sexual stasis. The guilt feeling originates from the sexual anxiety indirectly by way of intensified destructive aggression. In short, I pointed out the role played by destructiveness in the development of anxiety. Six months later, Freud demonstrated the connection between conscience-anxiety and the repressed instinct of destruction; at the same time, however, he minimized its connection with sexual anxiety. This was logical within his system. For, after all, he considered destruction a primary biological instinct, equal to sexuality. In the meantime, I had demonstrated the correlation between the *intensity of the destructive impulse and the intensity of sexual stasis,* and had differentiated "aggression" and "destruction." These differentiations, as theoretical and as specialized as they may appear, are of fundamental importance. They led in an entirely different direction from the Freudian conception of destruction.

The major aspects of my clinical findings were presented in my book *Die Funktion des Orgasmus.* I gave the manuscript to Freud in his apartment on May 6, 1926. This work had been dedicated to him. He seemed somewhat annoyed upon reading the title. He looked at the manuscript, hesitated a moment, and said, as if he were agitated, "So thick?" I felt uncomfortable. His reaction had not been rational. He was usually very polite and would not normally have made such a cutting remark. Prior to this, Freud had been in the habit of reading every manuscript in a few days and then making his comments in writing. In this instance, more than two months elapsed before I received his letter. It read as follows:

Dear Doctor: I have taken considerable time, but finally I have read the manuscript which you dedicated to me in commemoration of my birthday. I find the work valuable, rich in clinical material as well as in ideas. You know that I am definitely not opposed to your attempt at a solution which traces neurasthenia back to an absence of genital primacy. . . .

With regard to an earlier work on the problem of neurasthenia, Freud had written me:

I have known for quite some time that my postulation and conception of the actual neuroses was a superficial one and that it requires detailed corrections. Clarification was to be expected from further intelligent investigations. Your efforts give me the impression that you are entering upon a new and hopeful path. . . . I do not know whether your hypothesis really solves the problem. I had, and still have, certain doubts about it. You yourself fail to explain some of the most characteristic symptoms, and *your entire conception of the displacement of genital libido is still not quite palatable to me.* However, I hope that you will keep the problem in mind and eventually arrive at a satisfactory solution. . . . [italics Reich's]

This is what Freud had to say about a partial solution of the problem of neurasthenia in 1925, and about a detailed presentation of the orgasm problem and the role of somatic sexual stasis in the neurosis. The cooling in his attitude is quite evident. At first, I did not understand it. Why did Freud reject the solution contained in the "orgasm theory," which had been enthusiastically greeted by most young analysts? I had no idea that he and others were held back by the consequences my theory entailed for the whole theory of the neuroses.

On his seventieth birthday, Freud had told us we should not trust the world; acclaim did not mean anything. Psychoanalysis was merely being accepted so it could be destroyed more easily. What he really meant was the theory of sexuality. But it was precisely to the consolidation of the theory of sexuality that I had made a decisive contribution—and Freud rejected it. Therefore, I decided to hold on to the *Orgasm* manuscript for a few months and to think about it. It did not go to the printers until January 1927.

In December 1926, I gave a talk on character-analytic technique to Freud's inner circle. I concentrated my presentation on the problem whether, in the presence of a latent negative attitude, the analyst should interpret the patient's incestuous desires or whether it would be better to wait until the patient's distrust had been eliminated. Freud interrupted me. "Why don't you want to interpret the material in the sequence in which it appears? Of course, it is necessary to analyze and interpret the incest dreams as soon as they appear!" I had not expected this. I proceeded to give a precise and minute explanation of my standpoint. The whole thing was foreign to Freud. He did not understand why the analyst should not interpret the material in the sequence in which it appeared. This contradicted views he had expressed earlier in private conversations about technique. The mood of the meeting was not good. My opponents in the seminar gloated and felt sorry for me. I held my peace.

From 1926 on, the problems of the "theory of therapy" were given priority. The official report of the psychoanalytic clinic covering the period 1922–32 ran as follows:

> The causes of psychoanalytic successes and failures, the criteria of cure, the attempt to arrive at a typology of forms of illness in terms of their resistances and possibilities of cure, the problems of character analysis, character resistances, "narcissistic resistances," and the "affect block" were always subjected to a clinical and theoretical investigation on the basis of concrete cases. Partially in connection with this, we reviewed a number of publications dealing with the problems of technique.

The reputation of our seminar grew. The line of approach I was following produced a large number of subjects for investigation. These I assigned without any claims of priority. I took the collective work seriously. It was enough for me that I had made headway in a central field of research.

In the years which followed, a number of ambitious students who had participated in the seminar raised unjustified claims of originality. There was no reason to pay any attention to these claims. Generally speaking, those working in the field of psychoanalysis knew the origin of the basic ideas. Of the twenty students or so who were members of the Vienna seminar, not one of them continued in the path of character analysis.

In a letter, Freud acknowledged the originality of my work, in contrast to what was "common knowledge." But this common knowledge was insufficient for instruction in practical work. I contended that I was merely consistently applying analytic principles to the character. I did not know I was interpreting Freud's theory in a way he would soon reject. I still had no inkling of the incompatibility between the theory of the orgasm and the later psychoanalytic theory of neuroses.

5. THE GENITAL CHARACTER AND THE NEUROTIC CHARACTER. THE PRINCIPLE OF SELF-REGULATION

I was not able at that time to turn my intuitions about the physiological anchorings of psychic phenomena to practical or theoretical account. That is all they were then—intuitions. Hence, I worked on the development of my character-analytic technique. Clinically, the orgasm theory had been sufficiently substantiated to be able to provide a solid foundation for this technique.

My book *Character Analysis* was not published until April 1933. In 1928, the first essay on this subject entitled "The Technique of Interpretation and Resistance Analysis" was published in the psychoanalytic journal. At the end of the year, I revised this essay and presented it to the seminar on technique. It was the first of a number of articles which in the following five years made up the aforementioned book. It was supposed to be published by the psychoanalytic press. I was already in the process of reading the second galley proofs when the executive committee of the International Psychoanalytic Association decided not to allow the book to appear under its imprint. Hitler had just seized power.

The *principle of consistency* developed on the basis of typical errors of conventional, so-called orthodox psychoanalysis. The latter followed the rule of interpreting the material in the sequence in which the patient offered it, without regard to stratification and depth. I suggested that the resistances should be dealt with systematically, starting with that resistance closest to the psychic surface and having particular contemporary importance. The neurosis was to be undermined from a secure position. Every quantum of psychic energy which became liberated through the dissolution of defense functions had to strengthen the unconscious instinctual demands and thereby make them more accessible. A systematic removal of the layers of the character armor should take into account the stratification of neurotic mechanisms. Direct interpretations of unconscious instinctual material could only disrupt this work and therefore had to be avoided. The patient first had to establish contact with himself before he could grasp the connections between his various neurotic mechanisms. As long as the armor functioned, the patient could at best achieve only an intellectual comprehension of his situation. According to experience, this had minor therapeutic effect.

An additional rule was to proceed consistently from the warding off of sexual contents and not to go into prohibited sexual desires until the defense against them had been broken down. In the analysis of resistances, I recommended the strictest consistency, i.e., sticking to that element of defense which proved to be the most important and most disruptive at the moment. Since every patient had a character armor which reflected his individual history, the technique of destroying the armor had to be specific to each case, determined and developed from step to step. This precluded a schematic technique. The analyst bore the main burden of responsibility for the success of the therapy. Since the armor restricts the patient, his inability to express himself openly is a part of his illness. It is not ill will, as many analysts believed at that time. Correct dissolution of rigid psychic armorings must eventually lead to the release of anxiety. Once the stasis anxiety has been set free, there is every possibility of establishing free-flowing energy and, in conjunction with it, genital potency. It merely remained questionable whether the comprehension of the character armor also included the comprehension of the ultimate sources of energy. I had my doubts, and they proved to be justified. One thing I was sure about, however, was that the character-analytic technique was a considerable step forward toward the mastery of severe, encrusted neuroses. The stress was no longer on the content of neurotic fantasies but on the energy function. Since the majority of patients were incapable of following the so-called basic rule of psychoanalysis, i.e., "to say everything which comes to mind," I ceased to insist on it. Instead, I used as my points of attack not only what the patient communicated but everything he offered, in particular the way in which he made his communications or was silent. Even silent patients revealed themselves, expressed something which could be gradually unraveled and mastered. Alongside the "what" of the old Freudian technique, I placed the "how." I already knew that the "how," i.e., the form of the behavior and of the communications, was far more important than what the patient told the analyst. Words can lie. The expression never lies. Although people are unaware of it, it is the immediate manifestation of the character. I learned in the course of time to comprehend the form of the communications themselves as direct expressions of the unconscious. The need to convince and persuade the patient diminished in importance and soon became superfluous. Whatever the patient did not grasp spontaneously and automatically did not have any therapeutic value. Character attitudes had to be understood spontaneously. The intellectual understanding of the unconscious was superseded by the patient's immediate perception of his own expression. I ceased to use psychoanalytic terminology with my patients. This in itself precluded the possibility of concealing an affect behind a word. The patient no longer talked about his hate—he experienced it. He had no way of escaping it insofar as I correctly removed the armoring.

Narcissistic individuals were looked upon as ill suited for analytic treatment, but by breaking down the armor, these cases also became accessible. I was able to bring about cures in patients suffering from severe character disturbances, though they were regarded as inaccessible by analysts using conventional methods.[1]

The love and hate transferences to the analyst lost their more or less academic character. It is one thing to talk about the anal eroticism of one's childhood or to remember that one felt such things at one time; it is quite another thing to experience them in the session as an actual urge to break wind and even to have to yield to such an urge. In the latter instance, no convincing or persuading is necessary. I finally had to free myself from the academic attitude toward the patient and to tell myself that, as a sexologist, I had to deal with sexuality in the same way an internist has to deal with bodily organs. In the process, I discovered the severe hindrance to analytic work entailed by the rule, insisted on by most analysts, that the patient live in abstinence for the duration of the treatment. If this was to be the case, how were the genital disturbances to be understood and eliminated?

---

[1] Carl M. Herold underestimated the difference between character analysis and psychoanalytic technique when he described them as being merely technical finesses instead of a fundamental theoretical nature. ("A Controversy about Technique," *The Psychoanalytic Quarterly*, Vol. VIII, 1939, No. 2.) However, the following argument is correct:

"We often hear raised at this point in the controversy the objection that all this is not new and is practiced by every good analyst. This is a very elegant way of suggesting modestly that one is a really good analyst but it leaves unanswered the question why these really good analysts did not trouble themselves to state these things with such clarity, especially as they should have known that, among the younger analysts, there was a keen desire for such technical advice. This desire must indeed have been very strong, judging from the eagerness with which Reich's book and ideas were absorbed by the younger German analysts. They had been stuffed with complicated theories but given very few cues as to how to use them in practice. Reich offered a clear summing up of the theoretical aspects of the practical situation in which a young analyst finds himself, not elaborate enough perhaps to include all the intricate details, but simple enough to be readily usable in practical work."

I am not mentioning these technical details here, which are fully discussed in my book *Character Analysis,* for reasons pertaining to technique. I merely want to describe the reassessment in my basic attitude that enabled me to discover, formulate, and make applicable for my later work *the principle of sexual self-regulation.*

Many psychoanalytic rules had an inherently and strongly taboo character, which merely reinforced the patient's neurotic taboos in the sexual realm. Such, for instance, was the rule that the analyst should not be seen—should remain, so to speak, a blank sheet of paper upon which the patient inscribed his transferences. This procedure did not eliminate but rather reinforced the patient's feeling that he had to deal with an "invisible," unapproachable, superhuman, i.e., in terms of the child's way of thinking, a sexless being. Under these circumstances, how was the patient to overcome the sexual timidity that lay at the root of his illness? Dealt with in this way, everything pertaining to sexuality remained diabolic and forbidden, something which had to be "condemned" or "sublimated" at all cost. It was forbidden to look at the analyst as a sexual being. Under such circumstances, how could the patient dare to express his human criticism? All the same, the patients had a way of knowing about the analysts. But with this kind of technique, they seldom expressed what they knew. With me, however, patients quickly learned to overcome any reserve about criticizing me. Another rule was that the patient was only supposed "to remember," but never to "do anything." I was in agreement with Ferenczi in rejecting this method. There could be no doubt that the patient should be "allowed to do" also. Ferenczi got into difficulties with the association because, having a good intuition, he allowed the patients to play like children. I tried every conceivable means to free my patients from their characterological stiffness. My intent was to have them look upon me as a human being, not to fear me as an authority. This was part of the secret of my successes, which were generally acknowledged. Another part of the secret was that I used every available means appropriate to medical work to liberate my patients from genital inhibitions. I did not consider any patient cured who could not at least masturbate free of guilt feelings. I attached the greatest importance to the supervision of the patient's genital sex life at the time of treatment. (Hopefully, it is clear that this has nothing to do with the superficial masturbation therapy practiced by some "wild" analysts.) It was precisely by following this approach that I first learned to differentiate sham genitality from the natural genital attitude. Gradually, over long years of work, the traits of the "genital character," which I later set off against those of the "neurotic character," became clear to me.

I overcame my reserve toward the patient's actions and discovered an unexpected world. At the base of the neurotic mechanism, behind all the dangerous, grotesque, irrational fantasies and impulses, I discovered a simple, self-evident, decent core. I found it without exception in every case where I was able to penetrate to a sufficient depth. This gave me courage. I allowed the patients greater and greater rein, and I was not disappointed. True, there were dangerous situations now and then. However, the fact speaks for itself that, as extensive and protean as my practice has been, I have not had a single case of suicide. It was not until much later that I came to understand the cases of suicide that happened during treatment. Patients committed suicide when their sexual energy had been stirred up but was prevented from attaining adequate discharge. The universal fear of the "evil" instincts has had a severely detrimental effect on the work of psychoanalytic therapy. *Psychoanalysts had unquestioningly accepted the absolute antithesis between nature (instinct, sexuality) and culture (morality, work, and duty) and had come to the conclusion that "living out of the im-*

CHARACTER-ANALYTIC TECHNIQUE 175

pulses" was at variance with cure. It took me a long time to overcome my fear of these impulses. It was clear that the *asocial impulses which fill the unconscious are vicious and dangerous only as long as the discharge of biological energy by means of natural sexuality is blocked.* When this is the case, there are basically only three pathological outlets: unbridled, self-destructive impulsiveness (addiction, alcoholism, crime due to guilt feelings, psychopathic impulsiveness, sexual murder, child rape, etc.); instinct-inhibited character neuroses (compulsion neurosis, anxiety hysteria, conversion hysteria); and the functional psychoses (schizophrenia, paranoia, melancholia, or manic-depressive insanity). I am omitting the neurotic mechanisms which are operative in politics, war, marriage, child rearing, etc., all of which are consequences of the lack of genital gratification in masses of people.

With the ability to experience complete genital surrender, the patient's personality underwent such a thorough and rapid change that, initially, I was baffled by it. I did not understand how the tenacious neurotic process could give way so rapidly. It was not only that the neurotic anxiety symptoms disappeared—the patient's entire personality changed. I was at a loss to explain this theoretically. I interpreted the disappearance of the symptoms as the withdrawal of the sexual energy which had previously nourished them. But the character change itself eluded clinical understanding. The genital character appeared to function according to different, hitherto unknown laws. I want to cite a few examples by way of illustration.

Quite spontaneously, the patients began to experience the moralistic attitudes of the world around them as something alien and peculiar. No matter how tenaciously they might have defended premarital chastity beforehand, now they experienced this demand as grotesque. Such demands no longer had any relevancy for them; they became indifferent to them. Their attitude toward their work changed. If, until then, they had worked mechanically, had not demonstrated any real interest, had considered their work a necessary evil which one takes upon oneself without giving it much thought, now they became discriminating. If neurotic disturbances had previously prevented them from working, now they were stirred by a need to engage in some practical work in which they could take a personal interest. If the work which they performed was such that it was capable of absorbing their interests, they blossomed. If, however, their work was of a mechanical nature as, for example, that of an office employee, businessman, or middling attorney, then it became an almost intolerable burden. In such cases, I had a hard time mastering the difficulties which arose. The world was not attuned to the human aspect of work. Teachers who had been liberal, though not essentially critical of educational methods, began to sense a growing estrangement from, and intolerance of, the usual way of dealing with children. In short, the sublimation of instinctual forces in one's work took various forms, depending upon the work and the social conditions. Gradually, I was able to distinguish two trends: (1) a growing immersion in a social activity to which one was fully committed; (2) a sharp protest of the psychic organism against mechanical, stultifying work.

In other cases, there was a complete breakdown in work when the patient became capable of genital gratification. This appeared to confirm the malicious exhortations of the world that sexuality and work were antithetical. Upon closer examination, the matter ceased to be alarming. It turned out that the latter were always patients who had, until then, performed their work on the basis of a compulsive sense of duty, at the expense of inner desires they had repudiated, desires which were by no means asocial—quite the contrary. A person who felt himself best suited to be a writer had, if employed in an attorney's office, to muster all his energy to master his rebellion and to suppress his healthy impulses. Thus, I learned the important rule that not everything unconscious is asocial, and that not everything conscious is social. On the contrary, there are highly praiseworthy, indeed culturally valuable, attributes and impulses which have to be repressed for material considerations, just as there are flagrantly asocial activities which are socially rewarded with fame and honor. The most difficult patients were those who were studying for the priesthood. Inevitably, there was a deep conflict between sexuality and the practice of their profession. I resolved not to accept any more priests as patients.

The change in the sexual sphere was just as pronounced. Patients who had felt no qualms in going to prostitutes became incapable of going to them once they were orgastically potent. Wives who had patiently endured living with unloved husbands and had submitted to the sexual act out of "marital obligation" could no longer do so. They simply refused; they had had enough. What could I say against such behavior? It was at variance with all socially dictated views, for instance, the conventional arrangement whereby the wife must unquestioningly fulfill her husband's sexual demands as long as the marriage lasts, whether she wants to or not, whether she loves him or not, whether she is sexually aroused or not. The ocean of lies in this world is deep! From the point of view of my official position, it was embarrassing when a woman, correctly liberated from her neurotic mechanisms, began to make claims upon life for the fulfillment of her sexual needs, not troubling herself about morality.

After a few timid attempts, I no longer ventured to bring up these facts in the seminar or in the psychoanalytic association. I feared the stupid objection that I was imposing my own views upon my patients. In this case, I would have had to retort that moralistic and authoritarian influencing by means of ideologies lay not on my side but on the side of my opponents. Nor would it have served any purpose if I had wanted to lessen the impact of such facts by confronting official morality with more acceptable examples. For instance, I might have pointed out that orgasmotherapy imbued women with a seriousness about sex which made it impossible for them to go to bed with anybody who happened to come along. And I am speaking of women who, whether married or not, had been previously capable of spreading their legs at the drop of a hat simply because they did not experience any gratification. That is to say, they became "moral" and wanted only one partner who loved and gratified them. As I said, such examples would not have served any purpose. Where scientific work is under the purview of morality, it is guided not by facts but by moral codes. What rankles most in all this is the ostentation of "scientific objectivity." The more trapped one is in the net of dependencies, the more loudly one asserts that one is an "objective scientist." Once a psychoanalyst sent me a woman for treatment who was suffering from deep melancholia, suicidal impulses, and acute anxiety, explicitly stipulating that I "should not destroy the marriage." The patient, as I learned in the first session, had already been married for four years. Her husband had not yet deflowered her. Instead, he had engaged in all sorts of perverse activities which his wife, in her middle-class naïveté, had accepted as her unquestioning marital obligation. And the analyst had stipulated that this marriage should not be destroyed under any circumstances! The patient broke off the treatment after three sessions because she suffered from extremely acute anxiety and experienced the analysis as a seductive situation. I knew this, but there was nothing I could do about it. A few months later I learned that the patient had taken her life. This kind of "objective science" is one of the millstones around the neck of a drowning humanity.

I no longer had a clear conception of the relation of the

psychic structure to the existing social system. The change in the patient's attitude with respect to this moralistic code was neither clearly negative nor clearly positive. The new psychic structure appeared to follow laws which had nothing in common with the conventional demands and views of morality. It followed laws that were new to me, of which I had no inkling prior to this. The picture which these laws offered when taken altogether corresponded to a different form of sociality. They embraced the best principles of official morality, e.g., that women must not be raped and children must not be seduced. At the same time, they contained moral modes of behavior which, though flatly at variance with conventional conceptions, were socially unimpeachable. One such attitude, for instance, was that it would be base to live a chaste life due to external pressure, or to be faithful solely for reasons of marital obligation. The attitude that it is unsatisfying and repulsive to embrace a partner against his or her will appeared to be unassailable, even from the strictest moralistic point of view. Yet, it was incompatible with the legally protected demand of "marital obligation."

Allow these few examples to suffice. This other form of morality was not governed by a "Thou shalt" or "Thou shalt not"; it developed spontaneously on the basis of the demands of genital gratification. One refrained from an ungratifying action not out of fear, but because one valued sexual happiness. These people abstained from a sexual act even when they felt a desire for it, if the external or internal circumstances did not guarantee full gratification. It was as if moralistic injunctions had been wholly dispensed with and replaced by better and more tenable guarantees against antisocial behavior. They were guarantees which were not incompatible with natural needs; indeed, they were based precisely on principles that fostered the joy of life. The sharp contradiction between "I want" and "I must not" was eliminated. It was replaced by something which might almost be called *vegetative consideration:* "True, I would very much like to, but it would mean little to me; it would not make me happy." This was an entirely different matter. Actions were carried out in accordance with a self-regulating principle. This self-regulation, in turn, brought with it a certain amount of harmony because it eliminated and obviated the struggle against an instinct which, though inhibited, was constantly obtruding itself. The interest was merely shifted to a different goal or to a different love object which offered fewer difficulties of gratification. The precondition for this shift was that the interest, which was natural and of an inherently social nature, was neither repressed (i.e., withdrawn from consciousness) nor moralistically condemned. It was merely gratified elsewhere and under different circumstances.

If a young man was in love with an "untouched" girl from a so-called "good family," this was certainly something natural. If he wanted to embrace her, this impulse was not, to be sure, "socially acceptable"—but it was healthy. If the girl proved to be strong enough and healthy enough to deal with all the internal and external difficulties contingent upon her acceptance of him as an intimate friend, then everything would be all right. True, their behavior would be at variance with official morality, but it would be wholly in keeping with rational, healthy conduct. If, however, the girl proved to be weak, apprehensive, inwardly dependent upon her parents' opinion—in short, neurotic—then the embrace could entail only difficulties. If the young man is not enslaved by morality and does not conceive of the embrace as a "violation," he might do one of two things: (1) help the girl to gain the clarity he has gained; (2) simply forego the pleasure. In the latter case, which is just as rational as the former, he would eventually turn his attention to another girl where these difficulties did not exist. The neurotic—moralistic in the old sense of the word—young man would have behaved in a fundamentally different way in the same situation. He would have desired the girl and at the same time refrained from the fulfillment of his desire, thus creating a lasting contradiction. The moralistic renunciation would have worked against the impulse until the latter's repression would have put an end to the *conscious* conflict, replacing it by an unconscious conflict. The young man would have become progressively enmeshed in a difficult situation. Not only would he have refrained from the possibility of instinctual gratification, he would also have denied himself the possibility of seeking another object. A neurosis for both partners would have necessarily resulted. *The gap between morality and instinct would remain.* Or the instinct would be expressed in a disguised or distorted form. The young man might easily develop compulsive rape fantasies, actual rape impulses, or the characteristics of a double morality. He would go to prostitutes and run the risk of acquiring a venereal disease. There would be no possibility of inner harmony. From a purely social point of view, the result could be nothing but disastrous. "Morality" would not have been served in any respect whatever. There are any number of variations of this example. It applies to marriage as well as to every other sexual relationship.

Now let us contrast *moralistic regulation and sex-economic self-regulation.*

Morality functions as an obligation. It is incompatible with the natural gratification of instincts. Self-regulation follows the natural laws of pleasure and is not only compatible with natural instincts; it is, in fact, functionally identical with them. Moralistic regulation creates a sharp, irreconcilable psychic contradiction, i.e., morality contra nature. It thus intensifies the instinct, and this, in turn, necessitates increased moralistic defense. It precludes an efficient circulation of energy in the human organism. Self-regulation withdraws energy from an unrealizable desire by transferring it to a different goal or partner. Steadily alternating between tension and relaxation, it is consistent with all natural functions. The psychic structure molded by compulsive morality performs work perfunctorily, governed by an ego-estranged "should." The sex-economically regulated structure performs work in harmony with sexual interests, drawing from a great reserve of life energy. The moralistic psychic structure overtly adheres to the rigid laws of the moralistic world, adapts itself to them externally, and rebels internally. A person with such a structure is constantly at the mercy of antisocial inclinations, of both a compulsive and impulsive nature. The person with a healthy, self-regulated structure does not adapt himself to the irrational part of the world; he insists on the fulfillment of his natural rights. He appears sick and antisocial to neurotic moralists. In reality, he is incapable of antisocial actions. He develops a natural self-confidence, based on sexual potency. A moralistic structure always goes hand in hand with weak potency, and such a person is constantly forced to make compensations, i.e., to develop an artificial, stiff self-confidence. He is ill disposed toward the sexual happiness of others because he feels provoked by it and is incapable of enjoying it himself. Essentially, he engages in sexual intercourse to prove his potency. For the person who has a genital structure, sexuality is an experience of pleasure and nothing but that. Work is a pleasurable activity and achievement. For the moralistically structured individual, work is an irksome duty or solely a material necessity.

The nature of the character armor is also different. The person having a moralistic structure has to develop an armor which restricts and controls every action and functions automatically and independently of external situations. He cannot vary his attitudes even when he would like to. The compulsively moralistic official continues to be one in the conjugal bed also. The sex-economically regulated person is capable of closing himself to one situation and opening to another. He is in control of his armor because he does not have to hold back forbidden impulses.

I called one type a "neurotic" character, the other a "genital" character.[2] From this point on, the therapeutic task consisted in the transformation of the neurotic character into the genital character and in the replacement of moralistic regulation by sex-economic self-regulation.

It was well known at the time that moralistic inhibitions produce neuroses. Analysts spoke of the necessity of "smashing the superego." I did not succeed in convincing them that this was not enough, that the problem was more extensive and lay deeper. The moralistic regulation cannot be destroyed unless it is replaced by something different and better. And yet, it was precisely this something different that my colleagues regarded as dangerous, wrong, and "nothing new." In reality, they were afraid of the "meat grinder," of the serious confrontation with the present-day world, which categorizes and assesses everything in accordance with compulsive moralistic principles. At that time I myself was not too clear about the very far-reaching social consequences. I simply followed the traces of my clinical work with great determination. One cannot escape a certain kind of logic, even if one would like to.

It was not until a few years ago that I began to understand why free, self-regulated behavior fills people with enthusiasm but at the same time terrifies them. The fundamentally changed attitude toward the world, toward one's own experience, toward other people, etc., which characterizes the genital character, is simple and natural. It is immediately evident, even to people whose structure is completely different. It is a secret ideal in all people, and it always means the same thing, even if called by a different name. No one would

---

[2] The special article I wrote about these two types was published in the psychoanalytic journal and was well received by psychoanalysts. In 1933, it was incorporated into my book *Character Analysis*.

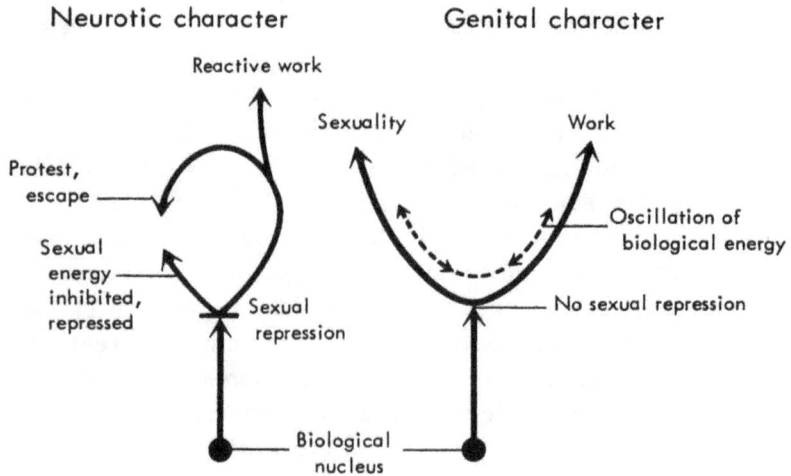

Diagram depicting the reactive and sex-economic performance of work

Reactive work performance: The work is performed in a mechanical, forced, dull way; it deadens the sexual desires and is diametrically opposed to them. Only small amounts of biological energy can be discharged in the performance. Work is essentially non-pleasurable. Sexual fantasies are strong and disrupt the work. Hence, they have to be repressed, creating neurotic mechanisms which further reduce the capacity for work. The reduction of one's work performance burdens every love impulse with guilt feelings. Self-confidence is weakened. This produces compensatory neurotic fantasies of grandeur.

Sex-economic work performance: In this case, biological energy oscillates between work and sexual activity. Work and sexuality are not antithetical; they foster one another by enhancing self-confidence. The respective interests are clear and concentrated, borne by a feeling of potency and a capacity for surrender.

gainsay the capacity for love, any more than he would gainsay sexual potency. No one would dare to postulate incapacity for love or impotence, the results of authoritarian upbringing, as goals of human striving. It is part of natural attitudes to be spontaneously social, and it is not exactly the ideal to force oneself to be social by suppressing criminal impulses. It is obvious to everyone that it is better and healthier not to have an impulse to rape in the first place than to have to inhibit it morally. For all that, no other point of my theory has endangered my work and existence as much as my contention that self-regulation is possible, naturally present, and universally feasible. If, of course, I had merely postulated a hypothesis about this, using sweet elegant words and pseudo-scientific phrases, I would have been universally acclaimed. My medical work required constant improvements in the technique of influencing people, and this prompted me to raise ever more deeply penetrating questions: *if the attributes of the genital character are so self-evident and desirable, why is the intimate relation between sociality and orgastic potency overlooked?* Why is it that the exact opposite view dominates everything that rules life today? *Why has the conception of a sharp antithesis between nature and culture, instinct and morality, body and spirit, devil and God, love and work, become one of the most salient characteristics of our culture and philosophy of life?* Why has it become incontestable and given legal protection? Why was the development of my scientific work followed with such great interest, only to be rejected in dismay and slandered and denigrated when it began to make serious headway? Originally, I thought the reason was ill will, treachery, or scientific cowardice. Not until many years later, years filled with horrible disappointments, did I understand this enigma.

Most of the troubled and disoriented reactions I had at that time toward my opponents, whose number increased from day to day, originated from the erroneous assumption that what is correct in principle can also be simply and naturally accepted and put into practice. If I had been able to grasp and formulate these obvious facts, if they fit in so well with the purposes of therapeutic work, why should not my colleagues grasp them also? My naïveté was fostered by the enthusiasm my colleagues had for my views, by their keen interest and affirmation. I had touched their simple human ideals and ideas. I was soon to find out that ideals are smoke and ideas are quickly changed. Far more persuasive were the concerns for one's livelihood and the ties to organizations, authoritarian attitudes, and . . . ? Something was missing.

What was affirmed and longed for in the ideal aroused anxiety and terror in reality. It was inherently alien to the existing structure. The entire official world fought against it. The mechanisms of natural self-regulation lay deeply buried in the organism, covered over and infused with compulsive mechanisms. The pursuit of money as the content and goal of life was at variance with every natural feeling. The world forced this upon people by educating them in specific ways and by placing them in conditions of life that fostered it. Thus, the gap which formed in social ideology between morality and reality, the demands of nature, and the idea of culture, existed in man himself, merely in a different form. To be able to cope with this world, people had to suppress what was most beautiful and most true, what was most basic in themselves; they had to strive to annihilate it, to surround it with the thick wall of the character armor. In doing so, they came to grief internally, and usually externally as well; but they also spared themselves the struggle with this chaos. There was a dim reflection of the deepest and most natural feelings for life, of natural decency, spontaneous honesty, mute and complete feelings of love. However, it was embodied in a "sentiment" which was all the more artificial the more thickly the psychic armor was developed against their own naturalness. Thus, even in the most exaggerated pathos, we find a tiny trace of what is really alive. And it is from this last dim spark of life that human mendacity and meanness derive the force which nourishes falsity. This became my firm conviction, for how else could it be explained that the ideology of human morality and honor had survived for such a long time and been defended by masses of people, in spite of the actual filthiness of their lives. Since people neither can nor are allowed to live their real life, they cling to the last glimmer of it, which reveals itself in hypocrisy.

On the basis of such considerations, the idea of the direct correlation between social structure and character structure developed. Society molds human character. In turn, human character reproduces the social ideology en masse. Thus, in reproducing the negation of life inherent in social ideology, people produce their own suppression. This is the basic mechanism of so-called tradition. I had no inkling of the importance this formulation would have for the comprehension of fascist ideology some five years later. I did not indulge in any speculations in the interest of political views. Nor did I construct a philosophy of life. The solution of every problem which came up in my clinical work led to this formulation. Thus, I was no longer surprised that the glaring inconsistencies in the moralistic ideology of society coincided in every detail with the contradictions in the human structure.

Freud had contended that the existence of culture as such is dependent upon the "cultural" repression of instincts. I had to agree with him, but with very definite reservations: present-day culture is, in fact, based on sexual repression. But the next question was: is the development of culture as such dependent upon sexual repression? And does not our culture rest on the suppression of unnatural, secondarily developed impulses? No one had yet spoken about what I had discovered in man's depth and was now in a position to develop. There was still no opinion about this. I soon noticed that, in discussions about "sexuality," people meant something other than what I had in mind. By and large, pregenital sexuality is antisocial and is at variance with natural feelings. But the condemnation extends to the genital embrace as well. Why, for instance, does a father look upon the sexual activity of his daughter as a defilement? It is not solely because he is unconsciously jealous. This would not explain the severity of his reaction, which sometimes includes murder. Genital sexuality is, in fact, looked upon as something low and dirty. For the average man, the sexual act is merely an evacuation or a proof of conquest. The woman instinctively rebels against this, justifiably so. And it is also precisely for this reason that the father conceives of his daughter's sexual activity as a defilement. Under such circumstances, there can be no correlation between sexuality and happiness. From this, everything written about the baseness of sexuality and its dangers can be explained. But this "sexuality" is a sick distortion of natural love. It has completely submerged everything that is deeply yearned for as genuine happiness in love. People have lost their feeling for natural sexual life. Their assessment of it is based on a distortion, which they rightly condemn.

Hence, to fight for or against sexuality is futile and hopeless. On the basis of such distortions, the moralist can, must, and should win out. The distortion cannot be tolerated. The modern woman is repelled by the sexuality of men who get their experience in brothels and acquire a revulsion toward sex from prostitutes. "Fucking" is a defilement. No sensitive woman wants "to let herself be fucked."

This is what causes an impasse in discussions and makes the struggle for a healthy life so difficult. This is where my opponents and I were speaking at cross purposes. When I speak of sex, I do not mean "fucking," but the embrace prompted by genuine love; not "urinating into the woman," but "making her happy." No headway can be made unless a distinction is drawn between the unnatural practices in sexual life, practices that have developed on a secondary level, and the deeply buried needs for love which are present in every person.

And so the question arose: how can principle be translated into reality, the natural laws of a few into the natural laws of everyone? It was clear that an individual solution of the problem was unsatisfactory and missed the essential point.

Inquiry into the social aspects of psychotherapy was new at that time. Accesses to the social problem were opened on three sides: the prophylaxis of neuroses, the closely related question of sexual reform,[3] and finally the general problem of culture.

---

[3] I gave a thorough presentation of the problem of sexual reform in my book *The Sexual Revolution*. It is, therefore, not discussed in the present volume.

Chapter VI

AN ABORTIVE BIOLOGICAL REVOLUTION

1. MENTAL HYGIENE AND THE PROBLEM OF CULTURE

The countless burning questions that came up in my social work prompted me to want to hear Freud's opinion. In spite of the encouragement he had given me in an earlier conversation regarding my plan to set up a center for the purpose of providing sexual counseling for the poor, I was not sure of his concurrence. Behind the scenes, the situation in the psychoanalytic organization was tense. I made an effort to induce my colleagues to take a clear stand, for I had no doubts about the social radicalness of my work and did not want to conceal it. I had already heard the first sexually defamatory slanders against me. Following the publication of a series of articles on the sex education of children in the *Zeitschrift für Psychoanalytische Pädagogik,* rumors were circulated that I allowed my children to witness sexual intercourse. It was also rumored that, abusing the transference situation, I engaged in sexual intercourse with my patients during the analytic sessions. And there was more of the same. It was the typical reaction of sexually frustrated people to the fight of healthy people for sexual happiness. I knew that this reaction was unparalleled in hate and bitterness. There

AN ABORTIVE BIOLOGICAL REVOLUTION 191

is nothing in the world which, in a mute and murderous way, is capable of causing so much human suffering. Murder in war gives the victim the sensation of heroic sacrifice. Men and women with healthy feelings for life must mutely bear the mark of filth branded upon them by those who, out of fear and guilt, are ridden by perverse fantasies. There was not a single organization in our society which would have defended the natural feelings for life. I did everything possible to shift the discussion from a personal to an objective level. The intent of these slanderous rumors was all too clear.

I gave my talk on the prophylaxis of neuroses to Freud's inner circle on December 12, 1929. These monthly meetings in Freud's house were open only to the officers of the Psychoanalytic Society. Everyone knew that words of far-reaching importance were spoken here and that important decisions were made. One had to consider very carefully what one said. Psychoanalysis had become a very controversial, worldwide movement. The responsibility was enormous, but it was not my nature to escape it by glossing over the truth: I had either to present the problem exactly as it was or to say nothing at all. But the latter was no longer possible. My sex-political work had gained autonomy—thousands of people flocked to my meetings to hear what psychoanalysis had to say about social and sexual misery.

The following are typical questions. They were asked by people of all circles and professions in open meetings, and they were answered.

What should one do when the woman, in spite of a conscious desire, has a dry vagina?
How often should one have sexual intercourse?
Can one have intercourse during the menstrual period?
What should a man do when the woman is unfaithful?

What should a woman do when the man does not gratify her? When he is too quick?

Is it all right to engage in sexual intercourse from behind?

Why is homosexuality punished?

What should a woman do when the man wants to and she does not?

Is there any remedy for insomnia?

Why do men so much love to talk among themselves about their relationships with women?

Is intercourse between brother and sister punished in the Soviet Union?

A worker was married to a woman who was severely ill. She was confined to her bed for years. There were three small children and an eighteen-year-old daughter. She took the place of the mother, cared for the children, and cared for the father. There were no problems. She slept with the father. Everything went well. She continued to care for the family, to cook for them, and to keep house for them. The father worked and provided for his sick wife. The daughter was nice to her younger brothers and sisters. People began to gossip. The vice squad was called in. The father was arrested, charged with incest, and put into prison. The children were put on welfare. The family went to pieces. The daughter had to become a servant in a strange household. Why is this so?

What should one do if one wants to make love and several other people are sleeping in the same room?

Why do physicians refuse to help when a woman becomes pregnant and does not want to or cannot have the child?

My daughter is just seventeen years old and already has a boy friend. Is there anything wrong with that? He won't marry her—that's for sure.

Is it very bad to have sexual relations with more than one person?

The girls make such a fuss. What should I do?

I am very lonely; I want very much to have a boy friend. But when one comes along, I am afraid.

My husband goes out with another woman. What should I do? I would like to go out with another man. Is there anything wrong with that?

I live on twenty schillings per week. My girl wants to go to the movies. There isn't enough money for that. I love my girl. What should I do to keep her from going to someone else?

I have been living with my wife for eight years now. We love one another, but we don't hit it off sexually. I have a strong desire to sleep with another woman. What should I do?

My child is three years old and is always playing with his penis. I try to punish him, but it is no use. Is that bad?

I masturbate every day—three times on some days. Is this injurious to my health?

Zimmermann [a Swiss reformer] says that, to avoid pregnancy, the man should prevent ejaculation by not moving inside of the woman. Is this true? It really hurts!

I read in a book for mothers that one should have intercourse only when one wants to have a child. That's ridiculous, isn't it?

Why is everything pertaining to sex so forbidden?

If sexual freedom were introduced, wouldn't this produce chaos? I would be afraid of losing my husband!

Woman is naturally different from man. Man has a polygamous predisposition—woman a monogamous predisposition. Bearing children is a duty. Would you allow your wife to sleep with another man?

You speak of sexual health. Do *you* allow your children to masturbate as much as they please? I'll bet you don't!

In the company of others, our husbands behave differently from the way they behave at home. At home, they are brutal tyrants! What should one do about this?

Are you married? Do you have children?

Wouldn't sexual freedom lead to the complete destruction of the family?

I suffer from uterine hemorrhages. The physician at the clinic is uncouth, and I have no money to consult a private physician. What should I do?

At what age can one begin to engage in sexual intercourse?

My period always lasts ten days and it is very painful. What should I do?

Is masturbation harmful? People say that it makes you goofy!

Why are parents so strict with us? I always have to be at home by eight o'clock! And I'm already sixteen years old.

When I attend meetings (I am a functionary and very much interested in politics), my wife is jealous. What should I do with her?

My husband always insists on making love to me. I don't always feel like it. What should I do?

I am engaged, and it happens with us that my fiancé does not find the right position in sexual intercourse, so that we get tired before the gratification and immediately stop. I want to point out that my fiancé is twenty-nine years old, but has never had intercourse before this.

Are people with reduced potency allowed to get married?

What should unattractive people do who can't find a boy friend or a girl friend?

What should an older untouched girl do? Obviously she can't offer herself to a man!

Is it possible that a man who lives like an ascetic can forgo sexual intercourse by taking cold baths every day, engaging in gymnastics, sports, etc.?

Is coitus interruptus harmful?

If coitus interruptus is practiced over a long period of time, will it lead to impotence?

What should be the relationship between boys and girls at a summer camp?

Does the sexual intercourse of an adolescent have any mental consequences?

Is it harmful to interrupt masturbation right before the ejaculation?

Is vaginal discharge caused by masturbation?

On those evenings, which were dedicated to the discussion of the prophylaxis of neuroses and the question of culture, Freud for the first time clearly expressed the views which were published in *Civilization and Its Discontents,* 1931, and were often glaringly at variance with the position he took in *The Future of an Illusion.* I had not "provoked" Freud, as some analysts accused me of doing. Nor were my arguments "dictated by Moscow," as others maintained. At that very time, I was using these same arguments to fight the economists in the socialist movement who, with their slogans about the "iron course of history" and the "economic factors," were alienating the very people whom they claimed to be liberating. I was merely making an effort to clarify the issues, and I have no regrets about it today. I was resisting the growing tendency to move away from the psychoanalytic theory of sex and to shy away from its social consequences.

By way of introduction, therefore, I asked that my presentation be regarded as a private and personal communication, since I had not yet published anything on this subject. Four questions demanded an answer:

1. *What are the ultimate consequences of psychoanalytic theory and therapy?* What are they, that is, if psychoanalysis retains the central importance of the sexual etiology of the neuroses?

2. *Is it possible to continue to merely limit oneself to the analysis of the neuroses of individual men and women in private practice?* Neurosis is an epidemic disease operating be-

neath the surface. Humanity as a whole is psychically ill.

3. *What is the nature of the role the psychoanalytic movement has to assume in the social framework?* There can be no doubt that it has to assume a role. We are speaking here of the important social question of psychic economy which is identical with sex-economy if the theory of sexuality is pursued to its ultimate conclusion.

4. *Why does society produce neuroses en masse?*

I answered these questions on the basis of experiences which I have often described elsewhere. According to the statistical data which I had gathered in various organizations and youth groups, it could be demonstrated that as many as *60 to 80 percent of these people were afflicted with severe neurotic illnesses*. And it must be borne in mind that these figures represent conscious neurotic symptoms only; they do not include character neuroses of which the members of these organizations were unaware. In meetings having a specifically sex-political character, the percentage was higher, above 80 percent. The reason for this, as could be assumed, was that a great many neurotically ill people came to such meetings. The argument that only neurotics attended such meetings, however, was refuted by the following fact: in meetings of closed organizations (e.g., free-thinker organizations, groups of schoolchildren, laborers, all kinds of politically oriented youth groups, etc.) which did not have any special attraction for neurotics, the percentage of symptom neuroses was only an average of 10 percent lower than that of the open meetings. In the six counseling centers in Vienna which were under my supervision, about 70 percent of those who came to us for help and advice were in need of psychoanalytic treatment. Only about 30 percent, consisting of men and women who suffered from stasis neuroses of a mild sort, could be helped through counseling and social help. This meant that even if sex-hygiene care were provided for the entire population, at best only some 30 percent of the people could be helped by quick medical intervention. The remaining 70 percent of the population (higher in the case of women, lower in the case of men) required psychoanalytic treatment which, in every case and with questionable results, necessitated an average of two to three years. It was senseless to set this as the goal of social-political work. Mental hygiene on this individual basis was only a dangerous utopia.

The situation demanded clear, extensive social measures aimed at the prevention of neuroses. The principles and means by which these measures would be applied, could, of course, be derived from the experience gained from individual patients, in the same way that efforts are made to combat a plague on the basis of experiences gained from individuals infected with it. There is a tremendous difference, however. Smallpox is prevented through quick vaccinations. The measures necessary to prevent neuroses present a somber, appalling picture. Still, they cannot be circumvented. The only prospect is to destroy the source from which neurotic misery issues.

What are the sources of the neurotic plague?

The most important source is authoritarian, sexually repressive family upbringing, with its unavoidable, sexual child-parent conflict and genital anxiety. Precisely because there could be no doubt about the correctness of Freud's clinical findings, there could be no doubt about the correctness of the conclusions I had drawn. I had, moreover, solved a problem which had remained unclear until then: the relation between the sexual child-parent attachment and the general social suppression of sexuality. We were dealing here with a fact characteristic of education as a whole, and hence the problem assumed a new perspective.

There could no longer be any doubt that people became neurotic on a mass scale. What was not clear and in need of explanation was how people could remain healthy under the prevailing conditions of education! To solve this far more interesting riddle, it was necessary to draw upon the relationship between authoritarian family upbringing and sexual suppression.

Parents suppress the sexuality of small children and adolescents, not knowing that they are doing so at the behest of authoritarian, mechanized society. Their natural expression blocked by forced asceticism and in part by the lack of fruitful activity, children develop a sticky attachment to the parents, marked by helplessness and guilt feelings. This, in turn, thwarts their liberation from the childhood situation, with all its concomitant sexual anxieties and inhibitions. Children brought up in this way become character-neurotic adults who, in turn, pass on their neuroses to their own children. And so it goes from generation to generation. This is how the conservative, life-fearing tradition is perpetuated. How, in spite of this, can people become and remain healthy?

The theory of the orgasm provided the answer: accidental or socially determined conditions occasionally enable the attainment of genital gratification; this, in turn, eliminates the energy source of the neurosis and weakens the tie to the childhood situation. Thus, in spite of the neurotic family situation, it is possible for some people to become and to remain healthy. The sexual life of the youth of 1940 is fundamentally more free, but also more conflict-laden, than that of the youth of 1900. The healthy person as well as the sick person goes through family conflict and sexual repression. It is a peculiar coinciding of circumstances, quite accidental in this society, which makes it possible for an organism, with the help of a sex-economic mode of life, to free itself from both ties. The industrial collectivization of work has been an important factor in this connection. But what is the fate of these healthy people later in life? They do not have an easy time of it, that is certain. However, with the help of the "spontaneous organotherapy of neurosis"—the term I used to designate the orgastic resolution of tensions—they overcome the pathological tie to the family as well as the effects of the sexual misery of society. There is a category of people in society who, living and working in scattered parts of the world without any connection with one another, are endowed with natural sexuality. They represent what I have termed the *genital character*. They are very frequently found among the industrial workers.

The mass plague of neuroses is produced in three main stages of human life: *in early childhood*, through the atmosphere of the neurotic home, in *puberty*, and finally in the *compulsive marriage* in its strict moralistic conception.

Strict and premature toilet training and insistence on "good behavior," absolute self-control, and good manners have a damaging effect in the first stage. They make the child amenable to the most important prohibition of the next period, the prohibition of masturbation. Other obstructions to the child's development may vary, but these are typical. The inhibition of natural childhood sexuality in all layers of the population provides the most fertile soil for the fixation to the neurotic home and its extension into the tie to one's "homeland." This is the origin of man's lack of independence in thought and action. Psychic mobility and energy go together with sexual vitality and are its precondition. On the other hand, sexual inhibition is the precondition of psychic inhibition and clumsiness.

In puberty, the damaging principle of education is repeated, leading to psychic stagnation and character armoring. It is repeated on the solid basis of the previous inhibition of childhood impulses. Contrary to psychoanalytic belief, *the puberty problem is socially and not biologically determined*. Nor is it determined by the child-parent conflict. Adolescents who find their way into the real life of sexuality and work sever the neurotic tie to the parents acquired in childhood. The others, severely affected by the specific frustration brought about by sexual inhibition, sink back into the infantile situation more than ever. It is for this reason that most neuroses and psychoses develop in puberty. Statistical investigations carried out by Barasch on the duration of marriages, with reference to the period at which genital sexual life began, confirm the close correlation between marriage and adolescent asceticism. The sooner an adolescent arrives at gratifying sexual intercourse, the more incapable he is of adapting himself to the strict demand of "only one partner, and this partner for a lifetime." However one may feel about this, it is a fact which can no longer be gainsaid. It means that *the demand of asceticism for adolescents has the intent of making adolescents amenable and marriageable.* And this is precisely what it does. In the process, however, it produces the very sexual impotence which, in turn, destroys marriages and heightens marriage crises.

One plays the hypocrite when one makes it legally possible for an adolescent to marry on the eve of his or her sixteenth birthday—thereby proclaiming that sexual intercourse is not damaging in this case—while at the same time demanding "asceticism to the day of marriage," even when this cannot take place until the man or woman is thirty years old. Then, all of a sudden, "sexual intercourse at an early age is damaging and immoral." No person capable of thinking for himself can accept such an explanation, any more than he can accept the neuroses and perversions produced in this way. Making the punishment of masturbation less severe is merely a convenient evasion of the issue, which is the fulfillment of the physical demands of budding youth. Puberty is sexual ripening, and initially that is all it is. The so-called cultural puberty of aesthetic psychologists is, to put it mildly, sheer nonsense. *Safeguarding the sexual happiness of maturing adolescents is a central point in the prophylaxis of neuroses.*

The youth of every generation has the function of representing the next step of civilization. The older generation attempts to keep the youth at its own cultural level. The motives for this are of a predominantly irrational nature: the older generation has had to become resigned—hence it feels threatened when the youth lives out what it could not achieve. The typical adolescent rebellion against the parental home is not a neurotic manifestation of puberty, but a preparation for the social function these young people will later have to fulfill as adults. They have to fight for their ability to progress. No matter what cultural and civilized tasks confront every new generation, it is always the older generation's fear of the sexuality and fighting spirit of the young which inhibits.

I was accused of being a utopian, of wanting to eliminate unpleasure from the world and safeguard pleasure only. However, I had put down in black and white that conventional upbringing makes people incapable of pleasure by armoring them against unpleasure. *Pleasure and joy of life are inconceivable without struggle, painful experiences, and unpleasurable self-confrontations.* Psychic health is characterized, not by the Nirvana theory of the Yogis and the Buddhists, the hedonism of the epicureans,[1] the renunciation of monasticism; it is characterized by the alternation between unpleasurable struggle and happiness, error and truth, deviation and rectification, rational hate and rational love; in short, by being fully alive in all situations of life.

The ability to endure unpleasure and pain without becoming embittered and seeking refuge in rigidification goes hand in hand with the ability to receive happiness and to give love.

---

[1] The term is used here in its vernacular meaning. In reality, Epicurus and his school have, apart from the name, nothing in common with the so-called epicurean philosophy of life. Epicurus' serious natural philosophy was misconstrued by the half-educated and uneducated masses of people. It was taken to mean the gratification of secondary impulses. There is no way of defending oneself against such falsifications of true ideas. Sex-economy is threatened with the same fate by those who suffer from pleasure anxiety and by a science which fears sexuality.

As Nietzsche put it, he who would "exult to high heaven" must be prepared to "grieve unto death." However, our European social philosophy and education turned adolescents, depending upon their social situation, either into fragile puppets or into dried-up, dull, chronically morose machines of industry and "business," incapable of pleasure.

One has to learn to see clearly into the problem of marriage. Marriage is neither a love affair pure and simple, as one group of people contends, nor is it a purely economic institution, as another group contends. It is a form which was imposed upon sexual needs through socio-economic processes.[2] Apart from the ideology acquired in early childhood and the moral pressure exerted by society, sexual and economic needs, particularly in women, produce the desire for marriage. Marriages fall to pieces as a result of the ever deepening discrepancy between sexual needs and economic conditions. The sexual needs can be gratified with one and the same partner for a limited time only. On the other hand, the economic tie, moralistic demand, and human habit foster the permanency of the relationship. This results in the wretchedness of marriage. *Pre*marital abstinence is supposed to prepare a person for marriage. But this very abstinence creates sexual disturbances and thereby undermines marriage. Sexual fulfillment can provide the basis for a happy marriage. But this same fulfillment is at variance with every aspect of the moralistic demand for lifelong monogamy. This is a fact, no matter how one feels about it. But there should be no hypocrisy. Under poor internal and external conditions, the above contradictions lead to resignation. This necessitates severe inhibition of the vegetative impulses. This, in turn, draws out from the depth all available neurotic mechanisms. Sexual partnership and human friendship are replaced by fatherliness or motherliness in the marital relationship and by mutual, slavish dependency—in

---

[2] Cf. Lewis Morgan, *Ancient Society*.

short, by disguised incest. Today, these are commonplace, long-since thoroughly described matters, of which only many priests, psychiatrists, social reformers, and politicians are still ignorant.

These internal injuries to the psychic structure, already extremely serious in themselves, are strongly reinforced by the external social conditions which caused them in the first place. Psychic misery is not the intention of sexual chaos, but it is an inseparable part of it. *Compulsive marriage and the compulsive family reproduce the human structure of the economically and psychically mechanized era.* In terms of sexual hygiene, everything is turned upside down in this system. Biologically, the healthy human organism requires three to four thousand sexual acts in the course of the thirty to forty years during which it is genitally active. Generally speaking, parents do not want more than two to four children. Moralism and asceticism postulate that, even in marriage, sexual pleasure should serve only the purpose of procreation. Carried to its ultimate conclusion, this means at most four sexual acts in one lifetime. The authorities say yes to this, and people suffer mutely, cheat, and become hypocrites. Yet no one puts up a forceful and energetic fight against such nonsense, which takes on the proportions of mass murder. This nonsense is manifested in the legal or moralistic prohibition of the use of contraceptives. This causes sexual disturbances and fear of pregnancy in women, which, in turn, resuscitate childhood sexual anxieties and destroy marriages. The elements of sexual chaos are interconnected. The childhood prohibition of masturbation reinforces in the woman the anxiety of having her vagina entered or touched. This causes women to be afraid of using contraceptives. Hence, we have the thriving practice of "criminal abortions," which, for their part, produce countless bases for neuroses. When there is a fear of pregnancy, neither the woman nor the man can experience gratification. Approximately 60 percent of the adult male population practice coitus interruptus. This produces sexual stasis and nervousness en masse.

And to all this science and medicine say nothing. More than that, they obstruct every serious scientific, social, or medical attempt to remedy the situation, by evading the issue, erudition, false theories, and direct endangerments of life. There is every reason to be indignant when one hears all the claptrap about "moralistic indications," the harmlessness of abstinence and coitus interruptus, etc., expounded in a highly dignified and authoritarian manner. I did not say this at Freud's apartment, but my objective description of the facts must have triggered off a feeling of indignation.

To all this is added the housing problem. According to the statistics of 1927, more than 80 percent of the population of Vienna lived four and more in one room. Thus, for 80 percent of the population, this meant a disturbance, indeed the impossibility, of regulated, physiologically adequate sexual gratification, even under the best inner conditions. There was complete silence about this in the fields of medicine and sociology.

Mental hygiene presupposes an ordered, materially secure life. A person harassed by basic material needs cannot enjoy any kind of pleasure and easily becomes a sexual psychopath. Thus, those who are in favor of the prophylaxis of neuroses must be prepared for a radical revolutionizing of everything that produces neuroses. This explains why the prophylaxis of neuroses was never a topic of serious discussion and why it was alien to human thought. My arguments had to have a provocative effect, whether I intended it or not. The facts alone contained all manner of provocation. I did not even mention the legally enforceable "marital obligation" and the "obedience owed to parents to the point of enduring physical punishment." Such things were not talked about in academic circles; they were looked upon as "unscientific and political."

What was awkward about my objectively unassailable position was that, while no one wanted to hear the facts I presented, no one could gainsay them. Everyone knew of course that individual therapy was of no consequence socially, that education was hopeless, and that ideas and lectures on sex education alone were not enough. With inevitable logic, this led to the *problem of culture.*

Until 1929, the relation of psychoanalysis to "culture" was not discussed. Not only had psychoanalysts not seen any contradiction between the two, they had averred that the Freudian theory "fostered culture", wholly disclaiming its criticism of culture. Between 1905 and about 1925, the enemies of psychoanalysis had continually called attention to the "danger to culture" which psychoanalysis would soon entail. The opponents of psychoanalysis and the attentive world had attributed to psychoanalytic theory more than it purported. This was due, on one hand, to the deep need people had for clarity about sexuality and, on the other, to the "sexual chaos" the "champions of culture" feared. Freud thought he could harness the danger by means of the theories of sublimation and of instinctual renunciation. The hubbub gradually subsided, especially as the theory of the death instinct came more and more into prominence and the theory of stasis anxiety faded more and more into the background. The theory of the biological will to suffer saved embarrassment. Its postulation and acceptance were proof that psychoanalysis could "adapt itself to culture." Now this harmony was being endangered by my work. Not to compromise themselves, psychoanalysts explained that my views were really quite "banal," or they said that my views were incorrect. But I had not made matters at all easy for myself. I had not merely contended that psychoanalysis was at variance with the existing culture and that it was "revolutionary." It was much more complicated than most people imagine today.

My views could not be dismissed; clinicians worked more

and more with the genital theory of therapy. Nor could they be denied. At best, their importance could be minimized. My work confirmed the revolutionary character of the natural-scientific theory of sex. On the other hand, it was proclaimed that Freud had just introduced a new cultural epoch. How, in view of this, could the correctness and practicality of my views be admitted? To do so would have been at variance with the psychoanalysts' material security, as well as with the contention that psychoanalysis only *fostered* "culture." No one asked what was being endangered in this "culture" and what was being fostered. Everyone overlooked the fact that, by its very development, the "new" criticized and negated the old.

The leading social scientists of Austria and Germany rejected psychoanalysis and competed with it in the attempt to elucidate problems of human existence. The situation was anything but simple. It is astonishing that I did not commit any serious blunders at that time. It would have been very tempting to make a short-sighted judgment and to come up with a widely acceptable statement, e.g., that sociology and psychoanalysis could be reconciled without any difficulty or that psychoanalysis, though correct as individual psychology, was socially unimportant. This was how the Marxists who were sympathetic toward psychoanalysis spoke. But this was not the way to go about it. I was too much of a psychoanalyst to accept a superficial solution and too much interested in the development of freedom in the world to be content with halfway measures. For the moment, I was satisfied that I had been able to incorporate psychoanalysis as such into the province of sociology, even if only as a method at that time.[3] Friends and foes alike were forever accusing me of being overhasty. However, even if their unconsidered accusations often made me angry, I saw no reason to be per-

---

[3] Cf. Reich, *Dialektischer Materialismus und Psychoanalyse*, "Unter dem Banner des Marxismus," 1929.

turbed by them. I knew that no one put in as much theoretical and practical effort as I. I allowed my manuscripts to lie in my desk drawer for years before I felt secure enough to publish them. Being clever was something I could leave to others.

The relationship between psychoanalysis and culture began to be clarified when a young psychiatrist gave a talk on *Psychoanalyse und Weltanschauung* at Freud's apartment. Only a very few people know that Freud's *Civilization and Its Discontents* grew out of these discussions on culture as a defense against my ripening work and the "danger" it entailed. Statements with which Freud had opposed my views appeared in the book.

While it is true that in this book Freud reaffirmed that natural sexual pleasure is the aim of human striving for happiness, it is also true that he tried to demonstrate the untenability of this principle. His basic theoretical and practical formula continued to read: man normally, and of necessity, advances from the "pleasure principle" to the "reality principle." He has to forgo pleasure and to adjust himself to reality. The irrational components of this "reality," which today celebrate orgies of annihilation, were not questioned, nor was a distinction made between those pleasures which are compatible with sociality and those which are not. In *Civilization and Its Discontents*, Freud sets forth the same arguments he used to reject the point of view I advocated in our discussions. In retrospect, I see that this confrontation had a positive value for the cultural-political movement. It clarified many things, particularly the fact that psychoanalysis could not continue to be effective as a "cultural-revolutionary" theory, without concretely criticizing and changing the conditions of education. How else could the misused word "progress" be interpreted?

The following was the view held by intellectuals at that time: science is concerned with problems of essence; ideology deals with questions of possibility. Essence (science) and possibility (politics) were said to be totally separate fields. The establishment of a fact did not spell out a possibility, i.e., did not indicate a goal which should be striven after. Every political orientation was free to do what it pleased with facts established by science. I spoke out against these ethical logicians who took refuge from reality in an abstract formula. When I ascertain that an adolescent becomes neurotic and disturbed in his work as a result of the abstinence demanded of him—this is "science." In an "abstract logical" sense, it can be concluded from this that the adolescent should continue to live abstinently or that he should give up abstinence. The conclusion arrived at is "political ideology" and its implementation is political practice. I, however, argued that there are scientific findings which allow only one practical conclusion. What appears to be logically correct can be wrong from a practical and objective point of view. If, today, someone came forth and established as fact that abstinence is injurious to adolescents, without drawing the conclusion that adolescents should cease to live abstinently, he would simply be laughed at. It is for this reason that it is so important to know the practical implications of a question. A physician must never assume an abstract point of view. He who refuses to accept the "should" which follows from the above finding with respect to adolescent abstinence must, whether he intends to or not, make a false statement of a purely "scientific nature." With the full force of his "scientific authority," he will have to contend that abstinence is not injurious to the adolescent. He has, in short, to veil the truth and to play the hypocrite. *Every scientific finding has an ideological presupposition and a practical social consequence.* At that time, it first became clear just how deep was the abyss separating abstract logical thinking and functional, natural-scientific thinking. Abstract logic often has the function of admitting scientific facts without allowing a single

AN ABORTIVE BIOLOGICAL REVOLUTION

practical conclusion to be drawn from them. For this reason, I preferred practical functionalism.

Freud took the following position: the "average man's" attitude toward religion was understandable. As a famous poet once put it:

> Wer Wissenschaft und Kunst besitzt,
> *hat* auch Religion,
> Wer jene beiden nicht besitzt,
> der *habe* Religion! [4]

This saying holds true for the present, as does everything else conservative ideology presumes to assert. The right of the conservatives is identical with the right of science and medicine to confront conservatism at such a deep level that the source of its arrogance—ignorance—is destroyed. Because we refuse to question the workingman's attitude of toleration, his pathological renunciation of the knowledge and cultural fruits of this world of "science and art," his helplessness, his fear of responsibility, and his craving for authority, we must look on while the world plunges into the abyss, at present in the form of the fascist plague. What meaning can science have if it looks down on such questions? Do they have a clear conscience, those scientists who could have worked out the answer but deliberately refused to fight against the psychic plague? Today, faced with universal danger, the whole world realizes what was barely speakable twelve years ago. Social life has put into sharp focus the problems which, at that time, were the concern of individual physicians only.

Freud justified the renunciation of happiness of masses of people as expertly as he defended the fact of childhood sexuality. A few years later, exploiting human ignorance and

---

[4] He who has Science and has Art, Religion, too, has he; /Who has not Science, has not Art, Let him religious be!—Goethe. (From the translation of *Das Unbehagen in der Kultur* by Joan Riviere.)

fear of happiness, a pathological genius plunged Europe into the abyss with the slogan of the "heroic renunciation of happiness."

> Life, as we find it, is too hard for us [Freud wrote]; it brings us too many pains, disappointments, and impossible tasks. In order to bear it we cannot dispense with palliative measures. . . . There are perhaps three such measures: powerful deflections, which cause us to make light of our misery; substitute satisfactions, which diminish it; and intoxicating substances, which make us insensitive to it. Something of the kind is indispensable.[5]

At the same time, in *The Future of an Illusion*, Freud rejected the most dangerous illusion, i.e., religion.

> The common man cannot imagine this Providence otherwise than in the figure of an enormously exalted father. Only such a being can understand the needs of the children of men and be softened by their prayers and placated by the signs of their remorse. The whole thing is so patently infantile, so foreign to reality, that to anyone with a friendly attitude to humanity it is painful to think that the great majority of mortals will never be able to rise above this view of life.

Thus, Freud's correct findings with respect to religious mysticism ended in resignation. And life outside was seething with struggles for a rational philosophy and a scientifically based social regulation. In principle, there was no difference between the two. Freud, however, not only refused to take sides, he also rejected "political" ideology and advocated the "scientific" view of life. He felt that he had nothing to do with politics. I sought to demonstrate that the striving for the democratization of the work process is and must be scientifically rational. At that time, the smashing of Lenin's social democracy, the development of dictatorship in the Soviet Union, and the abandonment of all principles of truth in sociological thinking, had already begun. These

---

[5] Sigmund Freud, *Civilization and Its Discontents*, translated from the German by James Strachey. New York: Norton & Company, 1962.

things could not be denied. I rejected Freud's political aloofness. It could be only dimly divined then that Freud's attitude, as well as the dogmatic attitude of the Soviet government, each in its own way, was justified. *The scientific, rational regulation of human existence is the highest goal. However, the acquired irrational structure of the masses, i.e., of those who embody the historical process, makes dictatorship possible through the very exploitation of this irrationalism.* It depends on who wields power, toward what goal, and against what forces. At any rate, Russia's initial social democracy was the most human approach possible under the existing historical conditions and given man's structure. Freud had explicitly admitted this. The degeneration of this social democracy into the dictatorial Stalinism of today cannot be denied, and is grist for the mill of the opponents of democracy. In the following years, Freud's pessimism appeared to be all too horribly justified: "There's nothing to be done." After the Russian experience, the development of genuine democracy appeared utopian. Those who did not have art and science had the "socialistic mystique," to which a tremendous world of scientific thought had degenerated. It is to be stressed that Freud's attitude merely reflected the basic general attitude of academic scientists. They had no confidence in the possibility of democratic self-education, nor in the mental capacities of the masses. Therefore, they did nothing to undermine the sources of dictatorship.

Since the beginning of my activity in the field of social hygiene, the idea had become more and more fixed in my mind that cultural happiness in general and sexual happiness in particular are the real content of life, and should be the goal of a practical politics of the people. Everyone, the Marxists included, were opposed to this idea. But the discovery which I had made in the depth of the human organism outweighed all objections, difficulties, and reservations. The entire output of culture, from the love story to the highest achievements of poetry, confirmed my view. The entire politics of culture (film, novels, poetry, etc.) revolve around the sexual element, thrive on its renunciation in reality and its affirmation in the ideal. The consumer goods and advertising industries capitalize on it. If all humanity dreams and poeticizes about sexual happiness, should it not also be possible to translate the dream into reality? The goal was clear. The facts discovered in the biological depth demanded medical attention. Why, in spite of this, did striving for happiness always appear merely as a fantastic vision that wrestled with hard reality? Freud became resigned in the following way:

In terms of human behavior itself, what is the purpose and goal of man's life? What does man want from life? What does he hope to accomplish in it? In 1930, these were the questions Freud asked after those discussions in which the effects of the sexual will to life of the broad masses were felt as far away as the quiet rooms of the scholar, precipitating a clash between antithetical views.

Freud had to admit, *"The answer to this can hardly be in doubt. They strive after happiness; they want to become happy and to remain so."* [6] Man wants to experience strong feelings of pleasure. It is simply the pleasure principle that determines the purpose of life. This principle governs the performance of the psychic apparatus from the very beginning.

There can be no doubt about its efficacy, and yet its program is at loggerheads with the whole world, with the macrocosm as much as with the microcosm. There is no possibility at all of its being carried through; all the regulations of the universe run counter to it. One feels inclined to say that the intention that man should be "happy" is not included in the plan of "Creation." What we call happiness in the strictest sense comes from the (preferably sudden) satisfaction of

---

[6] *Ibid.* [Italics are Reich's.]

needs which have been dammed up to a high degree, and it is by its nature only possible as an episodic phenomenon.

In this passage, Freud articulated a mood which constitutes a part of man's inability to be happy. The argument rings true, but it is incorrect. It seems to say that abstinence is a precondition of the experience of happiness. It overlooks the fact that the damming-up itself is experienced as pleasure *when there is the prospect of gratification and this gratification is not overly delayed*. On the other hand, the damming-up makes the organism rigid and incapable of pleasure when there is no prospect of gratification, and when the experience of happiness is threatened with punishment. The greatest experience of pleasure, the sexual orgasm, has the peculiarity that it presupposes a damming-up of biological energy. However, this peculiarity by no means leads to the Freudian conclusion that happiness is at variance with all the institutions of the world. Today, I can prove experimentally that this contention is incorrect. At that time, I merely sensed that Freud was concealing a reality behind a figure of speech. *To have admitted the possibility of human happiness would have been tantamount to admitting the incorrectness of the theory of the repetition compulsion and the theory of the death instinct.* It would have meant a critique of the social institutions which destroy the happiness of life. To retain his resigned position, Freud advanced arguments which he deduced from the existing situation, without questioning whether this situation is inherently necessary and immutable. I did not understand how Freud was able to believe that the discovery of child sexuality could have no world-changing effect whatever. He appeared to me to do a terrible injustice to his own works, and to feel the tragedy of this contradiction. When I disagreed with him and presented my arguments, he told me that either I was all wrong or that one day I would "have to bear the heavy burden of psychoanalysis all alone." Since I was not wrong, his prophecy proved true.

In his discussions as well as in his publications, Freud took refuge in the theory of biological suffering. He sought a way out of the catastrophe of civilization in an "effort on the part of Eros."

In a private conversation in 1926, Freud expressed the hope that the "experiment" of the Soviet Russian revolution would succeed. No one had any inkling at that time that Lenin's attempt to establish social democracy would end so disastrously. Freud knew, and had set down in writing, that mankind is sick. Neither the psychiatrist nor the politician had the faintest notion of how this universal sickness was related to the Russian and later to the German catastrophe. Three years later, conditions in Germany and Austria were already in such a state of turmoil as to distort every professional activity. The irrationalism in political life became more and more conspicuous. Analytic psychology penetrated more and more into social problems. In my work as a whole, I began to consider "man" not solely as a type, but as a being acting within a specific social context. I saw that neurotic and starving masses of people were falling into the hands of political exploiters. In spite of his knowledge of the psychic plague, Freud feared the inclusion of psychoanalysis in the political arena. His conflict, which was very deep, made me feel very close to him. Today, I also understand the necessity of his resignation. For a decade and a half, he had fought for the recognition of simple facts. His professional colleagues had slandered him, called him a charlatan, and questioned the sincerity of his intentions. Freud was not a social pragmatist, "only" a scientist, but he was a strict and honest scientist. The world could no longer gainsay the fact of unconscious psychic life. Thus, it resorted to its old game of corruption. It sent him many students, who came to a set table and did not have to bother about the cooking. They had but one interest: to popularize psychoanalysis as quickly as possible. They carried their conservative ties to this world into his organization, and Freud's work could not exist without organization. One after the other, they discarded or watered down the libido theory. Freud was well aware of the difficulties involved in championing the libido theory. But, in the interest of self-preservation and the consolidation of the movement, he could not permit himself to say what, in a more honest world, he would certainly have stood up for all alone. In his scientific work, he had gone far beyond the narrow intellectual framework of the traditional habits and modes of thought of the middle classes. His school pulled him back in again. Freud knew, in 1929, that, for all my youthful scientific enthusiasm, I was right. To admit this, however, would have meant to sacrifice half of the psychoanalytic organization.

Essentially, the problem was that of child upbringing and psychotherapy. Psychic illness—this much was beyond question—is a product of sexual repression. Analytic theory and therapy advocated the elimination of the repression of sexual instincts. The next question was: what happens to the instincts which are liberated from repression? According to psychoanalysis, they are condemned and sublimated. There was no mention of, nor could there have been any mention of, actual gratification, because the unconscious was conceived of solely as an inferno of asocial and perverse impulses.

I became more and more intent on finding an answer to this one question: *what happens to the natural genitality of small children and adolescents after it has been liberated from repression?* Was it too supposed to be "sublimated and condemned"? Psychoanalysts were never able to give me an answer to this question. Yet, it constituted the central problem of character formation.

All education suffers from the fact that social adjustment

requires the repression of natural sexuality, and that this repression makes people sick and asocial. Thus, it became necessary to ask why social adjustment demands repression. This demand is based on a fundamental error in the assessment of sexuality.

Freud's great tragedy was that he sought refuge in biologistic theories, instead of saying nothing or simply allowing everyone to do as he pleased. It was this that caused him to contradict himself.

Happiness, he said, is an illusion, because suffering threatens inevitably from three sides. First, "from one's own body, which is fated to decay and disintegrate . . ." Why, then, is science forever dreaming about the prolongation of life?

Second, "from the outside world, which can rage against us with overwhelming, unrelenting, destructive force. . . ." Why, then, have great humanitarians spent half their lives thinking about ways of improving this world? Why have millions of freedom-fighters given their lives in the fight against this threatening outside world, both in its social and technological context? Had not pestilence been finally checked, after all? Had not physical and social slavery been reduced? Was it never to be possible to master cancer and war, as pestilence had been mastered? Was it never to be possible to vanquish the moralistic hypocrisy that cripples our children and adolescents?

The third argument against the longing for human happiness was serious and remained unexplained. The suffering caused by one's relations to other people, Freud said, is more painful than any other. People are inclined to look upon it as a superficial annoyance, but it is no less fateful or avoidable than suffering of different origin. Here, Freud gives voice to his own bitter experiences with the human species. Here, he touched upon the sex-economic problem of structure, i.e., the irrationalism that determines man's behavior. I myself had a painful taste of it in the psychoanalytic organization, an organization whose professional task was supposed to consist of the medical mastery of irrational behavior. Now Freud was saying that this suffering was fateful and inevitable.

But why? What then was the purpose of viewing human behavior through the perspective of rational scientific methods? What was the purpose of advocating the education of man to rational, reality-oriented behavior? For some unexplainable reason, Freud failed to see the growing contradiction in his attitude. On one hand, he had been correct in tracing back man's acting and thinking to unconscious irrational motives. However, he had carried it too far: the impulse to chop down a tree to build a hut is not of irrational origin. On the other hand, there was a scientific view of the world in which the law he had discovered was not supposed to be valid. It was a science that transcended its own principles! Freud's resignation was nothing other than an evasion of the enormous difficulty presented by the pathology in human behavior, man's maliciousness. Freud was disillusioned. Initially, he believed that he had discovered the radical therapy of neuroses. In reality, it had been only a beginning. It was much more complicated than was indicated by the formula of making the unconscious conscious. He claimed that psychoanalysis could grasp not only medical problems, but universal problems of human existence. But he did not find his way into sociology. In *Beyond the Pleasure Principle,* he had entered into important biological questions hypothetically and had deduced the theory of the death instinct. It turned out to be a misleading hypothesis. Initially, Freud himself took a very skeptical view of it. The psychologization of sociology as well as of biology precluded every prospect of achieving a practical mastery of these enormous problems.

Moreover, from both his medical practice and people's attitudes toward his theory, Freud had come to know human beings as highly unreliable, malicious creatures. For decades he had been living isolated from the world to protect his psychic bearing. If he had entered into every irrational objection made against him, he would have been lost in destructive everyday battles. To isolate himself, he needed a skeptical attitude toward human "values"; he needed, indeed, a certain contempt for modern man. Learning and knowledge came to mean more to him than human happiness, especially in view of the fact that people themselves appeared not to make the best of happiness when it came their way. This attitude was definitely in keeping with the then prevalent attitude of academic superiority. There was also concrete evidence to support such an attitude. But one should not assess universal problems of human existence from the point of view of a scientific pioneer.

Two crucial facts prevented me from following Freud, though I understood his motives. One was the continually growing demand on the part of the culturally neglected, materially exploited, and psychically ruined masses of people to determine their own social existence. Their point of view was that of earthly happiness. Not to see and take this demand into account would have been to close one's eyes to the existing political mood. I had become too familiar with this mass awakening to discredit it or to misappraise its social potential. Freud's motives were unimpeachable. But the motives of the awakening masses were also unimpeachable. Simply to dismiss them meant ultimately to find oneself in the ranks of the non-working drones of society.

The second fact was that I had learned to see people from two perspectives: They were often corrupt, slavish, faithless, full of empty slogans, or simply dried up. But they were not like this by nature. They had become this way through the conditions of life. In principle, therefore, they could become something different: decent, honest, capable of love, sociable, mutually responsible, social without compulsion. We were dealing with characterological contradictions that reflected the contradictions of society. More and more I realized that what is called "wicked" and "antisocial" is a neurotic mechanism. A child plays in a natural way. He is inhibited by his environment. Initially, he defends himself against this inhibition. He is subdued and retains merely the defense against the limitation of pleasure, in the form of pathological, aimless, irrational reactions of spitefulness. In the same way, human behavior merely reflects the contradictions between life-affirmation and life-negation in the social process itself. The next question was: could the contradiction between striving for pleasure and social frustration of pleasure be resolved someday? Psychoanalytic research in the field of sexuality seemed to me to be the first step in the direction of such a change. But this approach to the problem had been all but excluded from the picture. Psychoanalysis became an abstract and then a conservative "theory of cultural adjustment," with many insoluble contradictions.

The conclusion was irrefutable: *man's longing for life and pleasure cannot be checked, whereas the social chaos of sexuality can be eliminated.*

Then Freud began to make absolute judgments, to provide justifications for ascetic ideologies. The "unrestrained gratification" of all needs, he stated, obtruded itself as the most seductive mode of life, but this would mean putting pleasure before caution and would have repercussions after a short time. To this, I could answer even at that time that it was necessary to distinguish *natural* needs for happiness from secondary *asocial* drives produced by compulsive education. Secondary, unnatural, asocial drives entailed and continue to entail moralistic inhibition. However, the gratification of natural needs can be governed by the principle of freedom, by the principle of "living out," if you like. It must merely be known what the word "drive" means in each case.

According to Freud, "The use of narcotics in the effort to achieve happiness and keep misery at bay is appreciated as a blessing to such a high degree that individuals as well as peoples have set aside a fixed place for it in their libido economy." He says nothing of the medical condemnation of this substitute pleasure, which destroys the organism! Not a word is mentioned about the preconditions that produce the need for narcotics, i.e., the frustration of sexual happiness. Not a word is mentioned in all psychoanalytic literature on the correlation between addiction and the lack of genital gratification!

Freud's assessment was hopeless. While he admitted that the striving for pleasure is ineradicable, he claimed that it is not the social chaos but the drive for happiness that should be influenced.

The complicated structure of the psychic apparatus, Freud argued further, made it possible to influence it in a number of ways. While instinctual gratification is happiness, the need for this gratification becomes the cause of severe suffering when the outside world forces us to live in want and frustrates the fulfillment of our needs. Thus, by influencing the instinctual impulses, i.e., not the world which forces people to live in want, one could hope to free oneself from a certain amount of suffering. The intent of this influencing was to master the inner sources of the needs. In an extreme way, this can be brought about by killing the instincts, as is taught by Oriental philosophy and put into practice by Yoga. These are the arguments of Freud, the man who incontestably put before the world the fact of child sexuality and sexual repression!

Here one no longer could or should follow Freud. On the contrary, it was necessary to gather all one's resources to

AN ABORTIVE BIOLOGICAL REVOLUTION

fight against the consequences of such a view spoken by an authority. I knew that one day all the life-fearing spirits of darkness would point to Freud as their authority. This was no way to deal with a human problem of the first magnitude, no way to defend the renunciation imposed upon the Chinese coolie, no way to indirectly condone the infant mortality in the brutal patriarchy of India, a patriarchy which had just suffered its first defeats. The most crucial problem of adolescence and stultifying childhood was the killing of spontaneous life impulses in the interest of a questionable refinement. This was something to which science must never consent. It must not make it so easy for itself, especially in view of the fact that Freud himself did not question the overwhelming, and fundamentally correct, role of human striving for happiness.

It is true, he wrote, that the striving for the positive fulfillment of happiness, the orientation which takes love as its center of gravity and expects all gratification from loving and being loved, is felt keenly enough by everyone. Sexual love, he said, provided the strongest sensations of pleasure and was the prototype of the striving for happiness in general. But there was a weak side to this view, otherwise it would never have occurred to anyone to leave this path in favor of another. A person is never less protected against suffering than when he loves, never more helplessly unhappy than when he loses the loved object or love. To become happy in accordance with the pleasure principle, Freud concluded, was not possible. Again and again, he maintained that human structure and the conditions of human existence were unchangeable. He was speaking of the attitudes he observed in the neurotic reactions of disappointment in women who were emotionally and materially dependent upon a man.

My detachment from Freud's point of view and the working out of the sex-economic solution of these problems fell into two parts: first, it was necessary to comprehend the striving after happiness biologically. In this way, it could be separated from the secondary distortions of human nature. Second, there was the momentous question as to the social feasibility of that which people so deeply long for and at the same time fear so much.

The first part was new ground in the field of biology. No one had yet investigated the pleasure mechanism from a biological point of view. The second part was new ground in the field of sociology, more specifically in the field of sexual policy. When people naturally strive for something that is rightfully theirs and they cannot attain it because the social modes of life prevent it, one question inevitably arises, namely: what measures have to be applied and what paths have to be pursued in order, eventually, to gain what is naturally striven for? This is as much the case in speaking of the attainment of sexual happiness as it is in speaking of the realization of economic interests. We need only that peculiar, slogan-saturated mentality to deny here what is otherwise readily conceded, e.g., when it is a matter of making money or preparing for war. A rational economic policy is needed to guarantee the distribution of goods. Sexual policy is nothing other than this, when the obvious principles which pertain to the fulfillment of economic needs are applied to the fulfillment of sexual needs. It was not difficult to recognize sexual policy as the core of cultural policy, to separate it from the shallow efforts of sexual reform and pornographic mentality, and to represent its simple scientific foundation.

Life and, with it, the striving for pleasure do not take place in a vacuum, but under definite, natural, and social presuppositions.

All cultural efforts, as expressed in literature, poetry, art, dance, and folk customs, are characterized by their concern with sexuality.

No interest influences man more strongly than the sexual interest.

The patriarchal laws pertaining to religion, culture, and marriage were predominantly laws against sexuality.

In the libido, the energy of the sexual instinct, Freudian psychology recognized the central motor of psychic phenomena.

In the strict sense of the word, primeval history and mythology are reproductions of the sexual economy of the human species.

The crucial question could no longer be evaded: *is sexual repression an indispensable component of cultural development?* If scientific research clearly answered this question in the affirmative, then any attempt at a positive cultural policy would be hopeless. However, this would also have to apply to every psychotherapeutic effort.

Such a view could not be correct. It was at variance with all human strivings, scientific findings, and intellectual achievements. Since my clinical work had firmly convinced me that the sexually gratified man is also the more productive man in the cultural sense, I could not possibly answer the above question according to Freud's line of reasoning. The question whether the suppression of child and adolescent sexuality was necessary was replaced by a far more important one: what were the human motives for so consistently and, until now, so successfully evading a clear answer? I sought to discover the unconscious motives of a man like Freud, who put himself and his authority at the apex of a conservative ideology and, with his theory of civilization, overthrew what he had achieved through diligent work as a natural scientist and physician. There could be no doubt that he had not done so out of intellectual cowardice or for conservative political reasons. He had acted within the framework of a science which, like every other science, was dependent upon society. The social barrier made itself felt not only in the therapy of neuroses, but also in the investigation of the origin of sexual repression.

In my sex-counseling centers, it became clear to me that *the suppression of child and adolescent sexuality had the function of making it easier for parents to insist on blind obedience from their children.*

In the earliest beginnings of economic patriarchy, the sexuality of children and adolescents was combatted by means of direct castration or genital mutilation in one form or another. Later, psychic castration through the inculcation of sexual anxiety and guilt feeling became the customary means. Sexual suppression has the function of making man amenable to authority, just as the castration of stallions and bulls has the function of producing willing draft animals. No one had thought about the devastating consequences of *psychic castration,* and no one can predict how human society will cope with them. Freud later confirmed the relation between sexual suppression and the attitude of submissiveness, after I had brought the issue to a head in my publications.[7]

> Fear of a revolt by the suppressed elements drives it to stricter precautionary measures. A high-water mark in such a development has been reached in Western European civilization. A cultural community is perfectly justified, psychologically, in starting by proscribing manifestations of the sexual life of children, for there would be no prospect of curbing the sexual lusts of adults if the ground had not been prepared for it in childhood. But such a community cannot in any way be justified in going to the length of actually *disavowing* such easily demonstrable, and, indeed, striking phenomena.[8]

Thus, the molding of a negative sexual character structure was the reál, unconscious goal of education. Psychoanalytic pedagogy could no longer be discussed, therefore, without taking into account the problem of character structure,

---

[7] Cf. Reich, *Geschlechtsreife, Enthaltsamkeit, Ehemoral,* Münsterverlag, 1930. Part I of *Die Sexualität im Kulturkampf,* Sexpol Verlag, 1936.
[8] Freud, *Civilization and Its Discontents.*

nor could the latter be discussed without deciding the social goal of education. Education always serves the purposes of the existing social system. If this social system is at variance with the interests of the child, then education has to leave the child's interests out of account. It has, in short, to turn against its own interest, i.e., to become unfaithful to itself, and either openly relinquish or hypocritically represent its declared goal, "the welfare of the child." This education did not distinguish between the "compulsive family" which suppresses the child and the "family" which is founded on deep relations of love between parents and children, relations that are always destroyed by compulsive familial relationships. It overlooked the enormous social revolutions which had taken place in man's sexual and family life since the turn of the century. With its "ideas" and "reforms," it hobbled behind and still hobbles behind the concrete changes that have occurred. In short, it became enmeshed in its own irrational motives, of which it neither was nor could be aware.

For all that, the contagion of neuroses is comparable to the contagion of a plague. It poisons everything created by striving, effort, thought, and work. It was possible to combat the plague without external obstruction because neither pecuniary interests nor mystical feelings were violated thereby. It is far more difficult to combat the contagion of neuroses. Everything which thrives upon man's mysticism clings to it and has power. Who could accept the argument that the psychic plague should not be combatted because mental hygiene measures impose too much of a strain on the masses? It is an excuse to say that there are not enough funds to carry out such measures. The sums of money squandered on war in a week's time would be enough to meet the hygienic needs of millions. We also have a way of underestimating the enormous forces which lie fallow in man himself and demand expression and confirmation.

Sex-economy had comprehended the biological goal of human striving, the realization of which was thwarted by the human structure itself, as well as by some institutions of the social system. Freud overruled the goal of happiness in favor of the contemporary human structure and the existing social chaos. Hence, there was nothing left for me other than to stick to the goal and to learn to know the laws according to which this human structure is molded and can be altered. It took me a long time to realize the magnitude of this problem, to realize above all that the *neurotic psychic structure has become somatic innervation,* "second nature," as it were. In spite of all his pessimism, Freud was not content to rest his position on a note of hopelessness. His final statement was:

> The fateful question for the human species seems to me to be whether and to what extent their cultural development will succeed in mastering the disturbance of their communal life by the human instincts of aggression and self-destruction. . . . And now it is to be expected that the other of the two "heavenly powers," eternal Eros, will make an effort to assert himself in the struggle with his equally immortal adversary.[9]

This was far more than a figure of speech, as was believed by psychoanalysts. It was far more than merely a clever observation. *"Eros" presupposes full sexual capacity.* And sexual capacity presupposes social concern and the general affirmation of life. In 1930, following the debates and radical clashes of opinion, it appeared to me that Freud secretly wished me success in my undertaking. He expressed himself vaguely, but the concrete weapons had been found which one day would help to fulfill this hope. *It is only the liberation of man's natural capacity for love that can vanquish sadistic destructiveness.*

---
[9] *Ibid.*

2. THE SOCIAL ORIGIN OF SEXUAL REPRESSION

At that time, of course, the question as to the feasibility of general human happiness here on earth could not be answered in a practical way. As we continue our presentation, the naïve person will now ask whether science had nothing else to worry about except the stupid question as to the "desirability" or "feasibility" of the earthly happiness of masses of people. His opinion is that this is self-understood. Nevertheless, it is not as simple as the vigorous, enthusiastic adolescent and the easygoing, happy-go-lucky person imagine. In the important centers that molded public opinion in Europe in 1930, the claim to earthly happiness on the part of masses of people was not looked upon as self-evident, nor was its lack looked upon as being worthy of question. There was at that time not a single political organization which would have regarded such questions in any other way than as "commonplace," "personal," "unscientific," and "non-political."

Be that as it may, it was precisely *this* question which the social events around 1930 made imperative. It was the fascist deluge which swept across Germany like a tidal wave, astonishing everyone and causing many to ask how such a thing was possible. Economists, sociologists, cultural reformers, diplomats, and statesmen sought for an answer in the old books. But the old books contained no explanation of these phenomena. There was not a single political model which provided an insight into the eruption of the irrational human emotions that fascism represented. Never before had high politics itself been called into question as an irrational formation.

In the present volume, I want to analyze merely those social events that had a forceful bearing upon the controversy which took place in Freud's study. I have to omit the broad socio-economic background.

Viewed socially, Freud's discovery of child sexuality and sexual repression was the first dim awareness of the sexual renunciation which had been going on for thousands of years. This awakening consciousness still appeared in a highly academic garb and had little faith in its own movements. The question of human sexuality had to be shifted from the dark corners of the social framework, where for thousands of years it had been leading a filthy, distorted, and festering life, to the very front of the shiny edifice grandiosely called "culture" and "civilization." Sexual murder, criminal abortions, the sexual agony of adolescents, the killing of all vital impulses in children, perversions en masse, pornography and the vice squad that goes with it, exploitation of the human longing for love by a cheap and prurient consumer industry and commercial advertising, millions of illnesses of a psychic and somatic nature, loneliness and psychic deformity everywhere, and—on top of this—the neurotic politicizing of the would-be saviors of mankind could hardly be looked upon as showpieces of civilization. The moral and social assessment of man's most important biological function was in the hands of sexually frustrated ladies and dignified, vegetatively inert privy councilors.

There was no quarrel with societies of sexually frustrated old ladies and other mummified creatures. But one protested against the fact that it was precisely these atrophied specimens of life who not only wanted but were in a position to dictate the behavior of healthy and vigorous individuals. Moribund and frustrated men and women appealed to the general sexual guilt feeling and pointed to the sexual chaos and the "downfall of civilization and culture." True, the masses of people were not really taken in by this claptrap, but they were silent because they were not really sure whether their own natural feelings of life might not be criminal after all. This is what they had always been told. Hence, Malinowski's investigations in the South Sea islands had an unusually beneficial effect. Their impact was of a serious nature. There was nothing of the sensational lasciviousness with which the sexually bankrupt traders experienced the South Sea girls or raved about Hawaiian hula dancers.

As early as 1926, Malinowski contested in one of his publications the biological nature of the sexual conflict between child and parent (the Oedipus conflict) discovered by Freud. He was right in contending that the relationship between children and parents changes with social processes; that it was, therefore, of a sociological and not biological nature. In short, the family in which the child grows up is itself the result of social development. Among the Trobrianders, for example, it is not the father but the brother of the child's mother who determines how the child should be brought up. This is an important characteristic of matriarchy. The father plays only the role of a friend to his children. The Oedipus complex of the Europeans does not exist among the Trobrianders. Naturally, the Trobriander child also comes into conflict with the taboos and precepts of the family, but these laws of conduct are fundamentally different from those of the Europeans. Apart from the taboo of incest between brother and sister, they contain no sexual prohibitions. The English psychoanalyst Ernest Jones sharply protested against this functional sociological contention, arguing that the Oedipus complex discovered in European man was the "fons et origo" of all culture. Hence, the present-day family was an immutable biological institution. At issue in this controversy was the decisive question: *does sexual repression have a biological origin, or is it sociologically determined and, therefore, changeable?*

Malinowski's principal work, *The Sexual Life of Savages,* appeared in 1929. This book contained a profusion of material which made it quite clear that sexual repression was of a sociological and not of a biological origin. Malinowski himself did not discuss this question in his book, but the material spoke for itself. In my essay "Der Einbruch der Sexualmoral" (second edition, 1934),* I attempted to demonstrate the *sociological origin of sexual negation* on the basis of available ethnological material. I shall summarize what is important for the present discussion.

The Trobriander children are not familiar with sexual repression and sexual secrecy. The sexual life of Trobriander children develops naturally, freely, and without interference *through all stages of life with full sexual gratification*. The children engage in sexual activity in keeping with their age. In spite of this, or, rather, precisely for this reason, the Trobriander society, in the third decade of this century, was ignorant of any sexual perversions, functional mental illnesses, psychoneuroses, sexual murder; they had no word for theft. In their society, homosexuality and masturbation were looked upon as incomplete and unnatural means of sexual gratification, as a proof that the capacity to experience normal gratification is hampered. The strict, compulsion-neurotic toilet training which saps the civilization of the white races is unknown to the Trobriander child. Hence, the Trobriander is *spontaneously* clean, orderly, naturally social, intelligent, and industrious. Non-compulsive, voluntary monogamous marriage, which can be dissolved at any time without difficulties, prevails as the social form of sexual life. There is no promiscuity.

A few miles from the Trobriand Islands, on the Amphlett Islands, there lived a tribe having a patriarchal, authoritarian family arrangement. All the characteristics of the European neurotics (distrust, anxiety, neuroses, suicides, perversions, etc.) were already evident in the natives of this island.

Our science, which is so steeped in sexual negation, has

---

* *The Invasion of Compulsory Sex-Morality,* New York: Farrar, Straus and Giroux, 1971.

thus far succeeded in nullifying the importance of decisive facts by placing side by side and equating what is important and what is unimportant, what is commonplace and what is extraordinary. The difference just described between the matriarchal, free organization of the Trobrianders and the patriarchal, authoritarian organization of the tribe living on the Amphlett Islands carries more weight in the assessment of mental hygiene than the most complicated and seemingly most exact curves and graphs of our academic world. *To what extent does a population enjoy natural sexuality?— that is the pivotal question of mental hygiene.*

Freud had contended that the sexual latency period of our children, roughly speaking between the ages of six and twelve, was of a biological nature. I had been attacked by psychoanalysts because I had ascertained in adolescents stemming from various strata of the population that there is no latency period when sexuality develops in a natural way. The latency period is an unnatural product of civilization. Now this was confirmed by Malinowski. The sexual activity of the Trobriander children is continuous; it merely varies from age group to age group. There is no latency period. Sexual intercourse begins when puberty demands it. The sexual life of the adolescents is monogamous; changing a partner takes place quietly, in an orderly fashion, without violence or jealousy. And, completely contrary to our civilization, the Trobriander society provides for the privacy and hygiene of adolescent sexuality, particularly with reference to living accommodations, and to other matters as well, as far as their knowledge of natural processes permits.

There is only one group of children excluded from this natural course. They are the children who are set aside for a prearranged, economically advantageous marriage, for a cross-cousin marriage. Such a marriage brings the chief economic advantages and constitutes the nucleus from which the patriarchal order develops. The cross-cousin marriage was found wherever ethnological research was able to prove the contemporary or historical existence of matriarchy (cf. Morgan, Bachofen, Engels, and others). Just like our own children, these children are compelled to live ascetic lives; they demonstrate the same neuroses and character traits known to us from character-neurotics. Their asceticism has the function of making them subservient. *Sexual suppression becomes an essential tool of economic enslavement.*

Thus, sexual suppression in the small child and in the adolescent is not the precondition for cultural adjustment, sociality, industriousness, and cleanliness, as psychoanalysis, in line with the traditional erroneous conception of education, contends. It is the exact opposite. With their complete freedom of natural sexuality, the Trobrianders have achieved a high stage of agriculture. More significantly, due to the absence of secondary drives, they have preserved a social condition that must appear like a dream to every European state of 1930 or 1940. Healthy children are sexually active in a natural and spontaneous way. Sick children are sexually active in an unnatural, i.e., perverse, way. Therefore, in our sexual education, we are faced not with the alternative of sexual activity or asceticism, but with the alternative of natural and healthy, or perverse and neurotic sexuality.

Sexual repression is of a socio-economic and not of a biological origin. Its function is to lay the foundation for an authoritarian, patriarchal culture and economic slavery, which we find especially pronounced in Japan, China, India, and other countries. In its sexual life, the primeval period of mankind adhered to natural laws, which established the foundation for a natural sociality. Using the energy of suppressed sexuality, the intermediary period of authoritarian patriarchal society of some four to six thousand years has produced the secondary, perverse, distorted sexuality of modern man.

3. FASCISTIC IRRATIONALISM

There is ample evidence to support the contention that the cultural upheavals of the twentieth century are determined by mankind's struggle to reclaim the natural laws of sexuality. This struggle for naturalness and the harmony of nature and culture is reflected in the various forms of mystical longing, cosmic fantasies, "oceanic" feelings, religious ecstasies, and, above all, in the advance toward sexual freedom. It is unconscious, imbued with neurotic contradictions and anxiety, and is often manifested in the forms that characterize the secondary perverse drives. A humanity which has been forced for thousands of years to deny its basic biological law and, as a consequence of this denial, has acquired a second nature which is anti-nature can only work itself up into an irrational frenzy when it wants to restore the basic biological function and, at the same time, is afraid of doing so.

The patriarchal, authoritarian era of human history has attempted to hold the asocial impulses in check by means of compulsive moralistic prohibitions. It is in this way that civilized man, if he can indeed be called civilized, developed a psychic structure consisting of three layers. On the surface, he wears an artificial mask of self-control, compulsive insincere politeness, and pseudo-sociality. This mask conceals the second layer, the Freudian "unconscious," in which sadism, avarice, lasciviousness, envy, perversions of all kind, etc., are held in check without, however, being deprived of the slightest amount of energy. This second layer is the artificial product of a sex-negating culture and is usually experienced consciously as a gaping inner emptiness and desolation. Beneath it, in the depth, natural sociality and sexuality, spontaneous joy in work, the capacity for love, exist and operate. This third and deepest layer, which represents the biological core of the human structure, is unconscious, and it is feared. It is at variance with every aspect of authoritarian education and control. At the same time, it is the only real hope man has of one day mastering social misery.

All discussions on the question of whether man is good or evil, a social or antisocial being, are philosophic gameplaying. Whether man is a social being or a mass of protoplasm reacting in a peculiar and irrational way depends on whether his basic biological needs are in harmony or at variance with the institutions he has created for himself. In view of this, it is impossible to free the workingman from the responsibility he bears for the regulation or lack of regulation of biological energy, i.e., for the social and individual economy of his biological energy. It has become one of his most essential characteristics that he is only too happy to shift this responsibility from himself to some Führer or politician, since he no longer comprehends and indeed fears himself and his institutions. He is helpless, incapable of freedom, and he craves authority, because he cannot react spontaneously; he is armored and wants to be told what to do, for he is full of contradictions and cannot rely upon himself.

The cultivated European bourgéoisie of the nineteenth and early twentieth centuries took over the compulsive moralistic forms of behavior from feudalism and made them the ideal of human conduct. Since the dawn of enlightenment, people have begun to search for truth and to cry out for freedom. As long as the compulsive moralistic institutions governed man externally as coercive law and public opinion, and internally as compulsive conscience, a sham peace prevailed, with occasional outbreaks from the subterranean world of secondary drives. During this period, the secondary drives remained curiosities, of psychiatric interest only. They became manifest as symptom neuroses, neurotic criminal actions, or perversions. When, however, social upheavals began to arouse in the people of Europe a longing for freedom, independence, equality, and self-determination, there

AN ABORTIVE BIOLOGICAL REVOLUTION

was also an inner urge to liberate the living organism itself. Social enlightenment and legislation, pioneer work in the field of social science, and freedom-oriented organizations strove to put "freedom" into this world. After World War I, which had destroyed many compulsive authoritarian institutions, the European democracies wanted "to lead people to freedom." But this freedom-striving European world committed a major assessment error. It failed to see what thousands of years of the suppression of the vital energies in man had bred beneath the surface. It failed to see the far-reaching, universal defect of character neurosis. The severe catastrophe of the psychic plague, i.e., the catastrophe of the irrational human character structure, swept over large parts of the world in the form of the victory of dictatorships. What the superficial veneer of good breeding and artificial self-control had held in check for such a long time now broke through into action, action implemented by the freedom-striving masses of people themselves—in the concentration camps; in the persecution of the Jews; in the annihilation of all human decency; in the sadistic, playful, mowing-down of entire cities by those who are capable of feeling life only when they goose-step, as in Guernica in 1936; in the stupendous betrayal of the masses by authoritarian governments claiming to represent the interests of the people; in the engulfing of tens of thousands of young people who, naïvely and helplessly, thought that they were serving an idea; in the destruction of billions of dollars worth of human labor, a fraction of which would have been sufficient to eliminate poverty the world over. In short, in a St. Vitus dance which will return again and again, as long as those who work and have knowledge fail to destroy the mass neurosis in themselves and outside of themselves, the neurosis which calls itself "high politics" and thrives upon the characterological helplessness of the citizens of the earth.

In 1928–30, at the time of the controversy with Freud, I

knew very little about fascism, about as little as the average Norwegian in 1939 or the average American in 1940. It was not until 1930–3 that I became familiar with it in Germany. I was helplessly perplexed when I rediscovered in it, bit by bit, the subject of the controversy with Freud. Gradually, I understood that this had to be so. At issue in the controversy was the assessment of the human structure, of the respective roles played by human striving for happiness and the irrationalism in social life. In fascism, psychic mass illness was thrust into the open.

The opponents of fascism—liberal democrats, socialists, Communists, Marxist and non-Marxist economists, etc.—sought the solution to the problem in the personality of Hitler or in the formal political errors of the various democratic parties of Germany. One, as well as the other, meant to trace back the deluge of the plague to individual shortsightedness or the brutality of a single man. In reality, Hitler was merely the expression of the tragic contradiction between longing for freedom and actual fear of freedom.

German fascism made it quite clear that it operated not with people's thinking and knowledge, but with their childish emotional reactions. Neither its political program nor any one of its many confused economic promises carried fascism to power and secured it in the period that followed. In the main, it was the appeal to a dark, mystical feeling, to a vague, nebulous, but extraordinary powerful longing. Those who did not grasp this did not grasp fascism, which is an international phenomenon.

The irrationalism in actions of the masses of the German people can be illustrated by the following contradictions: the masses of the German people wanted "freedom." Hitler promised them authoritarian, strictly dictatorial leadership, with the explicit exclusion of any freedom of speech. Seventeen million out of thirty-one million voters jubilantly carried Hitler to power in March 1933. Those who watched the events with open eyes knew that the masses of people felt helpless and incapable of bearing the responsibility for the solution of the chaotic social problems within the old political framework and system of thinking. The Führer should and would do it for them.

Hitler promised to eliminate democratic discussion of opinions. Masses of people flocked to him. They were tired of these discussions, because these discussions had always bypassed their personal everyday needs, that is, what was subjectively important. They did not want discussions about the "budget" and "high politics." What they wanted was concrete, true knowledge about life. Not getting it, they threw themselves into the hands of authoritarian leadership and the illusionary protection they were now promised.

Hitler promised to do away with individual freedom and to establish "national freedom." Masses of people enthusiastically exchanged the possibility of individual freedom for illusionary freedom, that is, freedom through identification with an idea. This illusionary freedom relieved them of all individual responsibility. They craved a "freedom" which the Führer was going to conquer and secure for them: the freedom to yell; the freedom to escape from truth into the lies of political principle; the freedom to be sadistic; the freedom to boast, in spite of one's actual nothingness, that one is a member of a superior race; the freedom to attract girls with uniforms instead of a strong sense of humanity; the freedom to sacrifice oneself for imperialistic aims instead of for the concrete struggle for a better life, etc.

The fact that masses of people had always been taught to acknowledge traditional political authority instead of authority based on factual knowledge constituted the basis on which the fascistic demand for obedience could operate. Hence, fascism was not a new philosophy of life, as its friends and many of its enemies wanted to make people believe; still less had it anything to do with a rational revolution against intolerable social conditions. *Fascism is merely the extreme reactionary consequence of all prior undemocratic forms of leadership within the framework of the social machinery.* Even the racial theory was nothing new; it was merely the logical and brutal continuation of the old theories of heredity and degeneration. Hence, it was precisely the hereditary-oriented psychiatrists and eugenicists of the old school who were so accessible to the dictatorship.

What was new in the fascist mass movement was the fact that extreme political reaction succeeded in making use of the deep longings for freedom of the masses of people. *Intense longing for freedom on the part of the masses, plus fear of the responsibility which freedom entails, produces fascist mentality,* whether this longing and fear are found in a fascist or in a democrat. New in fascism was that the masses of the people affirmed and concretely implemented their own suppression. The need for authority proved to be stronger than the will to independence.

Hitler promised male supremacy. Women were to be relegated to the kitchen and home, denied the possibility of material independence, and excluded from the process of molding social life. Women, whose personal freedom had been suppressed for centuries, and who had developed an especially strong fear of leading an independent existence, were foremost in hailing him.

Hitler promised the destruction of the socialistic and bourgeois democratic organizations. Socialistic and bourgeois democratic masses of people flocked to him because, though their organizations spoke a great deal about freedom, they never even mentioned the difficult problem of the human craving for authority and the helplessness of the masses in practical politics. The masses of the people had been disappointed by the irresolute attitude of the old democratic institutions. *Disappointment on the part of masses of people in liberal organizations, plus economic crisis, plus an irresistible will to freedom, produces fascist mentality,* i.e., the willingness to surrender oneself to an authoritarian father figure.

Hitler promised an all-out fight against birth control and the sexual reform movement. In 1932, Germany comprised some 500,000 people who were members of organizations fighting for rational sexual reform. But these organizations always shied away from the central element of the problem —the longing for sexual happiness. Years of work among the masses of the people taught me that it is precisely this problem they want to have discussed. They were disappointed when they were given learned talks on demography, instead of being told how they should raise their children to be vitally alive, how adolescents should cope with their sexual and economic needs, and how married people should deal with their typical conflicts. The masses of the people seemed to feel that the suggestions on "techniques of love," such as those given by Van de Velde, though profitable for the publisher, had nothing to do with what they were looking for, nor were they appealing. And so it happened that the disappointed masses of the people flocked to Hitler, who, even if mystically, appealed to their vital forces. *Preaching about freedom leads to fascism unless a consistent and determined effort is made to inculcate in the masses of people a willingness to assume responsibility for everyday life, and unless there is an equally consistent and determined fight to establish the social preconditions for this responsibility.*

For decades, German science had been fighting for the separation of the concept of sexuality from the concept of procreation. This struggle failed to bear fruit for the working masses, because it was of a purely academic nature and hence without social effect. Now Hitler came along and promised to make the idea of procreation, and not happiness in love, the basic principle of his cultural program. Brought up to be ashamed to call a spade a spade, compelled by all facets of the social system to say "eugenic higher breeding" when one meant "happiness in love," the masses flocked to Hitler, for he added a strong, even if irrational, emotion to the old concept. Reactionary concepts plus revolutionary excitement produce fascist feelings.

The Church had preached "happiness in the beyond" and, drawing upon the concept of sin, had planted deep in the human structure a helpless dependency on a supernatural, omnipotent figure. But the economic world crisis between 1929 and 1933 confronted the masses of the people with bitter earthly distress. It was neither socially nor individually possible for them to master this distress by themselves. Hitler appeared and declared himself to be an earthly, omnipotent, and omniscient Führer, ordained by God, who could remove this mundane misery. The stage had been set to drive new masses of people to him, people who were hemmed in between their own individual helplessness and the minimal real gratification which the idea of happiness in the beyond offered them. Hence, an earthly god who let them shout "Heil" with all their might had greater emotional significance than a God whom they could never see and who no longer helped them, even emotionally. *Sadistic brutality plus mysticism produces fascist mentality.*

For years, Germany had been fighting in its schools and universities for the principle of a liberal school system, for voluntary achievement, and for the self-determination of the students. In the broad sphere of education, the responsible democratic authorities clung to the authoritarian principle, which instilled in the student a fear of authority and, at the same time, incited him to engage in irrational forms of rebellion. The liberal educational organizations did not enjoy any social protection. On the contrary, they were wholly dependent upon private financial aid, in addition to being exposed to the gravest dangers. It was not surprising, therefore, that

AN ABORTIVE BIOLOGICAL REVOLUTION

these inchoate stirrings toward the non-compulsive restructuralization of the masses of the people remained a drop in the bucket. The youth flocked to Hitler by the thousands. He did not impose any responsibility upon them; he merely built upon their structures, which had been previously molded in the authoritarian families. Hitler was victorious in the youth movement because the democratic society had not done everything possible to educate the youth to lead a free and responsible life.

In place of voluntary achievement, Hitler promised the principle of compulsive discipline and mandatory work. Several million German workers and employees voted for Hitler. The democratic institutions had not only failed to cope with unemployment, they had shown themselves to be clearly afraid when it came right down to teaching the working masses of people to assume responsibility for their own work accomplishment. Brought up not to understand anything about the work process (indeed prevented from understanding it), accustomed to being excluded from having any part in the control of production and to merely receiving wages, these millions of workers and employees could easily accept the old principle in an intensified form. Now they could identify themselves with "the state" and "the nation," which were "great and strong." Hitler openly declared in his writings and speeches that since the masses of the people were childish and feminine, they merely repeated what was funneled into them. Masses of people hailed him, for here was a man who wanted to protect them.

Hitler demanded that all science be subordinated under the concept of "race." Large segments of German science deferred to this demand, for the theory of race was rooted in the metaphysical theory of heredity. It is this theory, with its concepts of "inherited substances" and "predispositions," that has repeatedly enabled science to shirk the responsibility for understanding life functions in their state of becoming and for actually comprehending the social origin of human behavior. It used to be customary to believe that when cancer, neurosis, or psychosis were declared to be hereditary, something highly significant had been said. *The fascist theory of race is merely an extension of the convenient theories of heredity.*

There was hardly another dogma of German fascism as capable of inspiring masses of people as that of the "surging of the German blood" and of its "purity." The purity of German blood meant freedom from "syphilis," from "Jewish contamination." In each and every one of us, there is a deep fear of venereal disease; it is a carry-over of childish genital anxiety. Hence, it is understandable that masses of people flocked to Hitler, for he promised them "purity of blood." Every human being senses in himself what are called "cosmic or oceanic feelings." Dry academic science felt it was too elevated to concern itself with such mysticism. This cosmic or oceanic longing which people feel is nothing other than the expression of their orgastic longing for life. Hitler appealed to this longing, and it is for this reason that the masses of people followed him and not the dry rationalists, who tried to suffocate these vague feelings of life with economic statistics.

From olden times, the "preservation of the family" has been an abstract slogan in Europe, behind which the most reactionary thoughts and actions were concealed. A person who criticized the compulsive authoritarian family and distinguished it from the natural relationship of love between children and parents was "an enemy of the fatherland," a "destroyer of the sacred institution of the family," an anarchist. As Germany became more and more industrialized, familial ties came into sharp conflict with this collective industrialization. There was no official organization that would have dared to single out what was sick in the family and to tackle the problem of parental suppression of children, family hatreds, etc. The typical authoritarian German family, particularly in the country and in small towns, hatched fascist mentality by the millions. These families molded the child according to the pattern of compulsive duty, renunciation, absolute obedience to authority, which Hitler knew how to exploit so brilliantly. By espousing the "preservation of the family," and at the same time drawing the youth away from the family into its youth groups, fascism made allowances for familial ties as well as rebellion against the family. By stressing the emotional identity of "family," "nation," and "state," fascism made possible a smooth transition from the structure of the family to the structure of the fascist state. True, not a single problem of the family nor the actual needs of the nation were solved by this, but it enabled masses of people to transfer their familial ties from the compulsive family to the larger "family," the "nation." The structural groundwork for this transfer had been well prepared over thousands of years. "Mother Germany" and "Father-God Hitler" became the symbols of deeply rooted infantile emotions. Identified with the "strong and unique German nation," every citizen—no matter how nondescript or miserable he felt himself to be—could mean something, even if in an illusionary way. Finally, the interest in "race" was capable of absorbing and concealing the unleashed sources of sexuality. Adolescents could engage in sexual intercourse now if they alleged that they were propagating children in the interest of racial breeding.

It was not only that man's natural vital forces remained buried; now they were forced to express themselves in far more disguised forms than ever before. As a result of this "revolution of the irrational," there were more suicides and socio-hygienic misery in Germany than ever before. The death of tens of thousands in the war in honor of the German race constitutes the apotheosis of this witches' dance.

The persecution of the Jews was part and parcel of the longings for "purity of blood," i.e., purity from sins. The Jews tried to explain or to prove that they too had strict moral codes, that they too were nationalistic, that they too were "German." Anthropologists who were against Hitler used skull measurements in an attempt to prove that the Jews were not an inferior race. Christians and historians attempted to explain that Jesus was of Jewish descent. In the persecution of the Jews, however, rational questions played no part; i.e., it was not a question whether the Jews too were decent, whether they were racially inferior, or whether they had *acceptable* cranial indexes. These were not at all a part of the issue. It was something else entirely. Precisely on this point, the consistency and correctness of sex-economic thinking proved valid.

When the fascist says "Jew," he means a definite irrational sensation. Irrationally, the "Jew" represents the "money-maker," the "usurer," the "capitalist." This is borne out by the depth-psychological treatment of Jews and non-Jews alike. At a deeper level, the concept "Jew" means "dirty," "sensual," "bestially sexual," but also "Shylock," "castrator," "murderer." Since the fear of natural sexuality is as deeply rooted as the horror of perverse sexuality, it is easily understood that the skillfully executed persecution of the Jews stirred the deepest sexual defense functions of people brought up in a sexually aberrant way. Drawing upon the concept "Jew," it was possible to fully incorporate the anticapitalistic and antisexual attitude of the masses of people into the machinery of the fascist deluge. *Unconscious longing for sexual joy in life and sexual purity coupled with fear of natural sexuality and horror of perverse sexuality produces fascist, sadistic anti-Semitism.* "Frenchman" has the same meaning for the German as "Jew" and "black man" have for the unconsciously fascistic Englishman. "Jew,"

"Frenchman," and "black man" are terms for "sexually sensual."

These were the unconscious factors which enabled the modern sex-propagandist of the twentieth century, the sexual psychopath and criminal pervert Julius Streicher, to put *Der Stürmer* into the hands of millions of German adolescents and adults. In the pages of *Der Stürmer* more than anywhere else, it became clear that sexual hygiene had ceased to be a problem of medical societies; it had, rather, become a question of decisive social significance. The following samples of Streicher's fantasy will suffice to elucidate. We quote from issues of *Stürmer* published in 1934:

Helmut Daube, 20, had just completed his first year at college. Toward two o'clock in the morning, he went home. At five in the morning, his parents found him lying dead on the street in front of their apartment building. His throat had been cut through to the spine, *his penis had been removed*. There was no blood. The hands of the unfortunate boy were cut. *He had been stabbed a number of times in the abdomen.*

One day the old Jew fell upon the unsuspecting non-Jewish girl in the attic, raped and abused her. As time went on, he would sneak into her room, which could not be locked.

A young couple went for a walk outside of Paderborn and found a *piece of flesh* on the path. Upon closer examination, they discovered to their horror that it was the *skillfully removed genital part of a female body.*

The Jew had *cut up* [the body] *into one pound pieces*. Together with his father, he had scattered the pieces throughout the entire area. They were found in a small wood, in fields, in brooks, in a pond, in a creek, in a drainpipe and in the cesspool. *The cut-off breasts were found in the hayloft.*

While Moses strangled the child with a handkerchief, *Samuel cut off a piece of his cheek with a knife*. The others collected the blood in a basin, at the same time pricking the naked victim with needles. . . .

The woman's resistance was not capable of cooling off his lust. On the contrary. He tried to close the window to prevent the neighbors from looking in. But then he again touched the woman in a vile, typically Jewish way. . . . He urgently persuaded the woman not to be so prudish. He locked all the windows and doors. His words and actions became more and more shameless. More and more he pushed his victim into the corner. All protestations were to no avail. He even laughed at her threats to cry out for help. He pushed the woman closer and closer to the couch. Verbally, he hurled the meanest and most obscene words at her. But then *he pounced upon the woman's body like a tiger and completed his diabolic work.*

Until this point, many readers of this newspaper undoubtedly believed that I was exaggerating when I spoke of the psychic plague. I can only assure them that I am not introducing this concept frivolously, nor merely as a subtle figure of speech. I am quite serious about it. During the past seven years, the *Stürmer* has not merely effectively confirmed the genital castration anxiety a million times over in the German and other masses of people who read it. Over and above this, it has stirred and nourished the perverse fantasies that slumber in every one of us. After the downfall of the chief perpetuators of the psychic plague in Europe, it will remain to be seen how this problem will be dealt with. It is not a German but an international problem, for the longing for love and the fear of genitality are international facts. In Scandinavia, I was sought out by fascist adolescents who had managed to preserve a trace of natural feeling for life, and asked what attitude they should take toward Streicher, the racial theory, and the other "niceties." Something was not quite right, they said. I summarized the necessary measures in a short résumé, which I want to append here:

What Is to Be Done?

General: This reactionary filth has to be opposed with a well-organized and objectively correct elucidation of the difference between *sick* and *healthy* sexuality. Every average person will understand this difference because he feels it instinctively. Every average person is ashamed of his perverse, pathological ideas of sex and desires clarity, help, and natural sexual gratification.

We have to clarify and help!

1. Collect all material which makes the pornographic character of Streicherism readily clear to every reasonable person. Circulate this material in leaflets! The healthy sexual interest of the masses has to be awakened, made conscious, and championed.

2. Collect and circulate all material which will show the population that Streicher and his accomplices are psychopaths and are committing grave crimes against the health of the nation! There are Streichers everywhere in this world.

3. Expose the secret of Streicher's effect upon the masses: he provokes pathological fantasies. The people will gladly purchase and read good educational material.

4. *The pathological sexuality which forms the soil of Hitler's racial theory and Streicher's crimes can be opposed most effectively by showing the people the natural and healthy processes and modes of behavior in sexual life.* The people will immediately grasp this difference and demonstrate a burning interest for it, once they have understood what they really want and are afraid to articulate; among other things:

a. Healthy and gratifying sexuality unconditionally presupposes the possibility of being alone and undisturbed with the loved partner. Thus, it is necessary to provide apartments for everyone who needs them, also for the youth.

b. Sexual gratification is not identical with procreation. The healthy person has sexual intercourse about three to four thousand times during his life, but an average of only two or three children. Contraceptives are absolutely necessary for sexual health.

c. Owing to their sexually suppressed upbringing, the vast majority of men and women are sexually disturbed, i.e., they remain ungratified by sexual intercourse. Thus, it is necessary to set up a sufficient number of clinics to treat sexual disturbances. *A rational, sexually affirmative sex education is imperative.*

d. Youth is made sick by its masturbation conflicts. Only self-gratification which is *free of guilt feelings* is not detrimental to one's health. *Youth has a right to a happy sexual life under the best conditions.* Prolonged sexual abstinence is definitely harmful. Pathological fantasies disappear only with gratifying sexuality.

Fight for this right!

I know that leaflets and clarifications alone are not enough. What is needed is general, socially protected work on the human structure which produces the psychic plague and makes it possible for psychopaths to function as dictators and modern sexual propagandists who poison the life of everyone. In short, what is needed is the liberation and social protection of natural sexuality in the masses of the people.

In 1930, human sexuality was a social Cinderella, a subject discussed by questionable reform groups. Now, in 1940, it has become a pivotal social problem. If it is correct that fascism has been successful in irrationally exploiting the sexual longing for life on the part of masses of people and, in having done so, has created chaos, then it must also be correct that the perversions which it allowed to break loose can be mastered through the universal rational solution of the sexual problem.

In their profusion of mental hygiene problems, the events in Europe between 1930 and 1940 confirmed the position I had taken in my discussions with Freud. What was painful in this confirmation was the powerlessness I felt and the conviction I had that natural science was still a long way off from really comprehending what, in this book, I call the "biological core" of the character structure.

On the whole, both as individuals and as physicians and teachers, our position with respect to the biological deviations of life is just as helpless as was the position of the individual in the Middle Ages with respect to infectious diseases. At the same time, we feel certain that the experience of the fascist plague will mobilize the forces in the world which are needed to come to terms with this problem of civilization.

The fascists claim they are going to carry out the "biological revolution." The truth is that fascism completely exposes the fact that the life function in man has become neurotic. From the point of view of the masses who follow it, an inflexible will to life is undoubtedly at work in fascism.

AN ABORTIVE BIOLOGICAL REVOLUTION

But the forms in which this will to life has manifested itself reveal all too clearly the consequences of an ancient psychic enslavement. *In fascism, only the perverse impulses have broken through. The post-fascist world will carry out the biological revolution which fascism did not produce but made necessary.*

The following chapters of this book deal with the functions of the "biological core." Its scientific comprehension and social mastery will be an achievement of rational work, militant science, and the natural function of love, an achievement of genuine democratic and collective efforts. The goal of these collective efforts is the earthly, material, and sexual happiness of masses of people.

CHAPTER VII

THE BREAKTHROUGH INTO THE BIOLOGICAL REALM

The theory of the orgasm confronted me with this question: what is to be done with the sexual energy liberated from repression in the process of cure? The world said no to everything that sexual hygiene demanded. The natural instincts are biological facts. They cannot be done away with and they cannot be fundamentally changed. Like all living beings, man needs, first and foremost, the appeasement of hunger and the gratification of sexual needs. Today's society makes the first difficult and frustrates the latter. There is a glaring contradiction between natural demands and certain social institutions. Man is immersed in this contradiction, leans more toward one side or the other, makes compromises that always backfire, escapes into sickness and death, or rebels senselessly and fruitlessly against the existing system. The human structure is molded in these struggles.

Biological as well as sociological demands are operative in the human structure. Everything that has social standing, title, and prestige champions the sociological demands against the natural demands. I was amazed that the overwhelming role of natural demands could have been so thoroughly overlooked. Even Freud, who of course had discovered very essential parts of these demands, became inconsistent. After 1930, the instincts were merely "mythical qualities" for him. They were "indeterminable," though "rooted in chemical processes." The contradictions were enormous. In clinical therapeutic work, the instinctual demands determined everything and society just about nothing. On the other hand there was no getting away from the fact that "society and culture," representing the so-called reality principle, also made demands. True, the instincts unconditionally and overwhelmingly determined existence—at the same time, however, they had to adapt themselves to the sex-negating reality. True, the instincts derived from physiological sources. At the same time, however, the id had an Eros and a death instinct which are engaged in an eternal struggle. The duality in Freud's concept of instinct was absolute. There was no functional connection between sexuality and its biological counterpart, the death instinct. The two were merely antithetical. Freud psychologized biology. He said that there were "tendencies" in the realm of the living which "intended" this and that. This was a metaphysical point of view. Its criticism was justified by the later experimental proof of the simple functional nature of instinctual processes. The attempt to explain neurotic anxiety in terms of the concepts of Eros and the death instinct was not successful. Freud eventually discarded the libido-anxiety theory.

The "partial drives" also created difficulties for Freud's theory of the instincts. Each one of them, even those which led to perversions, were said to be biologically determined. Thus, whether he intended to or not, Freud ultimately gave credence to many views of hereditary science. And in Freud himself, the theory of constitution gradually began to replace the dynamic conception of psychic illness. If a child smashed a glass, this act was said to be the expression of the destructive instinct. If he often fell down, this was said to be the effect of the mute death instinct. If his mother left him and the child played going away and coming back, this was said to be the effect of a "repetition compulsion beyond the pleasure principle."

The biological "repetition compulsion" beyond the pleasure principle was supposed to explain masochistic actions. There was supposed to be a will to suffer. This fit in with the theory of the death instinct. In short, Freud carried over laws he had discovered in the psychic function to its biological foundation. Since, according to this conception, society is structured like an individual, psychology became overburdened with methodology that could not withstand any criticism and, moreover, gave free rein to speculations about "society and Thanatos." In the process, psychoanalysis became more and more assertive in its claim that it could explain all existence. It simultaneously demonstrated an ever-growing aversion to the correct sociological and physiological, as well as psychological comprehension of one object: man. Nonetheless, there could be no doubt that man is distinguished from the other animals by a particular interlacing of biophysiological and sociological processes with psychological processes. The correctness of this structural principle of my theory was borne out by the solution of the problem of masochism. From then on, piece by piece of the psychic structure was elucidated as a dynamic unification of biophysiological and sociological factors.

1. THE SOLUTION OF THE PROBLEM OF MASOCHISM

For psychoanalysis, the pleasure in suffering pain was the result of a biological need. "Masochism" was said to be an instinct like any other instinct, merely directed toward a peculiar goal. Nothing could be done with this in therapy. For, if the analyst told the patient that he wanted to suffer "for biological reasons," there was nothing more to be done.

BREAKTHROUGH INTO THE BIOLOGICAL

The orgasmotherapeutic task confronted me with the question of why the masochist converted the otherwise clearly understandable desire for pleasure into a desire for unpleasure. A drastic incident freed me from the false line of questioning which had led psychology and sexology astray until then. In 1928, I treated a completely crushed individual who had a masochistic perversion. His incessant complaining and his demands to be beaten blocked every attempt to get through to him. After months of the usual psychoanalytic work, my patience gave out. When he once again demanded that I should beat him, I asked what he would say if I granted his wish. He beamed blissfully. I took a ruler and gave him two hard whacks on his buttocks. He let out a terrible yell. There was no trace of pleasure, and that was the last I heard of such demands. But he continued to complain and make reproaches. My colleagues would have been scandalized if they had heard of this incident. I did not regret it. All at once I understood that pain and unpleasure are not at all, as is contended, the instinctual goal of the masochist. When he is beaten, the masochist, like any normal person, experiences pain. There are entire industries that thrive upon the false appraisal of masochism they help to create. The question remained: *if the masochist does not strive for unpleasure, does not experience it pleasurably, why does he feel compelled to be tormented?* After a great deal of effort, I discovered the fantasy which lay at the basis of this perverse conduct. *The masochist fantasizes he is being tormented because he wants to burst. Only in this way does he hope to attain relaxation.*

The masochistic complaints proved to be the expression of a torturous and unresolvable inner tension. They are open or concealed pleas of desperation to be released from this instinctual tension. Since, owing to his pleasure anxiety, the ability to experience gratification through his own initiative and activity is blocked, the masochist anticipates the orgastic resolution, which he deeply fears, as a release from the outside brought about by another person. The desire to burst is counteracted by a deep fear of bursting. The masochistic character's self-disparagement now appeared in a hitherto unknown light. Self-aggrandizement is, so to speak, a biopsychic erection, a fantastic expansion of the psychic apparatus. A few years later I learned that underlying it is the perception of bioelectric charges. The opposite of this is self-disparagement, brought about by the fear of expanding to the point of bursting. Vain ambition and an inhibited seeking for greatness, rooted in anxiety, are the driving forces of masochistic self-disparagement. The masochist's provocation of punishment proved to be the expression of a deep desire to be brought to gratification against his own will. Characterologically masochistic women could engage in the sexual act only with the fantasy that they were being seduced or raped. The man is supposed to force them to do what they simultaneously desire and fear. To engage in the sexual act of their own volition is forbidden and laden with severe guilt feelings. The familiar vindictiveness on the part of the masochist, whose self-confidence is severely damaged, is realized by making the other person out to be bad, or by provoking him into cruel behavior.

The idea that the skin, especially the skin of the buttocks, becomes "warm," or "is burning," is frequently encountered among masochists. The desire to be rubbed with a hard brush or to be beaten until one's skin "bursts" is nothing other than the wish to bring about the release of a tension through bursting. Thus, the pain is by no means the goal of the impulse; it is merely an unpleasant experience in achieving release from the unmistakably real tension. Masochism is the prototype of a secondary drive, and forcefully demonstrates the result of the repression of the natural pleasure function.

Masochists exhibit a special form of orgasm anxiety. Other types of patients do not allow a sexual excitation in the genital to take place, as in compulsion neurotics, or they take refuge in anxiety, e.g., hysterical patients. The masochist persists in pregenital stimulation. He does not elaborate it into neurotic symptoms. This causes the tension to mount and, since the ability to experience relaxation diminishes, there is a corresponding increase in orgasm anxiety. Thus the masochist becomes entangled in a vicious cycle of the worst kind. The more he desires to extricate himself from the tension, the deeper he sinks into it. At the moment the orgasm is supposed to take place, the masochistic fantasies become much more intense. Often, it is only at this point that they become conscious. For instance, the man might fantasize that he is being forcefully dragged through fire; the woman that her abdomen is being slit open or that her vagina is bursting. Many are capable of experiencing a certain measure of gratification only with the aid of such fantasies. To be forced to burst means to use outside help in order to obtain relief from tension. Since fear of orgastic excitation is met with in every neurosis, masochistic fantasies and attitudes are part of every emotional illness.

It was strictly at variance with clinical experience to explain masochism as the perception of the inner death instinct or as the result of "fear of death." Masochists develop very little anxiety as long as they can fantasize masochistically. They are immediately afraid when a hysteria or compulsion neurosis begins to consume the masochistic fantasies. Pronounced masochism, on the other hand, is an excellent means of avoiding instinctual anxiety, since it is always the other person who causes the injury. Moreover, the twofold nature of the idea of *bursting* (desire for and fear of orgastic release) satisfactorily explains all aspects of the masochistic attitude.

The desire to explode or burst (or the fear of it), which I subsequently discovered in all my patients, puzzled me. According to prevailing psychological concepts, a psychic idea has to have a function and has to have an origin. We are in the habit of deducing ideas from graphic impressions. The idea originates in the outside world and is transmitted to the organism as a perception through the sense organs. It derives its energy from inner instinctual sources. No such external origin was found for the idea of bursting. This made it difficult to incorporate it clinically.

Nevertheless, I was able to record a number of important insights: masochism does not correspond to a biological instinct. It is the result of a disturbance in a person's capacity for gratification and a continuously unsuccessful attempt to correct this disturbance. It is a result and not a cause of the neurosis. Masochism is the expression of a sexual tension that cannot be relieved. Its immediate source is the pleasure anxiety or the fear of orgastic discharge. What characterizes it is that it seeks to bring about precisely what it fears most deeply: the pleasurable release of tension which is experienced and feared as bursting or exploding.

Comprehension of the masochistic mechanism opened the way for me into the field of biology. Man's pleasure anxiety became understandable as a fundamental change in the physiological function of pleasure. *Suffering and enduring suffering are results of the loss of the organic capacity for pleasure.*

Thus, without intending it, I had hit upon the dynamic nature of all religions and philosophies of suffering. When, in my capacity as a sex counselor, I came into contact with many Christian people, I grasped the connection between biological functioning and religion. Religious ecstasy is patterned precisely according to the masochistic mechanism. Release from inner sin, i.e., from inner sexual tension—a release one is not capable of bringing about by oneself—is expected from God, an all-powerful figure. Such release is desired with biological energy. At the same time, it is experienced as "sin." Thus, it cannot be realized through one's own volition. Someone else has to accomplish it, be it in the form of punishment, pardon, redemption, etc. We shall have more to say about this later. The masochistic orgies of the Middle Ages, the Inquisition, the chastisements and tortures, the penances, etc., of the religious betrayed their function. They were unsuccessful masochistic attempts to attain sexual gratification!

The orgasm disturbance of the masochist differs from the orgasm disturbance of other neurotics in that, at the moment of the highest excitation, the masochist is seized by spasm and maintains it. In this way, he creates a contradiction between the marked expansion that is about to occur and the sudden contraction. All other forms of orgastic impotence inhibit *before* the peak of excitation is reached. This subtle difference, which would seem to be of academic interest only, decided the fate of my scientific work. It is clear from my notes between 1928 and about 1934 that the groundwork for my experimental work in the field of biology, up to the point of the bion experiments, was prepared in this period. It is impossible to describe the whole process. I must simplify or, to put it in a better way, I have to describe my first fantasies, which I would never have dared to publish if they had not been confirmed by experimental and clinical work over the course of the following ten years.

2. THE FUNCTIONING OF A LIVING BLADDER

I had discovered the fear of bursting and the desire to be brought to the point of exploding in one case of masochism, then in all masochists, and finally traces of this fear and desire in all patients without exception, insofar as they demonstrated tendencies to masochistic suffering. The refutation of the idea that masochism is a biological instinct like other sexual instincts extended far beyond the critique of Freud's theory of the death instinct. As I have already pointed out, I was continually grappling with the question as to the origin of the idea of "bursting," which regularly emerged in all patients shortly before the attainment of orgastic potency. In most patients, this idea enters consciousness as a kinesthetic perception of the condition of one's own body. When it is clearly delineated, it is always accompanied by the idea of a *taut bladder*. Patients complain of "being tense to the point of bursting," "filled to the point of exploding." They feel themselves to be "blown up." They fear any attack upon their armoring because it makes them feel as if they were being "pricked open." Some patients said that they were afraid of "dissolving," of "melting," of losing their "grip on themselves" or their "contour." They clung to the rigid armorings of their movements and attitudes like a drowning man to a ship's plank. The most cherished wish of others was "to burst." This accounts for many suicides. The more acute the sexual tension becomes, the more markedly these sensations are experienced. They promptly disappear as soon as the orgasm anxiety has been eliminated and sexual relaxation can take place. When this happens, the hard character traits subside, the person becomes "soft" and "yielding," and simultaneously develops an elastic strength. The crisis of every successful character analysis always sets in precisely at that point when powerful preorgastic sensations are hindered from pursuing an orderly course by anxiety-induced spasms of the musculature. If excitation has mounted to the highest peak and requires complete discharge, the spasm of the pelvic musculature has the same effect as pulling the emergency brake of a car while traveling at seventy-five miles per hour; everything is thrown into confusion. The same thing happens to the patient in a genuine process of cure. He is faced with the decision of wholly discarding the inhibiting somatic mechanism or relapsing into his neurosis. *The neurosis is nothing other than the sum total of all chronically auto-*

matic inhibitions of natural sexual excitation. Everything else is the result of this original disturbance. In 1929, I began to comprehend that the original conflict in mental illness (the unresolved contradiction between striving for pleasure and moralistic frustration of pleasure) is physiologically and structurally anchored in a muscular disturbance. *The psychic contradiction between sexuality and morality operates in the biological depth of the organism as the contradiction between pleasurable excitation and muscular spasm.* The masochistic attitudes assumed great importance for the sex-economic theory of neuroses: there could not be a better example of this contradiction. Compulsion neurotics and hysterics, who circumvent the orgastic sensation by developing anxiety or neurotic symptoms, regularly go through a phase of masochistic suffering in the process of cure. They go through it when the fear of sexual excitation has been eliminated to such an extent that they yield to the preorgastic excitation in the genitals, without, however, allowing the climax of the excitation to take place free of inhibition, i.e., free of anxiety.

Moreover, masochism became a central problem of mass psychology. How it would be practically dealt with seemed of decisive importance. The working masses suffer severe deprivations of all kinds. They are ruled and exploited by a few people who wield power. In the form of the ideology and practice of various patriarchal religions, masochism proliferates like weeds and chokes every natural claim of life. It holds people in an abysmal state of submission. It thwarts their attempts to arrive at a common rational action and imbues them with fear of assuming responsibility for their existence. It causes the best strivings toward the democratization of society to fail. Freud explained the chaotic and catastrophic nature of social conditions on the basis of a death instinct, which wreaked havoc in society. Psychoanalysts contended that the masses were *biologically* masochistic. A punitive police force, some said, was a natural expression of biological mass masochism. People are in fact submissive to the authoritarian leadership of the state in the same way that the individual is obedient to the all-powerful father. Since, however, the rebellion against dictatorial authority, against the father, was regarded as neurotic, whereas conformity to its institutions and demands was regarded as normal, proofs against both of these contentions were needed: first, that there is no biological masochism; second, that conformity to present-day reality, e.g., irrational upbringing or irrational politics, is itself neurotic. I did not tackle the work with this intent in mind. In the interplay of manifold observations, far from the raging clash of ideologies, these two proofs were found. They were discovered in the simple answer to an almost stupid question: *How would an organic bladder behave if it was inflated with air from within and was unable to burst*—in other words, if its covering were capable of being stretched but not of being torn?

The picture of the human character as an armor around the core of the living organism was extremely significant. If such a bladder were put into an unresolvable condition of tension and it could express itself, it would complain. Rendered helpless, it would seek the causes of its suffering outside of itself and make reproaches. It would beg to be pricked open. It would provoke its surroundings until it believed it had reached its goal. *What it had failed to bring about spontaneously from the inside, it would passively and helplessly expect from the outside.*

Bearing this picture of an armored bladder in mind, let us imagine a biopsychic organism whose energy discharge is impaired. The surface membrane would be the character armor. The stretching is produced by the constant production of internal energy (sexual energy or biological excitation). The biological energy urges toward the outside, whether to seek pleasurable discharge or to seek contact with people and things. Thus, this urge to expand corresponds to the *direction from within outward*. The surrounding wall of the armor counteracts this urge. The armor not only prevents the bursting, it exerts a pressure from the outside toward the inside. Rigidification of the organism is its ultimate effect.

This picture coincided with the physical processes of internal pressure and surface tension. I had come into contact with this phenomenon in 1926, when I reviewed the highly significant book by Fr. Kraus,[1] the famous Berlin pathologist, for the psychoanalytic journal.

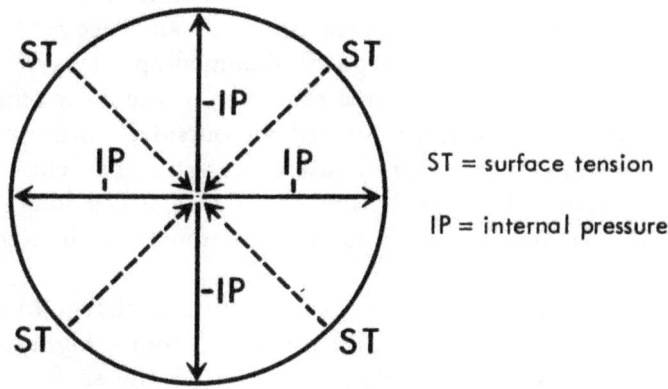

ST = surface tension

IP = internal pressure

The neurotic organism could be readily compared to such a simple system as that of a taut and, at the same time, peripherally armored bladder. This curious analogy between a physical phenomenon and the well-known characterological situation stood the test of clinical scrutiny. The neurotic patient has developed a "stiff" body periphery, while retaining a lively inner core. He feels "uncomfortable within his own skin," "inhibited," unable to "realize himself," as if he "were immured," "without contact," "tense to the point of

---

[1] Fr. Kraus, *Allgemeine und spezielle Pathologie der Person*. I. *Teil, Tiefenperson*. Leipzig: Thieme, 1926.

bursting." He strives with all available means "toward the world," but it is as if he "were tied down." More than that, his efforts to come into contact with life are often so painful, he is so ill equipped to endure the difficulties and disappointments of life, that he prefers "to crawl into himself." *Thus, the direction of the biological function "toward the world," "from the inside toward the outside," is counteracted by a "moving away from the world," a "withdrawal into the self."*

This equation between the highly complicated and the simple was fascinating. The neurotically armored organism cannot burst like an ordinary bladder to rid itself of its inner tension. It can become "masochistic" or it can "recover," i.e., permit the orgastic discharge of dammed-up energy. This orgastic discharge consists in a reduction of the inner tension by means of a "discharge toward the outside," in the form of convulsions of the entire body. It was still not clear what was discharged toward the outside. I was still a long way from the present insight into the functioning of biological energy.

I also conceived of the orgasm, with its discharge of substances from the body, as proliferations from a highly taut bladder. Following their detachment, both the surface tension and the inner pressure are reduced. It was clear that the ejaculation of semen alone could not be responsible for this, for the pleasureless ejaculation does not reduce the tension. I have never regretted this speculation. It led me to very concrete facts.

I remember in this connection an insignificant but impressive incident which took place in 1922. It was before the Berlin Congress of Psychoanalysts. I had, still entirely under the influence of Semon and Bergson, fabricated a naturalscientific fantasy. One has, I told friends, to take Freud's conception of the "sending out of libido" literally and seriously. Freud compared the stretching forth and pulling back of psychic interests to the stretching forth and pulling back of the pseudopodia in the amoeba. The stretching forth of sexual energy becomes visible in the erection of the male penis. Hence, the erection must be functionally identical with the stretching forth of the pseudopodia of the amoeba. On the other hand, erective impotence, in which the penis shrinks, as a result of anxiety, would be identical with the retraction of the pseudopodia. My friends were appalled at what they considered to be confused thinking. They laughed at me, and I was hurt. But thirteen years later I succeeded in experimentally confirming this assumption. I now want to describe how my findings led me to this confirmation.

3. THE FUNCTIONAL ANTITHESIS OF SEXUALITY AND ANXIETY

The equating of the erection of the penis with the protrusion of pseudopodia and its shrinking with their retraction caused me to assume a *functional antithesis between sexuality and anxiety*. The antithesis was expressed in the direction of biological activity. I could no longer free myself from this idea. Since everything I had learned from Freud about the psychology of instincts was in a state of flux, this image tied in with the deeply serious question as to the biological basis of psychic processes. Freud had postulated a physiological foundation for depth psychology. His "unconscious" was deeply immersed in biophysiological phenomena. In the psychic depth, the clear psychic tendencies gave way to a highly mysterious mechanism, which could not be grasped by psychoanalytic thinking alone. Freud had tried to apply the psychic concepts to the sources of life. This had to lead to a personification of the biological processes and bring back metaphysical assumptions which had been previously dispelled from psychoanalytic thinking. I had learned in the study of the orgasm function that, in the physiological realm, it is inadmissible to use the same approach and concepts one uses in the psychic realm. In addition to its causal legitimacy, every psychic phenomenon has a meaning in terms of its relationship to the environment. The psychoanalytic interpretation revealed this meaning. But in the physiological realm, there is no such meaning, nor can there be, without reintroducing a supernatural power. *The living merely functions. It does not have any "meaning."*

Natural science tries to exclude metaphysical hypotheses. Yet, when one cannot explain why and how the living organism functions, one looks for a "purpose" or a "meaning," which is then introduced into the functioning. I again found myself grappling with the problems of the early period of my work, the problems of mechanism and vitalism. I avoided giving a speculative answer. I still did not have a method with which to arrive at a correct solution of this problem. I was familiar with dialectical materialism, but I did not know how I could apply it in natural-scientific research. True, I had given a functional interpretation to Freud's discoveries. But to make the idea of the physiological foundation of psychic phenomena practically applicable, I had to discover the correct method. That the soma influences the psyche is correct, but it is one-sided. The reverse of this, i.e., that the psyche conditions the soma, can be seen again and again. To enlarge the psychic realm to such an extent as to make its laws valid in the somatic does not work. The concept that the psychic and the somatic were two independent processes, which merely interact with one another, was at variance with everyday experience. I had no solution. However, this much was clear: *the experience of pleasure, of expansion, is inseparably connected with living functioning.*

At this point, my new concept of the masochistic function aided me. The thought ran as follows: the psyche is determined by quality, the soma by quantity. In the former, it is the kind of idea or desire which is important; in the latter, it is solely the amount of the functioning energy which is important. Yet, the processes in the organism demonstrated that *the quality of a psychic attitude is dependent upon the amount of the somatic excitation from which it is derived.* In a condition of strong somatic tension, the idea of sexual pleasure and sexual intercourse is intense, vivid, graphic. After gratification, this idea can be reproduced only with difficulty. I formed an image of this as an ocean wave which, by its rising and falling, influences the movement of a piece of wood on the surface. It was nothing more than a vague clue that the psyche arises from or sinks into the deep biophysiological process, depending upon the state of the latter. It seemed to me that the appearance and disappearance of consciousness in the act of waking and going to sleep were expressive of this wave process. It was vague, elusive. It was merely clear that biological energy governs the psychic as well as the somatic. A *functional unity* prevails. To be sure, while it is possible for biological laws to be valid in the psychic realm, psychic characteristics cannot be valid in the biological realm. This forced me to reconsider the Freudian hypothesis pertaining to the instincts.

Imagination is undoubtedly a psychic process. There are unconscious ideas which can be inferred from their visible manifestations. According to Freud, the unconscious itself cannot be grasped. Yet, if it is "immersed" in the biophysiological realm, it must be possible to grasp it with a method applicable to the common factor which determines the biopsychic apparatus as a whole. This common factor cannot be the "meaning," nor can it be the "purpose." These are secondary functions. Viewed from a consistently functional point of view, there is no purpose or goal in the biological realm, but only *function* and *development,* which follow a natural course. There remained the dynamic structure, the interplay of forces. This was valid in all realms. One

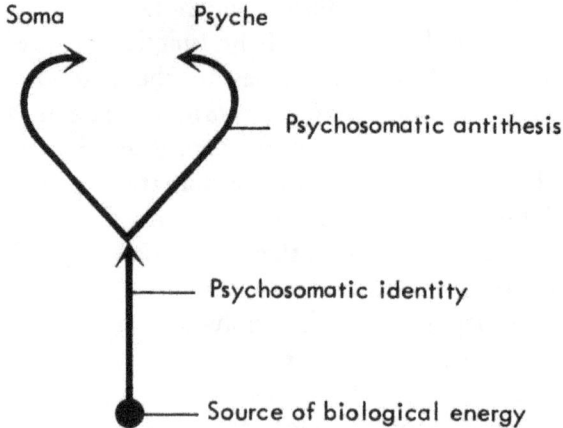

Diagram depicting psychosomatic identity and antithesis

could hold on to it. What psychology calls "tension" and "relaxation" is a counterplay of forces. My idea of the bladder, as simple as it was, was definitely in keeping with the idea of the unity of the soma and the psyche. But apart from the unity, there was also antithesis. This thought was the germ of my theory of sexuality.

In 1924, I had assumed that in the orgasm an excitation concentrates at the periphery of the organism, particularly at the genital organs, then flows back into the vegetative center and subsides there. Unexpectedly, a train of thought was completed. What appeared earlier as psychic excitation now emerged as a biophysiological current. The internal pressure and surface tension of a bladder are, after all, nothing other than functions of the center and periphery of an organism. They are functionally antithetical; they are opposed to one another. The "fate" of the bladder depends upon the relationship between internal pressure and surface tension, just as psychic health depends upon the balance of energy in the sexual sphere. *"Sexuality" could be nothing other than the biological function of expansion "out of the* self," *from the center toward the periphery*. In turn, *anxiety could be nothing but the reversed direction, i.e., from the periphery to the center, "back into the self."* They are antithetical directions of one and the same excitation process. This theory was quickly substantiated by a profusion of clinical findings. In sexual excitation, the peripheral vessels are dilated. In anxiety, one senses a centralized inner tension as if one would burst; the peripheral vessels are contracted. The sexually aroused penis expands. In anxiety, it retracts. The sources of functioning energy lie in the "biological energy center." It is at the periphery that we find its areas of functioning, in contact with the world, in the sexual act, in orgastic discharge, in work, etc.

These findings were already outside the framework of psychoanalysis. They shattered a number of previous conceptions. The psychoanalysts could not grasp what I was saying, and my position was too controversial. Hence, it became increasingly difficult to allow my views to exist in the same organization. Freud had rejected the attempt to include the libido process in the autonomic system. As a prominent psychoanalyst, I was not on particularly good terms with the orthodox psychiatrists and other clinicians. Owing to their mechanistic and non-analytic way of thinking, they would have comprehended very little of what I was saying. The newly born theory of sexuality found itself utterly alone. I was consoled by the numerous confirmations of my view which I found in experimental physiology. My theory seemed capable of reducing to the simplest terms the diverse findings accumulated by generations of physiologists. *At the center stood the antithesis between sympathetic and parasympathetic.*

4. WHAT IS "BIOPSYCHIC ENERGY"?

Some sixty years of sexology, forty years of psychoanalysis, and almost twenty years of my own work on the orgasm theory still had not succeeded in providing the clinician (who was supposed to cure human sexual disturbances, i.e., neuroses) with an answer to this question. Let us recall the point of departure of the orgasm theory. Neuroses and functional psychoses are sustained by surplus, inadequately discharged sexual energy. Initially it was called "psychic energy." No one knew what it really was. Psychic illnesses were undoubtedly rooted "in the body." Hence, there was good reason to assume that the psychic proliferations were nourished by an energy stasis. Only the elimination of this energy source of the neurosis through the establishment of full orgastic potency seemed to make the patient immune against a relapse. There could be no thought of preventing psychic illnesses on a mass scale without a knowledge of the biological foundation of these illnesses. The premise "given gratifying sexuality, there are no neurotic disturbances" was unassailable. Naturally, this contention had individual as well as social implications. The significance of the sexual question is obvious. Yet, in spite of Freud, official science wanted to know nothing about the implication of sexuality. Psychoanalysis itself showed an increasing tendency to shrink away from the question. In addition, the question was imbued with the outpourings of a pathological, distorted, somehow always pornographically tinged "sexuality," i.e., with the sexuality which governs human life. The clear-cut distinction between "natural" sexual expression and pathological, culturally anchored sexual expression, between the "primary" drives and the "secondary" drives, made it possible to persist and to pursue the problem to its core. Reflection alone would not have produced a solution, nor would the collation of the many brilliant insights in modern physiological literature that, from about 1925, appeared in increasing abundance and were condensed and compiled in Müller's *Die Lebensnerven*.

Once again clinical observation provided the correct line of approach. In Copenhagen, in 1933, I treated a man who offered considerable resistance to the uncovering of his passive homosexual fantasies. This resistance was overtly expressed in the extremely stiff attitude of his throat and neck ("stiff-necked"). A concentrated attack on his defense finally caused him to yield, though in an alarming way. For three days, he was shaken by acute manifestations of vegetative shock. The pallor of his face changed rapidly from white to yellow to blue. His skin was spotted and motley. He experienced violent pains in the neck and back of the head. His heartbeat was rapid and pounding. He had diarrhea, felt tired, and seemed to have lost control. I was uneasy. True, I had often seen similar symptoms, but never in such violent form. Something had happened here that, while somehow a legitimate part of the work, was not immediately intelligible. *Affects had broken through somatically after the patient had relinquished his attitude of psychic defense.* Apparently, the stiff neck, which emphasized austere masculinity, had bound vegetative energies which now broke loose in an uncontrolled and chaotic manner. A person with an ordered sexual economy is not capable of such a reaction. Only continuous inhibition and damming-up of biological energy can produce it. The musculature had served the function of inhibition. When the neck muscles relaxed, powerful impulses, as if unleashed from a taut coil, broke through. The alternating pallor and flushing of the face could be nothing other than the flowing back and forth of body fluids, i.e., the contraction and dilation of the blood vessels. This fits in extremely well with my earlier described views on the functioning of biological energy. The direction, "out of the self toward the world," alternated rapidly and continuously with the opposite direction, "away from the world —back into the self."

By means of tensions, the musculature can obstruct the flow of blood, in other words can reduce the movement of body fluids to a minimum. I checked a number of other patients to see whether this observation held true in their cases, too, and I also thought about patients whom I had treated earlier. All observations confirmed this phenomenon. In a short time, I had a profusion of facts at my disposal. They reduced themselves to a concise formulation: *sexual life energy can be bound by chronic muscular tensions. Anger and anxiety can also be blocked by muscular tensions.* From now on, I found that whenever I dissolved a muscular tension, one of the three basic biological excitations of the body, anxiety, hate, or sexual excitation, broke through. I had, of course, succeeded in doing this before through the loosening of purely characterological inhibitions and attitudes. But now the breakthroughs of vegetative energy were more complete, more forceful, experienced more affectively, and occurred more rapidly. In the process, the characterological inhibitions were loosened spontaneously. These findings, made in 1933, were published in an incomplete form in 1935. In 1937, I published them in more detail.[2] Quite rapidly, a number of decisive questions pertaining to the relationship between mind and body were clarified.

Character armorings were now seen to be functionally identical with muscular hypertonia. The concept, "functional identity," which I had to introduce, means nothing more than that muscular attitudes and character attitudes have the same function in the psychic mechanism: they can replace one another and can be influenced by one another. Basically,

---

[2] Cf. Reich, *Psychischer Kontakt und vegetative Strömung*, 1934; and *Orgasmusreflex, Muskelhaltung und Körperausdruck*, Sexpol Verlag, 1937.

they cannot be separated. They are identical in their function.

Postulations resulting from the connecting of facts immediately lead to further findings. If the character armor could be expressed through the muscular armor, and vice versa, then the unity of psychic and somatic functioning had been grasped in principle, and could be influenced in a practical way. From that time on, I was able to make practical use of this unity whenever necessary. If a character inhibition did not respond to psychic influencing, I resorted to the corresponding somatic attitude. Conversely, if I had difficulty in getting at a disturbing somatic attitude, I worked on its expression in the patient's character and was able to loosen it. I was now able to eliminate a typical friendly smile which obstructed the analytic work, either by describing the expression or by directly disturbing the muscular attitude, e.g., pulling up the chin. This was an enormous step forward. It took another six years to develop this technique into the vegetotherapy of today.

The loosening of the rigid muscular attitudes produced peculiar body sensations in the patients: involuntary trembling and twitching of the muscles, sensations of cold and hot, itching, the feeling of pins and needles, prickling sensations, the feeling of having the jitters, and somatic perceptions of anxiety, anger, and pleasure. I had to break with all the old ideas about the mind-body relationship, if I wanted to grasp these phenomena. They were not "results," "causes," "accompanying manifestations" of "psychic processes"; they were simply these phenomena themselves in the somatic realm. I categorized as "vegetative currents" all somatic phenomena which, in contrast to rigid muscular armorings, are characterized by movement. Immediately the question arose: are the vegetative currents merely the movements of fluid or are they more than that? I could not be satisfied with the explanation that these currents were merely mechanical movements of fluid. While purely mechanical movements could account for the hot and cold sensations, pallor, and blushing, the "simmering of the blood," etc., they could not explain the feeling of pins and needles, the sensation of prickling, shuddering, the sweet preorgastic sensations of pleasure, etc. The crucial problem of orgastic impotence was still unsolved: it is possible for the genital organs to be filled with blood without a trace of excitation. Hence, sexual excitation can certainly not be identical with, nor be the expression of the flow of blood. There are anxiety states without any particular pallor of the face or skin. The feeling of "tightness" in the chest ("angustiae," anxiety), the feeling of "constriction," could not be traced back solely to a congestion of blood in the central organs. If this were so, one would have to feel anxiety after a good meal, when the blood is concentrated in the stomach. In addition to the flow of the blood, there must be something else which, depending upon its biological function, causes anxiety, anger, or pleasure. In this process, the flow of blood merely represents an essential means. Perhaps this unknown "something" does not occur when the movement of the body fluids is hindered.

5. THE ORGASM FORMULA: TENSION → CHARGE → DISCHARGE → RELAXATION

The unknown "something" I was looking for could be nothing other than *bioelectricity*. This occurred to me one day when I tried to understand the physiology of the process of friction which takes place between the penis and the walls of the vaginal mucous membrane in the sexual act. Sexual friction is a fundamental biological process. It is found throughout the animal kingdom wherever reproduction takes place in the union of the two sexes. Two surfaces of the body rub against one another. In this process, *biological excitation* occurs, together with congestion, expansion, "erection." On the basis of pioneer experiments, the Berlin internist Kraus ascertained that the body is governed by electrical processes. It is made up of countless "border surfaces" between membranes and electrolytic fluids, having various densities and compositions. According to a well-known law of physics, electrical tensions develop at the borders between conducting fluids and membranes. Since the concentrations and organization of membranes are not homogeneous, differences develop in the tensions at the border surfaces, and, simultaneously, differences in potential of varying intensity. These differences of potential may be likened to the energy differences of two bodies at different heights. The body having the higher elevation is capable of performing more work as it drops than the body having the lower elevation. A weight of one kilogram will drive a stake deeper into the earth when it is dropped from a height of three meters than when it is dropped from a height of one meter. The "potential energy of position" is higher, and, therefore, the "kinetic energy" which is generated will also be greater when this potential energy is released. The principle of "potential difference" can be easily applied to the difference in electrical tensions. If I attach a wire from a highly charged body to a less highly charged one, a current will flow from the first to the second. In this process, static electrical energy is converted into current energy. Moreover, an equalization takes place between the two charges, in the same way that the water level in two vessels becomes the same if I connect the two by means of a pipe. The equalization of energy presupposes a difference in potential energy. Our body consists of billions of such potential surfaces having various potential energies. Consequently, the energy in the body is in constant motion from places of higher to places of lower potential. The tiny particles of body fluids, the ions, are the transmitters of the electrical charges in this continuous process of equalization. These are atoms which possess a fixed quantum of electrical charge, and, depending upon whether they are moving toward a negative or toward a positive pole, are called cations or anions. What has all this to do with the problem of sexuality? A great deal.

Sexual tension is felt throughout the body, but it is experienced most strongly in the regions of the heart and the abdomen. The excitation gradually becomes concentrated in the sexual organs. They become congested with blood, and electrical charges reach the surface of the genitals. We know that the sexual excitation of one part of the body by a gentle touch will excite other parts of the body. The process of friction increases the tension or excitation until it reaches a climax, the orgasm, a condition characterized by involuntary convulsions of the musculature of the genitals and of the entire body. It is known that muscular contraction is accompanied by the discharge of electrical energy. This discharge can be measured and represented in the form of a graphic curve. Some physiologists are of the opinion that the nerves store up excitation, while the muscle contraction discharges it, for it is not the nerve but only the muscle which can contract and is capable of discharging energy. In the process of sexual friction, energy is at first stored up in both bodies and then discharged in the orgasm. The orgasm can be nothing other than an electrical discharge. The physical structure of the genital organs is most particularly suited for this: great vascularity, dense ganglia, capacity for erection, and a musculature which is especially capable of spontaneous contractions.

If the process is investigated more closely, it is observed that there are four stages to the course of excitation:

1. The organs become filled with fluid: erection with *mechanical tension*.

2. This produces a strong excitation which I assumed to be of an electrical nature: *electrical charge*.

3. In the orgasm, the convulsion of the musculature discharges the sexual excitation: *electrical discharge*.

4. This modulates into a relaxation of the genitals through a flowing back of the body fluid: *mechanical relaxation*.

I called this four-beat process the *orgasm formula:* MECHANICAL TENSION → ELECTRICAL CHARGE → ELECTRICAL DISCHARGE → MECHANICAL RELAXATION.

The process it describes can be depicted simply. This brings me back to the function of a filled elastic bladder which I had fantasized six years prior to the discovery of the orgasm formula.

Let us imagine two spheres: one is rigid, made of metal, the other elastic, something like a living organism, an amoeba, a starfish, a heart.

Diagram depicting inorganic and organic living spheres

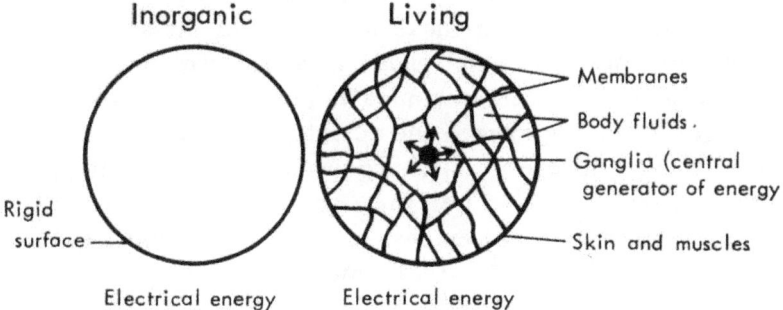

Electrical energy (Fig. 1): on the surface only, evenly distributed, charged from the outside, the entire system is rigid.

Electrical energy (Fig. 2): throughout whole body, unevenly distributed, supplied from its own inner source; the entire system is capable of expanding and contracting.

The metal sphere would be hollow, whereas the organic sphere would surround a complicated system of fluids and membranes of various densities having the ability to conduct electricity. The metal sphere would receive its electrical charge from the outside, e.g., from an electrostatic machine. But the organic sphere, e.g., a pig's bladder, would have a charging apparatus which operates automatically in the center. Hence, it would charge itself spontaneously from the inside. In keeping with basic laws of physics, the electric charge of the metal sphere would be on the surface and only on the surface, evenly distributed. The filled elastic bladder would be electrically charged through and through. Owing to the differences in density and the nature of the fluids and membranes, the charge would be greater in some areas and less in others. In this ideally conceived organism, the electrical charges would be in constant movement from places of higher to places of lower potential. In general, however, one direction would predominate: from the center, the operative source of the electrical charge, toward the periphery. Consequently, the bladder would be found most frequently in the condition of expansion and extension. Now and then, like the ciliate, it would return to the form of the sphere, in which, given equal body content, the surface tension is lowest. If the inner production of energy becomes too great, the bladder can, by contracting a number of times, discharge the energy toward the outside, in short, can regulate its energy. This energy discharge would be extremely pleasurable because it liberates the organism from dammed-up tension. In the state of extension, the bladder would be able to carry out various rhythmic movements, e.g., produce a wave of alternating expansion and contraction, as in the movement of a worm or in intestinal peristalsis.

It could also describe a wavy, serpentine movement, using the entire body.

In these movements, the charged organic bladder would display a unity. If it were capable of self-perception, it would experience the rhythmic alternation of extension, expansion, and contraction in a pleasurable way. It would feel like a small child who hops around rhythmically because he is happy. In the course of these movements, bioelectrical energy would continually oscillate between tension-charge and discharge-relaxation. It would be able to convert itself into heat, into mechanical kinetic energy, or into work. Such a bladder would feel at one with its surroundings, just like a small child. There would be direct contact with other organic spheres, for they would identify with one another on the basis of the sensations of movement and rhythm. Contempt for natural movements would be foreign to them, just as they would have no comprehension of unnatural behavior. Development would be provided for and guaranteed through the continuous production of internal energy, as in the budding of flowers, or progressive cell division after the introduction of energy by fertilization. Moreover, there would be no end to the development. Achievement would be within the framework of general biological activity; it would not be at variance with it.

Longitudinal extension over longer periods of time would cause this shape to become fixed and thereby bring about the development of a supportive apparatus in the organism. While this fixed extension would preclude a return to the spherical form, pulsating by means of flexion and stretching would continue undisturbed. This would guarantee the metabolism of energy. To be sure, a fixed supportive apparatus would already constitute one of the preconditions of being less protected against destructive inhibitions of motility.

However, it would not be an inhibition itself. Such an inhibition could only be compared with the restricting of a snake at one point of its body. Held fast, a snake would immediately lose its rhythm and the unity of the organic wave movements in the remaining free parts of its body.

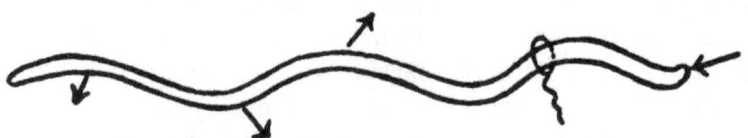

The animal body is comparable to the above described organic bladder. To complete the picture, we would have to introduce an automatically operating pumping system, like a heart, which causes the fluid to flow in a continuously rhythmic cycle, from the center to the periphery and back again: the cardiovascular system. The animal, even at the very lowest stage of development, possesses an apparatus that generates electricity from the center. It is the so-called vegetative ganglion, a conglomeration of nerve cells which, arranged at regular intervals and connected with all organs and their parts by means of very fine strands, governs the involuntary life functions. They are the organs of vegetative feelings and sensations. They constitute a coherent unity, a so-called "syncytium," which is divided into two antithetically functioning groups: the *sympathetic* and the *parasympathetic*.

Our imagined bladder can expand and contract. It can expand to an extraordinary degree and then, with a few contractions, relax. It can be flaccid, tense, relaxed, or excited. It can concentrate the electrical charges, together with the fluids which transmit them from one place to another, with varying intensity. It can keep certain parts in a state of continuous tension and other parts in a state of continuous motion. If one were to squeeze it in one part, increased tension and charge would immediately appear in another part. If, indeed, one were to exert and maintain continuous pressure over the entire surface, i.e., prevent it from expanding in spite of continuous inner production of energy, it would be in a perpetual state of anxiety; that is to say, it would feel constricted and confined. Were it able to speak, it would beg for "release" from this tormenting condition. The bladder would not care what happened to it as long as movement and change were reintroduced into its rigid, compressed condition. Since it would not be able to bring about this change of its own accord, someone else would have to do it, e.g., by tossing it around in space (gymnastics); by kneading (massage); by stabbing, if need be (fantasy of being pricked open); by injury (masochistic beating fantasy, hara-kiri); and, if nothing else helps, by dissolving, perishing, disintegrating (Nirvana, sacrificial death). A society consisting of such bladders would create the most idealistic philosophies about the "condition of non-suffering." Since any stretching out toward pleasure, or motivated by pleasure, could be experienced only as painful, the bladder would develop a fear of pleasurable excitation (pleasure anxiety) and create theories on the "wickedness," "sinfulness," and "destructiveness" of pleasure. In short, it would be a twentieth-century ascetic. Eventually, it would be afraid of any reminder of the possibility of the so ardently desired relaxation; then it would hate such a reminder, and finally it would prosecute and murder anyone who spoke about it. It would join together with similarly constituted, peculiarly stiff beings and concoct rigid rules of life. These rules would have the sole function of guaranteeing the smallest possible production of inner energy, i.e., of guaranteeing quietness, conformity, and the continuance of accustomed reactions. It would make inexpedient attempts to master surpluses of internal energy which could not be disposed of through natural pleasure or movement. For instance, it would introduce senseless sadistic actions or ceremonies which would be of an essentially automatic nature and have little purpose (compulsive religious behavior). Realistic goals are self-developing and, therefore, compel movement and restlessness in those who move toward them.

The bladder could be shaken by suddenly emerging convulsions, through which the dammed-up energy would be discharged. For instance, it might have hysterical or epileptic seizures. It might, on the other hand, become completely rigid and desolate, as in catatonic schizophrenia. In any event, this bladder would always be plagued by anxiety. Everything else follows inevitably from this anxiety, e.g., religious mysticism, belief in a Führer, meaningless martyrdom. Since everything in nature moves, changes, develops, expands, and contracts, the *armored* bladder would have an alien and hostile attitude toward nature. It would conceive of itself as "something very special," belonging to a superior race because it is dressed in a stiff collar or uniform. It would represent that "culture" or that "race" which is incompatible with nature, and nature would be looked upon as "base," "demonic," "impulsive," "uncontrolled," "ignoble." At the same time, however, the bladder, still feeling some last vestiges of nature in itself, would have to enthuse about it and to sentimentalize it, e.g., as "sublime love" or as the "surging of the blood." To associate nature with bodily convulsions would be a blasphemy. Yet, it would create industries for pornography, without being aware of the contradiction.

The tension-charge function brought together ideas which had made an impression on me in my study of classical biology. It was necessary to re-examine its theoretical tenability. From the point of view of physiology, my theory was substantiated by the well-known fact that muscles contract spontaneously. The muscular contraction can be brought about by electrical stimuli. According to Galvani, however, the contraction can also be brought about by injuring the muscle and connecting the end of the severed nerve to the muscle at the point of injury. The contraction is accompanied by the measurable expression of the so-called electrical *action current*. In injured muscles, there is also an *ordinary current*. It becomes manifest when the middle of the muscle surface is connected to the injured end by means of an electric conductor, e.g., copper wire.

The study of muscle contractions had been an important area of investigation in physiology for decades. I did not understand why muscle physiology did not find the connection with general animal electricity. If two nerve-muscle preparations are placed upon one another in such a way that the muscle of one touches the nerve of the other, and if, then, contractions are produced in the first muscle preparation by applying an electrical current to it, the second muscle preparation also contracts. The first muscle preparation contracts as a response to the electrical stimulus, and, in the process, itself develops a biological action current. This, in turn, acts as an electrical stimulus upon the second muscle preparation, which responds with a contraction, thus producing a second biological action current. Since the muscles in the body are in contact with each other and are connected with the total organism by means of body fluid, every muscle action would have a stimulating influence on the total organism. Naturally, this influence varies, depending upon the location of the muscle, the initial stimulus and its strength; but it always affects the total organism. As the prototype of this influencing, we have the orgastic contraction of the genital musculature, which is so strong that it is conveyed to the entire organism. I found nothing about this in the available literature. Yet, it appeared to be of decisive importance.

Closer observation of the cardiac action curve confirmed my assumption that the tension-charge process also governs the cardiac function. It runs as an electrical wave from the auricle, via the cardiac arteries, to the apex of the heart. The precondition for the onset of this contraction is the filling of the auricle with blood. The result of the charge and discharge is the forcing of the blood through the aorta due to the contraction of the heart.

Bulk-producing medicines have a purgative effect on the intestines. The swelling acts on the muscles like an electrical stimulus. They contract and relax in rhythmic waves ("peristalsis"). These contractions and relaxations cause the intestines to be emptied. The same applies to the urinary bladder. If it is filled with fluid, it contracts, thus causing the contents to be emptied.

In this description, an extremely important but unobserved fact was revealed. It can be considered the basic model for the refutation of the absolute "teleological" thinking in the field of biology. The urinary bladder does not contract "in order to fulfill the function of micturition" by virtue of divine will or supernatural biological powers. It contracts in response to a simple causal principle which is anything but divine. It contracts because its mechanical filling induces a contraction. This principle can be applied to any other function at will. One does not engage in sexual intercourse "in order to produce children," but because a congestion of fluid bioelectrically charges the genital organs and urges toward discharge. This, in turn, is accompanied by the discharge of sexual substances. Thus, sexuality is not in the service of procreation; rather procreation is an incidental result of the tension-charge process in the genitals. This may be depressing to champions of eugenic moral philosophy, but it is nonetheless true.

In 1933, I came upon an experimental work by the Berlin biologist Hartmann. In special experiments dealing with the sexuality of gametes, he demonstrated that the male and female functions in copulation are not fixed. A weak male gamete can behave in a feminine way toward a stronger male gamete. Hartmann left open the question as to what determines the groupings of gametes of the same sex, their "mating," if you like. He assumed the existence of "certain" still-uninvestigated "substances." I understood that the groupings were determined by electrical processes. A few years later, I was able to confirm this by means of an electrical experiment on bions. That the grouping in the copulation of gametes takes place in one way and not another is determined by bioelectrical forces. Around this same time, I received a newspaper clipping that reported on experiments carried out in Moscow. A scientist (his name has slipped my memory) succeeded in demonstrating that egg and sperm cells produce male or female individuals, depending upon the nature of their electrical charge.

Thus, *procreation is a function of sexuality,* and not vice versa, as was hitherto believed. Freud had maintained the same thing with respect to psychosexuality, when he separated the concepts "sexual" and "genital." But for a reason I was not able to understand, he later stated that "sexuality in puberty" is "in the service of procreation." Hartmann provided proof in the field of biology that it is not sexuality which is a function of procreation, but the reverse: procreation is a function of sexuality. I was able to add to this a third argument, based on the experimental investigations of various biologists: *the division of the egg, like cell division in general, is an orgastic process. It is governed by the tension-charge function.* The consequence of this finding for the moralistic appraisal of sexuality is evident: sexuality can no longer be regarded as an unfortunate concomitant of the preservation of the species.

When the egg has been fertilized, when it has absorbed the energy of the sperm cell, it first becomes tense. It absorbs fluid; its membrane becomes taut. This means that the surface tension and the inner pressure increase simultaneously. The greater the pressure of the content of the bladder, which here represents the egg, the more difficult it is for the surface to "hold" the system "together." These are processes which are still definitely governed by the counteraction between inner pressure and surface tension. If stretched further, a purely physical bladder would *burst*. In the egg cell, the process now commences which is so characteristic of the living function: *the stretching or expansion provokes a contraction.* The growth of the egg cell is ascribable to the active absorption of fluid, which always proceeds only to a certain point. The nucleus of the cell begins to "radiate," i.e., to produce energy. Gurwitsch called this phenomenon *mitogenetic radiation*. Mitosis means division of the nucleus of the cell. Later, I learned to observe and to assess the vitality of bion cultures on the basis of the degree of certain radiation phenomena inside the formation. The extreme filling of the cell, i.e., *mechanical tension,* is accompanied by an *electrical charge*. At a certain point, the membrane begins to contract. As a matter of fact, it begins to contract at that point where the sphere has attained the greatest circumference and the greatest tension. This is always the equator or, if one prefers, a meridian of the sphere. This contraction is not, as one can observe, gradual and constant; it is a struggling, contradictory process. The tension of the membrane at the site of the contraction struggles against the internal pressure which has become stronger precisely owing to this contraction. It is quite clear that inner pressure and surface tension have a mutually intensifying effect upon one another, that they strengthen one another. This produces the visible vibrations, undulation and contraction.

The constriction (indentation) increases. The inner tension mounts. If the egg cell could speak, it would express anxiety. There is only one possibility of resolving this inner tension (apart from bursting): the "division" of the one big bladder with its taut surface into two smaller bladders, in which the *same volume content is surrounded by a much*

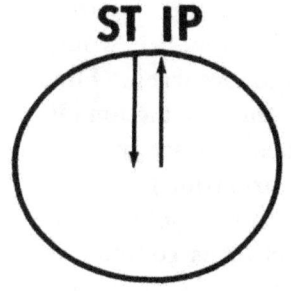
I. Egg cell

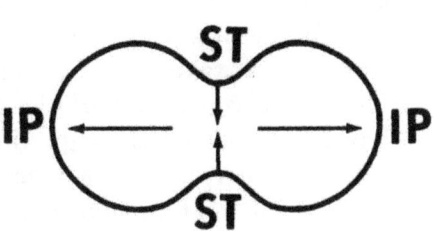
II. Onset of process division

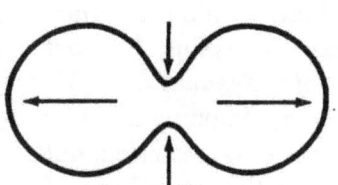
III. End of process division

IV. Two daughter cells

Inner Pressure (IP) and Surface Tension (ST) in the Division of the Egg

I. Equilibrium between IP and ST in the tension-charge. Beginning of the process of swelling
II. IP > ST, ST counteracts IP by means of "contraction"
III. Division; ST becomes greater; balance between ST and IP through expansion of surface
IV. Relaxation; ST = IP; the same volume now distributed in two daughter cells with a larger combined surface

larger and therefore less taut membrane. The egg division corresponds to the resolution of a tension. The nucleus, in its spindle formation, goes through this process prior to the division of the cell as a whole. The spindle formation is regarded by many biologists as an electrically determined process. If it were possible for us to measure the electrical condition of the nucleus after the cell division, we would very likely ascertain that a discharge had occurred. That this process takes place is suggested by the "reduction division," in which half of the chromosomes (whose number has been doubled through the spindle formation) are extruded. Each of the two daughter cells now contains the same number of chromosomes. Reproduction is completed.

Hence, cell division also follows the four-beat of the orgasm formula: tension → charge → discharge → relaxation. It is the most important process in the sphere of living functioning. The orgasm formula could also be called the "life formula." I did not want to publish anything about this at that time. Rather, I confined myself to hints within the framework of clinical presentations, merely publishing a short work, *Die Fortpflanzung als Funktion der Sexualität,* 1935, based on the experiments carried out by Hartmann. The matter appeared so decisive that, until I had carried out special experiments to confirm or refute the hypothesis, I wanted to forgo publication. I was later able to demonstrate important connections between the vegetative currents, the contractions in protozoa, and the dynamic interplay between surface tension and inner pressure in the energy-charged, organic bladder.

6. PLEASURE (EXPANSION) AND ANXIETY (CONTRACTION): PRIMARY ANTITHESIS OF VEGETATIVE LIFE

In 1933, my idea of the unity between psychic and somatic functioning became clear in the following way.

The fundamental biological functions of contraction and expansion were applicable to the psychic as well as to the somatic realm. Two series of antithetical effects emerged, their elements representing various depths of biological functioning.

Investigation shows that the impulses and sensations are not produced by the nerves, but are merely transmitted by them. Impulses and sensations are biological actions of the total organism. They are present in the living system long before the development of an organized nervous system. Protozoa demonstrate fundamentally the same actions and impulses as metazoa, in spite of the fact that they do not have an organized nervous system. The great achievement of Kraus and Zondek was in demonstrating that the functions of the autonomic nervous system can not only be stimulated or retarded by chemical substances; more important, they can be replaced by them.

On the basis of his experiments, Kraus came to the conclusion that the action of nerves, drugs, and electrolytes can be substituted for one another in the biological system with respect to the hydration or dehydration of the tissues (which is, as we have already pointed out, the basic function of life).

What follows is a comparative table (see following page), compiled in terms of the total function.

The facts represented in this table show:

1. The antithesis between the potassium (*parasympathetic*) group and the calcium (*sympathetic*) group: expansion and contraction.

2. The antithesis between periphery and center with respect to excitation.

3. The functional identity of the sympathetic and parasympathetic with the functions of substances having a chemical stimulus.

4. The dependency of the innervation of the individual

VEGETATIVE GROUP	GENERAL EFFECT ON TISSUES	CENTRAL EFFECT	PERIPHERAL EFFECT
Sympathetic Calcium (group) Adrenalin Cholesterin H-ions	Reduction of surface tension Dehydration Striated musculature: flaccid or spastic Reduction of electrical excitability Increase of oxygen consumption Increase of blood pressure	Systolic Heart musculature is stimulated	Vasoconstriction
Parasympathetic Potassium (group) Cholin Lecithin OH-ions	Increase of surface tension Hydration Muscles: increased tonicity Increase of electrical excitability Decrease of oxygen consumption Decrease of blood pressure	Diastolic Heart musculature relaxed	Vasodilatation

organs on the functional unity and antithesis of the total organism.

As we have already pointed out, all biological impulses and organ sensations can be reduced to *expansion* (elongation, dilatation) and *contraction* (shrinking, constriction).

How are these two basic functions related to the autonomic nervous system? Investigation of the very complicated vegetative innervations of the organs shows that the parasympathetic (vagus) always functions where there is expansion, dilatation, hyperemia, turgor, and pleasure. Conversely, the *sympathetic* nerves function whenever the organism contracts, blood is withdrawn from the periphery and pallor, anxiety, and pain appear. If we go one step further, we grasp that the *parasympathetic nervous system operates in the direction of expansion, "out of the self—toward the world," pleasure and joy; whereas the sympathetic nervous system operates in the direction of contraction, "away from the world—into the self," sadness and unpleasure.* The life process consists of a continuous alternation between expansion and contraction.

Further investigation shows the identity between parasympathetic function and sexual function on one hand, and sympathetic function and the function of unpleasure or anxiety on the other. We see that in the experience of pleasure, the blood vessels dilate at the periphery, the skin becomes flushed, pleasure is experienced from its mildest form to the highest degree of sexual ecstasy. In the condition of anxiety, pallor, contraction of the blood vessels, and unpleasure go together. In pleasure, "the heart expands" (parasympathetic dilatation) and the pulse beat is quiet and full. In anxiety, the heart contracts and beats rapidly and forcibly. In the former, it forces the blood through wide vessels; its work is therefore easy. In the latter, it forces the blood through narrowed vessels; its work is hard. In the former, the blood is predominantly distributed toward the periphery; in the latter, the constricted vessels cause a congestion of the blood toward the heart. Thus, it is readily understandable that with anxiety there is a feeling of oppression and, conversely, with a feeling of oppression there is anxiety. It is the picture of so-called cardiovascular hypertension with which organic medicine is so much concerned. *This hypertension corresponds to a general condition of sympatheticotonic contraction in the organism.*

	Anxiety syndrome	*Pleasure syndrome*
Peripheral vessels	contracted	dilated
Cardiac action	accelerated	slowed down
Blood pressure	increased	decreased
Pupils	dilated	constricted
Secretion of saliva	decreased	increased
Musculature	paralyzed or in spasm	state of tonus, relaxed

On the highest psychic level, biological expansion is experienced as pleasure; contraction is experienced as unpleasure. In the realm of *instinctual phenomena*, expansion functions as sexual excitation, and contraction functions as anxiety. On a deeper physiological level, expansion corresponds to parasympathetic functioning, and contraction to sympathetic functioning. According to discoveries made by Kraus and Zondek, the parasympathetic function can be replaced by the potassium ion group, and the sympathetic function can be replaced by the calcium ion group. Thus, we arrive at a convincing and impressive picture of *unitary functioning from the highest psychic sensations to the deepest biological reactions.*

The following is a table listing the two series of functions arranged according to their depth:

Pleasure	*Unpleasure and Anxiety*
Sexuality	Anxiety
Parasympathetic	Sympathetic
Potassium	Calcium
Lecithin	Cholesterin
Cholin	Adrenalin
OH-ions (hydrating bases)*	H-ions (dehydrating acids)
Function of expansion	*Function of contraction*

* The pH is always basic (7.2—7.8).

On the basis of this formulation of the unitary antithetical body-mind functioning, a number of previously misunderstood contradictions of the autonomic nerve innervation were clarified. Formerly, the organism's autonomic nerve innervation appeared to lack unity and coherence. In one instance, it was said that the parasympathetic nervous system caused muscles to contract. In another instance, the same function was ascribed to the sympathetic nervous system. In one instance, the functions of the glands were said to be stimulated by the parasympathetic nervous system (genital glands); in another instance, they were said to be stimulated by the sympathetic nervous system (sweat glands). A tabular comparison of the sympathetic and parasympathetic innervations of the autonomically functioning organs brings out even more clearly the apparent illogicality.

In the course of demonstrating the two directions of biological energy, a fact has appeared to which we have given little attention. The vegetative periphery has been clearly described. Still undetermined is the site at which the biological energy concentrates as soon as a condition of anxiety

Functioning of the Autonomic Nervous System

Sympathetic Effect	Organ	Parasympathetic Effect
Inhibition of the m. sphincter pupillae: *dilated pupils*	Musculature of the iris	Stimulation of the m. sphincter pupillae: *narrowing of the pupils*
Inhibition of the lachrymal glands: "dry eyes." Depression	Lachrymal glands	Stimulation of the lachrymal glands: "glowing eyes." Joy
Inhibition of the salivary glands: "parched mouth"	Salivary glands	Stimulation and increased secretion of the salivary glands: "making mouth water"
Stimulation of the sweat glands in face and body: "skin is moist and cold"	Sweat glands	Inhibition of the sweat glands in face and body: "skin is dry"
Contraction of the arteries: "Cold sweat," pallor, anxiety	Arteries	Dilatation of the arteries: "freshness and flushing of skin, increased turgor without perspiration
Musculature of hair follicle is stimulated: hair bristles, "goose pimples," chills	Arrectores pilorum	Inhibition of arrectores pilorum: skin becomes smooth and warm
Inhibition of the contractive musculature: bronchi are relaxed	Bronchial musculature	Stimulates the contraction of the bronchial musculature: bronchi are narrowed
Stimulates cardiac action: palpitation, rapid heart beat	Heart	Slows cardiac action: quiet heart, slower pulse
Inhibits peristalsis: reduces secretion of digestive glands	Digestive tract from esophagus to rectum, liver, pancreas, kidneys, all digestive glands	Stimulates peristalsis: increases secretion of digestive glands
Increases adrenal secretion: anxiety reaction	Suprarenal gland	Reduces adrenal secretion: pleasure reaction
Inhibits musculature of the bladder, stimulates urinary sphincter: inhibits micturition	Urinary bladder	Stimulates musculature of the bladder, inhibits the sphincter: stimulates micturition

(*cont. on next page*)

Functioning of the Autonomic Nervous System

Sympathetic Effect	Organ	Parasympathetic Effect
Tightening of the smooth musculature, reduces secretion of all glands, decrease of blood supply, dry vagina: reduction of sexual feeling	Female sex organs	Relaxation of the smooth musculature, stimulates all gland functions, increases blood flow, moist vagina: increase of sexual feeling
Tightening of the smooth musculature of the scrotum, reduction of gland functions, decrease of blood supply, flaccid penis: "diminished sexual desire"	Male sex organs	Relaxation of the smooth musculature of the scrotum, increases all secretions, increases blood flow, erection: "intensified sexual desire"

arises. There must be a *vegetative center* from which the biological energy issues and to which it returns. This question provides the connecting link to well-known facts of physiology. In the abdominal region, the so-called seat of the emotions, we find the generators of biophysical energy. They are the large centers of the autonomic nervous system, essentially the solar plexus, the hypogastric plexus, and the lumbosacral plexus. A glance at the anatomy of the vegetative nervous system will easily convince us that the vegetative ganglia are most dense in the abdominal and genital regions. The diagrams on the following pages show the functional relation between center and periphery.

The attempt to introduce meaning into the apparent illogicality succeeded when I investigated the vegetative innervation of the respective organs, first with reference to the biological expansion and then with reference to the contraction of the total organism. In other words, I asked myself how the respective organs would normally function in pleasure and in anxiety, and in which way the autonomic innervation would have to take place in the process. When investigated with reference to the total function of the organism,

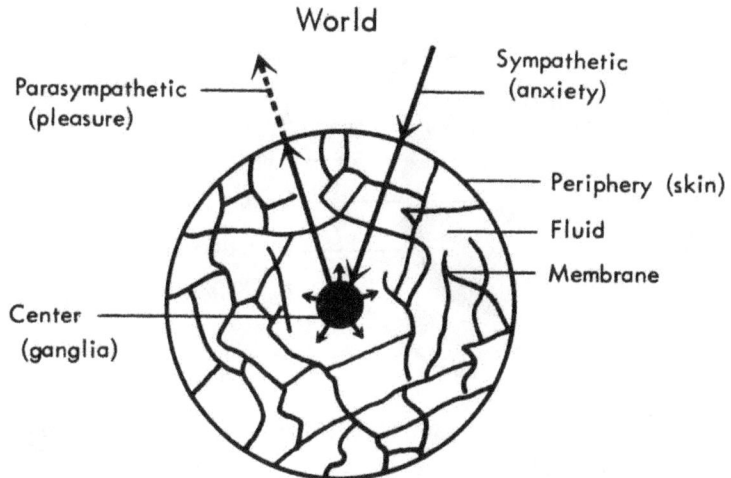

Diagram a): The basic functions of the vegetative nervous system

the seemingly contradictory innervation proved to be entirely logical and understandable.

This can be most convincingly demonstrated by the antithesis between the innervation of the heart, i.e., the "center," and of the blood vessels and muscles, i.e., the "periphery." The parasympathetic nervous system dilates the blood vessels, enhancing the flow of blood to the periphery and inhibiting the action of the heart. The sympathetic nervous system contracts the peripheral blood vessels, thereby impeding

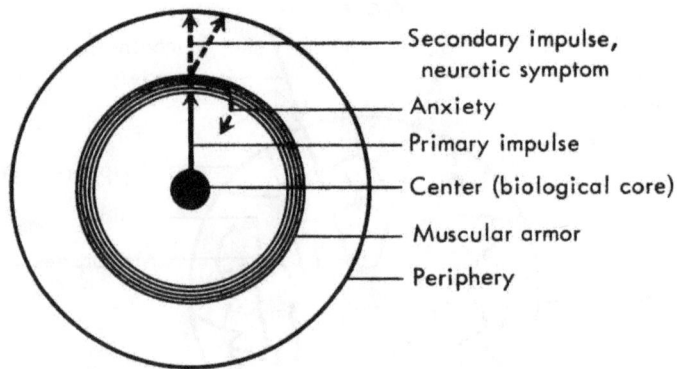

Diagram b): The same functions in an armored organism. The inhibition of the primary impulse produces a secondary impulse and anxiety

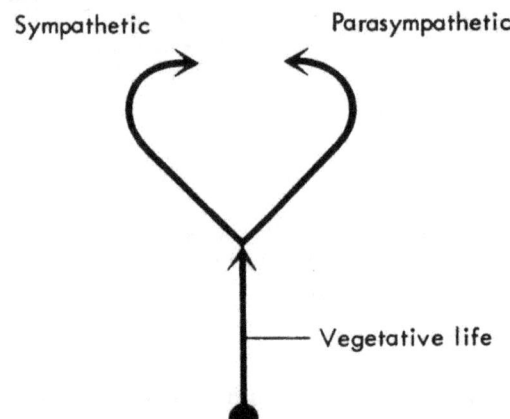

Diagram c): The unity and antithesis of the autonomic nervous system

the flow of the blood to the periphery and stimulating the action of the heart. In terms of the total organism, the antithesis in the innervation is understandable, for in anxiety, the heart has to overcome the peripheral inhibition, whereas in pleasure, it can work quietly and slowly. *There is a functional antithesis between periphery and center.*

The sympathetic anxiety function becomes coherent and meaningful when we bear in mind that the same nerve which inhibits the salivary gland stimulates adrenal secretion (i.e., produces anxiety). This is also true in the case of the urinary bladder. The sympathetic nervous system stimulates the muscle which prevents micturition. The parasympathetic nervous system has the opposite effect, relaxing or inhibiting the same muscle. In terms of the total organism, it is also significant that in pleasure the pupils are narrowed by the parasympathetic (corresponding to the diaphragm of a camera), thus sharpening vision. In apprehensive paralysis, on the other hand, vision is dimmed, due to the dilatation of the pupils.

The reduction of the autonomic innervations to the basic biological functions of expansion and contraction of the total organism was of course an important step forward, and at the same time a good test of the tenability of my biological hypothesis. According to this hypothesis, the parasympathetic nervous system always stimulates the organs when, whether to make them tense or to bring about a relaxation, the total organism is in a state of pleasurable expansion. On the other hand, the sympathetic nervous system stimulates all organs in a biologically significant way when the total organism is in a state of anxious contraction. This enables us to comprehend the life process, respiration in particular, as a condition of continuous oscillation, in which the organism is continually alternating between parasympathetic expansion (*exhalation*) and sympathetic contraction (*inhalation*). In making these theoretical deductions, I pictured to myself the rhythmic movement of an amoeba, a jellyfish, or an animal heart. The function of respiration is too complicated to be briefly described here in terms of these new insights.

Expansion and movement   Return to spherical shape produced by strong electrical stimulus

The flow of plasma in the amoeba in expansion and contraction

If the biological oscillation is disturbed in one direction or the other, i.e., if the function of expansion or the function of contraction predominates, then there must also be a disturbance of the general biological balance. Persistence of the state of expansion is indicative of a general *parasympatheticotonia*. Conversely, the persistence of a state of anxious contraction indicates *sympatheticotonia*. Thus, all somatic conditions which are known clinically as cardiovascular hypertension became understandable as conditions of chronic sympatheticotonic attitudes of anxiety. Central to this general sympatheticotonia is orgasm anxiety, that is, fear of expansion and involuntary convulsion.

The physiological literature contained many reports on investigations and findings pertaining to the manifold facts of autonomic innervation. Initially, my theory of sex-economy was notable not because it had discovered new facts in this field, but because it had reduced generally known innervations to a universally valid basic biological formula. The theory of the orgasm could take pride in having made an important contribution to the understanding of the physiology of the organism. This unification led to the discovery of new facts.

I wrote a short monograph, *Der Urgegensatz des vegetativen Lebens,* and published it in Denmark, in 1934, in the *Zeitschrift für Sexualökonomie und Politische Psychologie,* a periodical which came into existence following my break with the International Psychoanalytic Association. It was not until several years later that this article received attention and recognition in biological and psychiatric circles.

A detailed report on the painful proceedings at the thirteenth psychoanalytic congress in Lucerne, in August 1934, was given in the above-named periodical. For purposes of general orientation, therefore, I can be very brief here. When I arrived in Lucerne, I learned from the secretary of the German Psychoanalytic Society, of which I had been a member, that I had been expelled in 1933, following my relocation to Vienna. I had not been notified of this, and no one had found it necessary to inform me of the reasons for my expulsion. Finally I was told that my work on mass psychology,[3] which was directed against the irrationalism of fascism, had placed me in a much too exposed position. Hence, my membership in the International Psychoanalytic Association was no longer tenable. Four years later, Freud had to flee Vienna for London, and the psychoanalytic groups were crushed by the fascists. By joining the Norwegian group, I could have been reinstated as a member of the International Psychoanalytic Association. In the interest of preserving my independence, I rejected this possibility.

Subsequently, I avoided contact with my earlier colleagues. Their behavior was neither better nor worse than is usual in such cases. It was low and uninteresting. A good dose of banality is all that is needed to hush up a matter. Only *one* psychoanalyst, in the general embarrassment, hit

---

[3] Cf. Reich, *The Mass Psychology of Fascism,* Farrar, Straus and Giroux, 1970.

upon the bright idea that I was schizophrenic; he was eagerly intent upon making his diagnosis known the world over. However, since I knew I had the key to the biological function of neurosis, there was no need for me to be irritated by these indecencies.

CHAPTER VIII

THE ORGASM REFLEX AND THE TECHNIQUE OF CHARACTER-ANALYTIC VEGETOTHERAPY

1. MUSCULAR ATTITUDE AND BODY EXPRESSION

In character-analytic work, we begin by trying, in a consistent and systematic way, to isolate from one another the interlaced character attitudes and to unmask them one by one as defense functions in terms of their *contemporary* meaning and effectiveness. Our purpose is to release the affects which at one time were subject to severe inhibition and fixation. This is accomplished by loosening the incrustations of the character. Every successful dissolution of a character incrustation first liberates the emotions of anger or anxiety. By also treating these liberated emotions as psychic defense mechanisms, we eventually succeed in restoring to the patient his sexual motility and biological sensitivity. Thus, *by dissolving chronic character attitudes, we bring about reactions in the vegetative nervous system*. The breakthrough into the biological realm is that much more complete and energy-charged, the more thoroughly we treat not only the character attitudes, but also the muscular attitudes corresponding to them. This causes a part of the work to be shifted from the psychological and characterological realms to the immediate dissolution of the *muscular armor*. It has, of course, been clear for some time that the muscular rigidity, wherever it appears, is not a "result," an "expression," or a "concomitant" of the mechanism of repression. In the final analysis, I could not rid myself of the impression that somatic rigidity represents the most essential part in the process of repression. All our patients report that they went through periods in childhood in which, by means of certain practices in vegetative behavior (holding the breath, tensing the abdominal muscular pressure, etc.), they learned to suppress their impulses of hate, anxiety, and love. Until now, analytic psychology has merely concerned itself with *what* the child suppresses and what the motives are which cause him to learn to control his emotions. It did not inquire into the *way* in which children habitually fight against impulses. *It is precisely the physiological process of repression* that deserves our keenest attention. It never ceases to be surprising how the loosening of a muscular spasm not only releases the vegetative energy, but, over and above this, reproduces a memory of that situation in infancy in which the repression of the instinct occurred. It can be said *that every muscular rigidity contains the history and the meaning of its origin*. It is not as if we had to derive from dreams or associations how the muscular armor developed; the armor is the form in which the infantile experience is preserved as an impairment of functioning. For instance, the neurosis is not solely the expression of a disturbance of psychic equilibrium; it is, rather, in a far more justified and deeper sense, the *expression of a chronic disturbance of the vegetative equilibrium and of natural motility*.

The term "psychic structure" has, in the course of the past years of our research, acquired a special meaning. We understand by this term the characteristic features of a person's *spontaneous* reactions, i.e., what characterizes him as the result of the antithetical forces functioning within him. In other words, *the psychic structure is at the same time a biophysiological structure* which represents a specific state indicative of the interplay of a person's vegetative forces. There can be no doubt that most of what people are in the habit of describing as "disposition" or "instinctual constitution" will prove to be acquired vegetative behavior. The restructuralization we bring about is nothing other than a change in the interplay of forces in the vegetative life apparatus.

For character-analytic therapy, the muscular attitudes take on another importance also. They offer the possibility of avoiding, when necessary, the complicated detour via the psychic structure and of breaking through to the affects directly from the somatic attitude. In this way, the repressed affect appears before the corresponding remembrance. Such an approach provides a sure guarantee for the liberation of the affects, provided that the chronic muscular attitude has been successfully understood and dissolved. When one attempts to liberate the affects solely by means of work in the psychological realm, one releases the affects as a matter of chance. The character-analytic work on the layers of the character incrustation is more effective the more completely it helps to dissolve the corresponding muscular attitude. In many cases, a psychic inhibition will give way only to direct loosening of the muscular contraction.

The muscular attitude is identical with what we call "body expression." Very often it is not possible to know whether or not a patient is muscularly hypertonic. Nonetheless, his whole body or parts of it "express something." For instance, his forehead might appear "flat," or his pelvis might convey the impression of being "lifeless." His shoulders might appear "hard" or "soft." It is not easy to say what makes it possible for us to gain a direct impression of a person's body expression and to find the right words to express what we perceive. In this connection, we are reminded of the loss of spontaneous expression in children, the first and most important manifestation of the final sexual suppression which takes place in the fourth to fifth year of life. This quality is always first experienced as "dying," "being armored," or "being immured." In some cases, this feeling of "dying" or "being dead" may be later partially compensated for by camouflaging psychic attitudes, e.g., superficial joviality or contactless sociability.

The spasm of the musculature is the somatic side of the process of repression, and the basis of its continued preservation. It is never individual muscles which become spastic, but rather muscle groups that belong to a functional unity, in the vegetative sense. When, for example, an impulse to cry is to be suppressed, it is not solely the lower lip which is tense but also the entire musculature of the mouth and jaw, as well as the corresponding musculature of the throat; in short, those organs which are brought into action as a functional unit in the act of crying. We are reminded in this connection of the well-known phenomenon that hysterical persons demarcate their somatic symptoms not according to anatomical but according to functional areas. A hysterical blushing does not follow the ramification of a certain artery; rather it involves almost exclusively the neck or forehead. The vegetative body function is ignorant of the anatomical demarcations, which are artificial designations.

The total expression of the body can usually be condensed in a word or formula which, sooner or later in the course of the character-analytic treatment, suggests itself. Strangely enough, they are usually formulas and names derived from the animal kingdom, such as "fox," "pig," "snake," "worm," etc.

The spastic muscle group does not reveal its function until the work of elucidation has reached it in a "logical way." For instance, it would be fruitless to attempt to dissolve an abdominal tension right at the outset of the treatment. The dissolving of the muscle spasm obeys a law, all the preconditions of which are not yet known. Insofar as one can venture a judgment on the basis of experiences to date, the dissolving of the muscular armor generally begins with those parts of the body, usually the head, which are furthest away from the genitals. It is the facial attitude that is most conspicuous. Facial expression and tone of voice are also those functions which the patient himself most frequently and most carefully pays attention to and feels. The attitudes of the pelvis, shoulders, and abdomen are usually concealed.

I want now to describe the most important characteristics and mechanisms of a number of typical muscular attitudes; the list is far from exhaustive.

Head and neck: severe headache is a symptom found in many patients. Very often it is localized above the neck, over the eyes, or on the forehead. In psychopathology, these headaches are usually described as "neurasthenic symptoms." How do they come about? If one tries to strain the musculature of the neck for a long period of time, as if to ward off an imminent blow, one soon senses the emergence of pain at the back of the head; as a matter of fact, above the spot at which the musculature is being tensed. Hence, pain at the back of the head can be traced to an overstraining of the neck muscles. This attitude expresses a continual anxiety that something dangerous could happen from behind, e.g., that one could be seized by the neck, knocked over the head, etc.

The supraorbital headache, which is felt as "a tight band around the head" is produced by a chronic raising of the eyebrows. This sensation can be duplicated by keeping the eyebrows raised over a period of time. It also produces a continual tension in the muscles of the forehead, as well as in the entire musculature of the scalp. This attitude expresses continuous anxious expectancy in the eyes. Eyes wide with fear would correspond to the extreme expression of this attitude.

Fundamentally, these two symptoms, which are expressed

in attitudes of the head, belong together. In sudden fright, the eyes are opened wide, and, at the same time, the musculature of the scalp is tensed. Some patients have a facial expression that could be described as "haughty." The dissolution of this expression shows it to be a defense attitude against nervous or apprehensive attentiveness in the face. Some patients feign "the forehead of a thinker." It is unusual to find such a patient who, in his childhood, has not created a fantasy of being a genius. Usually, this facial attitude is the result of a defense against anxiety, mostly of a masturbational nature. In other patients, we observe a "smooth," "flat," or "expressionless" forehead. Fear of being struck over the head is always the motive for this expression.

Of far greater importance, and also appearing with greater frequency, are spasms of the mouth, chin, and throat. Many people have a masklike facial expression. The chin is thrust forward and looks broad; the neck just below the chin has a lifeless appearance. The two lateral neck muscles, which run down to the breastbone, stand out as thick cords; the floor of the mouth is tense. Such patients often suffer from nausea. Their voices are usually low, monotonous, or "thin." This attitude can also be tested on oneself. Imagine that you are suppressing an impulse to cry. The muscles of the floor of the mouth will become very tense, the entire musculature of the head will be put in a condition of continual tension, the chin will be thrust forward, and the mouth will be tight.

In this condition, one will try in vain to speak loudly and resonantly. Children often acquire such conditions at a very early age, when they are forced to suppress violent impulses to cry. Continual concentration of attention on a certain part of the body invariably results in a fixation of the corresponding innervation. If the said attitude is the same as the one which a person would take under other circumstances, a coupling of the two functions often occurs. Quite frequently, I have found the coupling of nausea and the impulse to cry. Closer investigation reveals that the two provoke approximately the same response in the muscles of the floor of the mouth. There is no possibility of eliminating nausea if the tension on the floor of the mouth is not discovered, because this nausea is the result of the inhibition of another impulse, namely the impulse to cry. Before the chronic sensation of nausea can be eliminated, the inhibition of the impulse to cry has to be completely dissolved.

The way one speaks is of special importance in the region of the head and face. It can usually be traced back to spasms of the muscles of the jaw and throat. In two patients, I was able to ascertain a violent defense-reflex in the neck which appeared immediately when I touched, however slightly, the region of the larynx. Fantasies of being choked or having the throat cut were found in both patients.

The total expression of the face must be given considerable attention, independently of the individual parts. We are familiar with the depressed face of the melancholic person. It is remarkable how an expression of languor can be combined with the most extreme and chronic tension of the musculature. There are people who affect a continuously radiating face; there are those whose cheeks are "stiff" or "sagging." The patients themselves usually find the corresponding term, if their attitude is continuously pointed out and precisely described to them, or if it is imitated for a while.

A female patient having "stiff cheeks" said, "My cheeks are heavy with tears." Suppressed crying easily leads to a masklike tightness of the facial muscles. In very early childhood, children develop a fear of the "funny faces" they were once so happy to make, but were threateningly told not to. The result of an inhibition of the corresponding impulse is that they keep their faces stiffly controlled.

2. ABDOMINAL TENSION

I shall defer a description of the symptoms of the chest and the shoulders, because it is more advantageous to consider them after discussion of the abdominal musculature. There is not a single neurotic person who does not show a "tension in the abdomen." It would have little meaning here to list and describe the symptoms, without understanding their function in neurosis.

Today, it seems incomprehensible to me that it could have been possible to resolve neuroses even to some extent without being familiar with the importance of the *solar plexus;* abdominal tension has become such an indispensable factor in our work. The respiratory disturbances in neuroses are the symptoms which result from abdominal tensions. Imagine that you have been frightened or that you anticipate great danger. You will involuntarily suck in your breath and hold it. Since respiration cannot cease entirely, you will soon breathe out again, but the exhalation will not be complete. It will be shallow. You will not exhale fully, only by snatches—not in one breath. In a state of apprehension, the shoulders are involuntarily pulled forward and remain in this cramped attitude. In some instances, the shoulders are also pulled up. If this attitude is maintained for a period of time, a pressure is felt in the forehead. I treated several patients in whom I did not succeed in eliminating the pressure in the forehead until I had discovered the attitude of fearful expectancy in the musculature of the chest.

What is the function of this attitude of "shallow breathing"? If we examine the position of the internal organs and their relation to the solar plexus, we shall immediately comprehend the situation we are dealing with here. In a state of fright, one involuntarily breathes in; we are reminded of the involuntary inhalation which takes place in drowning and actually causes death. The diaphragm contracts and exerts pressure upon the solar plexus from above. The function of this muscular action becomes completely understandable when we examine the results of the character-analytic investigation of early infantile defense mechanisms. It is by holding their breath that children are in the habit of fighting against continual and tormenting conditions of anxiety which they sense in the upper abdomen. They do the same thing when they sense pleasurable sensations in the abdomen or in the genitals, and are afraid of these sensations.

Respiratory inhibition and the fixation of the diaphragm is doubtlessly one of the first and most important acts in suppressing pleasurable sensations in the abdomen, as well as curtailing "abdominal anxiety." Added to this respiratory attitude is the effect of abdominal pressure. Everyone is familiar with these vegetative sensations in the abdomen. They are described in various ways. We hear complaints about an unbearable "pressure" in the abdomen or laments about a girdle around the upper abdomen which "constricts." In others, there is a certain place in the abdomen which is very sensitive. Everyone is afraid of being kicked in the stomach, and this fear becomes the center of copious fantasies. Some feel blocked in the stomach, or else feel that a foreign object is there. They say, "There is something in my stomach that can't come out"; "I feel as if I had a dinner plate in my stomach"; "My belly is dead"; "I have to hold my belly"; etc. Almost all children's fantasies about pregnancy and birth cluster around their vegetative abdominal sensations.

If, without frightening the patient, pressure is put on the abdominal surface with two fingers, about three centimeters below the lower end of the sternum, sooner or later a reflex-like resistive tension or a persistent resistance is noticed. The abdominal content is being protected. Patients who complain about a chronic girdle-like tension, or a feeling of pressure, show a rigid upper abdominal musculature that is as hard as a board. Thus, a double pressure is exerted upon the solar plexus—by the abdominal musculature from the front and by the diaphragm from above. As I have already established, the electrical potential of the skin of the abdomen is reduced by 10 to 30 mv when direct pressure is applied, as well as when the person breathes in deeply.

I once treated a female patient who was on the verge of a severe melancholic illness. Her musculature was in a condition of chronic tension. She was depressed and, throughout a whole year, could not be induced to permit the stirring of even the slightest emotion. For a long time, I did not understand how she managed to cope with the most difficult situations without affect. Finally, the situation became clear. At the slightest stirring of feeling, she would "adjust something in her stomach," hold her breath, and stare blankly into space. Her eyes looked empty; they seemed to be "turned inward." The abdominal wall became tense, and the buttocks were pulled in. She said later, "I make my belly dead; then I don't feel anything any more—otherwise my belly has a bad conscience." What she meant was, "Otherwise it has sexual feelings *and, therefore,* a bad conscience."

The way in which our children achieve this "shutting-off feeling in the stomach," with the help of respiration and abdominal pressure, is typical and universal. Vegetotherapy has to fight hard against this technique of controlling emotions, against this universal "Yogism."

How is it possible for the respiratory block to suppress or completely eliminate affects? This question was of decisive importance. For it was clear now that, as the physiological mechanism for the suppression and repression of affects, the inhibition of respiration was the basic mechanism of neurosis in general. Simple deliberation indicated that biologically, respiration has the function of introducing oxygen into the organism and of removing carbon dioxide. The oxygen of the introduced air brings about the combustion of the digested foodstuffs. Chemically speaking, combustion means everything which takes place in the fusion of substances with oxygen. This process generates energy. Without oxygen, there is no combustion and, therefore, no production of energy. In the organism, energy is produced through the combustion of foodstuffs. In that way, heat and kinetic energy are generated. Bioelectricity is also produced in this process of combustion. In reduced respiration, less oxygen is introduced, actually only as much as is necessary for the preservation of life. With less energy in the organism, the vegetative excitations are less intense and, therefore, easier to control. Viewed biologically, the inhibition of respiration in neurotics has the function of reducing the production of energy in the organism and, hence, of reducing the production of anxiety.

3. THE ORGASM REFLEX—A CASE HISTORY

To describe the direct release of sexual (vegetative) energies from the pathological muscular attitudes, I am choosing a patient in whom orgastic potency was established rapidly. I want to make it quite clear at the outset that this case does not claim to represent the great difficulties which are usually encountered in overcoming disturbances of the orgasm.

A twenty-seven-year-old technician came to me because of his addiction to alcohol. He suffered from the fact that he had to give in almost every day to the urge to become inebriated; he feared the complete ruin of his health and capacity for work. When he was with his friends, he could do nothing against the temptation to get drunk. His marriage was a shambles. His wife was an extremely complicated hysteric who did not make life easy for him. It was immediately evident that the wretchedness of this marriage constituted an important motive for his escape into alcoholism. He further complained that he "did not feel life." In spite of his unhappy marriage, he could not bring himself to form a liaison with another woman. He did not derive any pleasure from his work; he performed it mechanically, listlessly, without any interest. He said that if it went on like this, he would soon break down. This condition had already lasted a number of years, and had become appreciably worse in the last months.

Conspicuous among his pathological traits was the fact that he was incapable of any aggression. He always felt compelled to be "nice and polite," to agree with everything people said, even when they expressed opposite, mutually contradictory opinions. He suffered under the superficiality that ruled his life. He could not really and seriously devote himself to any cause, idea, or work. He spent his leisure hours in cafés and restaurants, engaging in empty, meaningless chatter and exchanging stale witticisms. True, he sensed there was something pathological in his attitude; at the same time, he was not fully aware of the pathological meaning of these traits. He was suffering from the widespread illness, a misconstrued contactless sociality, which becomes rigid compulsion and inwardly devastates many people.

The general impression given by this patient was marked by the uncertainty of his movements; the forced jauntiness of his walk made him appear somewhat awkward. The attitude of his body was not rigid; rather it expressed submission, as if he were continually on his guard. His facial expression was empty and without any particular distinguishing features. There was a slight shininess to the skin of his face; it was drawn tight and had the effect of a mask. His forehead appeared "flat." His mouth gave the impression of being small and tight. It hardly moved in the act of speaking; his lips were narrow, as if pressed together. His eyes were devoid of expression.

In spite of this obviously severe impairment of his vegetative motility, one sensed a very lively, intelligent nature beneath the surface. It was doubtlessly this factor that enabled him to tackle his difficulties with great energy.

The ensuing treatment lasted six and one half months, with one session each day. I want to try to describe its most important stages.

At the very first session, I was faced with the question of whether I should first consider his psychic reserve or his very striking facial expression. I decided in favor of the latter, leaving it to the further course of the treatment as to when and in what form I would deal with his psychic reserve. Following the consistent description of the rigid attitude of his mouth, a clonic twitching of his lips set in, weak at first but growing gradually stronger. He was surprised by the involuntary nature of this twitching and defended himself against it. I told him to give in to every impulse. Thereupon, his lips began to protrude and retract rhythmically and to hold the protruded position for several seconds as if in a tonic spasm. In the course of these movements, his face took on the unmistakable expression of an infant. The patient was startled, grew fearful, and asked me what this might lead to. I allayed his fears and asked him to continue to give in to every impulse and to tell me whenever he sensed the inhibition of an impulse.

During the following sessions, the various manifestations in his face became more and more distinct, and they gradually aroused the patient's interest. This must have some special meaning, he said. What was very peculiar, however, was that he appeared not to be emotionally affected by these somatic manifestations; indeed, he was able to speak to me calmly following such a clonic or tonic excitation of his face. During one of the subsequent sessions, the twitching of his mouth increased to a suppressed crying. He also uttered sounds like the outbreak of a long-suppressed, painful sob. My insistence that he give in to every muscular impulse bore fruit. The described activity of his face grew more complicated. While his mouth became twisted into a spasmodic crying, this expression did not resolve itself into tears. To our surprise, it passed over into a distorted expression of anger. Strangely enough, however, the patient did not feel the slightest anger, though he knew quite well that it was anger.

When these muscular actions grew especially strong, making his face blue, he became apprehensive and restless. He repeatedly wanted to know where this was leading and what was happening to him in these actions. I began now to draw his attention to the fact that his fear of an unexpected happening was entirely in keeping with his general character attitude, namely that he was dominated by a vague fear of the unforeseeable, of something that might suddenly overwhelm him.

Since I did not want to abandon the consistent pursuit of a somatic attitude once I had attacked it, I had first to ascertain how his muscular facial actions were related to the general defense attitude of his character. If the muscular rigidity had not been so distinct, I would have begun by working on the character defense as manifested in his reserve. However, I was now forced to conclude that there was obviously a split in the psychic conflict which dominated him. The defense function was performed at this time by his general psychic reserve, while that which he warded off, i.e., the vegetative excitation, was revealed in the muscle actions of his face. Fortunately, it occurred to me that not only the warded-off affect but also the defense was represented in his muscular attitude. The smallness and cramped attitude of his mouth could, of course, be nothing other than the expression of its opposite, the protruding, twitching, crying mouth. I now proceeded to carry out the experiment of consistently destroying the defense forces, not from the psychic but from the muscular side.

Thus, I worked on all the muscular attitudes of his face which, I assumed, represented spasms, i.e., hypertonic defenses against the corresponding muscular actions. Several weeks passed before the actions of the musculature of his face and neck intensified into the following picture: the contracted attitude of his mouth first gave way to a clonic twitching and then became transformed into a protrusion of the lips. This protrusion resolved itself into crying, which, however, did not break out completely. In turn, the crying was replaced by an exceedingly strong reaction of anger on his face. His mouth became distorted, the musculature of his jaws became as stiff as a board, and he grit his teeth. In addition, there were other expressive movements. The patient sat half up on the couch, shook with anger, raised his fist as if he were going to strike a blow, without, however, following through. Then, out of breath, he sank back exhausted. The whole action dissolved into a whimpering kind of weeping. These actions expressed "impotent rage," as is often experienced by children with adults.

When this attack had subsided, he spoke about it tranquilly, as if nothing had happened. It was clear that somewhere there was a break in the connection between his vegetative muscular excitation and the psychic perception of this excitation. Naturally, I continually discussed with him not only the sequence and the content of his muscular actions, but also the strange phenomenon of his psychic detachment from these actions. What was particularly striking to both of us was the fact that, in spite of his lack of emotional involvement, he had an immediate comprehension of the function and meaning of these episodes. I did not even have to interpret them to him. On the contrary, he surprised me again and again with elucidations that were immediately evident to him. I found this most gratifying. I recalled the many years of painstaking work of interpreting symptoms, in the process of which the analyst inferred an anger or anxiety on the basis of associations or symptoms and then, through months and years, tried, at least to some extent, to make the patient aware of it. How seldom and how ineffectively one succeeded in those days in arriving at anything more than an intellectual understanding. Thus, I had good reason to be pleased that the patient had an immediate grasp of the meaning of his action, without any explanation on my part. He knew that he was expressing an overwhelming anger which he had kept locked up in himself for decades. The emotional detachment subsided when an attack produced the remembrance of his older brother, who had very much dominated and mistreated him as a child.

He understood now without any promptings from me that he had at that time suppressed his anger against his brother, who had been his mother's darling. To ward off this anger, he had adopted toward his brother an agreeable and loving attitude, which was at violent odds with his true feelings. He had not wanted to incur his mother's displeasure. The anger which had not been expressed at that time now rose up in his actions, as if unaffected by the intervening decades.

At this point, we have to pause a moment and form a clear picture of the psychic situation with which we are dealing. Analysts who use the old technique of symptom interpretation know that they work with remembrances and have to leave it more or less to chance whether

1. the corresponding remembrances of earlier experiences also emerge, and

2. the emerging experiences are actually those in which the strongest and, in terms of the patient's future, the most important excitations were developed.

In vegetotherapy, on the other hand, the vegetative behavior necessarily produces the memory which was decisive for the development of the neurotic character trait.

It is known that the approach which proceeds solely on the basis of remembrances accomplishes this task to a very limited degree. In assessing the changes in a patient after years of this kind of treatment, one realizes that they are not worth the expenditure of so much time and energy. The patients in whom one succeeds in getting directly at the vegetative sexual energy bound in the musculature produce the affect before they know what affect they are dealing with. Furthermore, the memory of the experience which originally produced the affect automatically emerges without any effort. An example of this would be our patient's remembrance of the situation with his brother, who was preferred by the mother. This fact cannot be overemphasized; it is as important as it is typical. It is not that under certain circumstances a memory brings about an affect, but that *the concentration of a vegetative excitation and its breakthrough reproduces the remembrance.* Freud continually stressed that, in analysis, the analyst was dealing solely with "derivatives of the unconscious," that the unconscious was like "a thing in itself," i.e., was not really tangible. This contention was correct, but not absolute. It pertained to the methods used at that time, by which the unconscious could be inferred only through its derivatives, and could not be grasped in its actual form. Today, we succeed in comprehending the unconscious not in its derivatives, but in its reality, by directly attacking the binding of vegetative energy. For instance, our patient did not deduce his hatred of his brother from vague associations having but little affect.

Rather, he acted as he would have acted in the original situation, as he would have acted if his hatred of his brother had not been offset by the fear of losing his mother's love. Moreover, we know that there are childhood experiences which have never become conscious. It became evident from the subsequent course of the analysis that, while the patient had always been intellectually conscious of his envy of his brother, he had no awareness of the extent and intensity of the rage he had actually mobilized in himself. As we know, the effects of a psychic experience are determined not by its content, but by the amount of vegetative energy which is mobilized by this experience. In the compulsion neurosis, for instance, even incest desires are sometimes conscious. We contend, however, that they are "unconscious" because they have lost their emotional charge. And we have all had the experience that, using the conventional analytic method, it is not possible to make the compulsion neurotic conscious of the incest desire, except in an intellectual form. Frankly speaking, this means that the repression has not been eliminated. To illustrate, let us return to the further course of this treatment.

The more intense the muscular actions of the face became, the more the somatic excitation, still wholly cut off from psychic recognition, spread toward the chest and abdomen. Several weeks later, the patient reported that in the course of twitchings in his chest, but especially when these twitchings subsided, he sensed "currents" moving toward his lower abdomen. During this time, he left his wife with the intention of forming a liaison with another woman. However, it was revealed in the course of the following weeks that the intended liaison had not materialized. Initially, the patient was indifferent to this. Only after I had drawn his attention to it did he try, after venturing a number of seemingly plausible explanations, to take an interest in the matter. But it was quite evident that an inner prohibition prevented him from dealing with this problem in a really affective manner. Since it is not customary in character-analytic work to deal with a subject, no matter how topical, unless the patient enters upon it of his own accord in a fully affective way, I postponed a discussion of this problem and continued to pursue the approach dictated by the spreading of his muscular actions.

The tonic spasm of the musculature spread to his chest and upper abdomen. In these attacks, it was as if an inner force lifted him up from the couch against his will and held him up. The muscles of his abdominal wall and chest were boardlike. It took some time before I understood why a further spreading downward of the excitation failed to occur. I had expected that the vegetative excitation would now spread from the abdomen to the pelvis, but this did not happen. Instead, there were strong, clonic twitchings of the musculature of the legs, and a marked intensification of the patellar reflex. To my complete amazement, the patient told me that he experienced the twitchings of his leg musculature in a highly agreeable way. Quite involuntarily, I was reminded of epileptic clonisms, and my view was confirmed that in both the epileptic and epileptiform muscular convulsions, we are dealing with the release of anxiety which can only be experienced in an agreeable, i.e., pleasurable manner. There were times in the treatment of this patient when I was uncertain whether or not I was confronted with a true epileptic. Superficially, at least, the patient's attacks, which commenced tonically and occasionally subsided clonically, showed very little difference from epileptic seizures. I want to stress that, at this stage of the treatment, which had been in progress for roughly three months, the musculature of his head, chest, and upper abdomen, as well as the musculature of his legs, particularly of his knees and upper thighs, had become mobile. His lower abdomen and pelvis were and remained immobile. The gap between his muscular actions and the patient's perception of them also remained unchanged. The patient knew about the attack. He was able to comprehend its significance, but he did not experience it emotionally. The main question continued to be: what caused this gap? It became increasingly clear that the patient was resisting the comprehension of the whole in all of its parts. We both knew that he was very cautious. It was not only in his psychic attitude that this caution was expressed, nor in the fact that up to a certain point he was cooperative and adapted himself to the requirements of the work, and that when the work transgressed certain limits he somehow became unfriendly and cold. This "caution" was also contained in his muscular activity; it was, so to speak, doubly preserved. He himself described and comprehended his situation as follows: he is a boy being pursued by a man who wants to beat him. While making his escape, he dodges to the side a number of times, glances apprehensively over his shoulder, and pulls in his buttocks, as if to put them out of reach of the pursuer. In conventional analytic language, it would have been said that behind his fear of the blows, there is a fear of a homosexual attack. As a matter of fact, the patient had spent roughly a year in symptom interpretation analysis, during which his passive homosexuality had been continually interpreted. "In itself," this interpretation had been correct. From the point of view of our present knowledge, however, it is clear that it had been meaningless. There were too many factors in the patient which opposed a really affective comprehension of his homosexual attitude. For example, his characterological caution and the muscular binding of his energy, which were still far from resolved.

Now I began to deal with his caution, not from the psychic side, as I am usually in the habit of doing in character analysis, but from the somatic side. For instance, I pointed out again and again that, while it was true he revealed his anger in his muscular actions, he never followed through, never really struck with his clenched and raised fist. Several times, at the very moment the fist was about to strike the couch, his anger disappeared. From now on, I concentrated my effort on the blocking of the completion of the muscular action, always guided by the understanding that it was precisely his caution which he was expressing in this inhibition. After consistently working on the defense against the muscular action for a number of sessions, the following episode from his fifth year of life suddenly occurred to him: as a small boy he had lived near a cliff, which dropped off precipitously to the sea. One day, he was intensely involved in building a fire at the edge of the rocks; he was so immersed in his play that he was in danger of falling into the sea. His mother appeared in the doorway of their home, saw what he was doing, was frightened, and sought to draw him away from the cliff. She knew him to be a hyperactive child, and, precisely for this reason she was very much afraid. She lured him to her in a sweet voice, promising to give him candy. When he ran up to her, instead of keeping her promise, she gave him a terrible beating. This experience had made a deep impression on him, but now he understood it in connection with his defensive attitude toward women and the caution he demonstrated toward the treatment.

Yet, this did not put an end to the matter. The caution continued. One day, in the interval between two attacks, he humorously told me that he was an enthusiastic trout fisherman. He gave me a very impressive description of the joys of trout fishing; he enacted the corresponding movements, describing how one catches sight of the trout and how one throws out the line. In the act of telling and demonstrating this to me, he had an enormously greedy, almost sadistic expression on his face. It struck me that, while he gave an exact description of the entire procedure, he omitted one detail, namely the moment at which the trout bites into the hook. I understood the connection, but saw that he was unaware of the omission. In conventional psychoanalysis, the analyst would have told him the connection or would have encouraged him to comprehend it himself. For me, however, it was precisely this point that was of utmost importance, namely to find out why he had not described the actual catch, why he had omitted this detail. Roughly four weeks elapsed before the following took place: the twitching of various parts of his body lost more and more their spasmodic tonic character. The clonus also diminished and strange twitchings appeared in the abdomen. They were not new to me, for I had seen them in many other patients, but not in the connection in which they now revealed themselves. The upper part of his body jerked forward, the middle of his abdomen remained still, and the lower part of his body jerked toward the upper part. The entire response was an organic unitary movement. There were sessions in which this movement was repeated continuously. Alternating with this jerking of his entire body, there were sensations of current in some parts of his body, particularly in his legs and abdomen, which he experienced as pleasurable. The attitude of his mouth and face changed a little. In one such attack, his face had the unmistakable expression of a fish. Without any prompting on my part, before I had drawn his attention to it, the patient said, "I feel like a primordial animal," and shortly afterward, "I feel like a fish." What did all this mean? Without having any inkling of it, without having worked out a connection through associations, the patient represented in the movements of his body an obviously hooked, flapping fish. Expressed in the language of analytic interpretation, it would be said "he acted out" the caught trout. Everything about him expressed this: his mouth was spasmodically protruded, rigid, and distorted. His body jerked from the shoulders to the legs. His back was as stiff as a board. Not entirely intelligible in this phase was the fact that, with each jerk of his body, the patient for a time thrust his arms forward as if embracing someone. I no longer remember whether I drew the patient's attention to the relationship between these actions and the story of the trout, or whether he grasped it of his own accord. But he very definitely felt the connection immediately and had not the slightest doubt that he represented the trout as well as the trout fisherman.

Naturally, the whole incident was directly related to his disappointments in his mother. From a certain point in childhood, she had neglected him, treated him badly, and often beaten him. Quite often, he had expected something very nice or good from her, and had received the exact opposite. His caution became understandable now. He did not trust anyone; he did not want to be caught. This was the deepest reason for his superficiality, his fear of surrendering, of assuming real responsibility, etc. In the process of working through this connection, his personality underwent a conspicuous change. His superficiality disappeared; he became serious. The seriousness appeared very suddenly during one of the sessions. The patient said literally, "I don't understand; everything has become so deadly serious all of a sudden." Thus, he did not merely recall the serious emotional attitude he had had at a certain period of his childhood; he actually changed from being superficial to being serious. It became clear that his pathological relationship to women, i.e., his fear of forming a liaison with a woman, of giving himself to a woman, was connected with this anxiety which was rooted in his character and had become part of his structure. He was a man whom women found very attractive; strangely enough, he had made little use of this fact.

From now on, the somatic sensations of current increased visibly and rapidly, first in his abdomen, then also in his legs and upper body. He described these sensations not only as currents, but also as voluptuous and "sweet." This was especially the case when strong, lively, and rapid abdominal twitchings occurred.

Let us pause a moment to review the patient's situation at this stage of the treatment.

The abdominal twitchings were nothing other than the expression of the fact that the tonic tension of the musculature of his abdominal wall was subsiding. The entire reaction was like a reflex. When his abdomen was tapped lightly, the twitching was immediately evoked. After several twitchings, the abdominal wall was soft and could be pressed in deeply. Previously, it had been extremely taut and displayed a phenomenon which, conditionally, I should like to call abdominal defense. This phenomenon exists in all neurotics, without exception, whenever they are told to breathe out fully and a slight pressure is applied to the abdominal wall approximately three centimeters below the end of the sternum. When this is done, there is either a strong resistance inside the abdomen or pain is experienced similar to that felt when pressure is exerted on the testicles. A glance at the position of the abdominal contents and of the solar plexus shows us that, together with other phenomena still to be discussed, abdominal tension has the function of enclosing the plexus. The abdominal wall exerts pressure on it. The same function is fulfilled by the tense and downward-extended diaphragm. This, too, is a typical symptom. A tonic contraction of the diaphragm is discernible, without exception, in all individuals who are neurotic; it is expressed in a tendency to breathe out only in a shallow and interrupted manner. The diaphragm is raised in exhalation; the pressure on the organs below it, including the solar plexus, is diminished. Apparently, a freeing of the autonomic plexus from the pressure exerted upon it is dependent upon the relaxation of the diaphragm and the musculature of the abdominal wall. It is manifested in the appearance of a sensation like that experienced in the upper abdomen in swinging, in the descent of an elevator, and in falling. On the basis of my experiences, I have to assume that we are dealing here with an extremely important phenomenon. Almost all patients remember that as children they held down and suppressed these sensations in the upper abdomen which are felt quite intensely in anger or anxiety. They learned to do this spontaneously by holding their breath and pulling in their abdomen.

Knowledge of how pressure on the solar plexus develops is indispensable for an understanding of the further course of our patient's treatment. What followed was definitely in agreement with the above assumption; indeed, it confirmed it. The more carefully I had the patient observe and describe the behavior of the musculature in the region of his upper abdomen, the more intense the jerking became, the more intense also became the sensations of currents following their cessation, and the more the wavelike, serpentine movements of the body spread. But his pelvis continued to remain stiff, until I began to make the patient aware of the rigidity of his pelvic musculature. During the movements, the entire lower part of his body jerked forward. The pelvis, however, did not move by itself; it moved together with his hips and thighs. I asked the patient to pay attention to the inhibition which obstructed the separate movement of his pelvis. It took him about two weeks to thoroughly perceive the muscular block in his pelvis and to overcome the inhibition. He gradually learned to include his pelvis in the twitchings. Now, a previously unfamiliar sensation of current also appeared in his genitals. He had erections during the session and a strong urge to ejaculate. Thus, the jerkings of his pelvis, his upper body, and abdomen were the same as those which are produced and experienced in orgastic clonus.

From this point on, the work was concentrated on the patient's behavior in the sexual act, which he was asked to describe precisely. This description exposed what is found not only in all neurotics, but in the overwhelming majority of all men and women: *movement in the sexual act is artificially forced, without the person being aware of it.* Usually, it is not the pelvis itself that moves, but the abdomen, pelvis, and upper thigh as one unit. This does not correspond to the natural vegetative movement of the pelvis in the sexual act; it is, on the contrary, an inhibition of the orgastic reflex. It is voluntary movement, as opposed to involuntary reflex action. Its function is to reduce or wholly cut off the orgastic sensation of current in the genitals.

Proceeding on the basis of these experiences, I was now able to make rapid headway with the patient. It became evident that his pelvic floor was held in a state of chronic tension. It was this case that finally enabled me to understand an error which I had committed formerly. In my previous efforts to eliminate the orgastic inhibitions, I had, of course, treated the contraction of the pelvic floor and had attempted to loosen it. However, I had been continually haunted by the impression that this was not enough, that the result was somehow incomplete. Now I understood that *the pressure exerted upon the solar plexus from above by the diaphragm, from the front by the abdominal wall and, from below, by the contracted pelvic floor considerably reduced the abdominal cavity.* I shall speak later about the significance of these findings with respect to the development and preservation of neurotic situations.

After a few more weeks, I succeeded in completely dissolving the patient's muscular armor. The isolated abdominal twitchings decreased to the extent to which the sensations of current in the genitals increased. His emotional life grew more serious. In this connection, he remembered an experience from the time he was about two years old.

He was alone with his mother at a summer resort. It was a clear starry night. His mother was asleep and breathing deeply; outside he could hear the steady pounding of the waves on the beach. The mood he had felt then was the same deeply serious, somewhat sad and melancholy mood which he experienced now. We can say that he remembered one of the situations from earliest childhood in which he had still allowed himself to experience his vegetative (orgastic) longing. Following the disappointment in his mother, which had occurred when he was five years old, he had begun to fight against the full expression of his vegetative energies and had become cold and superficial. In short, he had developed the character which he presented at the outset of the treatment.

Following the increase of the sensations of current in the genitals, the feeling of a "peculiar contact with the world" intensified. He assured me that there was a complete identity between the emotional seriousness which overcame him now and the sensations which he had experienced as a small child with his mother, especially on that night. He described it as follows: "It is as if I were at one with the world. It is as if everything inside of me and outside of me were whirling. It is as if all stimuli emerged much slower, as in waves. It is like a protective husk around a child. It is incredible how I now sense the depth of the world." There was no need for me to tell him; he grasped it spontaneously: *the feeling of unity with the mother is the same as the feeling of unity with nature.* The equating of mother and earth or universe takes on a deeper meaning when it is understood from the point of view of the vegetative harmony between self and world.

On one of the following days, the patient experienced a severe attack of anxiety. He jumped up, his mouth contorted with pain; beads of perspiration covered his forehead; his musculature was as stiff as a board. He hallucinated an animal, an ape. In doing so, his hand had the bent attitude of an ape's paw, and he uttered sounds from the depth of his chest, "as if without vocal cords," he himself said afterward. It was as if someone had come very close to him and threatened him. Then, trance-like, he cried out, "Don't be angry, I only want to suck." The anxiety attack subsided, the patient grew calm again, and in subsequent sessions, we concentrated our work on this experience. Among many other things, he remembered that at about the age of two (which was established by the fact that they had lived in a particular apartment at that time), he had seen Brehm's *Tierleben* for the first time and had looked at a gorilla with great admiration and astonishment. He was not aware of having experienced the same anxiety then, but the anxiety that occurred in the session undoubtedly corresponded to that experience.

In spite of the fact that anxiety had not become manifest at that time, it had subsequently dominated his entire life. Now it had finally broken through. The gorilla represented his father, the threatening figure who wanted to obstruct his sucking. Thus, his relationship to his mother had remained fixated at this level and had broken through right at the beginning of the treatment in the form of sucking movements of his mouth. But this did not become spontaneously intelligible to him until after his entire muscular armor had been dissolved. It was not necessary to spend five years searching for the early sucking experience on the basis of memory traces. In the treatment, he actually was an infant with the facial expression of an infant, and the anxieties he had experienced as an infant.

I can briefly summarize the remainder of the treatment. Following the dissolution of the two main fixations in the childhood situation, his disappointment in his mother and his fear of yielding, genital excitation increased rapidly. Within a few days, he met a pretty young woman, with whom he easily formed a friendship. After the second or third sexual act, he came to the treatment beaming and reported in complete amazement that his pelvis had moved "so curiously by itself." From his detailed description it was apparent that he still had a slight inhibition at the moment of ejaculation. However, since the pelvic movement had already been liberated, it required but little effort to eliminate this final inhibitory trace. It was a matter of not holding back at the moment of ejaculation, but of surrendering himself completely to the vegetative movements. He had not the slightest doubt that the twitchings he had experienced during the treatment had been nothing other than the suppressed vegetative orgastic movements of coitus. However, as it was later shown, the orgasm reflex had not developed wholly free of disturbance. The orgastic contractions were still jerky. He was still very hesitant to allow his head to fall back, i.e., to assume the attitude of surrender. However, the patient soon overcame this resistance against a soft, coordinated course of the movement. Following this, the final trace of his disturbance, which had not appeared so clearly before, was resolved. The hard, forceful form of the orgastic convulsion corresponded to a psychic attitude which said, "A man is hard and unyielding; any form of surrender is feminine."

Immediately following this realization, his infantile conflict with his father was resolved. On one hand, he felt sheltered and protected by his father. He knew that, no matter how difficult matters might be, it would always be possible to "retreat" to the parental home. At the same time, he strove to stand on his own feet and to be independent of his father. He looked upon his need to be protected as feminine, and he wanted to rid himself of it. Thus, the desire to be independent and the need for passive-feminine protection conflicted with one another. Both were contained in the form of the orgasm reflex. The resolution of the psychic conflict took place hand in hand with the elimination of the hard, thrustlike form of the orgasm reflex, and its unmasking as a warding off of the gentle, surrendering movement. When he finally experienced surrender in the reflex, he was deeply baffled by it. "I would never have thought," he said, "that a man can surrender, too. I have always regarded surrender as a characteristic of the female sex." In this way, his own warded-off femininity was connected with the natural form of orgastic surrender, and thus disturbed the latter.

It is interesting to note how society's double standard of morality was reflected and anchored in this patient's structure. In customary social ideology, we also find that surrender is emotionally associated with femininity, and unyielding hardness is associated with masculinity. Accordingly, it is inconceivable that an independent person can give himself and that a person who does give himself can be independent. Just as, on the basis of this false association, women protest against their femininity and want to be masculine, men rebel against their natural sexual rhythm out of fear of appearing feminine; and it is from this false assessment that the difference in the view of sexuality in man and in woman derives its seeming justification.

During the ensuing months, every change became integrated in the transformation of his personality. While he did not deny himself an occasional social drink, he ceased to drink excessively. He made a suitable arrangement with his wife and formed a happy liaison with another woman. Most important, he showed great interest and enthusiasm in a new job.

The superficiality of his character had completely disappeared. He was no longer capable of engaging in empty talk in cafés or of undertaking other things that did not have some objective interest. I want to make it quite clear that it would not have occurred to me to guide or to influence him morally. I myself was surprised by the spontaneous transformation of his personality. He became objective and serious. He grasped the basic concepts of sex-economy less on the basis of his treatment, which was of short duration, than spontaneously on the basis of his changed structure, the feeling of his body, i.e., on the basis of the vegetative motility he now experienced.

Over the course of the next four years, the patient showed considerable improvement in the integration of his personality, in his capacity for happiness, and in the rational management of difficult situations.

I have now been practicing the technique of vegetotherapy for six years with students and patients and can see that it provides great advantages for the treatment of character neuroses. The results are better than they were previously, and the duration of the treatments are shorter. A number of physicians and teachers have already learned to use character-analytic vegetotherapy.

4. THE ESTABLISHMENT OF NATURAL RESPIRATION

Before I describe the details of this technique, it is necessary to give a brief summary of a few fundamental facts. A knowledge of these facts will clarify every individual technical measure which, taken by itself, appears to be meaningless.

The vegetotherapeutic treatment of muscular attitudes is interlaced in a very definite way with the work on character attitudes. Thus, it in no way excludes the character-analytic work. Rather it supplements it or, expressed differently, vegetotherapy means the same work at a deeper layer of the biological system. For, according to our therapeutic views, the character armor and the muscular armor are functionally identical. There would be good reason to call vegetotherapy "character analysis" in the realm of biophysical functioning.

However, the identity between character armor and muscular armor has a counterpart. Character attitudes can be dissolved by the overcoming of muscular armorings, just as muscular attitudes can be dissolved through the removal of character attitudes. Once the force of muscular vegetotherapy has been experienced, there is a temptation to give up the work on character incrustations altogether and to concentrate solely on vegetotherapy. But practical experience soon teaches us that it is just as inadmissible to exclude one form of work as it is to exclude the other. With one patient, work on the muscular attitude will predominate from the beginning, while with another, work on the character attitudes will be emphasized. We also encounter a third type of patient with whom the work on the character and the work on the musculature proceed partly simultaneously and partly alternatingly. But it is the work on the muscular armoring that gains the greater importance and scope toward the end of the treatment. It is concentrated on the task of restoring the orgasm reflex, which is naturally present but disturbed in all neurotic patients. This task is accomplished in various ways.

In the effort to release the orgasm reflex, a great number of details are learned which provide the correct understanding of natural movement, as opposed to unnatural, neurotically restricted movement. Sometimes the vegetative impulse and the vegetative inhibition of the same impulse can be localized in the same muscle group. For instance, the impulse to butt a person in the stomach with one's head, as well as the inhibition of this impulse, might be contained in a stooped attitude of the head. The conflict between impulse and defense, with which we are so familiar in the psychic realm, has a direct correlation in physiological behavior. At other times, impulse and inhibition are distributed among various muscle groups. For example, there are patients in whom the vegetative impulse is expressed in involuntary twitchings of the muscles of the upper abdomen. However, the inhibition of this vegetative impulse is found in a different place, e.g., in a spasm of the uterus which can be felt as a well-delineated spherical lump when one carefully palpates the lower abdomen. It is a vegetative hypertonic condition of the musculature; the lump disappears as the orgasm reflex develops. In fact, the lump will occasionally appear and disappear several times within the same session.

It is particularly important to mention this, for the release of the orgasm reflex is essentially brought about by an intensification of the vegetative inhibitions. The patient, of course, knows nothing about his muscular blocks. He must first feel them before he is in a position to focus his attention on them. There would be no point in intensifying his vegetative impulses before the inhibitions have been dissolved.

We want to cite an example to facilitate our understanding of this phenomenon. A snake or a worm demonstrates a uniform, wavelike, rhythmic movement which governs the entire organism. Now let us imagine that some segments of the body are paralyzed or somehow restricted, so that they are not able to move with the rhythm of the entire body. In such a case, the other parts of the body would not, as before, move in one unit; the total rhythm would be disturbed, owing to the exclusion of individual muscle groups. Thus, the completeness of the body harmony and motility is dependent upon the uniformity, totality, and freedom from disturbance of the impulses of the body. A person who holds back in the pelvis is inhibited in his bearing and movements, no matter how mobile he may appear. The orgasm reflex consists precisely of the fact that a wave of excitation and movement runs from the vegetative center over the head, neck, chest, upper and lower abdomen, to the pelvis and then to the legs. If this wave is obstructed, slowed down, or blocked at some point, the reflex is "disrupted." Our patients usually demonstrate not one but many such blocks and inhibitions of the orgasm reflex at various parts of the body. There are two points where the inhibition is always found: the throat and the anus. That this is connected with the embryonic character of both openings can only be conjectured, in as much as the throat and the anus are the two openings of the primordial intestinal tract.

The vegetotherapist locates the individual sites at which the orgasm reflex is inhibited and intensifies the inhibitions. Then the body itself seeks the path prescribed by the course of the vegetative excitation. It is amazing how "logically" the body integrates the total reflex. When, for example, a stiffness of the neck has been dissolved, or a spasm of the throat or chin has been eliminated, some impulse almost invariably becomes manifest in the chest or shoulders. However, it is not long before this impulse, too, is obstructed by a corresponding inhibition. If, now, this new inhibition is removed, an impulse makes itself felt in the abdomen until it, too, meets an inhibition. Hence, it becomes clear that it is not possible to loosen the vegetative motility of the pelvis until the inhibitions which lie above it have been eliminated.

This description should not be viewed too schematically. Although there can be no doubt that every dissolution of an inhibition enables a part of a vegetative impulse to become manifest "farther down," it is also true that often a throat spasm can be dissolved completely only after stronger vegetative impulses have already broken through in the abdomen. In the breakthrough of new vegetative impulses, previously concealed inhibitions clearly emerge. In many cases, a severe throat spasm is not discovered until the vegetative excitation in the pelvis has developed to a certain extent. This increase in vegetative excitation mobilizes the remainder of the available inhibitory mechanisms.

Particularly important in this connection are the *substitute movements*. Very often a vegetative impulse is feigned where there is only an acquired, half-voluntary movement. The basic vegetative impulse is liberated only after the substitute movement has been unmasked and eliminated. For instance, many patients suffer from a chronic tension of the musculature of the jaws, which makes the lower half of the face look "mean." In attempting to push the chin downward, a strong resistance, a rigidity, is noticed. If the patient is told to open and close his mouth, he carries out this movement only after some hesitation and with evident effort. But the patient must first be made to experience this artificial form of opening and closing his mouth before he can be convinced that the motility of his chin is inhibited.

Hence, the voluntary movements of muscle groups can function as a warding off of involuntary movements. It is also possible for involuntary muscle actions to function as a warding off of other involuntary muscle actions, e.g., a rhythmic movement of the musculature of the eyelids ("tic") can function as a warding off of strained staring. Then again, voluntary muscle actions can coincide entirely with the direction of involuntary muscle actions; thus, the conscious imitation of a pelvic movement can release an involuntary vegetative pelvic movement.

The basic principles in freeing the orgasm reflex are:

1. To seek out those places where the unitary character of the orgasm reflex is interrupted.

2. To intensify the involuntary inhibitory mechanisms and impulses, e.g., the forward movement of the pelvis, which are capable of completely releasing the blocked vegetative impulse.

The most important means of freeing the orgasm reflex is *a breathing technique,* which evolved spontaneously through the work. There is not a single neurotic person who is capable of breathing out deeply and evenly in one breath. Patients have concocted every conceivable means of preventing deep exhalation. They exhale in a fragmentary manner, or quickly revert to a position of inhalation. Some patients describe the inhibition they sense in this kind of breathing as follows: "It is as if an ocean wave dashed against a rocky shore. It doesn't go any farther."

This inhibition is experienced in the upper or middle region of the abdomen. In breathing out deeply, strong feelings of pleasure or anxiety appear in the abdomen. But it is precisely the avoidance of these feelings that is accomplished by the respiratory block. By way of preparing for and bringing about the orgasm reflex, I first have my patients breathe in and out deeply and encourage them "to breathe all the way through." If the patient is told to breathe deeply, he usually forces his breath in and out artificially. This voluntary behavior serves only to obstruct the natural vegetative rhythm of breathing. It is unmasked as an inhibition; the patient is asked to breathe "in an entirely normal way," i.e., not to engage in any respiratory exercises, as he would like to. After five to ten breaths, respiration usually deepens, and the first inhibitions emerge. When a person breathes out naturally and deeply, his head spontaneously moves back at the end of the breath. Patients cannot let their heads move back spontaneously in a natural way. They stretch their heads forward to avoid "moving back," or they move them with a violent jerk to the side; in any case, in a way different from natural movement.

In deep exhalation, the shoulders relax in a natural way and move gently and lightly forward. It is precisely at the end of the exhalation that our patients hold their shoulders tight or lift them up; in short, they carry out various movements of the shoulders to prevent the spontaneous vegetative movement from taking place.

Another means of releasing the orgasm reflex is to apply a gentle pressure to the upper abdomen. I place the fingertips of both hands approximately in the middle of the upper abdomen between umbilicus and sternum, and tell the patient to breathe in and out deeply. During exhalation, I gradually apply a gentle pressure to the upper abdomen. This produces very different reactions in various patients. In some, the solar plexus proves to be highly sensitive to pressure; in others, there is a countermovement in which the back is arched. These are the patients who suppress every orgastic excitation in the sexual act by pulling back the pelvis and arching the back. Then, there are patients in whom continual pressure upon the upper abdomen produces wavelike contractions in the abdomen. This sometimes releases the orgasm reflex. If deep exhalation is continued for some time, an abdominal wall which is tense and hard will invariably soften. It can be pressed in more easily. The patients report that they "feel better," a statement that cannot be taken at face value. In my practice, I make use of a formulation which patients grasp spontaneously. I tell them to "give in" completely. The attitude of yielding is the same as that of surrender: the head glides backward, the shoulders move forward and upward, the middle of the abdomen draws in, the pelvis moves forward, and the legs move apart spontaneously. Deep exhalation spontaneously produces the attitude of (sexual) surrender. This explains the inhibition of the orgasm in those people, incapable of surrendering, who hold their breath as the excitation mounts to a climax.

Many patients keep their backs arched, so that the pelvis is pushed back and the upper abdomen is pushed forward. If the therapist places his hand under the middle of the patient's back, and tells him to press down on it, resistance will be noticed. Yielding in the bodily attitude is expressively the same thing as the attitude of surrender in the sexual act, or in the state of sexual excitation. Once the patient has grasped and assumed the attitude of surrender, the first precondition for the establishment of the orgasm reflex has been created. A relaxed opening of the mouth seems to contribute to the establishment of the attitude of surrender. In the course of this work, numerous inhibitions, previously unseen, appear. For example, many patients knit their eyebrows, stretch their legs and their feet in a spastic manner, etc. Hence, the elimination of the inhibitions and the establishment of the orgasm reflex cannot be separated from one another.

Rather, it is only in the process of reunifying the disrupted organic rhythm of the total body that all the muscular actions and inhibitions are unmasked which had previously obstructed the sexual function and vegetative motility of the patient's life.

It is only in the course of this work that the machinations are revealed which the patients used as children to master their instinctual impulses and the "butterflies in their stomachs." As heroically as they once wrestled with the "devil" in themselves, i.e., sexual pleasure, they now senselessly defend themselves against the cherished capacity for pleasure. I shall mention only a few of the typical forms of the somatic mechanisms of repression. If the excitations in the abdomen become too strong in the process of releasing the orgasm reflex, some patients stare blankly into a corner or out of a window. If one inquires further into this behavior, the patients remember that this is something they practiced consciously as children when they had to learn to control anger toward their parents, brothers and sisters, or teachers. Holding one's breath for a long time was considered an heroic achievement of self-control, as was making the head and shoulders rigid. "Grit your teeth" became a moralistic command. Here, language is a direct reflection of the somatic process of self-control. Certain phrases, commonly heard in conventional upbringing, exactly represent what we describe as muscular armoring: "A man must exercise self-control"; "a big boy doesn't cry"; "pull yourself together"; "don't let yourself go"; "don't be a yellow belly"; "don't vent your spleen"; "grit your teeth"; "grin and bear it"; "hold your head high"; etc. Initially, such typical admonitions are rejected by children, then accepted and carried out against their will. They always weaken the backbone of the child's character, crush his spirit, destroy the life in him, and turn him into a well-behaved puppet.

An educated mother told me about her eleven-year-old

daughter, who had been strictly forbidden to masturbate until she was five years old. When she was around nine, she saw a children's play in which there was a magician whose fingers were artificially elongated and unevenly shaped. Even at that time, she had been disturbed by his very large forefinger and, in later anxiety fantasies, the magician had always reappeared.

"You know," she told her mother, "when I get afraid, it always starts in my stomach [she bent over as if in pain]. Then I have to hold still. I mustn't move anything. I am only allowed to play with the little part down there [she means the clitoris], that I push back and forth like crazy. The magician says, 'You must not move. Only down there, you may move.' When the fear gets worse, I want to switch on the light. But every big movement makes me afraid again. Only when I make very small movements, it gets better. But when there is light again and I have rubbed enough down below, I grow calmer and then afterward it is all over. The magician is just like Nana, she too always says, 'Don't move, lie still.' [She imitates a stern face.] When I had my hands underneath the covers one time, she came and pulled them out."

Because she had her hand on her genitals practically every minute of the day, her mother asked her why she did that. The girl was not even aware she had her hand there so often. Then she described the nature of her various sensations. "Sometimes I just want to play, then I don't have to rub. But when I am frozen stiff with fear, then I have to push and pull down below like crazy. When everybody is away, and there is no one with whom I can talk to about anything, then the fear gets worse and I always have to do something down below." Somewhat later she added, "When the fear is there, I get very stubborn. Then I want to fight against something, but I don't know against what. Don't think that I want to fight against the magician [the mother had not mentioned him]; I am much too afraid of him.

It is something which I don't know." This child gives a good description of her abdominal sensations and the way in which she, with the help of the fantasy of the magician, tried to control them.

Another example will illustrate what importance respiration has for the activity of the abdominal vegetative ganglia. In the course of repeated deep exhalations, one patient became aware of a strong sensitivity in the pelvic region. He reacted to this by severely restricting his breathing. If one touched his upper thigh or lower abdomen ever so lightly, he would contract instantaneously. However, if I made him breathe out deeply several times, he would not react to touch. If the breath was held again, the irritability of his pelvic region promptly reappeared. This could be repeated at will. This clinical detail is very revealing. Deep inhalation produces a damming-up of the biological activity of the vegetative centers, resulting in increased reflex irritability. Repeated exhalation reduces the stasis and, with it, the anxious irritability. Thus, the blocking of deep exhalation creates a contradiction: the block serves to dampen the pleasurable excitations arising from the central vegetative apparatus. However, it is precisely this block that creates an increased susceptibility to anxiety and reflex irritability. This enables us to comprehend a further aspect of the conversion of suppressed sexual excitation into anxiety, just as does the clinical finding that, in the process of re-establishing the capacity for pleasure, it is the physiological anxiety reflexes we encounter first. Anxiety is the negative counterpart of sexual excitation; at the same time, it is identical with it in terms of energy. So-called nervous irritability is nothing other than a series of short circuits in the discharge of the electricity of the tissues, caused by the blocking of the energy from orgastic discharge. One is "electrically charged."

I once had a patient in whom the central and most persistent character resistance was expressed in a continual chatter.[1] However, his mouth was felt as "alien" and "dead," as if it "did not belong." The patient repeatedly passed his hand over his mouth as if to convince himself that it was still there. His pleasure in telling gossipy stories was unmasked as an attempt to overcome the feeling of a "dead mouth." After this defense function had been eliminated, his mouth began spontaneously to assume an infantile attitude of sucking, which alternated with a mean, hard facial expression. During these changes, his head was inclined sharply to the right. One day I had the impulse to feel the patient's neck to convince myself that there was nothing wrong with it. To my enormous surprise, the patient immediately assumed the attitude of a hanged person: his head sank limply to the side, his tongue protruded, his mouth remained rigidly opened. And this happened, although I had merely touched his neck. A straight path led from this incident to his early childhood fear of being hanged for a transgression (masturbation).

The reflex just described occurred only when the breath was held and deep exhalation was avoided. The reflex reaction disappeared as the patient gradually began to overcome the fear of breathing out. Thus, the neurotically inhibited respiratory activity is a central factor of the neurotic mechanism in general. It blocks the vegetative activity of the organism, thus creating the energy source for symptoms and neurotic fantasies of all kinds.

Another patient suffered from a very "bad feeling about himself." He felt he was a "pig." Essentially, his neurosis consisted in abortive attempts to overcome his poor opinion of himself by being importunate toward others. His pathological behavior had but one result: people insulted him mercilessly. This intensified and confirmed the poor opinion he had of himself. Now he began to muse about

---

[1] Talking is one of the favorite means of suppressing vegetative sensations. This explains compulsive neurotic talking. In such cases, I tell the patient to keep quiet, until a condition of restlessness appears.

what people were saying about him, why they were so mean to him, how he could improve the situation, etc. In the process, he became aware of a pressure in his chest. The harder he tried to overcome his lack of self-esteem through compulsive ruminating, the more intense the pressure became. It took a long time to discover the connection between the compulsive ruminating and the "pressure in his chest." This whole experience was preceded by a somatic sensation of which he had never been conscious: "Something begins to stir in the chest, then it shoots up to the head; I feel as if my head were going to burst open. A kind of mist settles around my eyes. I can't think any more. I lose all feeling of what is going on around me. It is as if I were going to sink, as if I were losing contact with myself and everything around me." Such reactions always appeared when an excitation failed to reach the genitals and was diverted "upward." This is the physiological basis for what psychoanalysts called "displacement from below upward." This neurotic condition led to fantasies of being a genius, dreams about a glorious future, etc.; they were all the more grotesque, the less they were in keeping with his actual achievements.

There are people who claim they have never experienced the familiar feeling of gnawing or longing in the upper abdomen. They are usually hard, cold, and ill-natured persons. I had two patients who had developed a pathological compulsion to eat as a means of suppressing their abdominal sensations. They would gorge themselves as soon as a sensation of anxiety or depression appeared. Following an unsatisfying sexual act, some women (I have not yet had occasion to observe this in men) have, as one such patient expressed it, "to shove something into the stomach." In others, there is a feeling of "having something in the intestines which can't come out."

5. THE MOBILIZATION OF THE "DEAD PELVIS"

The orgasm reflex does not suddenly emerge completely intact; rather it is a product of the gradual integration of separate parts involved in the total function. Initially, there is merely a wave of excitation which runs from the neck, over the chest and upper abdomen, to the lower abdomen. The pelvis is immobile during this action. Some patients describe it as follows: "It is as if the movement were stopped at a certain spot down below." The pelvis does not participate in the wavelike course of the excitation. If an effort is made to locate the inhibition which causes this, it is usually found that the pelvis is held in a retracted position. An arching of the spine, causing the abdomen to protrude, sometimes goes together with this retraction of the pelvis. For instance, it is easy to push one's hand between the patient's back and the couch. The immobility of the pelvis creates the impression of deadness. In the majority of cases, this is combined with a feeling of "emptiness in the pelvis" or a feeling of "weakness in the genitals." This phenomenon is especially pronounced in patients who suffer from chronic constipation. We shall have a better understanding of this connection when we bear in mind that chronic constipation corresponds to an overexcitation of the sympathetic. The same applies to the holding back in the pelvis. The patients are unable to move the pelvis. Instead, they move the abdomen, pelvis, and upper thighs as one unit. Accordingly, the first task of therapeutic work is to make the patients fully aware of the absence of pelvic excitation. As a rule, they offer considerable resistance to moving the pelvis by itself, particularly to moving it forward and upward. Comparison of patients suffering from genital anesthesia shows that the lack of sensation in the genitals, i.e., the feeling of emptiness, debility, etc., is that much more intense the more the pelvis has forfeited its motility. Such patients are always severely disturbed in the sexual act. The women lie motionless, or they try to overcome the inhibition of vegetative motility in the pelvis by means of forced movements of trunk and pelvis. In men, the disturbance is expressed in hurried, abrupt, and voluntary movements of the entire lower part of the body. The sensation of vegetative orgastic current cannot be demonstrated in any of these patients.

It is necessary to lay particular stress upon some details of this phenomenon. The genital musculature (bulbo-cavernosus and ischio-cavernosus) is tense, and this tenseness precludes the contractions brought on by friction. The musculature of the buttocks is also tense. Patients often attempt to overcome the flaccidity of these muscles by trying to produce voluntary contractions and relaxations in them.

The pelvic floor is pulled up. This contracted position of the pelvic floor below, together with the downward fixation of the diaphragm above and the tension of the abdominal wall in front, blocks the movement of vegetative current in the abdomen.

This attitude of the pelvis always appears in childhood as a result of two fundamental disturbances of development. Its groundwork is prepared by brutal toilet training in which the child is forced to control his bowel movements at a very early age. Severe punishment for bed wetting also causes a spasm of the pelvis. Far more important, however, is the spasm of the pelvis that is initiated as soon as the child begins to combat the intense genital excitations which urge toward masturbation.

Every sensation of genital pleasure can be deadened through the chronic contraction of the pelvic musculature. This is proven by the fact that sensations of current in the genitals begin to appear when the pelvic spasm is relieved. To bring this about, it is first necessary to make the patient aware of the pelvic attitude, i.e., the patient must have the immediate sensation that he or she is "holding" the pelvis "still." In addition, all voluntary movements which prevent the natural vegetative movements of the pelvis have to be exposed. The voluntary movement of the abdomen, pelvis, and upper thighs as a single unit is undoubtedly the most important and frequent means of preventing the pelvis from moving by itself. It is utterly useless to have the patient carry out pelvic exercises, as some gymnastics instructors attempt. As long as the concealing and defensive muscular attitudes and actions have not been eliminated, the natural movement of the pelvis cannot develop.

The more intensely the inhibition of the pelvic movement is worked on, the more completely the pelvis participates in the wave of excitation. It begins to move forward and upward without any conscious effort on the part of the patient. It is as if it were drawn up toward the umbilicus by an external force. At the same time, the upper thighs remain motionless. It is extremely important to grasp the difference between the defensive movement of the pelvis and its natural vegetative movement. When the wave runs from the neck over the chest and abdomen to the pelvis, then the character of the entire reflex is changed. If, until this point, the orgasm reflex was experienced in an essentially unpleasurable way, occasionally even as painful, it now begins to become pleasurable. If, until this point, defensive movements appeared, e.g., protruding abdomen and arched back, now the entire trunk presents the appearance of a fish in motion. The sensations of genital pleasure and the sensations of current in the total organism, which now grow increasingly strong, leave no doubt that we are dealing with the natural vegetative movement of coitus. The character of this movement differs completely from all earlier reflexes and reactions of the body. The feeling of emptiness in the genitals gives way gradually or rapidly to a sensation of fullness and urgency. This brings about the spontaneous establishment of the capacity for orgastic experience in the sexual act. The very movement which, carried out by individual muscle groups, represents pathological reactions of the body and serves to ward off sexual pleasure, is, in a wavelike movement of the total body, the basis of the capacity for spontaneous vegetative pleasure. The *arc de cercle* of the hysteric, in which the abdomen and the chest are arched forward while the shoulders and the pelvis are pulled back, now becomes comprehensible as the exact opposite of the attitude in the orgasm reflex.

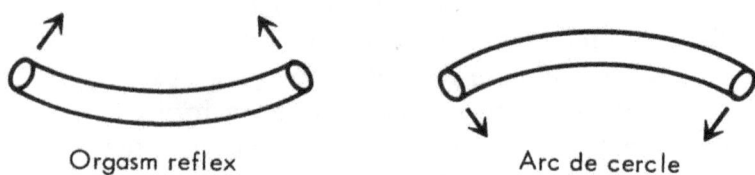

Orgasm reflex Arc de cercle

As long as these facts were still unknown to me, I was forced to have the patient overcome the inhibition of the pelvic movement partly by means of "exercises." The incompleteness of the results caused me to reject these artificial measures and to search for the inhibitions of natural motility. The warding off of the orgasm reflex causes a number of vegetative disturbances, e.g., chronic constipation, muscular rheumatism, sciatica, etc. In many patients, constipation disappears, even if it has existed for decades, with the development of the orgasm reflex. Its full development is often preceded by nausea and feelings of giddiness, in addition to spastic conditions of the throat, isolated twitchings of the abdominal musculature, the diaphragm, the pelvis, etc. But all these symptoms disappear as soon as the orgasm reflex has been fully developed.

The "stiff, dead, retracted pelvis" is one of man's most frequent vegetative disturbances. It is responsible for lumbago as well as for hemorrhoidal disturbances. Elsewhere, we shall demonstrate an important connection between these disturbances and genital cancer in women, which is so common.

Thus, the "deadening of the pelvis" has the same function as the deadening of the abdomen, i.e., to avoid feelings, particularly those of pleasure and anxiety.

Now that the various manifestations and forms of the attitude and expression of the body, with respect to the orgasm reflex and the defense against it, can be understood, many phenomena in therapeutic work are made comprehensible. I am reminded of a diaphragmatic tic in a forty-five-year-old woman whom I treated at the Vienna Psychoanalytic Clinic some fourteen years before and partially cured by making it possible for her to masturbate. I described this case in the article "Der Tic als Onanieäquivalent," published in the *Zeitschrift für Sexualwissenschaft,* 1924. The patient had suffered from very disturbing diaphragmatic movements, accompanied by noises, since her adolescence, i.e., for more than thirty years. There was a remarkable abatement in the tic as it became possible for her to masturbate. It is clear to me today that the improvement was due to the partial loosening of the chronic inspiratory position of the diaphragm. At that time, I could merely say, in a very general way, that sexual gratification had eliminated a portion of the sexual stasis and thus weakened the tic. But I would not have been able to say anything about the form in which this stasis had been maintained, where it had discharged itself, and how the sexual gratification had reduced the stasis. The tic had represented an inadequate effort to overcome the diaphragmatic contraction.

My present experiences remind me of the cases of epilepsy with abdominal aura in which I could not comprehend what part of the body was involved, what was its function, and what was its relationship to the vegetative nervous system. It has become clear now that the epileptic seizures represent convulsions of the vegetative apparatus in which the dammed-up biopsychic energy is discharged solely through the musculature, with the exclusion of the genitals. The epileptic seizure is an extragenital, muscular orgasm.[2] This also clarified those cases in which occasional involuntary fluttering of the abdominal musculature can be observed in the course of the treatment. These movements are attempts to bring about a relaxation of the tense abdominal wall.

Though never overtly expressed, there was in many patients a hidden maliciousness which, though I sensed it, I would not have been able to localize. Treatment of the vegetative behavior makes it possible to determine where the meanness is located somatically. There are patients who express friendliness with their eyes and cheeks, but whose chin and mouth express the exact opposite. The expression of the lower half of the face is completely different from that of the upper half. The dissolution of the attitude of the mouth and chin releases an unbelievable amount of anger.

In other patients, one senses the falsity of conventional politeness; it conceals the opposite, a cunning malice, which might be expressed in chronic constipation. The bowels are immobile, and their function must be kept active through the constant use of purgatives. As children, such patients had to control their anger and "to lock their wickedness in the stomach." The way in which patients describe their body sensations is almost always an exact repetition of often-heard sentences from their early toilet training, e.g., "the belly is naughty when it makes 'poo-poo.'" A "well-brought-up" child is very prone to respond to these admonitions with a "poo." But he must soon rid himself of this habit, and he can do this only by "hiding the 'poo' in the belly." To accomplish this, the child has to suppress every excitation he senses in the abdomen, including genital excitation, by withdrawing into

---

[2] Cf. Reich, "Über den epileptischen Anfall," *Internationale Zeitschrift für Psychoanalyse,* 17, 1931.

himself, "making the belly crawl into itself." The abdomen becomes hard, tense; it has "locked in the wickedness."

It would be worthwhile to describe, historically and functionally, the complicated development of the symptoms of body attitudes as they are manifested in various patients. For the moment, let it suffice to indicate a few typical facts.

It is extremely instructive to see that the body is just as capable of functioning as a unified organism as it is of dividing itself, one part functioning parasympathetically, the other sympathetically. I once treated a female patient who, at a certain stage of the treatment, was already completely relaxed in the upper abdomen; she experienced the familiar sensations of current, and the abdominal wall could be pressed in easily. There were no longer any interruptions in the sensation between the upper abdomen, the chest, and the neck. But the lower abdomen behaved as if it were separated from these parts by a line. When the lower abdominal wall was pressed in, a hard lump about the size of an infant's head could be felt. It would be impossible today to give an exact anatomical explanation of how such a lump is produced, i.e., which organs are involved in its formation, but it can be palpated unequivocally. During a later phase of the treatment, there were days when the lump alternately appeared and disappeared. It always appeared when the patient was afraid of, and therefore struggled against, emerging genital excitation. It disappeared when she felt capable of allowing genital excitation to become manifest.

The somatic manifestations of schizophrenia, particularly its catatonic form, will have to be discussed in a separate essay based on new material. The catatonic stereotypes, perseverations, automatisms of all kind, can be traced back to muscular armorings and breakthroughs of vegetative energy. This is especially true of the catatonic rage reaction. In the simple neurosis, there is only a surface restriction of vegetative motility, which allows room for inner excitations and discharges in "fantasy." If the armoring reaches into the depth, if it blocks central areas of the biological organism and *completely* takes hold of the musculature, there are only two possibilities: forceful breakthrough (violent rage, which is experienced as release) or the gradual, complete deterioration of the vital apparatus.

A number of organic diseases, such as gastric ulcer, muscular rheumatism, and cancer, tie in with the problem at this point.

I have no doubt that, in their clinical practice, psychotherapists can observe any number of such symptoms. However, these symptoms cannot be treated individually; they can be understood only in connection with the total biological functioning of the body, and in relation to the functions of pleasure and anxiety. It is impossible to master the vast complexity of body attitudes and expressions, if anxiety is looked upon as a cause and not essentially as the result of sexual stasis. *"Stasis" means nothing other than an inhibition of vegetative expansion and a blocking of the activity and motility of the central vegetative organs.* The discharge of excitation is blocked; the biological energy is bound.

The orgasm reflex is a unitary response of the total body. In the orgasm, we are nothing but a pulsating mass of plasm. After fifteen years of research on the orgasm reflex, it was finally possible to penetrate to the biological core of psychic illnesses. The orgasm reflex is found in all creatures that copulate. Among more primitive biological organisms as, for example, protozoa, it is found in the form of plasmatic contractions.[3] The most elementary stage at which it can be found is the division of single cells.

There are some difficulties in arriving at an answer to the question of what takes the place of contraction in more highly organized organisms, when the organism can no

---
[3] Cf. Reich, *Die Bione*. Sexpol Verlag, 1938.

longer contract to a spherical form like a protozoon. From a certain stage of development, the metazoa have a skeletal frame. This obstructs the function, native to molluscs and protozoa, of becoming spherical in the act of contracting. Let us imagine a flexible tube, into which our biological bladder has developed. Let us further imagine that we introduce a rod into it which is capable of bending only in one direction. This would represent the spine. Let us imagine that the impulse to contract is now introduced into this longitudinally stretched bladder. We can see that the bladder has but one possibility when, in spite of its inability to become spherical, it wants to contract. *It has to bend, to the greatest possible extent, and rapidly.*

Viewed biologically, the orgasm reflex is nothing else. The body attitude displayed in it is characteristic of many insects, and is particularly evident in the attitude of the embryo.

Hysterical persons have a special tendency to develop muscular spasms in parts of the organism that have an annular musculature, most notably the throat and the anus. Embryologically, these two places correspond to the two openings of the primal intestine.

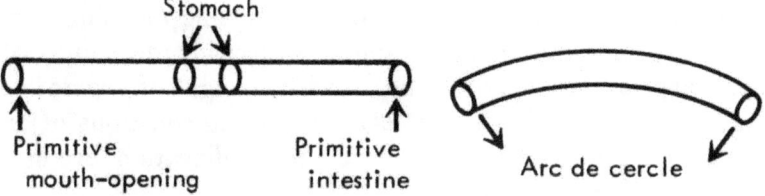

In addition, annular musculature is found at the entrance to and exit from the stomach. Spasms develop at these two openings which often have severe consequences for one's general condition. Those places of the body that are especially disposed to continual contractions and biologically correspond to very primitive stages of development are the most frequent locations of spastic disorders. If the throat and the anus are blocked, the orgastic contraction becomes impossible. The somatic "holding back" is expressed in an attitude that is the exact opposite of the orgasm reflex: the back is arched, the neck stiff, the anus blocked, the chest forward, the shoulders tensed. The hysterical arc de cercle is the exact opposite of the orgasm reflex and is the prototype of the defense against sexuality.

Every psychic impulse is functionally identical with a definite somatic excitation. The view that the psychic apparatus functions solely by itself and influences the somatic apparatus, which likewise functions by itself, cannot be in keeping with the actual facts. A leap from the psychic to the somatic is not conceivable, for the presupposition of two separate realms does not apply here. Nor can the content of a psychic function, such as the idea of hitting somebody, induce somatic expression, unless it is itself already the expression of a vegetative impulse to move. How an idea originates from a vegetative impulse is one of the most difficult questions of psychology. On the basis of clinical experiences, it is clear that the somatic symptom, as well as the unconscious psychic idea, is a sequel of a contradictory vegetative innervation. This is not at variance with the fact that the somatic symptom can be eliminated by making its psychic meaning conscious, for any change in the sphere of psychic ideas must of necessity be functionally identical with changes of vegetative excitation. Thus, it is not solely the making conscious of an unconscious idea that cures, but the modification brought about by the excitation.

Hence, we have the following sequence of functions when

an idea in the psychic realm exerts an influence on the soma:

1. The psychic excitation is functionally identical with the somatic excitation.
2. The fixation of a psychic excitation is produced by the establishment of a specific state of vegetative innervation.
3. The altered vegetative state changes the functioning of the organ.
4. The "psychic meaning of the organic symptom" is nothing other than the somatic attitude in which the "psychic meaning" is expressed. Psychic reserve expresses itself in vegetative rigidity. Psychic hatred expresses itself in a definite vegetative attitude of hate. They are inseparable and identical.
5. The fixed vegetative state has a repercussive effect on the psychic state. The perception of a real danger functions identically with a sympatheticotonic innervation. This, in turn, intensifies the anxiety. The intensified anxiety requires an armoring, which is synonymous with a binding of vegetative energy in the muscular armor. This armoring, in turn, disturbs the possibility of discharge and increases the tension, etc.

Bioenergetically, the psyche and the soma function as a mutually conditioning as well as a unitary system.

Let us use a specific clinical case to make this clearer.

A female patient who was exceptionally pretty and sexually attractive complained about feelings of being ugly, because she did not feel her body as a unified whole. She described her condition as follows: "Every part of my body goes its own way. My legs are here and my head is there, and I never quite know where my hands are. I don't have my body together." In short, she suffered from the well-known disturbance of self-perception, which is especially pronounced in schizoid depersonalization. During the vegetotherapeutic work, the various functions of the muscular attitudes of her face demonstrated a very peculiar relationship. Right at the beginning of the treatment, the "indifference" of her facial expression was conspicuous. Gradually, the expression of indifference became so strong that the patient began to suffer from it quite noticeably. When spoken to, even about serious matters, she always stared into a corner of the room or out of the window, with an expression of indifference on her face. At those times, her eyes had an empty, "lost" look. After this expression of indifference had been thoroughly analyzed and eliminated, another trait appeared in her face, only intimations of which had been visible before. The region of her mouth and chin were "vicious," while her eyes and forehead were "dead." These words reflected the patient's inner feelings. To begin with, I separated the attitude expressed in her mouth and chin. In the course of this work, increasingly strong reactions of a previously suppressed fierce desire to bite became manifest. She had developed these impulses toward her husband and her father, but had not allowed them to be expressed. The impulses of anger expressed in the attitude of her chin and mouth had been previously camouflaged by an attitude of indifference in her face as a whole; and it was the elimination of this indifference that brought to light the angry expression of her mouth. The indifference had the function of keeping the patient from being continually at the mercy of the tormenting sensation of hate around her mouth. After treating the region of her mouth for about two weeks, the malicious expression disappeared completely in connection with the working out of the patient's very strong reaction of disappointment. One of her character traits was the compulsion to continually demand love. She would become angry when her impossible demands were not gratified. After the attitude of her mouth and chin had been dissolved, preorgastic contractions appeared in her whole body, at first in the form of serpentine, wavelike movements which also included the pelvis. However, genital excitation was inhibited at a definite place. In the search for the inhibiting mechanism, the expression of her forehead and eyes gradually became very pronounced. It became an expression of vicious, observant, critical, and attentive staring. With that, the patient realized she had constantly "to be on guard" and she had never been capable of "losing her head."

The emergence and coming into focus of somatic vegetative impulses is no doubt the strangest phenomenon we encounter in vegetotherapy. It is very difficult to describe; it has to be clinically experienced. Thus, the "dead" forehead had concealed the "critical forehead." The next thing was to find out what function the "critical," malicious forehead had. The analysis of the details of the function of her genital excitation revealed that her forehead paid strict "attention to what her genital was doing." Historically, the severe expression of her eyes and forehead was derived from an identification with her very moralistic and ascetically oriented father. Already at a very early age, her father had continually impressed upon her that it was dangerous to give in to sexual desires; more than anything else, he had depicted the ravages of the body produced by syphilis. Thus, her forehead stood guard in place of her father when she wanted to give in to a sexual impulse. The interpretation that she identified with her father was in no way sufficient. The most important question was why she had carried out this identification precisely on the forehead and what maintained the function. We have to make a clear distinction between the historical explanation of a function and its contemporary dynamic explanation. These are two entirely different things. We do not eliminate a somatic symptom merely by making it historically comprehensible. We cannot get along without the knowledge of the contemporary function of the symptom. (Not to be confused with the "contemporary conflict"!) The derivation of the attentiveness of her forehead from her infantile identification with her critical father would not have had the slightest effect upon the orgastic disturbance. The subsequent course of this patient's treatment proved the correctness of this view; to the same extent to which the observant and critical expression replaced the dead expression, the total defense in the genital region became intensified. Gradually, the severe expression alternated with a cheerful, somewhat childlike expression of her forehead and eyes. Thus, one time she was in accord with her genital desire; another time she was critical and adverse toward it. With the replacement of the critical attitude of her forehead by the cheerful attitude, the inhibition of genital excitation also disappeared.

I have presented this case in such detail because it is characteristic of a number of disturbances of the tension-charge process in the genital apparatus. "Keep your wits about you" is a widespread attitude.

Our patient suffered from the sensation of having a divided, non-integrated, non-unified body. Hence, she also lacked the consciousness and sensation of her sexual and vegetative gracefulness. How is it possible that an organism which constitutes a unified whole can "fall to pieces" in its perception? The term "depersonalization" indicates nothing, for it itself requires explanation. What we must ask ourselves is how it is possible for parts of the organism to function by themselves, independent of the total organism. Psychological explanations do not help us here, for in its emotional function the psyche is completely dependent upon the functions of expansion and contraction of the autonomic nervous system. Its structure is non-homogeneous. Experimentation and clinical evidence show that the tension-charge process can comprise the entire body, as well as individual groups of organs. It is possible for the vegetative apparatus to be parasympathetic in the upper abdomen and sympathetic, hypertonic in the lower abdomen. It is also possible for it to create tension in the muscles of the shoulders, while causing a relaxation or even flaccidity in the legs. And the vegetative apparatus is capable of doing this simply because it is not a homogeneous apparatus. In sexual activity, the zone of the mouth can be excited, while the genitals are completely unexcited or even adverse to the sexual activity. Or the reverse of this could be the case. On the basis of these clinical facts, we have sound criteria for determining whether a function is "healthy" or "sick" in terms of sex-economy. The capacity of the vegetative organism to participate in the tension-charge function in a unified and total way is undoubtedly the basic characteristic of psychic and vegetative health. On the other hand, we have to describe as pathological the exclusion of individual organs or even groups of organs from the totality and unity of the vegetative tension-charge function, when it is chronic and continually disturbs the total function.

Clinical observation further teaches us that disturbances of self-perception do not really disappear until the orgasm reflex has been fully developed into a unified whole. Then it is as if all organs and organ systems of the body are integrated by a single function, with respect to contraction as well as expansion.

Thus, depersonalization becomes understandable as a lack of charge, i.e., as a disturbance of the vegetative innervation of individual organs or organ systems (e.g., the fingertips, the arms, the head, the legs, the genitals, etc.). The lack of unity in self-perception is also caused by the fact that the current of excitation in the body is interrupted in one place or another. This is especially true of two regions of the body. One is the neck which, when it is spastic, blocks the excitation wave in its path from the chest to the head; the other is the musculature of the pelvis which, when it is contracted, disturbs the course of the excitation from the abdomen to the genitals and the legs.

On the basis of psychoanalytic research, we understand the individual history of a neurosis, the external conditions of its genesis, the inner motive of the psychic conflict, and, finally, the consequences of sexual repression, e.g., neurotic symptoms and character traits. However, psychoanalytic research does not enable us to comprehend the *mechanism* by which a child's fate, an external trauma or an internal psychic conflict, chronically *retains* a pathological reaction.

We see women living under the best external sexual and economic conditions and nonetheless holding on to their neuroses. We see children of all economic strata, occasionally living under favorable sex-economic conditions, who not only become neurotic but remain neurotic. Moreover, we witness the hitherto mystically conceived and represented "repetition compulsion," i.e., the compulsion of so many people to continually put themselves in detrimental situations. None of these phenomena can be explained on the basis of previous views.

The most impressive evidence of the tendency to hold on to a neurosis is seen at the end of treatment, when the attempt is made to establish the capacity for orgastic surrender. Precisely at that point, when the patient should be on the verge of health, the worst possible reactions set in against it. The patients are dominated by a fear of pleasure, which is diametrically opposed to the pleasure principle of life.

The fear of punishment for sexual activities, which the patient experiences as a child, becomes chronically anchored in the form of pleasure anxiety. We recall that, when its course is inhibited, pleasure has the characteristic of turning into unpleasure. When, in spite of continual very high sexual excitation, a person is not capable of experiencing final gratification, a fear eventually develops not only of the final gratification, but also of the excitation which precedes it. The pleasurable excitation process itself becomes a source of unpleasure. The normal sensation of pleasure is inhibited by a muscular spasm which can become extremely painful, quite apart from the fact that it increases the stasis. It is the fixation of a condition of physiological spasm in the genitals that causes children and adolescents to reject sexual activity. This fixation causes every pleasurable excitation to be converted into its opposite, no matter how correct one's intellectual and emotional attitude might be. Also connected with this spastic state is the inability to endure even mild excitations. It is in the function of the muscular spasm during the intensification of pleasure that we must look for the structural and physiological basis of characterological resignation and modesty.

Thus, psychopathological conditions and symptoms are the results of a disturbance of the vegetative (sex-economic) regulation of energy. Every impairment of total somatic sensation simultaneously affects self-confidence and the unity of body feeling. At the same time, these impairments urge the body to make compensations. The feeling of vegetative integrity, which becomes the natural and optimal basis of strong self-confidence, is disturbed in all neurotics. This is expressed in the most varied forms, including a complete splitting of the personality. Between the simplest sensations of being cold or stiff on one hand, and schizophrenic splitting, contactlessness, and depersonalization on the other, there are no principle but merely quantitative differences, which are also expressed qualitatively. The sensation of integrity is connected with the sensation of having an immediate contact with the world. The unification of the orgasm reflex also restores the sensations of depth and seriousness. The patients remember the time in their early childhood when the unity of their body sensation was not disturbed. Seized with emotion, they tell of the time as children when they felt at one with nature, with everything that surrounded them, of the time they felt "alive," and how finally all this had been shattered and crushed by their education. In the disruption of the unity of body feeling by sexual suppression, and in the continual longing to re-establish contact with oneself and with the world, lies the root of all sex-negating religions. "God" is the mysticized idea of the vegetative harmony between self and nature. From this viewpoint, religion can be reconciled with natural science only if God personifies the natural laws and man is included in the natural process.

I must leave it to others more versed in Indian and Chinese culture to trace the connections in detail. The clinical findings I have attempted to describe here open a wide perspective for the understanding of those human cultures in which strict familial patriarchy, the most severe sexual suppression of small children and adolescents, and the ideology of reserve and "self-control" are part and parcel of all cultural circles. This is especially true of the cultures of India, China, and Japan. When a strict, sex-negating patriarchy wants to reproduce itself, it must severely suppress the sexual impulses of children. This results in acute anxiety and anger, both of which are detrimental to the culture of the patriarchal family and necessitate the ideology of self-control, the power not to move a muscle no matter how great the pain; indeed, they necessitate the overcoming of emotionality altogether, pleasure as well as suffering. This is the essence of the Buddhist ideology of Nirvana. This ideology also provides an insight into the breathing exercises of the Yogas. The breathing technique taught by Yogas is the exact opposite of the breathing technique we use to reactivate the vegetative emotional excitations in our patients. The aim of the Yoga breathing exercise is to combat affective impulses; its aim is to obtain peace. The rite is reminiscent of the ambiguity of compulsive actions. The counterpart of the longing for Nirvana is, as I have been told, the act of putting oneself into a state of tranquility, indeed ecstasy, by means of a definite breathing technique. The mask-like, rigid facial expression of the typical Indian, Chinese, and Japanese finds its extreme antipode in the capacity for intoxicated ecstasy. That the Yoga technique was able to spread to Europe and America is ascribable to the fact that the people of these cultures seek a means of gaining control over their natural vegetative impulses and at the same time of eliminating conditions of anxiety. They are not that far from an inkling of the orgastic function of life.

Very briefly, I want to allude to another phenomenon here which plays a destructive role in our present-day social life: namely, the "military attitude," especially as it is prescribed and carried out by the fascists. The "rigid military attitude" is the exact opposite of the natural, loose, agile attitude. The neck has to be rigid, the head stretched forward; the eyes have to stare rigidly straight ahead; the chin and mouth have to have a "manly" expression; the chest has to be thrust out; the arms have to be held closely and rigidly against the body; the hands have to be stretched along the crease of the pants. Doubtlessly, the most important indication of the sexually suppressive intent of this military technique is the proverbial command: stomach in, chest out. The legs are stiff and rigid. Picture, if you will, the position of patients who are struggling with and are making every effort to control affective impulses. Their shoulders are hard, their necks tense, their abdomens sucked in, their pelvises retracted, arms held rigidly against their bodies, their legs rigidly stretched. Indeed, the identity goes further: the stretching of the ankles is a typical clinical indication of the artificial control of affects. It is also a strict requirement of the Prussian goose step. People who are brought up in such a way, and are forced to retain this physical attitude, are incapable of natural vegetative impulses. They become machines, blindly carrying out mechanized manual exercises; obediently snapping out, "Yes, sir, Captain"; mechanically shooting their own brothers, fathers, mothers, sisters. Bringing people up to assume a rigid, unnatural attitude is one of the most essential means used by a dictatorial social system to produce will-less, automatically functioning organisms. This kind of upbringing is not confined to individuals; it is a problem which pertains to the core of the structure and formation of modern man's character. It affects large cultural circles, and destroys the joy of life and capacity for happiness in millions upon millions of men and women. Thus, we see a single thread stretching from the childhood practice of holding the breath in order not to have to masturbate, to the muscular block of our patients, to the stiff posturing of militarists, and to the destructive artificial techniques of self-control of entire cultural circles.

I have to content myself with this sketch. There can be no doubt that the importance of the attitude of the body for the structural reproduction of the social order will one day be understood and practically mastered on a large scale.

As intensely as they long for vegetative liveliness and freedom, children shrink from it and voluntarily suppress their impulses when they do not find a congenial environment in which to live out their fresh vitality relatively free of conflicts. It is one of the great secrets of mass psychology that the average adult, the average child, and the average adolescent are far more prone to resign themselves to the absence of happiness than to continue to struggle for the joy of life, when the latter entails too much pain. Thus, until the psychic and social preconditions necessary for vital life have been understood and established, the ideology of happiness must remain mere verbalization.

No purpose is served when "rebellious characters" rail against education. What we need is:

1. The most precise understanding of the mechanisms by which emotions are pathologically controlled.

2. The gathering of the widest possible experience in

practical work with children to discover what attitude the children themselves take toward their natural impulses under the existing conditions.

3. The working out of the educational conditions necessary to establish a harmony between vegetative motility and sociality.

4. The creation of the general socio-economic foundation for the above.

Man has made enormous progress in the construction and control of machines. It is hardly forty years since he began to comprehend himself. Unless he can develop the capacity to regulate his own biological energy, it will not be possible to master the psychic plague that is laying waste our century. The path of scientific research and mastery of life's problems is long and arduous; it is the exact opposite of the ignorance and impertinence of politicians. We have reason to hope that science will one day succeed in utilizing biological energy as it now does electricity. Not until then will the human psychic plague meet its master.

6. TYPICAL PSYCHOSOMATIC DISEASES: RESULTS OF CHRONIC SYMPATHETICOTONIA

We now have sufficient information about the nature of sympatheticotonia to take a cursory look at a number of organic diseases which owe their existence to man's orgastic impotence. Orgasm anxiety produces chronic sympatheticotonia; this, in turn, produces orgastic impotence, which, for its part, reinforces the sympatheticotonia. Its basic characteristic is the chronic inspiratory attitude of inhalation of the thorax and the curtailment of full (parasympathetic) exhalation. Essentially, the sympatheticotonic inspiratory attitude has the function of blocking the organ sensations and affects that normal exhalation would evoke.

The following malfunctionings result from the chronic attitude of anxiety.

1. *Cardiovascular Hypertension*

The peripheral blood vessels are chronically contracted and thus restricted in their pulsatory movement. This means that the heart is continually overexerted, having to pump blood through rigid blood vessels. Tachycardia, high blood pressure, and feelings of constriction in the chest are also symptoms of hyperthyroidism. Of importance in this connection is the extent to which the disturbance of the thyroid function is primary and the extent to which it is only a secondary symptom of general sympatheticotonia. Arteriosclerosis, a disease in which there is a calcification of the walls of the blood vessels, is also found with surprising frequency in people who have suffered from functional hypertension for many years. It is quite likely that even valvular disease and other forms of organic heart disease represent a reaction of the organism to chronic hypertension of the vascular system.

2. *Muscular Rheumatism*

In the long run, the chronic attitude of inhalation is not enough to master the bioenergetic excitations of the autonomic life system. It is reinforced by chronic muscular tension, i.e., the muscular armor. If hypertonicity of the musculature continues for years and decades, it leads to chronic contracture and to rheumatic nodules as a result of the depositing of solid substances in the muscle bundles. In this last stage, the rheumatic process is no longer reversible. It is conspicuous in the vegetotherapy of rheumatism that it typically takes hold of those muscle groups which play an essential part in the suppression of the affects and organ sensations. Muscular rheumatism is particularly common in the musculature of the neck ("stiff-necked," obstinate) and between the shoulder blades, where the pulling back of the shoulders gives the impression, from the viewpoint of character analysis, of "self-control" and "holding back." This illness usually involves the two thick muscles of the neck which run from the occiput to the clavicle (Mm. sternocleidomastoidei). These muscles become chronically hypertonic when anger is unconsciously and continuously suppressed. A rheumatic patient hit upon the descriptive term of "spite muscles" for these muscle groups. Added to these is the chronic spasm of the masseters, which gives the lower half of the face an obstinate and sullen expression.

Especially affected in the lower part of the body are those muscles which retract the pelvis and thus produce a lordosis. We already know that the chronic retraction of the pelvis has the function of suppressing genital excitation. Lumbago requires detailed investigation in this connection. It is found very frequently in patients whose buttocks musculature is in a state of chronic tension which holds back anal sensations. Another muscle group in which we frequently find muscular rheumatism comprises the deep and superficial adductors of the upper thighs, which keep the legs pressed together. They have the function, especially in women, of suppressing genital excitation. In vegetotherapeutic work, we have adopted the term "morality muscles" to describe them. The Viennese anatomist Julius Tandler jokingly referred to them as *custodes virginitatis* ("guardians of virginity"). In people suffering from muscular rheumatism, but also in an extremely large number of character neurotics, these muscle groups can be palpated as thick, chronically tense, sensitive bulges located on the inner sides of the upper part of the thighs. Also a part of this group are the muscles which, as flexors of the knee joints, run from the lower pelvic bone to the upper end of the tibia. They become chronically contracted when the organ sensations of the pelvic floor are suppressed.

The large anterior chest muscles (pectorales) are in a

state of chronic tension and stand out rigidly when the attitude of inhalation is chronically fixated. Intercostal neuralgias can be traced to this disturbance and overcome by relieving the muscular tension.

3. *Pulmonary Emphysema*

We have every reason to assume that pulmonary emphysema, characterized by the barrel-form of the air-filled thorax, is a result of a chronic and extreme attitude of inspiration. It must be borne in mind that any chronic fixation of a certain attitude impairs the elasticity of the tissues; this is the case in emphysema with respect to the elastic fibers of the bronchi.

4. *Nervous Bronchial Asthma*

Its connections with sympatheticotonia are not yet clear.

5. *Peptic Ulcer*

According to the table on page 291, chronic sympatheticotonia is accompanied by a surplus of acidity. This can be seen in gastric hyperacidity. Alkalization is reduced. The mucous membrane of the stomach is exposed to the effect of the acid. Typically, the peptic ulcer is located approximately in the middle of the posterior wall of the stomach, in front of the pancreas and the solar plexus. There is every indication that in sympatheticotonia the autonomic nerves at the posterior wall retract, thus reducing the resistance of the mucous membrane to the attack of the acid. Peptic ulcer as the by-product of a chronic affective disturbance is so frequent that there can no longer be any doubt as to its psychosomatic nature.

6. *Spasms of Annular Muscles*

a. Spastic attacks at the entrance to the stomach, cardiospasm, and at the exit of the stomach, pylorospasm.

b. Chronic constipation, as a result of the cessation or reduction of the tension-charge function in the intestines. It is always accompanied by general sympatheticotonia and a chronic inspiratory attitude. It is one of the most widespread chronic diseases.

c. Hemorrhoids, as a result of a chronic spasm of the anal sphincter. The blood in the veins peripheral to the spastic anal sphincter is mechanically dammed up, causing the vessel walls to dilate.

d. Vaginismus, as the expression of a contraction of the annular musculature of the vagina.

7. *Blood Diseases*

In his well-known work, *Die Lebensnerven,* Müller describes a number of blood diseases, such as chlorosis and other forms of anemia, as sympatheticotonic diseases.

8. *Excess of Carbon Dioxide in the Blood and Tissues*

On the basis of Warburg's pioneer work on tissue asphyxiation in cancer (CO_2 excess), it has become clear that the chronic restriction of exhalation due to sympatheticotonia represents an essential element of the disposition to cancer. The reduced external respiration results in a poor internal respiration. Organs whose respiration is chronically impaired and bioenergetic charge reduced are more susceptible to cancer-producing stimuli than organs with good respiration. The connection between the expiratory inhibition of sympatheticotonic character neurotics and the respiratory disturbance of cancerous organs discovered by Warburg became the point of departure for the sex-economic study of cancer. However, we cannot pursue this subject any further here. Only the extremely important fact that cancer in women predominantly affects the genital organs belongs in the context of this book.

It goes without saying that this summary is in no way intended to take the place of the necessary detailed investigation that no one person could ever accomplish. Such an investigation requires the cooperation of many physicians and scientists. It has merely been my intent to indicate an important field of organ pathology, which is closely related to the subject of the function of the orgasm; to emphasize hitherto overlooked connections; to appeal to the conscience of the

```
                ┌─────────────────────────────────────────────┐
                │ Disturbance of the function of tension and charge │
                └─────────────────────────────────────────────┘
                                     │
                                     ▼
                    ┌────────────────────────────────┐
                    │     Chronic inspiratory attitude    │
                    │         Pleasure anxiety            │
                    │     Chronic sympatheticotonia       │
                    └────────────────────────────────┘
                         ↙                    ↘
```

"Psychic disturbances"   "Somatic disturbances"

Impotence and frigidity   Disposition to cancer (CO_2-excess)
Symptom neurosis   Cardiovascular hypertension
Character neurosis   Hyperthyroidism
Perversion   Emphysema
Psychopathy   Rheumatism
Pseudo-debility   Constipation, hemorrhoids
Psychosis   General disturbance of vegetative
Neurotic criminality   equilibrium
                                     Chorea
                                     Epilepsy
                                     Raynaud's disease
                                     Chlorosis
                                     Peptic ulcer
                                     Tic
                                     Obesity

Diagram depicting the social causation of diseases through the disturbance of the tension-charge function

medical profession to take the sexual disturbances of men and women as seriously as they deserve; and to impress upon medical students the necessity of studying the theory of the orgasm and general sexology correctly, to enable them to meet the tremendous need of the population. The medical man must be careful not to confine himself to the microscopic slide, but to correlate what he sees in the microscope with the autonomic life function of the total organism. He should master this total function in its biological and psychic components and realize that the influence exerted by society on the tension-charge function of the organism and its organs has a decisive influence on the health or sickness of those whom he has in his care. Psychosomatic medicine, today the special province of enthusiasts and specialists, could soon be what it promises to become: *the general framework for the medicine of the future.*

It is quite evident that this general framework cannot be safeguarded if the sexual function of the living organism continues to be confused with the pathological expressions of neurotic men and women and the pornographic industry.

Chapter IX

FROM PSYCHOANALYSIS TO BIOGENESIS

1. THE BIOELECTRIC FUNCTION OF PLEASURE AND ANXIETY

Until 1934, I had applied my clinical theory, which had been obtained in the field of sex-economy, only to the general field of biophysiology. This was by no means a culmination of the work. On the contrary, now more than ever, it seemed absolutely necessary to provide experimental proof of the correctness of the orgasm formula. In the summer of 1934, the director of the Psychological Institute of the University of Oslo, Dr. Schjelderup, came to Denmark to participate in a course in this new field which I was giving to Scandinavian, German, and Austrian colleagues. He wanted to learn the technique of character analysis, but was unable to continue the work in Denmark; thus I accepted his suggestion that I continue my experiments at the Institute in Oslo. In Oslo I taught character analysis and, as recompense for this, I was given the opportunity to carry out the physiological experiments I had planned.

I realized that in the beginning I would need the technical assistance of specialists in each phase of the experiments. A preliminary discussion with the assistant of the Physiological Institute of Oslo showed me I would have no trouble reaching an understanding with the expert physiologists. My theory sounded plausible to him. The basic question was whether sexual organs in a state of excitation would show an increase of bioelectric charge. On the basis of my theoretical data, the physiologist sketched a plan for an apparatus. The magnitude of the phenomena to be measured was unknown. Such experiments had never been carried out. Would the surface charges in the sexual zone be one thousandth of a volt or one half a volt? The physiological literature provided no clues to the answering of such questions. Even the idea of a charge on the surface of the organism was not generally known. When, in December 1934, I asked the director of a physiological institute in London how the charge of the skin could be measured, he found the question itself peculiar. Tarchanoff and Veraguth, even before the turn of the century, had discovered the "psychogalvanic phenomenon," which revealed that psychic excitations become manifest as potential oscillations on the skin. However, sexual pleasure had never been measured.

After considering the matter for several months, it was decided to build an apparatus consisting of a chain of electron tubes. The idea was that the electric potential of the body would disturb the steady current ("anode current") of the tubes, would be amplified by the apparatus, transmitted to an electromagnetic oscillograph, and made visible on a strip of paper by reflection from a mirror. The apparatus was ready in February 1935. Some of my Norwegian friends and students and I served as subjects of the experiment.

It was surprising that the electrical cardiac-action curves were exceptionally small in comparison with the oscillations of the surface charges. After a number of tentative preliminary experiments, the picture became clear. I shall pass over the many details of trial and error and present only the essential findings. The experiments were carried out over a period of two years. I published the results in a monograph to which anyone interested in the technical arrangements and control experiments is referred.[1]

The entire surface of the organism constitutes a "porous membrane." This membrane exhibits an electric potential with respect to any part of the body where the epidermis has been abraded. Under normal circumstances, the undamaged skin possesses a steady or basic potential. This potential represents the normal biological potential of the body surface. It is symmetrical on both sides of the body and is approximately the same over the entire surface of the body (cf., Fig. 2, p. 388). It differs only slightly (10 to 20 mv) from person to person. The steady potential appears on the electrogram as an even, horizontal line. At regular intervals, the peaks of the electrocardiogram are superimposed on the steady potential. The cardiac peaks correspond to a change in the steady potential of the skin through the electrical pulsations transmitted by the heart.

There are certain parts of the surface where the reaction is fundamentally different from the other surfaces of the skin. These are the erogenous zones: the lips, mucous membrane of the anus, the nipples, the surface of the penis, the mucous membrane of the vagina, the ear lobes, the tongue, the palms, and—strangely enough—also the forehead. Their charge can be within the range of the potential of the other parts of the skin, but they can also exhibit a much higher or a much lower steady potential than the ordinary skin. In vegetatively alive, uninhibited men and women, the potential of one and the same sexual zone is seldom constant. Oscillations of up to 50 mv and more can be observed in the sexual zones. This is definitely in keeping with the fact that the sexual zones are endowed with a high and extremely variable intensity of sensation and capacity for excitation.

---

[1] Cf. Reich, *Experimentelle Ergebnisse über die elektrische Funktion von Sexualität und Angst.* Sexpol Verlag, 1937.

Subjectively, the excitation of the sexual zones is experienced as a streaming of current, an itching, a surging, a feeling of soothing warmth or of "sweetness." The areas of the skin that are not specifically erogenous exhibit these characteristics to a far lesser extent or not at all.

Whereas skin ordinarily registers the amplitude of its biological charge in a fairly undeviating horizontal line (cf. Fig. 1, p. 388), the various potentials of the erogenous zones exhibit a more or less steeply ascending or descending, gentle wavelike line. Let us call this steady changing of the potential "wandering" or "drifting" (cf. Fig. 3, p. 389).

Insofar as it does not approximate the amplitude of the other parts, the potential of the erogenous zone drifts i.e., it increases or decreases. The ascent of the wavelike curve indicates an increase, its descent a decrease of the charge at the surface. *The potential at an erogenous zone does not increase unless a streaming sensation of pleasure is experienced at that zone.* For instance, a nipple can become erect without an increase in potential taking place. The increase in the potential at the sexual zone is always accompanied by an intensification of the sensation of pleasure and, conversely, a decrease of the potential with a decline of the pleasurable sensation.

These experimental findings confirm the tension-charge formula. They indicate that the congestion or tumescence in an organ is not in itself sufficient to transmit the vegetative sensation of pleasure. *An increase in the bioelectric charge has to be added to the mechanical congestion of the organ to make the process perceptible as a sensation of pleasure.* The psychic intensity of the sensation of pleasure corresponds to the physiological magnitude of the bioelectric potential.

Control experiments on non-living matter demonstrated that this slow organic drifting of the potential is a specific characteristic of living matter. Non-living material does not react to "stimuli" at all, or it reacts like electrically charged bodies, e.g., a flashlight, with predictably angular, erratic, irregular fluctuations of potential (cf. Figs. 6 & 7, p. 390).

Let us call the potential that drifts upward the *preorgastic potential*. It is different in the same sexual organ at various times. It is also different in the same organ in different people. It corresponds to the preorgastic excitation or current in the vegetatively active organ. The increase in charge is the organ's response to an agreeable stimulus.

If an electrode is attached to an erogenous zone evenly and without pressure, and this zone is then tickled with a dry pledget of cotton, so that a sensation of pleasure is produced, the potential demonstrates a wavelike oscillation, the so-called *tickling phenomenon* (cf., Fig. K to *, p. 391). Tickling represents a variation of sexual friction, a basic life phenomenon. The sensation of itching also belongs here, for it automatically produces the impulse to scratch or rub. Both bear a relationship to sexual friction.

From our clinical experience in orgasmotherapy, we know that the sensations of sexual pleasure cannot always be brought about consciously. Nor can a bioelectric excitation be immediately produced in an erogenous zone by means of pleasurable stimuli. It depends entirely upon the state of the organ whether or not it will respond with excitation to a stimulus. This peculiar feature has to be given strict attention in experimentation.

The tickling phenomenon can be demonstrated on all parts of the surface of the organism. It is absent when moistened, inorganic material is rubbed with dry cotton. The positive ascending curve of the tickling oscillation is usually steeper than the descending curve. The wavelike line of the tickling phenomenon produced by a zone which is not specifically sexual is more or less horizontal. In sexual zones, the tickling oscillation is superimposed on the wandering electrical excitation, in the same way as the peaks of the cardiac action.

Pressure of any kind reduces the charge of the surface. If the pressure is removed, the charge returns exactly to the original level. Thus, if a pleasurable upward drift of the potential is interrupted by pressure, there is a sharp drop in the potential. If the pressure is removed, the drift continues at the level at which it was interrupted (cf. Fig. 9, p. 391).

The level of increase of an electrical excitation in an erogenous zone is dependent upon the softness of the stimulus —the gentler the stimulus, the steeper the increase. The level of increase is also dependent upon the psychophysical readiness of the zone to respond to the stimulus. The greater the readiness, the steeper, i.e., the more rapid, the increase.

Whereas pleasurable stimuli always yield an increase of potential, stimuli that cause anxiety or unpleasure reduce the surface charge more or less rapidly and steeply. Naturally, this reaction also depends upon the readiness of the organism to react. *Affect-blocked and vegetatively rigid men and women, e.g., catatonics, produce no or only very weak reactions.* In these individuals, the biological excitation of the sexual zones lies within the range of excitation of the remainder of the body surface. Thus, in investigating the phenomena of electrical oscillation, it is necessary to select persons specifically suited for this type of experimentation. Negating reactions of anxiety in the form of rapid reduction of the surface charge could be ascertained in the mucous membrane of the vagina, the tongue, and the palms. Unexpected fright, produced by screaming, the bursting of a balloon, the stroke of a loud gong, are particularly well suited as stimuli.

Like anxiety and pressure, vexation also causes the bioelectrical charge to be reduced at zones capable of being sexually stimulated. In a state of apprehension, all electrical reactions are reduced; increases in the positive surface charge cannot be brought about. Reactions of anxiety are usually easier to evoke than reactions of pleasure. Most significant are the reductions of the charge in the case of fright (cf. Figs. 10 & 11, p. 392).

It is much more difficult to produce reactions of pleasure after a reaction of fright has occurred. It is as if the vegetative system had become "cautious."

A concentrated solution of sugar used as an electrode fluid on the tongue produces a rapid increase in the potential of the tongue. If a salt solution is applied immediately afterward, the potential drops in the opposite, negative direction (cf. Figs. 12 & 13, p. 393). If now sugar is again applied, an increase in the potential is no longer achieved. The tongue is "cautious" or "disappointed." If sugar alone is placed on the tongue of a subject a number of times in succession, the level of increase in potential is reduced with each new experiment. It is as if the tongue had become "used to" the agreeable stimulus. Disappointed and habituated organs react sluggishly to pleasurable stimuli.

In its flaccid state, the male sexual organ reveals a much lower potential than other parts of the skin surface. If the root of the penis is squeezed, thus producing a congestion of blood in it, no drift of the potential occurs. This control experiment confirms that increased bioelectric charge at the surface is brought about by pleasurable excitation and not by mere mechanical congestion.

If, instead of direct attachment of the electrode to the sexual zone, an indirect connection is used, the same phenomena are produced. If a male and a female subject dip a finger of either hand in an electrode fluid which is connected to an oscillograph, the touching of their lips in the act of kissing produces a strong positive wandering potential. In short, the phenomenon is independent of the locality to which the electrode is brought into contact with the skin. If one of the subjects of the experiment performs the action unwillingly, the same stimulus produces a descending reaction of unpleasure, instead of an ascending reaction of pleasure. The same results are produced when the two persons bring their free hands into contact with one another. Gentle stroking yields positive oscillations. Pressure or strong rubbing of the palms cause reductions in the charge.

How is bioelectric energy transmitted from the vegetative center to the vegetative periphery, and vice versa?

According to the traditional view, the bioelectric energy moves along the paths of the nerve fibers, presupposing that the nerve fibers are non-contractile. Thus far, however, all observations necessitate the assumption that the *syncytial vegetative plexuses are themselves contractile; i.e., they can expand and contract.* Accordingly, the amoeba continues to exist in all animals, including man, in the form of the contractile autonomic nervous system. This assumption is confirmed microscopically. For example, movements of expansion and contraction in small translucent worms can be easily observed under the microscope. These movements of the autonomic life apparatus take place independently of the movements of the total body, and they precede them.

If the subject in an experiment is told to breathe in deeply, or to press as if to defecate, and the differential electrode is placed at the middle of the abdominal skin above the umbilicus, *there is a more or less sharp decrease in the surface potential in inhalation, which increases again in exhalation.* This result was repeatedly obtained in a large number of subjects. However, it was not obtained in persons having a severe affect-block or a pronounced muscular rigidity. This finding, added to the clinical observation that inhalation reduces affects, led to the following assumption:

In inhalation, the diaphragm is depressed and exerts pressure on the abdominal organs; it constricts the abdominal cavity. In exhalation, on the other hand, the diaphragm is elevated; the pressure on the abdominal organs is reduced and the abdominal cavity is thereby enlarged. In breathing, the cavities of the chest and abdomen are alternately enlarged and constricted, a fact which shall be considered elsewhere. Since pressure always lowers the potential, there is nothing particularly remarkable about the lowering of the potential of the skin in inspiration. What is remarkable is that the potential decreases, although the pressure is exerted not on the surface of the skin, but in the center of the organism.

The existence of *a continuous bioelectric field of excitation between center and periphery* is the only possible explanation for the fact that inner pressure is manifested on the abdominal skin. The transmission of bioenergy cannot be relegated solely to the nerve tracts; rather it follows the path of all membranes and fluids of the organism. This ties in very well with our earlier representation of the organism as a membranous bladder, and confirms the theory of Fr. Kraus.

This hypothesis received further confirmation when the investigation of a number of emotionally disturbed patients with restricted expiratory movement showed minimal or no fluctuations in the charge of the abdominal skin.

Let us summarize these findings with reference to our basic problem.

It is only biological pleasure, accompanied by the sensation of current and sensualness, that produces an increase in the bioelectric charge. All other excitations, pain, fright, anxiety, pressure, vexation, depression, are accompanied by a reduction of surface charge of the organism.

There are basically four kinds of reduction of charge at the periphery of the organism:

a. A withdrawal of the surface charge prior to an intended strong charge. This reaction is comparable to the suspended tension of a tiger on the verge of leaping.

b. In contrast to the preorgastic excitation, the orgastic discharge demonstrates a lowering of the potential. The orgasm's bioelectric curve corresponds to the curve of the sensations.

c. In a state of anxiety, the peripheral charge is lowered.

d. In dying, the tissues lose their charge; we observe negative reactions. *The source of energy is extinguished.*

Surface Charge

Increased	*Decreased*
Pleasure of any kind	Central tension before an action
	Peripheral orgastic discharge
	Anxiety, vexation, pressure, unpleasure, depression
	Death (extinction of the source of energy)

Thus, *sexual excitation is functionally identical with the bioelectric charge of the periphery of the organism.* Freud's concept of the libido as a measure of psychic energy is no longer merely a simile. It refers to concrete bioelectric processes. Sexual excitation alone represents bioelectric functioning in the direction of the periphery ("from within outward").

Pleasure and *anxiety* are the two primal excitations or *primal emotions* of living substance. Their bioelectric functioning aligns them, in principle, with the general electrical phenomena of nature.

Subjects in an experiment who are not emotionally disturbed and who are capable of orgastic sensations, i.e., persons who are not emotionally cold, are capable of stating what is objectively taking place at the apparatus in an adjacent room on the basis of their subjective sensations in the process of excitation. *The intensity of the sensation of pleasure corresponds to the quantity of the bioelectric charge at the surface, and vice versa.* The sensation of "being cold," "being dead," the "contactlessness" of the psychiatric patient, are expressions of a deficiency of bioelectric charge at the periphery of the body.

The *tension-charge* formula is valid. Biological excitation is a process which, in addition to mechanical tumescence, also requires bioelectric charge. *Orgastic gratification is a bioelectric discharge, followed by a mechanical detumescence.*

The biological process of expansion, illustrated by organ erection or the extension of pseudopodia in the amoeba, is the overt manifestation of a movement of bioelectric energy from the center to the periphery of the organism. What moves here, in both the psychic as well as the somatic sense, is the bioelectric charge itself.

Since only vegetative sensations of pleasure are accompanied by an increase of the charge at the surface of the organism, *pleasurable excitation has to be regarded as the specifically productive process in the biological system.* All other affects, e.g., unpleasure, vexation, anxiety, pressure, are, in terms of energy, opposed to this process and hence represent life-negating functions. Thus, *the process of sexual pleasure is the life process per se.* This is not a manner of speaking; it is an experimentally proven fact.

Anxiety, as the basic direction opposed to that of sexuality, coincides with the process of dying. It is not identical with dying, for the central source of energy, the process of charge, is extinguished in dying. In anxiety, on the other hand, the energy source in the center of the organism is dammed up, owing to the withdrawal of excitation from the periphery, thus creating the subjective sensation of constriction (*angustiae*).

These findings provide the concept of *sex-economy* with a concrete, natural-scientific meaning. Sex-economy refers to the manner in which bioelectric energy is regulated or, what is the same thing, to the regulation of a person's sexual energy. It refers to the way in which the individual deals with his bioelectric energy, how much he dams up and how much of it he discharges orgastically. Since the organism's bioelectric energy is the basic fact from which we have to proceed, we gain a new insight into the nature of organic disease.

From this point on, neuroses appear in a fundamentally different light than they did in psychoanalysis. They are not solely the results of unresolved psychic conflicts and infantile fixations. *These fixations and psychic conflicts cause fundamental disturbances in the regulation of bioelectric energy and, in this way, become somatically anchored.* For this reason, it is not possible, nor is it admissible, to separate psychic and somatic processes. Psychic disturbances are biological illnesses that are expressed in the somatic as well as in the psychic realm. A deflection in the natural course of the biological energy lies at the basis of these disturbances.

Mind and body constitute a functional unity, having at the same time an antithetical relationship. Both function on the basis of biological laws. The modification of these laws is a result of social influences. *The psychosomatic structure is the result of the clash between social and biological functions.*

The function of the orgasm becomes the yardstick of psychophysical functioning, because the function of biological energy is expressed in it.

2. THE THEORETICAL SOLUTION OF THE CONFLICT BETWEEN MECHANISM AND VITALISM

When it was established that the tension-charge formula was valid for all involuntary functions of living substance, one was prompted to ask whether it was also applicable to processes in non-living matter. Neither in the literature of physics nor in conversations with physicists could references to an inorganic function be found in which a mechanical tension (brought about by a filling with fluid) would lead to an electrical charge and culminate in an electrical discharge and mechanical relaxation (emptying of fluid). While it is true that all the physical elements of the formula are found in inorganic nature, they are found only individually and not in the particular sequence in which they appear in living matter. (For instance, we find mechanical tension caused by filling, and relaxation brought about by emptying. We also find electrical charge and discharge.) Thus, it seemed quite evident that *the particular combination of mechanical and electrical functions had to be specific to living functioning.*

I was now in the position to make a significant contribution to the age-old controversy between the vitalists and the mechanists. The vitalists had always contended that non-living matter is fundamentally different from living matter. They always adduced a metaphysical principle, such as "entelechy," to explain living functioning per se. On the other hand, the mechanists contended that, physically and chemically, living matter is in no way different from non-living matter; it simply had not yet been sufficiently investigated. Thus, the mechanists denied that there is a fundamental difference between living and non-living matter. The tension-charge formula was able to prove the correctness of both views, though in a manner different than either would have thought.

Living matter does indeed function on the basis of the same physical laws as non-living matter, as the mechanists contended. At the same time, it is fundamentally different from non-living matter, as the vitalists maintained. *In living matter, the functions of mechanics (tension-relaxation) and those of electricity (charge-discharge) are combined in a way which is alien to non-living matter.* However, this difference in the functioning of living matter cannot, as the vitalists believe, be traced back to a metaphysical principle existing beyond matter and energy. Rather, it can be comprehended on the basis of laws governing matter and energy. *In its functioning, living matter is simultaneously identical with and different from non-living matter.*

It is to be expected that the vitalists and spiritualists will take issue with this statement by pointing out that *consciousness and self-perception* are still unexplained. This is correct, but it does not justify the assumption of a metaphysical principle. Moreover, consciousness and self-perception can anticipate a final clarification. The electrical experiments demonstrated that the biological excitation of pleasure and the biological excitation of anxiety are functionally identical with their perception. We are justified in assuming, therefore, that even the most primitive organisms have *organ sensations* of pleasure and anxiety.

3. "BIOLOGICAL ENERGY" IS ATMOSPHERIC (COSMIC) ORGONE ENERGY

I have reached the end of the description of the orgasm theory. It is still in the process of development. The results of the bioelectric experiments left a number of difficult problems unsolved. Two peculiar facts revealed by the following experiments cannot be explained within the framework of known forms of energy. First:

1. If the surface of the body is tickled close to an attached electrode which is connected to an oscillograph, the tickling phenomenon is revealed as an oscillation of the electrical potential of the skin.

2. *If the same experiment is carried out with a moistened cloth, the tickling phenomenon does not occur. Thus, a moistened cloth does not "live."*

3. If, however, one places a hand on the moistened cloth, attaches the electrodes at about 30 cm. distance from each

other and "tickles" the cloth with a dry pledget of cotton approximately 2 to 5 cm. away from the hand, the tickling phenomenon is again demonstrated.

To explain this, it could be readily pointed out that the phenomenon takes place because the body is connected to the arrangement. However, this explanation is not satisfactory.

The tickling phenomenon on the skin could be explained on the basis of the oscillations of bioelectric energy in the organism, oscillations produced by the body in response to the tickling stimulus. In the third experiment, this reaction is relayed from within the boundaries of the organism to a region outside of it, namely to the non-living, moistened cloth. It is as if the moistened cloth "lived" when it was touched by a living organism. The cloth responded to the tickling stimulus in the same way as the living organism.

The second fact revealed by the electrical experiments appears even more significant. Electromagnetic energy moves at the speed of light, i.e., at approximately 186,000 miles per second. Observation of the nature of the curves and the time measurements which characterize the movement of bioelectric energy demonstrate that *the movement of bioelectric energy is fundamentally different from the known speed and type of movement of electromagnetic energy*. Bioelectric energy moves extremely slowly, at a speed measurable in millimeters per second. (The speed can be measured by counting the number of cardiac peaks, cf. Fig. 8, p. 391.) The form of the movement is slow and wavelike. It resembles the movements of an intestine or a snake. The movement also corresponds to the slow surging of an organ sensation or vegetative excitation. It could be maintained that it is the great resistance of the animal tissues that slows down the speed of the organism's electric energy. This explanation is unsatisfying. When an electric stimulus is applied to the body, it is *experienced immediately* and responded to.

In an unusual way, the knowledge of the biological tension-charge function led me to the discovery of energy processes in bions, in the human organism, and in the radiation of the sun.

In the summer of 1939, I published a short paper, *Drei Versuche mit Gummi am statischen Elektroskop*. Rubber and cotton exposed to a bion culture obtained from ocean sand produced a sharp deflection of the indicator of a static electroscope. The same substances brought into contact with a vegetatively undisturbed human body, particularly in the region of the abdomen and genitals, for approximately fifteen to twenty minutes, will similarly influence the electroscope. In the final analysis, the sand from which the bions develop through heating and swelling is nothing other than solidified solar energy. Now, the idea occurred to expose rubber and cotton to bright sunshine, after they had been shown to be indifferent at the electroscope. It was demonstrated that the sun emits an energy which influences rubber and cotton in the same manner in which it influences the bion culture and the human organism after full respiration in a vegetatively undisturbed state. I called this energy, which is capable of charging organic matter, orgone.

At this point, the investigation of the living organism went beyond the boundaries of depth psychology and physiology; it entered unexplored biological territory. For the past five years, the investigation of the *bion* has absorbed all available attention. The "bions" are microscopic vesicles charged with orgone energy; they are developed from inorganic matter through heating and swelling. They propagate like bacteria. They also develop spontaneously in the earth or, as in cancer, from decayed organic matter. My book *Die Bione*, 1938, shows the importance of the tension-charge formula for the experimental investigation of the natural organization of living substance from non-living matter.

Orgone energy is also demonstrable visually, thermically, and electroscopically, in the soil, in the atmosphere, and in plant and animal organisms. The flickering of the sky, which some physicists ascribe to terrestrial magnetism, and the glimmering of stars on clear dry nights, are direct expressions of the movement of the atmospheric orgone. The "electric storms" of the atmosphere which disturb electrical equipment during intensified sun-spot activity are, as can be experimentally demonstrated, an effect of the atmospheric orgone energy. Previously, they had been tangible only as disturbances of electrical currents.

The color of orgone energy is *blue* or *blue-gray*. In our laboratory, atmospheric orgone is accumulated or concentrated by means of an apparatus specifically constructed for this purpose. We succeeded in making it visible by arranging certain materials in a specific way. The inhibition of the orgone's kinetic energy is expressed as an increase in temperature. Its concentration or density is indicated on the static electroscope by the differences in the speed of the discharge. The spontaneous discharge of electroscopes in non-ionized air, a phenomenon designated as "natural leak" by physicists, is the effect of atmospheric orgone and has nothing to do with dampness. The orgone contains three kinds of rays: blue-gray, foglike vapors; deep blue-violet expanding and contracting dots of light; and white-yellow, rapidly moving rays of dots and streaks. The blue color of the sky and the blue-gray of atmospheric haze on hot summer days are direct reflections of the atmospheric orgone. The blue-gray, cloudlike Northern lights, the so-called St. Elmo's fire, and the bluish formations recently observed in the sky by astronomers during increased sun-spot activity are also manifestations of orgone energy.

The hitherto misunderstood formations of clouds and thunderstorms are dependent upon changes in the concentration of the atmospheric orgone. This can be simply demonstrated by measuring the speed of the electroscopic discharges.

The living organism contains orgone energy in each one of its cells, and continuously charges itself orgonotically from the atmosphere by means of respiration. The "red" blood corpuscles are microscopic, orgone-charged vesicles having a blue glimmer; they carry biological energy from the surface of the alveoli of the lungs to the body tissues. The chlorophyll of plants, which is related to the iron-containing protein of animal blood, contains orgone and absorbs orgone directly from the atmosphere and from solar radiation.

When magnified at more than $2000\times$, the existence of orgone energy in cells and colloids can be demonstrated in the blue (blue-gray or blue-green) coloration of the protoplasm and in the content of organic vesicles. All cooked food consists of blue, orgone-containing vesicles. The vesicles of humus or of gonadal cells and energy vesicles or bions obtained through the heating and swelling of inorganic matter also contain orgone. Protozoa, cancer cells, etc., also consist of orgone-containing, blue energy vesicles. Orgone has a parasympatheticotonic effect and charges living tissue, particularly the red blood corpuscles. It kills cancer cells and many kinds of bacteria. Our experiments with cancer therapy are based on these biological characteristics.

Numerous observations by biologists (Meisenheimer, Linné, and others) make it possible to understand the blue coloration of frogs in a state of sexual excitation or the blue luminescence of plant buds as biological (orgonotic) excitation of the organism. The bion cultures obtained from sea sand, in which I discovered orgone radiation in January 1939, had the same effect on color film in complete darkness as sunlight; i.e., it made the film blue.

The human organism is surrounded by an orgonotic energy field whose range depends on the organism's vegetative liveliness. Proof of this is simple. The orgone excites organic substances, e.g., cellulose. Thus, placing a one-foot-square cellulose plate about 3 to 5 cm. in front of a silver electrode, which is connected to the grid of an oscillograph, we observe that movements of inorganic substances in front of the cellulose do not produce any oscillation on the oscillograph, provided the inorganic material is moved in such a way that no part of our organism moves in front of the plate. However, if we move our finger or hand toward or away from the cellulose plate at a distance of 0.5 to 3 meters, we can, without establishing any metallic connection, obtain lively deflections of the light or galvanometer indicator. If we remove the cellulose plate, the effects at a distance are reduced to a minimum, or they disappear completely. *In contrast to electromagnetic energy, orgone energy is capable of charging non-conducting organic material.*

The second volume of this book will describe how bion research led to the discovery of atmospheric orgone energy, how the existence of orgone can be objectively demonstrated, and the importance of its discovery for the understanding of biophysical functioning. However, it was the consistent pursuit of the biological phenomenon of the orgasm that led to the discovery of the orgone, thus to the cosmic energy which has a specific biological effect.

Having arrived at the conclusion of this book, the reader, like the author himself, will not be able to avoid the impression that the study of the orgasm, the stepchild of natural science, has led us deep into the secrets of nature. The investigation of living matter went beyond the confines of depth psychology and physiology and entered unexplored *biological* territory. Sexuality and the living process became identical, and a new avenue of approach to the problem of biogenesis was opened. What was psychology became *biophysics* and a part of genuine, experimental natural science. Its core remains, as always, the *enigma of love,* to which we owe our being.

FROM PSYCHOANALYSIS TO BIOGENESIS 387

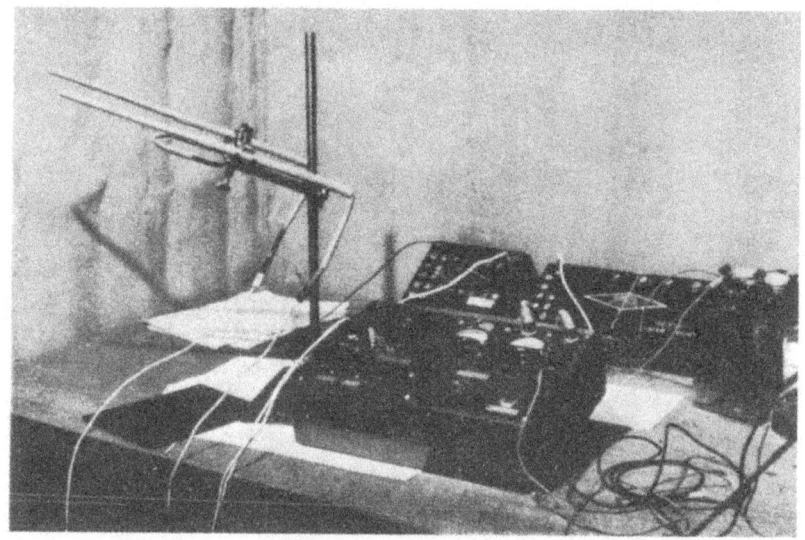

Amplifier and silver electrodes.

Oscillograph, paper film apparatus and electrode.

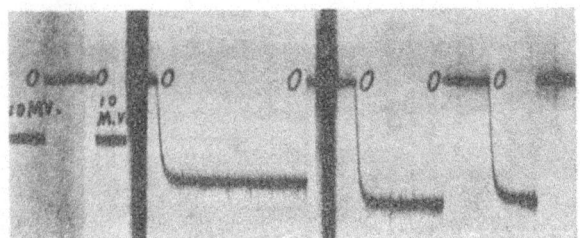

Fig. 1. Average skin potential (skin of the abdomen, right and left).

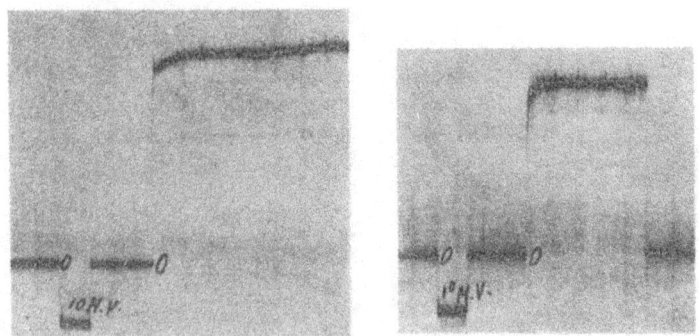

Fig. 2. Symmetrical normal potentials of a right and left palm.

FROM PSYCHOANALYSIS TO BIOGENESIS

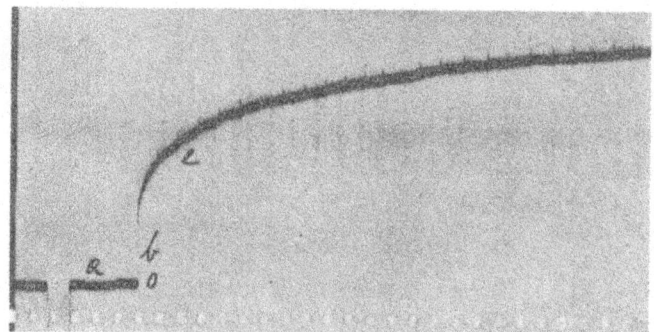

Fig. 3. "Wandering" of the potential of a palm.

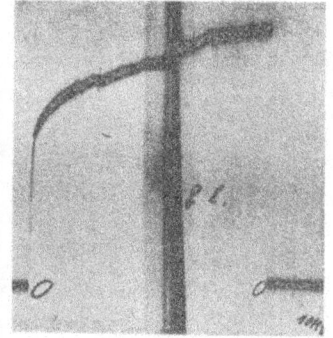

Fig. 4. Mucous membrane of the anus in a woman in a state of sexual excitation.

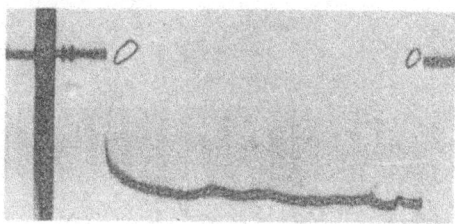

Fig. 5. The same mucous membrane in a state of depression (menstruation).

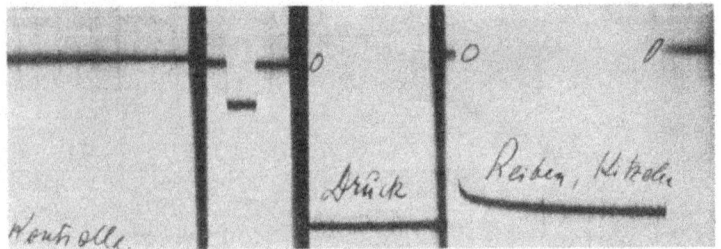

Fig. 6. Control experiment with wet towel.

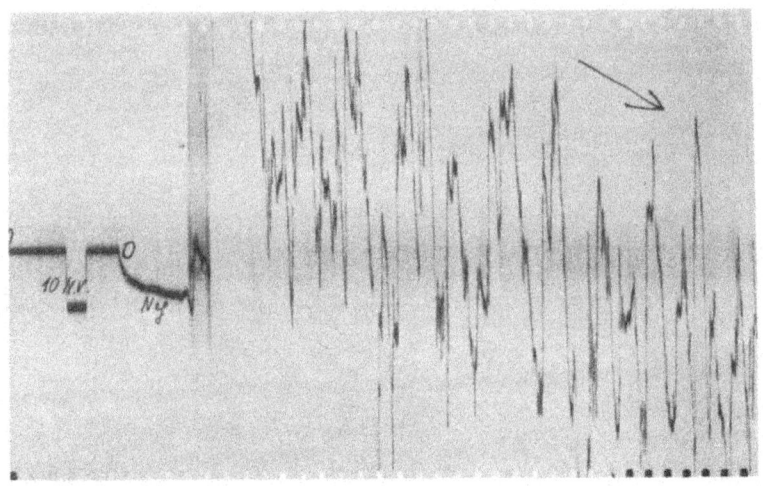

Fig. 7. Changes of potential produced by an electric flashlight.

FROM PSYCHOANALYSIS TO BIOGENESIS

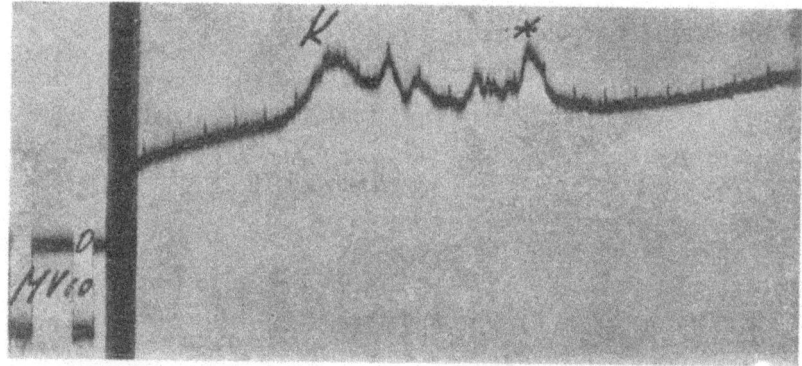

Fig. 8. Mucous membrane of the lip. K to * = tickling phenomenon. (The cardiac peaks are visible at regular intervals).

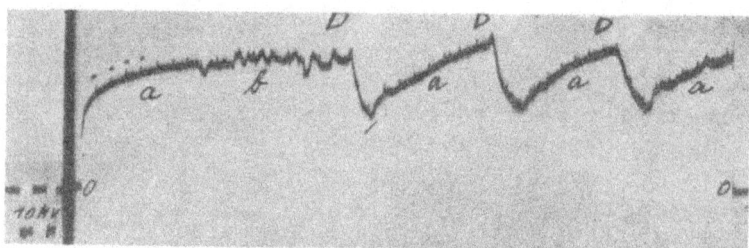

Fig. 9. Mucous membrane of the tongue. a = wandering; b = tickling phenomenon; D = pressure.

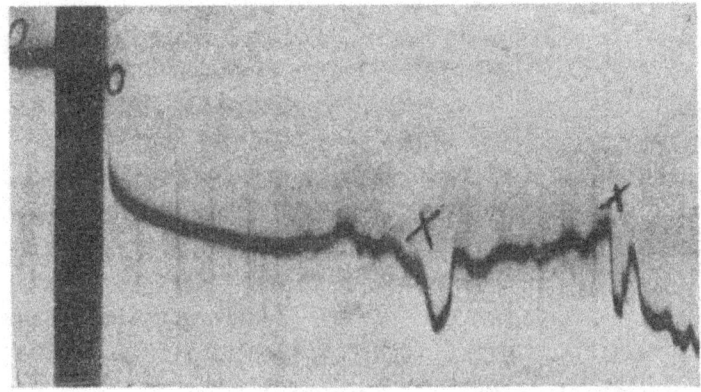

Fig. 10. x = reaction of vaginal mucous membrane to a stimulus of annoyance.

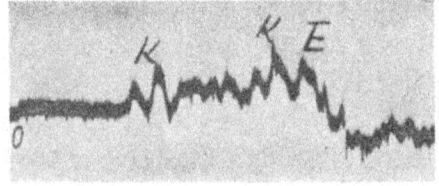

Fig. 11. *Tongue.* K = tickling; E = fright.

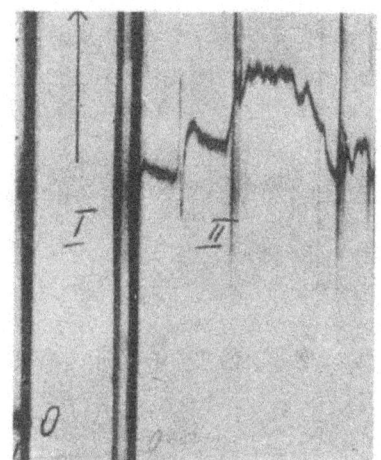

Fig. 12. Reaction of tongue to sugar (about + 70 MV; in this experiment, the first application of sugar resulted in a reaction way out of the field: I, arrow).

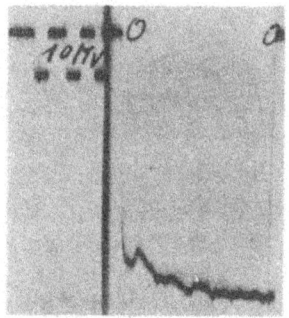

Fig. 13. Reaction of same tongue to salt (— 60 MV).

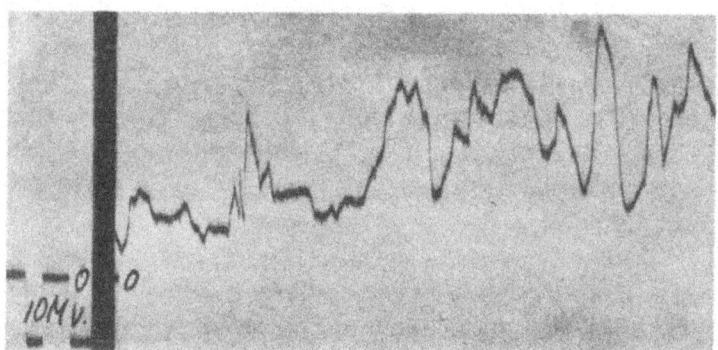

Fig. 14. Excitation with a kiss (changes in the bio-electrical excitation of the lips, up to 40 MV).

INDEX

Abraham, Karl, 58; on character traits, 73; on melancholia, 80; on duration of treatment, 86; at Psychoanalytic Congress (1924), 129

Actual neurosis, 88, 113, 136; cure of, 89; *see also* Stasis neurosis

Adler, Alfred, 34, 151; theory of the "nervous character," 72; character theory, 148, 150

Aggression, 154 ff

Alexander, Franz, 59, 128, 129

Allers, Rudolf, 92

Antisemitism, 244

Anxiety, anxiety neurosis, 88, 93, 133 ff, 378; and sexuality, 263 ff, 338; and muscular tension, 270; and pleasure, 287 ff, 368 ff

Authoritarian dictatorship, 11

Authoritarian family, and structuring of masses, 8, 241; and the neurotic plague, 197; and fascism, 243

Bachofen, J. J., 232
Barasch, 200

Beethoven, Ludwig van, 28
Bergson, Henri, 23, 262
Bioenergy, biological energy, ix, 379, 383; transmission of, 376; *see also* Orgone
Bions, bion research, 9, 257, 383; and Brownian movement, 92
Bleuler, E., 62
Bloch, Jwan, 22
Bohr, 40
Bucura, 34

Cancer, 5, 9; and sexual gratification, 96; tissue asphyxiation in, 365
Cardiovascular hypertension, 362
Castration, 31
Catatonic stupor, 64
Character analysis, character analytic, theory of structure, 36; development of, 61, 117; concept of "affect block," 86; task of, 154; technique, 171, 299 ff; crisis in, 258
Character armor, characterological armoring, 7, 186, 260; theory of, 138; stratification of, 144; function of, 145; dissolu-

tion of, 170; in moralistic structure, 182; in sex-economically regulated structure, 182; and muscular hypertonia, 270; *see also* Muscular armor

Character, character structure, of modern man, 7, 360; theory of, 34; in Psychoanalytic Association, 72; impulsive, 80; definition of, 145; and social structure, 187; and education, 224; *see also* Human structure

Chrobak, 95

Compulsive character, compulsion neurotic, therapeutic difficulties in, 82, 137; in the genital embrace, 104; genital disturbance in, 164; and incest desires, 316

Constipation, 365

Darwin, Charles, theory of natural selection, 28

Death instinct, early hints of, 59; and sexual instinct, 124; in psychoanalytic theory, 126, 154; and orgasm, 155; as destructive impulse, 157

Deutsch, Helene, 131

de Vries, 28

Driesch, Hans, 23

Du Teil, Roger, 99 fn

Economo, 62, 66

Einstein, Albert, 40

Emotional plague, vii

Engels, Friedrich, 232

Epilepsy, epileptic seizures, 345

Exhibitionism, 81

Fascism, fascistic irrationalism, 227, 233 ff

Ferenczi, Sandor, on "free association," 49; and genital sexuality, 81; theory of genitality, 131; and character, 149; "active technique," 152, 173

Fliess, Wilhelm, 29

Forel, August, 22

Freud, Sigmund, 19; first reading of, 22; and sexuality, 29, 283; and "libido," 29, 215, 262, 377; interpretation of symbols, 32; analytic technique, 32, 48; on cure, 33; personality of, 34, 47; on madness, 41; as a speaker, 45; on "drives," 53; "The Ego and the Id," 59, 123; and the death instinct, 59, 126, 128, 217, 251, 259; and "character," 72; on instincts, 81, 126, 187; *History of an Infantile Neuroses,* 86; and causal psychotherapy, 87; on actual neuroses, 88, 166; on neurasthenia, 88, 166; on psychoneurosis, 89; and philosophic discussions, 91; and Charcot, 95; on organotherapy, 114; on libido development, 132; theory of anxiety, 134; *Hemmung, Symptom und Angst,* 136; contradiction in, 139, 213, 217, 250; and the "unconscious," 140, 263, 265, 315; "primary masochism," 149, 252; and liberated natural sexuality, 152; and *Die Funktion des Orgasmus,* 166; on interpretation, 167; and prophylaxis of neuroses, 191; sublimation theories, 205; *Civilization and its Discontents,* 207, 224; on religion, 210; and politics, 210, 214; pessimism and resignation, 211; and Russian Revolution, 211, 214; tragedy of, 216; on narcotics, 220; theory of civilization, 223; discovery of child sexuality, 228; and sexual latency, 231

Galileo, 19
Galvani, 280
Genital character, 169 ff; attitude of, 176; characterized by, 183
Genitality, theory of, 82
Grimm, George, 26
Groddeck, 65
Gurwitsch, 284

Hartmann, Heinz, 282, 286
Heisenberg, 40
Hemorrhoids, 365
Herold, Carl M., 172 fn
Hertwig, O., 25
Hitler, Adolf, 19, 169
Hitschmann, Eduard, 60, 74
Human structure, 250, 260; *see also* Character structure
Hysterical character, hysteric, hysteria, childhood of, 79; therapeutic difficulties in, 82; sexual etiology of, 95; genital disturbance in, 164; "*arc de cercle,*" 344, 350; muscular spasms in, 349

Ibsen, Henrik, and *Peer Gynt,* 38, 69; and Brand, 45
Impulsive character, *Der triebhafte Charakter,* 76; 79
International Psychoanalytic Association, 58, 59, 61, 72, 124, 129, 132, 169, 177; Congress in Lucerne, 1934, 297

Jaspers, K., 91
Jesus, 244
Johnson, V., 99 fn
Jones, Ernest, 229
Jung, C. G., 151

Kammerer, Paul, 26, 28, 34
Kant, 38
Kipling, Rudyard, 44
Kraepelin, 28
Kraus, Fr., 261, 273, 287, 289, 376

Lange, F. A., 24
Lenin, N., 210
Libido concept, theory to pre-Freudian writers, 29, 36; and biogenesis, 36; destruction of, 124; 215
Linné, 385
Löwenfeld, 89
Lumbago, 363

Malinowski, Bronislaw, and the Oedipus complex, 229; *The Sexual Life of Savages,* 230
Marriage problem, 202
Masochism, masochistic, 252 ff; beating fantasy, 81; and reli-

gion, 256; in mass psychology, 259

Masters, W., 99 fn

Masturbation, 55, 84, 97, 174; in neurasthenia, 89; prohibition of, 199, 203; and diaphragmatic tic, 345

Meisenheimer, 385

Mendel, 28

Mental hygiene, 190 ff, 204, pivotal question of, 231

Moll, Albert, 22; and sexuality, 27

Morgan, Lewis H., 232

Müller, L. R., 269, 365

Müller-Lyer, 30

Muscular armor, 271, 299 ff; and orgasm reflex, 330; and rheumatism, 362; *see also* Character armor

Muscular rheumatism, 362

Napoleon, 19

Narcotics, 220

"Negative therapeutic reaction," 59, 128, 149

Nero, 19

Neurasthenia, 28, according to Freud, 88; genital disturbance in, 164

Neurotic character, 169 ff

Nietzsche, Friedrich, 202

Numberg, Hermann, 61

Nymphomania, 79, 107

Oedipus complex, according to Adler, 35; and energy stasis, 113; patients' use of, 120; among the Trobrianders, 229

Orgasm anxiety, definition of, 161; forms of, 162; in masochists, 254; and sympatheticotonia, 296, 361; see pleasure anxiety

Orgasm formula, 9, 272 ff

Orgasm reflex, 4, 70, 299 ff, 309 ff, 348; and natural movement, 330; and breathing, 333

Orgasm theory, development of, 84, 101; in sex-economy, 115; and character-analytic techniques, 122; and pregenitality, 132; and health, 198; and sexual energy, 250; point of departure of, 268

Orgastic impotence, 6, 272; role in sex-economy, 101; and psychic illness, 110; in the masochist, 257; and chronic sympatheticotonia, 361

Orgastic potency, natural-scientific substantiation of, 4; in relation to psychic health, 6, 268; differentiation from orgastic impotence, 52; 95 ff; definition of, 102; as goal of therapy, 112, 123, 151; and negative therapeutic reaction, 128; establishment of, 129; and sadism, 158; and sociality, 185

Orgone, orgone energy, 381 ff; discovery of, ix; radiation, 4, 9; *see also* Bioenergy

Orgone biophysics, introduction to, ix

Pasteur, 19

Patriarchy, emergence of, 8

INDEX

Peptic ulcer, 364
Phallic, narcissistic character, genital disturbance in, 164
Pilcz, 28
Planck, Max, 40
Pleasure anxiety, 7, 161, 279, 356; in the masochist, 253; *see also* Orgasm anxiety
Pleasure principle, 212, 221, 356
Pötzl, 63
Prophylaxis of neuroses, 189, 204; and Freud, 191; central point in, 200
Psychic structure, layering of, 233
Psychoanalytic theory, and female sexuality, 21
Puberty problem, 199
Pulmonary emphysema, 364

Rank, Otto, *Trauma der Geburt,* 131; 152
Reik, Theodor, 59, 126, 129; and the death instinct, 127
Resistance analysis, 48, 121
Roheim, Géza, on potency, 98

Sadism, 81, 154 ff
Schizophrenia, schizophrenic, Freud's theory of, 41; Tausk's theory of, 46; sexual etiology of, 68; and organ sensations, 70; somatic manifestations of, 347
Schilder, Paul, 62; and the Freudian unconscious, 63
Schjelderup, H., 368
Self-regulation, principle of, 169, 180; in contrast with moral regulation, 181
Semon, Richard, 22, 262
Sex-economy, sexual economy, sex-economic, and sexuality, 3; development of, 4, 83, 88, 115; theory of, 6, 80; and political organizations, 10; and the Freudian "unconscious," 63; cancer research, 64; theory of character, 138; and destructiveness, 155; self-regulation, 181; and psychic economy, 196; threat to, 201; and mythology, 223; and human striving, 225; ordered, 269; and innervations, 296; criteria for health or pathology, 355; meaning of, 378
Sex-politics, sex-political, 191
Stasis, definition of, 348
Stasis neurosis, 88, 93, 112; *see also* Actual neurosis
Steinach, E., 26, 28, 34
Steiner, Rudolf, 26
Stekel, Wilhelm, 34, 90, 151
Streicher, Julius, 245
Swoboda, Hermann, 28

Tandler, Julius, 30, 363
Tarchanoff, 369
Tausk, Viktor, 46, on schizophrenia, 97
Transference, 118, 172
Trobriander society, 230 ff

Vaginismus, 365
Van de Velde, 239
"Vegetative currents," 271

Vegetotherapy, character-analytic vegetotherapy, 5, 60, 330; basic principle of, 8; and "Yogism," 308; and memory, 314
Veraguth, 369
Vienna Psychoanalytic Clinic, 73
Vienna Psychoanalytic Society, 20, 45, 53, 57, 97
Vienna seminar on sexology, 20–21, 30
Vienna seminar on technique, origin of, 60, 117; and the death instinct, 129, 168, 177

Wagner-Jauregg, 62; and sexual symbolism, 64, 66
Warburg, Otto, 365
Work democracy, 12, 15
Wulffen, 28
Wundt, Wilhelm

Yoga, 358

Zondek, 287, 289

ABOUT THE AUTHOR

Wilhelm Reich was born in Austria on March 24, 1897, the son of a prosperous farmer. His early years were spent in a rural atmosphere close to animals and natural phenomena and this may well have determined his later interest in biology and natural science. After his service in the First World War, he entered the Medical School of the University of Vienna from which he was graduated in 1922. He met Freud in 1920 and soon became a prominent participant in the early psychoanalytic and mental-health movements. Freud's idea of a psychic energy, his libido theory, provided the stimulus for Reich's clinical and experimental studies into the exact nature of this energy, which was most vividly expressed in the orgasm function. These studies led eventually to the discovery of the life energy to which he gave the name *orgone*.

Forced to flee Nazi Germany in 1933, Reich pursued his work in Scandinavia until September, 1939, when he moved to the United States and established his laboratory in Forest Hills, New York. He later transferred it to Rangeley, Maine. In 1954, the Federal Food and Drug Administration filed a complaint for an injunction against him attacking specifically and clearly designed to discredit his discovery of orgone energy. He refused to be forced into court as a "defendant" in matters of basic natural research and a Decree of Injunction was issued *on default*. He was subsequently accused of criminal contempt in disobeying this injunction, and following a jury trial in May, 1956, in which his plea was "not guilty," he was sentenced to two years' imprisonment. He died on November 3, 1957, in the Federal Penitentiary at Lewisburg, Pennsylvania.